Lesson Guide

Volume I

Book Staff and Contributors

Kristen Kinney   *Senior Content Specialist*
Amy Rauen   *Instructional Designer*
David Shireman   *Instructional Designer*
Michelle Iwaszuk   *Instructional Designer*
Kandee Dyczko   *Writer*
Tisha Ruibal   *Writer*
Julie Philpot   *Editor*
Suzanne Montazer   *Creative Director*
Sasha Blanton   *Senior Print Designer, Cover Designer*
Julie Jankowski   *Print Designer*
Michelle Beauregard   *Project Manager*
Carrie Miller   *Project Manager*

John Holdren   *Senior Vice President for Content and Curriculum*
Maria Szalay   *Senior Vice President for Product Development*
David Pelizzari   *Vice President of Content and Curriculum*
Kim Barcas   *Vice President of Creative Design*
Seth Herz   *Director, Program Management*

Lisa Dimaio Iekel   *Production Manager*
John G. Agnone   *Director of Publications*

About K12 Inc.

K12 Inc., a technology-based education company, is the nation's leading provider of proprietary curriculum and online education programs to students in grades K–12. K12 provides its curriculum and academic services to online schools, traditional classrooms, blended school programs, and directly to families. K12 Inc. also operates the K12 International Academy, an accredited, diploma-granting online private school serving students worldwide. K12's mission is to provide any child the curriculum and tools to maximize success in life, regardless of geographic, financial, or demographic circumstances. K12 Inc. is accredited by CITA. More information can be found at www.K12.com.

ISBN 1-60153-109-5

Printed by RR Donnelley, Roanoke, VA, USA, May 2010, Lot 052010

Contents

Long Vowels and Sight Words

Ending Blends and Sight Words

Beginning Blends and Sight Words

Word Endings and Sight Words

Difficult Spellings & r-Controlled Vowels and Sight Words

Long *e* and Sight Words

Long *e* & Long *i* and Sight Words

Long *u* and Syllable Types

Long *u* & Double *o* and Syllable Types

Double *o* and Syllable Types

Schwa and Syllable Types

M·A·R·k¹²™
Reading

Introduction

Welcome to the *MARK¹² Reading* program, designed to help struggling readers significantly increase their reading ability. Before you begin the program, please be sure to read these introductory sections. You will learn how the activities support struggling readers by improving both reading and spelling skills.

About Remediation

Research suggests that about half of young learners experience difficulty in learning to read. Some of these difficulties may be neurologically based, but most derive from a lack of early instruction in the core skills of reading, including decoding (sounding out and taking apart words), vocabulary, fluency, and comprehension.

The good news, however, is that reading difficulties can be remediated. As many research studies confirm, most students, given intense, focused instruction in the core reading skills, can significantly improve their reading ability. The *MARK¹² Reading* program provides the concentrated focus on critical skills; students who devote sufficient time and effort to the program should make significant progress in improving their reading.

Talk with your students about the importance of reading. For people of any age, learning to read is rarely easy, but reading is a critical skill for both academic and social success. As the noted researcher Louisa C. Moats has stated plainly (in *Straight Talk About Reading*), "Reading is the most important skill for success in school and society." By making the commitment to complete the *MARK¹² Reading* program, you and your students are laying the foundation for success in school and beyond.

MARK¹² *Reading*: Overview of Program Components

The *MARK¹² Reading* program provides intensive reading instruction for students in grades 3, 4, and 5. The daily, two-hour lessons build in a sequence that can be adapted to the needs of individual students. The program is flexible because it is organized in three distinct but closely related parts: online reading instruction, offline reading instruction, and offline language arts.

Online Reading Instruction: Independent Work

The online portion of the program is designed for students to complete independently. During online instructional time, students work at the computer to complete Warm-Up, Code Work, Word Work, Sound Work, Speed Work, and Wrap-Up activities. (See *Lesson Components* for explanations of these activities.) Whenever a student completes an online lesson, the system provides a Performance Review with details about the student's performance. Used in conjunction with the Lesson Guide, the Performance Review helps you determine what to teach during the offline reading instruction.

Offline Reading Instruction: Working Together

The offline portion of the program is designed for students to complete *together with you*. Students begin by reviewing and, if necessary, revisiting the objectives of the online material before moving to offline activities. Using the Performance Review and the Lesson Guide, you can make efficient use of your student's time by deciding which activities deserve most attention. If your student performs extremely well on a specific online task, you may only touch on that task during the offline instruction. But if your student struggles with a specific online task, you can follow the instructions in the Lesson Guide to reinforce the concept in a focused, one-on-one, offline instructional session with your student.

Offline Language Arts

The Language Arts portion of the *MARK¹² Reading* program provides offline activities in Composition; in Grammar, Usage, and Mechanics; and in comprehension and analysis of readings in the *Classics for Young Readers* series. This content is similar to the grade-level content in the standard K¹² Language Arts program, but presents less material than the standard program and offers readings revised for increased readability.

Lesson Components

Online and Offline:

Reading Warm-Up – fluency and comprehension skills
Code Work – review, direct instruction, and assessment of phonics-based objectives
Word Work – review, direct instruction, and assessment of sight words or word structure
Sound Work – focused phonological awareness practice
Speed Work – focused fluency practice

Online only:

Wrap-Up – daily assessment of content in the day's lesson
Morris DeCode – a review game at the end of each unit

Offline only:

Grammar, Usage, and Mechanics (GUM) – rules and conventions of writing, including sentence structure and sentence types, parts of speech, punctuation, capitalization, synonyms, antonyms, and homonyms
Classics for Young Readers – classical fiction and nonfiction stories and articles, with accompanying comprehension questions
Composition – writing as process, including creative writing, book reviews, persuasive writing, and writing to a prompt
Unit Assessment – a four-page test of the master objectives covered in a specific unit

Online Reading Instruction

Lesson Components

The online portion of the lesson should take approximately 60 minutes for the student to complete. In this section, you will find details about each component.

ONLINE	**Student & Computer**	**:60** minutes
	Adult : *Check Performance Review*	
OFFLINE	**Student & Adult : Review online work**	**:30** minutes
	• Reading Warm-Up	
	• Code Work	
	• Word Work	
	• Speed Work	
	Grammar, Usage, and Mechanics (GUM)	**:30** minutes
	Instructional Time	**2:00** hours

Warm-Up

Each *MARK¹² Reading* lesson begins with an 8–10 minute Warm-Up activity that focuses attention, increases fluency, and develops comprehension skills.

In the Warm-Up, students follow this procedure:

★ Click the speaker button and listen to the text read aloud with proper intonation and pacing.

★ After listening, click and hold the red Record button, then read the onscreen text aloud. The computer will record the student's voice. To end the recording, release the red Record button. The recording is automatically saved when you release the red Record button.

★ If the student makes a mistake and wishes to make a new recording, click and hold the red Record button again. This will erase the previous recording and begin a new one.

★ To play back and listen to the recording, click the green Play arrow. The student should then click the Forward arrow at the bottom of the page to move on to the next page of the story.

★ As the Learning Coach, you can access the recordings by following the link to the Activity in the Performance Review. You can listen to the student's recordings by clicking the green Play arrow.

> **Note:** Each student will need a headset and a microphone to complete the Warm-Up activities. You might need to mute the computer speakers in order to record without feedback.

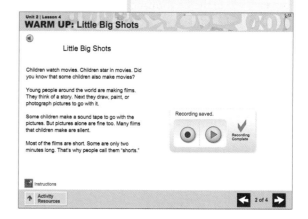

Before moving on to Code Work, students answer five questions about the Warm-Up reading. These questions develop comprehension skills and ensure that students pay close attention during the reading and recording of the passage.

Code Work

Code Work provides direct and systematic instruction in phonological awareness (Unit 1) and phonics (Units 2— 22). Students first complete a practice activity that reinforces earlier concepts. Then they move on to the instructional portion of Code Work. Students listen and watch as the onscreen instruction explains rules of letters and sounds.

Students are then given opportunities to practice what they have just learned, often by clicking and dragging letter tiles to build words.

After completing the Code Work activities, students take a mini-assessment that asks them to answer five to eight questions.

Students should complete the online Code Work activities and the mini-assessment independently, without your assistance or collaboration. The program is gathering information on the student's performance, which you can examine in the Performance Review, thus enabling you to focus the offline instruction on the student's specific needs.

Reading Diacritical Marks

Diacritical marks appear over letters to indicate how they should be pronounced. You will see the following diacritical marks in the *MARK[12] Reading* program:

/ā/ – The short line over the letter *a* is called a macron. When a macron appears over a vowel, it indicates that the vowel is long. In this example, the long *a* sound, as in *cake*, should be read.

/ă/ – The small curved mark over the letter *a* is called a breve. When a breve appears over a vowel, it indicates that the vowel is short. In this example, the short *a* sound, as in *cat*, should be read.

/ə/ – This symbol represents the schwa sound. The schwa is the vowel sound in an unaccented, or nonstressed, syllable. For example, the second (nonstressed) syllable in the word *wagon* is –*on*, and it contains the schwa. Typically, the schwa sound is similar to a short *u* (/ŭ/) or short *i* (/ĭ/) sound, but it can be represented by any vowel.

/o͞o/ – This symbol represents the short double *o* sound, as in *book*.

/o͞o/ – This symbol represents the long double *o* sound, as in *moon*.

/**th**/ - This symbol represents the voiced sound of the digraph *th*, as in *the*, *that*, and *these*.

Word Work

Word Work increases students' vocabulary and understanding of word structure in order to assist with decoding and figuring out word meanings. Students learn about sight words, syllable types, contractions, suffixes, prefixes, base words, and root words.

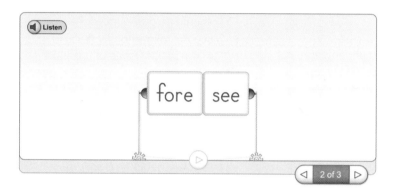

Students begin by briefly reviewing previous content, and then move to the instructional activities. As in Code Work, in Word Work students first listen and watch, then build words, and then complete a mini-assessment. Again, you will find student performance data in the Performance Review.

Sound Work

Sound Work is designed to improve students' phonological awareness, or, the ability to identify and manipulate sounds in words. Without phonological awareness, many students struggle with phonics. For each online Sound Work activity, there is a complementary offline Sound Work activity page that you must print from the Performance Review. Instructions can be found in the Sound Work section of the lesson plan in the Lesson Guide.

Speed Work

Speed Work improves students' *fluency*—the ability to read smoothly and quickly. Fluent readers can devote more attention to comprehension. Without fluency, readers focus on decoding words at the expense of comprehending them.

The student should print a fluency chart by clicking the Print Fluency Chart button. The student can print additional fluency charts as needed. On each chart, the student should fill in his or her name and the date.

At the start of each Speed Work activity, the student is prompted to begin: "Ready! Set! Read!" The decodable text appears onscreen, while a timer runs at the top of the screen. The student reads through each screen of the text, clicking the Next button to move through the pages. When he or she finishes, the student clicks the Stop button. The computer provides a fluency rate (the number of words read per minute), which the student writes down on the fluency chart.

Fluency goals for students vary by grade. In general, the expectations through the course of the *MARK¹² Reading* program are as follows:

★ Third-grade students: 77–110 words per minute

★ Fourth-grade students: 93–118 words per minute

★ Fifth-grade students: 104–124 words per minute

Wrap-Up

The online portion of each lesson concludes with a Wrap-Up, a 10-question assessment of the content presented during the day's Code Work and Word Work activities. You will find student performance data in the Performance Review.

Performance Review

Before moving to the offline portion of the lesson, it is important that you check the Performance Review. You can find the Performance Review on the screen immediately following the Wrap-Up.

To access the Performance Review, you, the Learning Coach, must be logged in. If the student is logged in, you will be prompted to enter your user name and password before accessing the Performance Review.

When you check the Performance Review, make a note of students' scores on the Warm-Up, Code Work, and Word Work activities. For each student, these scores help determine how many offline activities the student should complete.

Unit 2 | Lesson 4
PERFORMANCE REVIEW: /ā/ and Prefix *un-*

Assessment Results

Type	Average	YTD
Warm Up	70%	80%
Code Work	75%	85%
Word Work	100%	90%
Wrap Up	90%	85%

Review Your Student's Recordings
Little Big Shots

Materials

Lesson Guide

Warm-Up: Little Big Shots

Speed Work: Dave's Day

Online Tile Kit

↑ Lesson Materials   ↑ Lesson Resources   ➡

Offline Reading Instruction

Following the online work, the *MARK¹² Reading* program continues with 30 minutes of offline reading instruction, during which you work with the student.

ONLINE	Student & Computer	:60 minutes
	Adult : *Check Performance Review*	
OFFLINE	Student & Adult : Review online work	:30 minutes
	• Reading Warm-Up	
	• Code Work	
	• Word Work	
	• Speed Work	
	Grammar, Usage, and Mechanics (GUM)	:30 minutes
	Instructional Time **2:00** hours	

Lesson Guide

During the offline portion of the lesson, follow the instructions in the *MARK¹² Reading* Lesson Guide. In the Lesson Guide, each lesson is organized as follows:

Short Vowels and Sight Words Review 1

ONLINE	Student & Computer	:60 minutes	Materials
	Adult : *Check Performance Review*		• *MARK¹² Reading Activity Book*, pages 1–4
	Student & Adult : Review online work	:30 minutes	
OFFLINE	• Reading Warm-Up		
	• Code Work		
	• Word Work		
	• Speed Work		
	Grammar, Usage, and Mechanics (GUM)	:30 minutes	
	Instructional Time **2:00** hours		

Goals

In this lesson, students will read about the growth of wild corn. Students will also work with the short vowel sounds /ă/, /ĕ/, /ĭ/, /ŏ/, and /ŭ/ before reviewing the sight words *again*, *friend*, and *goes*. In today's *MARK¹² Reading Activity Book* pages, you will work with students to reinforce the short vowel sounds and sight words, as well as to understand homophones.

Advance Preparation

Based on the Performance Review, if students need to complete Code Work activity 4, you will need to gather 10 index cards. Write one vowel (*a, e, i, o, u*) on each card. Each vowel will be written on two cards, making a total of 10 cards. If students need to complete Word Work activities 2, 3, 4, or 5, you will need to gather six index cards. On each card, write one of the following sight words: *again, friend, goes*. Each word should be written on two cards, making a total of six cards.

| ONLINE | Student & Computer |

Students will work online to complete Warm-Up, Code Work, Word Work, and Speed Work activities, and a Wrap-Up assessment on their own. Be sure to read the Performance Review before beginning the offline portion of today's lesson.

Short Vowels and Sight Words Review 1   1

Overview: Skim this section for a glance at the activities, materials, goals, advance preparation, and tips for instruction for the day's lesson.

Warm-Up: Check the student's Reading Warm-Up score in the Performance Review. If the student scored well, move on to the next activity. Otherwise, follow the instructions.

Warm-Up

Taming Wild Corn: Small Corn

Look at the Performance Review. If the student achieved a perfect score on today's Warm-Up, move on to Code Work. If the student scored 60 percent or 80 percent, print the story and review the comprehension questions with the student. If the student scored less than 60 percent, print the story, have the student read the story aloud, and then work through the comprehension questions together, before moving on to Code Work.

Objectives
- Improve reading and comprehension skills.

Code Work

Short Vowels

Look at the Performance Review. If the student achieved a perfect score on today's Code Work activities, complete the first two activities from the list below. If the student scored less than 100 percent but more than 85 percent, complete the first three activities from the list below. If the student scored 85 percent or less, complete all four of the activities listed below.

Objectives
- Identify and use /ă/, /ĕ/, /ĭ/, /ŏ/, and /ŭ/.

Code Work and Word Work: Check the student's Code Work and Word Work scores in the Performance Review. If the student did well (as defined in the Lesson Guide), he or she should complete the Activity Book pages, and then move on to the next activity. If the student did not perform optimally (as defined in the Lesson Guide), follow the instructions.

Word Work

Sight Words

Look at the Performance Review. If the student achieved a perfect score on today's Word Work activities, complete the first activity from the list below. If the student scored less than 100 percent but more than 85 percent, complete the first three activities from the list below. If the student scored 85 percent or less, complete all five of the activities listed below.

Objectives
- Increase reading and oral vocabulary.
- Identify sight words.

Speed Work

My Pals Sam and Pam

Look at the Performance Review or check the student's fluency chart. Fluency scores (words read per minute) should not fall below 80. If the student scored below 80 words per minute, print a copy of the Speed Work story and have the student read the story silently before reading it aloud. Otherwise, move on to Grammar, Usage, and Mechanics.

Objectives
- Increase reading fluency rate.

Speed Work: Check the student's fluency chart from Speed Work. If the student's scores are not improving or seem excessively high or low, follow the instructions. A fluency range of 60–130 is typical. If students are scoring too low, they may not be attending to the activity or they may be struggling with the content. If students are scoring too high, they may be skipping screens of text, ignoring the text, or finding the text too easy.

Online Tile Kit or Paper Letter Tiles

During the offline Code Work and Word Work activities, you may be instructed to use the Online Tile Kit or Paper Letter Tiles. You and the student can choose which version of the letter tiles you prefer to use.

To access the Online Tile Kit, click on the link located in the Performance Review.

The Paper Letter Tiles are located at the back of the *MARK¹² Reading Activity Book*. Before you begin the program, remove these pages and cut out the letter tiles. The letter tiles are divided into sections. You may want to put each section of cut-out letter tiles in separate envelopes or sealable plastic bags, and label each bag.

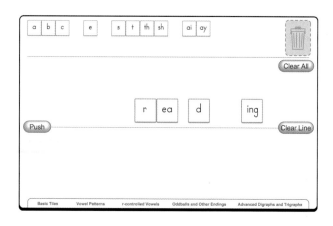

A note about MARK¹² Reading Activity Book pages:

K¹² recommends that you read the instructions to students and observe as students work through the first few items on each Activity Book page. If you see that students are performing well, further observation is not necessary. If students are struggling, provide additional encouragement and questioning to guide students to better understanding. Leaving a student to make his or her "best guess" about answers only serves to reinforce incorrect behaviors and misunderstandings. By observing and guiding, you reinforce the positive and avoid potentially negative consequences of uncorrected errors.

A note about MARK¹² Reading Dictation:

Preceding a list of words or sentences you will often see the direction, "Dictate the following to students." When dictating to students, you should first read the word or sentence aloud to the students. Students should repeat the word or sentence back to you before writing it on their paper. If it is *not* a Unit Assessment, as the students write the word or sentence, you should correctly write the word or sentence on a piece of scrap paper. Repeat with all words or sentences provided. When the students have finished writing all of the dictated words or sentences, they should compare their version to the correct version you wrote. Be sure students make any necessary corrections to their work.

A note about MARK¹² Reading Tear-Out Readers:

For some lessons, the Lesson Guide asks that you remove a story from the Activity Book for students to practice reading. *MARK¹² Reading* Tear-Out Readers provide students with structured, decodable text that reinforces the concepts taught in the day's lesson. These pages are designed to be torn out of the Activity Book, folded in half to form a booklet, and then read and reread until the student has mastered the text. Encourage students to revisit the Tear-Out Reader stories often; the best way to become a fluent reader is to read, read, and read again.

Offline Language Arts Instruction

In this final 30-minute portion of the lesson, students use offline materials to practice a variety of language arts skills. Each lesson includes at least one of the following:

ONLINE	Student & Computer	**:60** minutes
	Adult : *Check Performance Review*	
OFFLINE	Student & Adult : Review online work	**:30** minutes
	• Reading Warm-Up	
	• Code Work	
	• Word Work	
	• Speed Work	
	Grammar, Usage, and Mechanics (GUM)	**:30** minutes
	Instructional Time **2:00** hours	

★ Grammar, Usage, and Mechanics (GUM): rules and conventions of writing

★ Composition: practice in writing sentences, paragraphs, and essays

★ Classics Session: comprehension and analysis of readings, both fiction and nonfiction, from *Classics for Young Readers*

In general, you will work one-on-one with students during this time.

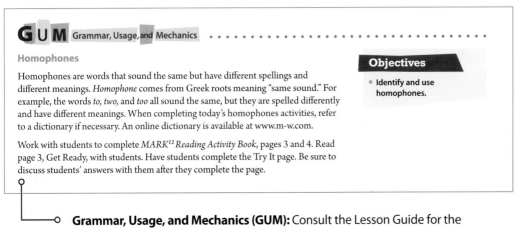

G U M Grammar, Usage, and Mechanics ·

Homophones

Homophones are words that sound the same but have different spellings and different meanings. *Homophone* comes from Greek roots meaning "same sound." For example, the words *to*, *two*, and *too* all sound the same, but they are spelled differently and have different meanings. When completing today's homophones activities, refer to a dictionary if necessary. An online dictionary is available at www.m-w.com.

Work with students to complete *MARK¹² Reading Activity Book*, pages 3 and 4. Read page 3, Get Ready, with students. Have students complete the Try It page. Be sure to discuss students' answers with them after they complete the page.

Objectives
• Identify and use homophones.

Grammar, Usage, and Mechanics (GUM): Consult the Lesson Guide for the GUM lesson. In general:

• Preview the Activity Book content.
• Read through the Get Ready section with the student.
• Have the students complete the Try It guided practice activity.
• Review the student's work and discuss any difficulties.

Composition

Composition instruction is addressed by the book *Just Write*. K[12] recommends that you follow the instructions in the workbook and work for 30 minutes each Composition day on the activities presented in *Just Write*. In the Lesson Guide, you will be prompted to gather your materials and begin where you left off on the previous Composition day.

MARK[12] Reading
Classics for Young Readers

The *MARK[12] Reading* program provides students with retold versions of readings from K[12]'s *Classics for Young Readers* series. Students may write in these books.
The *MARK[12] Reading Classics for Young Readers* series is intended to expose students to high-quality literature that their K[12] peers are reading in the grade-level Language Arts courses. The readings and activities aim to increase vocabulary, fluency, and comprehension skills. The stories are presented in one of two formats—either Listen or Read.

Listen stories, Session 1

★ Download the MP3 audio file from the online lesson. ("MP3" designates a kind of compressed audio file.)

★ Transfer the file to a format that works for you. You may choose to burn it to a CD to use in a CD player, or you may choose to leave it in MP3 format and load it to an MP3 player (such as an iPod®). You can also save the file to your computer and listen directly from your computer.

★ Have students listen to the story while following along in *MARK[12] Reading Classics for Young Readers*.

★ Have students write a summary of the story. Be sure to review the summary with students.

Listen stories, Session 2

★ Have students listen to the story again.

★ Have students answer the comprehension questions that follow the story. Students can write their answers in the space provided.

★ Review and discuss answers with students. Answers can be found in the Lesson Guide.

Read stories, Session 1

★ Discuss with students the keywords presented in the Lesson Guide.

★ Have students read the story. Students should be able to read these stories with minimal assistance. If necessary, read the story with the student.

★ Review the discussion questions with students. You will find these questions below the keywords in the Lesson Guide.

★ Have students write a summary of the story. Review the summary with students.

Read stories, Session 2

★ Discuss with students the keywords presented in the Lesson Guide.

★ Have students reread the story.

★ Have students answer the comprehension questions that follow the story. Students can write their answers in the space provided.

★ Review and discuss answers with students. Answers can be found in the Lesson Guide.

Session 1: Summary

Have students write a summary of the story. Summarizing what one has read leads to increased comprehension. You may want to provide the students with a notebook specifically for writing these summaries. Students should write these summaries in their own words. A good summary contains the story title, setting, and main characters. It includes a recap of main events, presented in the order in which they occurred. Proper grammar, usage, mechanics, and spelling are included. A checklist of these details is provided online. It can be found in the Performance Review on days the student should write a summary. Print a copy of the checklist to guide you as you review the written summary with the student.

Session 2: Comprehension Questions

Students should answer the comprehension questions that follow the story. Students can write their answers in the space provided. Review and discuss answers with students. Answers can be found in the Lesson Guide.

Unit Assessments

The *MARK[12] Reading* curriculum is divided into 22 units. Each unit ends with a Unit Assessment. On these days, the online and offline instructions vary slightly.

For students working independently online, the only difference comes at the end of the online lesson; rather than completing a daily Wrap-Up assessment, the student is provided with a Morris DeCode review game. This game is a one-player review of the content covered in the entire unit. When students have completed the Morris DeCode game, they are ready to move offline.

On Unit Assessment days, the assessments are provided instead of offline Code Work and Word Work activities. You are prompted to remove the assessment pages from the Activity Book and read the instructions to students before administering the assessment. This step is especially important because some activities require you to dictate, or read aloud, certain words to students, while others simply require you to read instructions to students. In the cases where assessment items must be dictated to students, this information is printed in the Lesson Guide in the Unit Assessment box. It is important that you carefully score each student's assessment and then enter the scores in the online assessment input tool.

Words to Know

Phonics – study of sounds and the letters that represent them

Phonological awareness – ability to identify and manipulate sounds in words

Fluency – ability to read smoothly and quickly

Structural Analysis – decoding (taking apart) words by letters and sounds or by word parts (roots, bases, suffixes, prefixes)

Dictation/Dictate – reading words aloud for others to write down

Base word – the part of a word that contains a prefix or a suffix or both. A base word can stand on its own. For example, in the word *happiness*, *happy* is the base word.

Root – a word part that gives a word meaning. In the word *toxic*, the root *tox* gives the word *toxic* its meaning. A root cannot stand on its own—it must always have an affix.

Affix – a word part attached to a word or word part to create a new word. Prefixes come at the beginning of a word, and suffixes come at the end of a word. In the word *unhappiness*, *un* is the prefix, *happy* is the base word, and *ness* is the suffix.

Syllable – a unit of spoken language; a syllable contains only one vowel sound.

Closed Syllable – a syllable that ends with a consonant, making the vowel sound a short vowel; in the word *mister*, the first syllable (*mis*) is a closed syllable.

Open Syllable – a syllable that ends with a vowel, making the vowel sound a long vowel; in the word *refer*, the first syllable (*re*) is an open syllable.

Vowel Team Syllable – a syllable that contains a vowel spelled with two or more letters; in the word day, the –*ay* forms the vowel team.

Consonant –*le* Syllable – a syllable type that comes at the end of a word; in the word *purple*, the second syllable (–*ple*) is a consonant –*le* syllable.

r-Controlled Vowel Syllable – a syllable containing a vowel followed by the letter r, which affects the pronunciation of the vowel. In the word *burglar*, the two syllables (*bur* and *glar*) contain an r-controlled vowel.

Vowel-consonant–*e* (v-c-e) Syllable – a syllable that contains a vowel, then a consonant, followed by a silent *e*, making the vowel sound long. In the word *sunrise*, the second syllable (*rise*) is a v-c-e syllable.

Sound Work and Sight Words 1

ONLINE	Student & Computer		**:60** minutes	
	Adult : *Check Performance Review*			
OFFLINE	Student & Adult : Review online work		**:30** minutes	
	• Reading Warm-Up			
	• Code Work			
	• Word Work			
	• Sound Work			
	Grammar, Usage, and Mechanics (GUM)		**:30** minutes	
		Instructional Time **2:00** hours		

Materials

- Online Tile Kit or Paper Letter Tiles
- Index cards
- *MARK¹² Reading Activity Book*, pages 1–4

Tip

In this unit, the emphasis in Code Work is on individual sounds. For more information, see the Phonological Awareness section of the Introduction.

Goals

In this lesson, students will read about a dog named Sam. Students will also review the alphabet and sounds before learning the sight words *and, the,* and *is*. In today's Grammar, Usage, and Mechanics, you will work with students to identify four types of sentences (*statements, questions, commands,* and *exclamations*).

Advance Preparation

Based on the Performance Review, if students need to complete Word Work activity 2, create sight word cards for the following words: *and, the,* and *is*. If students need to complete Word Work activity 3, you will need a timer and the Online Tile Kit or Paper Letter Tiles. If students need to complete Word Work activity 5, you will need to create a second set of sight word cards for the words *and, the,* and *is*.

ONLINE	**Student & Computer**

Students will work online to complete Warm-Up, Code Work, Word Work, and Sound Work activities, and a Wrap-Up assessment on their own. Be sure to read the Performance Review before beginning the offline portion of today's lesson.

Today you will work with students to complete Code Work, Word Work, and GUM activities. Be sure to read the online Performance Review before beginning the Code Work and Word Work activities.

Warm-Up ·

My Dog Sam

Look at the Performance Review. If the student achieved a perfect score on today's Warm-Up, move on to Code Work. If the student scored 60 percent or 80 percent, print the story and review the comprehension questions with the student. If the student scored less than 60 percent, print the story, have the student read the story aloud, and then work through the comprehension questions together, before moving on to Code Work.

Objectives

- Improve reading and comprehension skills.

Code Work ·

Sounds /m/, /t/, /n/, /p/, /h/, /d/, Long *e*, and Short *o*

Look at the Performance Review. If the student achieved a perfect score on today's Code Work activities, complete the first two activities from the list below. If the student scored less than 100 percent but more than 85 percent, complete the first three activities from the list below. If the student scored 85 percent or less, complete all five of the activities listed below.

Objectives

- Identify letters of the alphabet.
- Identify the word that separately spoken phonemes create.
- Identify the number of sounds within words.
- Identify individual sounds within words.

1. Have students complete page 1 in *MARK¹² Reading Activity Book*. Tell students to listen to the letters that are read to them and write each letter on the lines provided. Dictate the following letters to students: *a, e, i, o, u, f, h, l, t, z, y, x, w, v, n, m, k, s, r, p, c, q, j, g, b,* and *d.*

2. Have students listen as you say the individual sounds in words. Ask students to tell you the whole word. For example, say to students, /h/, /ē/, /t/. Students should answer *heat.* Repeat with one-syllable words.

3. Have students listen as you say the individual sounds in words. Ask students to tell you the number of sounds in each word. For example, say to students, /d/, /ē/, /p/, *deep.* Students should answer three. Repeat this process with five to seven one-syllable words.

4. Say the word *meet.* Tell students to change the first sound in *meet* to the sound /n/ and then name the new word (*neat*). Ask students to change the last sound in *neat* to the sound /d/ (*need*). Ask students to change the middle sound in *need* to /ŏ/ (*nod*). Ask students to change the first sound in *nod* to /t/ (*Todd*). Finally, ask students to change the last sound in *Todd* to /p/ (*top*).

5. Have students say the individual sounds in the following words: *meet, mean, team, teen, neat, need, Pete, heat, heap, mop, Tom, top, hop,* and *odd.*

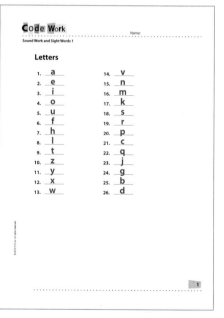

Code Work   Name: _____
Sound Work and Sight Words 1

Letters

1.	a	14.	v
2.	e	15.	n
3.	i	16.	m
4.	o	17.	k
5.	u	18.	s
6.	f	19.	r
7.	h	20.	p
8.	l	21.	c
9.	t	22.	q
10.	z	23.	j
11.	y	24.	g
12.	x	25.	b
13.	w	26.	d

Word Work

Sight Words

Look at the Performance Review. If the student achieved a perfect score on today's Word Work activities, complete the first activity from the list below. If the student scored less than 100 percent but more than 85 percent, complete the first three activities from the list below. If the student scored 85 percent or less, complete all five of the activities listed below.

1. Have students complete page 2 in *MARK¹² Reading Activity Book*. For items 1–3, dictate the words *and, the,* and *is* to students and have students write each word on the lines provided. For items 4–6, have students unscramble each sight word and write the unscrambled words on the lines provided. For items 7–9, ask students to read each word aloud and then say each word in a sentence.

2. Using the sight word cards for *and, the,* and *is,* read each word to students and have students write the words. Give students the cards, and instruct students to look for spelling mistakes. Students should correct any mistakes.

3. Gather the sight word cards and a timer. Have students read all of the sight word cards as accurately and quickly as possible. Make note of the time, as well as any errors students have made. Use the Online Tile Kit or Paper Letter Tiles to review words read incorrectly.

4. Gather the cards for the sight words *and, the,* and *is.* Show the first card to students, and ask students to read the word. If students read the word correctly, place in one pile. If students read the word incorrectly, place in a separate pile. On the back of the cards that were read correctly, make a note of the date and put aside. (Once students have read the word correctly five consecutive days, you can remove the word from the pile of cards students are working on.) Review any words students read incorrectly, and keep the cards for next time.

5. Gather the two sets of sight word cards for the words *and, the,* and *is,* and place all of the cards face down on the table or another flat surface. Have students choose a card, read the word aloud, and then choose a second card. After students read the second card aloud, if the two cards match, students should keep the cards. If they do not match, students should return them to the table. Continue until all cards have been collected.

Sound Work

Sounds: /m/, /t/, /n/, /p/, /h/, Long *e*, /d/, and Short *o*

Print a copy of today's Sound Work activity and work through it with students. Answer any questions students may have about Sound Work. Then, move on to Grammar, Usage, and Mechanics.

Grammar, Usage, and Mechanics ·

Types of Sentences

Sentences begin with a capital letter and end with punctuation. The type of sentence determines the type of punctuation used to end the sentence.

Type of Sentence	Punctuation
Statement: I like candy.	period
Question: What's your favorite food?	question mark
Command: Go home.	period
Exclamation: I won!	exclamation point

Work with students to complete pages 3 and 4 in *MARK¹² Reading Activity Book.* Read page 3, Get Ready, with students. Have students complete the Try It page, reading questions aloud as necessary. Be sure to discuss students' answers when the page is completed.

G U M Grammar, Usage, and Mechanics   Name:
Sound Work and Sight Words 1

Get Ready

■ There are four kinds of **sentences** that have different jobs.

    statements
    questions
    commands
    exclamations

Remember, a sentence is a group of words that expresses a complete thought. A sentence always starts with a capital letter. A sentence always ends with the appropriate punctuation mark. How do you know what kind of punctuation? It depends on the type of sentence.

■ **Statements** are telling sentences and end with a period.

    I like candy.

■ **Questions** are asking sentences and end with a question mark.

    Do you like candy?

■ **Commands** tell what to do and end with a period.

    Eat your dinner.

■ **Exclamations** express strong emotion and end with an exclamation mark.

    You did great work today!

3

G U M Grammar, Usage, and Mechanics   Name:
Sound Work and Sight Words 1

Try It

Draw a line from each sentence type to the appropriate punctuation.

    command   ?
    exclamation   .
    question   .
    statement   !

Listen as each sentence is read to you. Write the appropriate punctuation at the end of each sentence.

1. Sit down and talk to me .
2. What movie did you go to see ?
3. That sounds exciting !
4. I would like to see that movie, too .

4

Sound Work and Sight Words 2

ONLINE	**Student & Computer**	**:60** minutes	
	Adult : *Check Performance Review*		
OFFLINE	**Student & Adult : Review online work**	**:30** minutes	
	• Reading Warm-Up		
	• Code Work		
	• Word Work		
	• Sound Work		
	Classics Session 1	**:30** minutes	
		Instructional Time **2:00** hours	

Materials

- *MARK*[12] *Classics for Young Readers*
- *MARK*[12] *Reading Activity Book*, pages 5–8

Goals

In this lesson, students will read about camping in the backyard. Students will also review rhyming words and sounds before reviewing the sight words *and, the,* and *is.* In today's Classics activity, you will work with students on the story, "The Necklace of Truth."

Advance Preparation

Based on the Performance Review, if students need to complete Word Work activity 2, gather the sight word cards for the following words: *and, the,* and *is.* If students need to complete Word Work activity 3, you will need a timer and the Online Tile Kit or Paper Letter Tiles. If students need to complete Word Work activity 5, gather the second set of sight word cards for the words *and, the,* and *is.*

ONLINE | Student & Computer

Students will work online to complete Warm-Up, Code Work, Word Work, and Sound Work activities, and a Wrap-Up assessment on their own. Be sure to read the Performance Review before beginning the offline portion of today's lesson.

Today you will work with students to complete Code Work, Word Work, and *MARK¹² Classics for Young Readers* activities. Be sure to read the online Performance Review before beginning the Code Work and Word Work activities.

Warm-Up ·

Backyard Camping

Look at the Performance Review. If the student achieved a perfect score on today's Warm-Up, move on to Code Work. If the student scored 60 percent or 80 percent, print the story and review the comprehension questions with the student. If the student scored less than 60 percent, print the story, have the student read the story aloud, and then work through the comprehension questions together, before moving on to Code Work.

 ode Work ·

Sounds /b/, /f/, Long *a*, /g/, Short *o*, and /j/

Look at the Performance Review. If the student achieved a perfect score on today's Code Work activities, complete the first two activities from the list below. If the student scored less than 100 percent but more than 85 percent, complete the first three activities from the list below. If the student scored 85 percent or less, complete all four of the activities listed below.

1. Have students complete page 5 in *MARK¹² Reading Activity Book*. Tell students to listen to each pair of words that is read to them. Dictate the first word pair shown on the answer key to students. If the two words in the pair rhyme, students should write a check mark on the line provided. If the two words do not rhyme, students should write an X on the line provided. Continue with all word pairs.

2. Have students complete page 6 in *MARK¹² Reading Activity Book*. Tell students to write the missing lowercase or missing uppercase letter for each letter on the lines provided.

3. Dictate the following words to students, one at a time, and have students say the individual sounds in each word: *tame, bait, fate, gape, Jane, goat, dome, boat, hope, jog, made, job, gain, page,* and *hope.*

4. Say the word *mate*. Tell students to take away the first sound in *mate* and then say the new word (*ate*). Ask students to change the last sound in *ate* to the sound /p/ (*ape*). Ask students to change the last sound in *ape* to /m/ (*aim*). Ask students to add the sound /n/ to the beginning of the word *aim* (*name*). Ask students to change the first sound in *name* to /f/ (*fame*). Ask students to change the last sound in *fame* to /t/ (*fate*). Ask students to change the first sound in *fate* to /g/ (*gate*). Finally, ask students to change the middle sound in *gate* to /ō/ (*goat*).

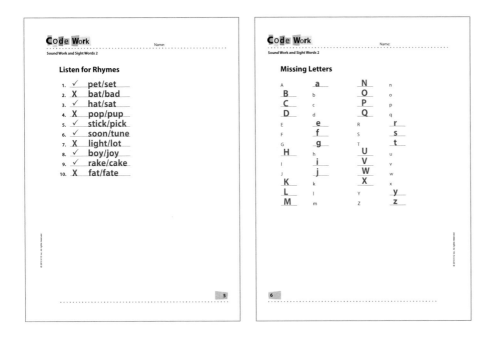

 Word Work

Look at the Performance Review. If the student achieved a perfect score on today's Word Work activities, complete the first activity from the list below. If the student scored less than 100 percent but more than 85 percent, complete the first three activities from the list below. If the student scored 85 percent or less, complete all five of the activities listed below.

1. Have students complete page 7 in *MARK¹² Reading Activity Book*. Tell students to listen to the word that is read to them. Dictate to students the word *the*. Students should write the word in the first column and then read the word aloud. Students should then place a check mark in the second column. Next, students should cover the word, and try to write it again in the third column. Students should then uncover the word and check their spelling. If they wrote it correctly, they should place a check in the fourth column. Repeat with the words *and* and *is*.

2. Have students complete page 8 in *MARK¹² Reading Activity Book*. For items 1–3, have students say each word in a sentence. For items 4–6, have students write the words *is, and,* and *the* on the lines provided.

3. Using the sight word cards for *the, and,* and *is,* read each word to students and have students write the words. Give students the cards, and instruct students to look for spelling mistakes. Students should correct the mistakes.

4. Gather all of the sight word cards students have worked on to date and a timer. Have students read all of the sight word cards as accurately and quickly as possible. Make note of the time, as well as any errors students have made. Use the Online Tile Kit or Paper Letter Tiles to review words read incorrectly.

5. Gather the cards for the sight words *and, the,* and *is,* and up to two additional sight words students have yet to master. Show the first card to students, and ask students to read the word. If students read the word correctly, place in one pile. If students read the word incorrectly, place in a separate pile. On the back of the cards that were read correctly, make a note of the date and put aside. (Once students have read the word correctly five consecutive days, you can remove the word from the pile of cards students are working on.) Review any words students read incorrectly, and keep the cards for next time.

Word Work

Name:

Sight Words: Spell and Check

Listen and Write	Read	Cover and Write	Check
the	✓	the	✓
and	✓	and	✓
is	✓	is	✓

7

Word Work

Name:

Sight Words Practice

1. is
2. and
3. the

4. is
5. and
6. the

8

Sound Work ·

Sounds: /b/, /f/, Long *a*, /g/, Short *o*, and /j/

Print a copy of today's Sound Work activity and work through it with students. Answer any questions students may have about Sound Work. Then, move on to Classics Sesssion 1.

Objectives

- Increase reading fluency rate.

Classics Session 1 ·

The Necklace of Truth

Today's story, "The Necklace of Truth," is a story of a young girl who learns the importance of telling the truth. Review the keywords with students. Read the story with students, and then use the Discussion Questions below as a guide to share ideas about the story. Have students read the story again before writing a summary of the story.

Objectives

- Improve reading and comprehension skills.

Keywords

clasp, n. – a type of hook that holds two things together
To take off my necklace, I unhooked the **clasp**.

stern, adj. – strict, no-nonsense; very serious
"You must clean up your room before you go play," she said in a **stern** voice.

satin, n. – a smooth, shiny material
Her red **satin** dress shimmered under the lights on the dance floor.

confess, v. – to admit to
"I confess," my mom giggled. "I ate the last cookie!"

Discussion Questions

1. Pearl's parents were unhappy at the beginning of the story. How did they most likely feel at the end of the story? Answers may include that Pearl's parents are most likely relieved and happy at the end of the story because Pearl no longer lies.

2. What does the following sentence from the story mean?
   Merlin was a great friend of truth.
   Answers may include that it means Merlin believed honesty was the best policy. He knew lying was wrong. He would not lie himself and thought others should never lie.

3. What does the following sentence from the story mean?
   A wizard knows a liar from miles away.
   Answers may include that it means that it is easy to recognize a liar.

4. Why do you think Pearl lies so much? What are some reasons people lie?
   Answers will vary.

5. Why is it important to always tell the truth? Answers will vary.

Students should write a summary of the story to complete today's Classics activity.

Sound Work and Sight Words 3

ONLINE	Student & Computer	:60 minutes
	Adult : *Check Performance Review*	
OFFLINE	Student & Adult : Review online work	:30 minutes
	• Reading Warm-Up	
	• Code Work	
	• Word Work	
	• Sound Work	
	Classics Session 2	:30 minutes
	Instructional Time **2:00** hours	

Materials

- *MARK[12] Classics for Young Readers*
- *MARK[12] Reading Activity Book*, pages 9–10

Tip

Today's lesson includes work on syllables. All words are made of syllables. A syllable always has a vowel sound. Some words have one syllable, some have more.

Goals

In this lesson, students will read about a boy named Tom who gets lost while on a bike ride. Students will also review syllables and sounds before learning three new sight words: *on, to,* and *in*. In today's Classics activity, you will work with students to complete comprehension questions about "The Necklace of Truth."

Advance Preparation

Based on the Performance Review, if students need to complete Word Work activity 2, create sight word cards for the following words: *on, to,* and *in*. If students need to complete Word Work activity 3, you will need a timer and the Online Tile Kit or Paper Letter Tiles. If students need to complete Word Work activity 5, create a second set of sight word cards for the words *on, to,* and *in*.

ONLINE   Student & Computer

Students will work online to complete Warm-Up, Code Work, Word Work, and Sound Work activities, and a Wrap-Up assessment on their own. Be sure to read the Performance Review before beginning the offline portion of today's lesson.

Today you will work with students to complete Code Work, Word Work, and *MARK¹² Classics for Young Readers* activities. Be sure to read the online Performance Review before beginning the Code Work and Word Work activities.

Warm-Up ·······················

Lost

Look at the Performance Review. If the student achieved a perfect score on today's Warm-Up, move on to Code Work. If the student scored 60 percent or 80 percent, print the story and review the comprehension questions with the student. If the student scored less than 60 percent, print the story, have the student read the story aloud, and then work through the comprehension questions together, before moving on to Code Work.

Code Work ·······················

Sounds /s/, /ă/, /w/, /z/, /ī/, & /l/

Look at the Performance Review. If the student achieved a perfect score on today's Code Work activities, complete the first two activities from the list below. If the student scored less than 100 percent but more than 85 percent, complete the first three activities from the list below. If the student scored 85 percent or less, complete all four of the activities listed below.

1. Have students complete page 9 in *MARK¹² Reading Activity Book*. To complete the items, ask students the following questions. If the answer is "yes," students should write a *Y* on the line provided. If the answer is "no," students should write an *N* on the line provided. Do you hear the sound /s/ in the word *wipes*? Repeat the question using the following: /ŏ/ in the word *mat*; /w/ in the word *wide*; /z/ in the word *as*; /ĭ/ in the name *Sam*; /l/ in the word *candle*; /ă/ in the word *lamp*; /ī/ in the word *dime*; /w/ in the word *what*, and /ă/ in the word *dog*.

2. Ask students to identify the number of syllables in the words: *hammer* (2), *life* (1), *alphabet* (3), *mother* (2), and *camera* (3).

3. Say the word *wise*. Tell students to change the first sound in *wise* to the sound /l/. Ask students to name the new word (*lies*). Ask students to change the last sound in *lies* to the sound /t/ (*light*). Ask students to change the middle sound in *light* to /ŏ/ (*lot*). Ask students to change the first sound in *lot* to /b/ (*bought*).

4. Help students count the number of sounds in words. For example: *Hammer*: /h/, /ă/, /m/, /r/. *Hammer has 4 sounds*. Repeat with words from activity 2. *Life*: /l/, /ī/, /f/ (3); *Alphabet*: /ă/, /l/, /f/, /ŭ/, /b/, /ĕ/, /t/ (7); *Mother*: /m/ /ŭ/, /th/ /r/ (4); *Camera*: /k/ /ă/ /m/ /r/ /ŭ/ (5).

Code Work   Name: _____

Sound Work and Sight Words 3

Listen for Sounds

1. __Y__
2. __N__
3. __Y__
4. __Y__
5. __N__
6. __Y__
7. __Y__
8. __Y__
9. __Y__
10. __N__

9

Word Work

Sight Words

Look at the Performance Review. If the student achieved a perfect score on today's Word Work activities, complete the first activity from the list below. If the student scored less than 100 percent but more than 85 percent, complete the first three activities from the list below. If the student scored 85 percent or less, complete all five of the activities listed below.

Objectives

- Read sight words.
- Increase reading vocabulary.

1. Have students complete page 10 in *MARK¹² Reading Activity Book*. For items 1–6, dictate the words shown in the answer key to students. Tell students to write each word on the lines provided. For items 7–12, tell students to unscramble each sight word and write the unscrambled words on the lines provided. For items 13–18, tell students to read each word aloud and then say each word in a sentence.

2. Using the sight word cards for *on, to,* and *in,* read each word to students and have students write the words. Give students the cards, and instruct students to look for any spelling mistakes. Students should correct the mistakes.

3. Gather all of the sight word cards students have worked on to date and a timer. Have students read all of the sight word cards as accurately and quickly as possible. Make note of the time, as well as any errors students have made. Use the Online Tile Kit or Paper Letter Tiles to review words read incorrectly.

4. Gather the cards for the sight words *on, to,* and *in,* and up to two additional sight words students have yet to master. Show the first card to students, and ask students to read the word. If students read the word correctly, place in one pile. If students read the word incorrectly, place in a separate pile. On the back of the cards that were read correctly, make a note of the date and put aside. (Once students have read the word correctly five consecutive days, you can remove the word from the pile of cards students are working on.) Review any words students read incorrectly, and keep the cards for next time.

5. Gather the two sets of sight word cards for *on, to,* and *in,* and place all of the cards face down. Have students choose a card, read the word aloud, and then choose a second card. After students read the second card aloud, if the two cards match, students should keep the cards. If they do not match, students should return them to the table. Continue until all cards are collected.

Word Work

Name:

Sound Work and Sight Words 3

Sight Words Practice

1. in
2. and
3. on
4. the
5. is
6. to

7. ot to
8. ni in
9. no on
10. si is
11. dna and
12. het the

13. to
14. is
15. the
16. on
17. and
18. in

10

Sound Work

Sounds: /s/, Short *a*, /w/, /z/, Long *i*, and /l/

Print a copy of today's Sound Work activity and work through it with students. Answer any questions students may have about Sound Work. Otherwise, move on to Classics Session 2.

Objectives

- Increase reading fluency rate.

Classics Session 2

The Necklace of Truth

Review the keywords with students. Have students reread the story on their own. After rereading the story, students should complete the comprehension questions in *MARK¹² Classics for Young Readers* book on their own. Afterward, if time allows, have students read the story aloud to you.

- Improve reading and comprehension questions.

W Write

The Necklace of Truth

1. Whose idea is it to take Pearl to the wizard?
   A. Pearl's
   B. Merlin's
   C. Pearl's father
   D. Pearl's mother

2. Why do Pearl's parents take her to Merlin?
   Pearl's parents take her to Merlin because they know she lies. They are hopeful that Merlin can cure her.

3. What does Merlin give Pearl?
   Merlin gives Pearl a necklace.

4. How does Pearl describe the coach and driver that she claims Merlin sent for her?
   Pearl says the coach seats were red satin. Six white horses pulled the coach. The driver wore a vest lined with gold.

The Necklace of Truth   5

---

5. How does the necklace show that Pearl is lying?
   The necklace changes to show that Pearl is lying. One time the diamond turned dull. When Pearl stretched the truth, the necklace stretched. When Pearl lied, the necklace shortened.

6. Why did the children stop laughing at Pearl?
   A. They knew they told lies, too.
   B. They wanted to help her tell the truth.
   C. They saw her crying and felt sorry for her.
   D. They were afraid the necklace might choke them.

7. Pearl told many lies. Which of the following is **not** a lie Pearl told?
   A. Merlin had a garden of gems at his palace.
   B. Merlin sent a coach pulled by six white horses.
   C. Merlin said the present was a gift for the truthful.
   D. Merlin told Pearl she was the smartest little girl he knew.

8. Why does Merlin take the necklace back?
   A. He believes Pearl is cured.
   B. He thinks the necklace is not working.
   C. He needs the necklace for another little girl.
   D. He does not think Pearl will ever learn to be truthful.

6   The Necklace of Truth

Sound Work and Sight Words 4

ONLINE	Student & Computer	**:60** minutes	
	Adult : *Check Performance Review*		
OFFLINE	Student & Adult : Review online work	**:30** minutes	
	• Reading Warm-Up		
	• Code Work		
	• Word Work		
	• Sound Work		
	Composition	**:30** minutes	
		Instructional Time **2:00** hours	

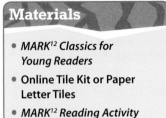

Materials

- *MARK¹² Classics for Young Readers*
- *Online Tile Kit or Paper Letter Tiles*
- *MARK¹² Reading Activity Book*, pages 11–14
- *Just Write*

Tip

*If students struggle with /th/ and /th/, have them place their fingers on their voice box while saying the words **thin** and **this**. The student will not feel the voicebox move with the sound /th/, as in **thin**, but will feel it move with the sound /th/, as in **this**.*

Goals

In this lesson, students will read about a little girl who likes to climb trees. Students will also learn new sounds before reviewing the sight words *on, to,* and *in.* In today's *MARK¹² Reading Activity Book* pages, you will work with students to review sounds and work with sight words.

Advance Preparation

Based on the Performance Review, if students need to complete Word Work activity 2, gather the sight word cards for the following words: *on, to,* and *in.* If students need to complete Word Work activity 3, you will need a timer and the Online Tile Kit or Paper Letter Tiles. If students need to complete Word Work activity 5, gather the second set of sight word cards for the words *on, to,* and *in.*

ONLINE   Student & Computer

Students will work online to complete Warm-Up, Code Work, Word Work, and Sound Work activities, and a Wrap-Up assessment on their own. Be sure to read the Performance Review before beginning the offline portion of today's lesson.

Today you will work with students to complete Code Work, Word Work, and Composition activities. Be sure to read the online Performance Review before beginning the Code Work and Word Work activities.

Warm-Up ·

May In the Tree

Look at the Performance Review. If the student achieved a perfect score on today's Warm-Up, move on to Code Work. If the student scored 60 percent or 80 percent, print the story and review the comprehension questions with the student. If the student scored less than 60 percent, print the story, have the student read the story aloud, and then work through the comprehension questions together, before moving on to Code Work.

Objectives

- Improve reading and comprehension skills.

Code Work ·

/th/, /th/, /k/, /ĕ/, /v/, and /r/

Look at the Performance Review. If the student achieved a perfect score on today's Code Work activities, complete the first two activities from the list below. If the student scored less than 100 percent but more than 85 percent, complete the first three activities from the list below. If the student scored 85 percent or less, complete all four of the activities listed below.

Objectives

- Identify the new word when onset or rime changes.
- Identify the word from separately spoken phonemes.
- Identify the new word when one sound is changed.

1. Have students complete pages 11 and 12 in *MARK¹² Reading Activity Book*. For page 11, tell students to listen to each word read to them. Read aloud each word shown in the answer key, beginning with *ties*. As each new word is read, either the beginning, middle, or end sound of the prior word will change. If the beginning sound changes, tell students to mark the first box in the row. If the middle sound changes, tell students to mark the second box. If the end sound changes, tell students to mark the last box. For page 12, tell students to listen to each word read to them. Read aloud each word shown on the answer key. Tell students to write the number of syllables in each word on the lines provided.

2. Ask students to change the first sound of a word to make a new word. For example, *chat* can become *bat, cat, fat, hat, mat, nat, pat, rat, sat,* and *vat*.

3. Have students tell you the words that individual sounds make. For example, if you say /ch/ ... /ĭ/ ... /p/, students should answer *chip*.

4. Say the word *thick*. Tell students to change the first sound in *thick* to the sound /ch/. Ask students to name the new word (*chick*). Ask students to change the last sound in *chick* to the sound /p/. Students should answer *chip*. Ask students to change the middle sound in *chip* to /ŏ/. Students should answer *chop*. Ask students to change the first sound in *chop* to /k/. Students should answer *cop*. Ask students to change the middle sound in cop to /ă/. Students should answer *cap*. Ask students to change the last sound in *cap* to the sound /t/. Students should answer *cat*. Finally, ask students to change the first sound in *cat* to /th/. Students should answer *that*.

Sound Chains

1.	X			ties
2.			X	wise
3.	X			white
4.		X		bite
5.	X			boat
6.			X	coat
7.	X			cope
8.		X		hope
9.	X			hop
10.	X			chop
11.		X		pop
12.			X	pup
				putt

11

Counting Syllables

1. 3 elephant
2. 1 dog
3. 2 monkey
4. 1 cat
5. 2 rabbit
6. 4 alligator
7. 2 ostrich
8. 1 bear
9. 3 chimpanzee
10. 2 lion
11. 1 fox
12. 2 tiger

12

Word Work

· ·

Sight Words

Look at the Performance Review. If the student achieved a perfect score on today's Word Work activities, complete the first activity from the list below. If the student scored less than 100 percent but more than 85 percent, complete the first three activities from the list below. If the student scored 85 percent or less, complete all five of the activities listed below.

Objectives

- **Read sight words.**
- **Increase reading vocabulary.**

1. Have students complete pages 13 and 14 in *MARK¹² Reading Activity Book*. For page 13, tell students to find the words from the word box in the word search and circle them. Words may go left to right or up and down. For page 14, tell students to listen to the words that are read to them and write each word on the lines provided. Read the words shown in the answer key to students.

2. Using the sight word cards for *on, to,* and *in,* read each word to students and have students write the words. Give students the cards, and instruct students to look for any spelling mistakes. Students should correct the mistakes.

3. Gather all of the sight word cards students have worked on to date and a timer. Have students read all of the sight word cards as accurately and quickly as possible. Make note of the time, as well as any errors students have made. Use the Online Tile Kit or Paper Letter Tiles to review words read incorrectly.

4. Gather the cards for the sight words *on, to,* and *in,* and up to two additional sight words students have yet to master. Show the first card to students, and ask students to read the word. If students read the word correctly, place in one pile. If students read the word incorrectly, place in a separate pile. On the back of the cards that were read correctly, make a note of the date and put aside. (Once students have read the word correctly five consecutive days, you can remove the word from the pile of cards students are working on.) Review any words students read incorrectly, and keep the cards for next time.

5. Gather the two sets of sight word cards for the words *on, to,* and *in,* and place all of the cards face down. Have students choose a card, read the word aloud, and then choose a second card. After students read the second card aloud, if the two cards match, students should keep the cards. If they do not match, students should return them to the table. Continue until all cards are collected.

Word Work

Name:

Sound Work and Sight Words 4

Word Search

| the | to | on | and | is | in |

i	s	b	o	n
j	t	h	e	z
q	v	x	k	m
t	o	h	i	n
a	n	d	w	r

13

Word Work

Name:

Sound Work and Sight Words 4

Dictation

1. the
2. and
3. is
4. on
5. in
6. to

14

Sound Work •

Sounds: /th/, /th/, /k/, Short e, /v/, and /r/

Print a copy of today's Sound Work activity and work through it with students. Answer any questions students may have about Sound Work. Otherwise, move on to Composition.

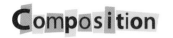omposition ··

Gather students' composition materials and begin where they left off.

bjectives

- Develop composition skills.

20   **Sound Work and Sight Words**

Sound Work and Sight Words 5

ONLINE	Student & Computer	**:60**	minutes
	Adult : *Check Performance Review*		
OFFLINE	Student & Adult : Review online work	**:30**	minutes
	• Reading Warm-Up		
	• Code Work		
	• Word Work		
	• Sound Work		
	Grammar, Usage, and Mechanics (GUM)	**:30**	minutes
	Instructional Time **2:00** hours		

Materials

- **Online Tile Kit or Paper Letter Tiles**
- *MARK[12] Reading Activity Book*, pages 15–18

Goals

In this lesson, students will read about a lion named Leo. Students will also learn new sounds before being introduced to the sight words *it, he,* and *was.* In today's *MARK[12] Reading Activity Book* pages, you will work with students to review sounds and work with sight words before completing work on identifying subjects.

Advance Preparation

Based on the Performance Review, if students need to complete Word Work activity 2, create sight word cards for the following words: *it, he,* and *was.* If students need to complete Word Work activity 3, you will need a timer and the Online Tile Kit or Paper Letter Tiles. If students need to complete Word Work activity 5, create a second set of sight word cards for the words *it, he,* and *was.*

ONLINE   Student & Computer

Students will work online to complete Warm-Up, Code Work, Word Work, and Sound Work activities, and a Wrap-Up assessment on their own. Be sure to read the Performance Review before beginning the offline portion of today's lesson.

Today you will work with students to complete Code Work, Word Work, and GUM activities. Be sure to read the online Performance Review before beginning the Code Work and Word Work activities.

Warm-Up ....

Leo the Lion

Look at the Performance Review. If the student achieved a perfect score on today's Warm-Up, move on to Code Work. If the student scored 60 percent or 80 percent, print the story and review the comprehension questions with the student. If the student scored less than 60 percent, print the story, have the student read the story aloud, and then work through the comprehension questions together, before moving on to Code Work.

Objectives

- Improve reading and comprehension skills.

Code Work. ....

/ĭ/, /ŭ/, /ch/, and /y/

Look at the Performance Review. If the student achieved a perfect score on today's Code Work activities, complete the first two activities from the list below. If the student scored less than 100 percent but more than 85 percent, complete the first three activities from the list below. If the student scored 85 percent or less, complete all five of the activities listed below.

Objectives

- Identify sounds in words.
- Identify the word that separately spoken phonemes create.

1. Have students complete page 15 in *MARK¹² Reading Activity Book*. Tell students to listen to the words that are read to them. Read aloud the words shown in the answer key. Tell students to write the number of sounds heard in each word on the lines provided.

2. Have students say the individual sounds in the following words: *chin, yum, hitch, chip, thick, yet, red, rub, yak, chap, these, thud, yes,* and *rose.*

3. Ask students to listen as you say the individual sounds in words. Have students tell you the whole word. For example, say to students, /ch/, /ĭ/, /p/. Students should answer *chip.*

4. Have students listen as you say the individual sounds in words. Ask students to tell you the number of sounds in each word. For example, say to students, /p/, /ĭ/, /ch/, *pitch.* Students should answer three.

5. Say the word *fed.* Tell students to change the first sound in *fed* to /h/. Ask students to name the new word (*head*). Tell students to change the last sound in *head* to /m/. Ask students to name the new word (*hem*). Tell students to change the middle sound in *hem* to /ĭ/. Ask students to name the new word (*him*). Tell students to change the first sound in *him* to /j/. Ask students to name the new word (*Jim*). Tell students to change the middle sound in *Jim* to /ă/ (*jam*).

Code Work		Name:
Sound Work and Sight Words 5		

Counting Sounds

1.	3	chip
2.	3	much
3.	4	fifth
4.	4	river
5.	2	itch
6.	3	thick
7.	3	shed
8.	2	shy
9.	5	visit
10.	3	catch
11.	3	wise
12.	2	the

15

Word Work

Objectives

Sight Words

Look at the Performance Review. If the student achieved a perfect score on today's Word Work activities, complete the first activity from the list below. If the student scored less than 100 percent but more than 85 percent, complete the first three activities from the list below. If the student scored 85 percent or less, complete all five of the activities listed below.

Objectives
- Read sight words.
- Increase reading vocabulary.

1. Have students complete page 16 in *MARK¹² Reading Activity Book.* Tell students to see how fast they can read all of the words on the page. Time students and record their time for the first round. After students have read the words once, tell them to read the words again and try to beat their first time. Record students' time for the second round.

2. Using the sight word cards for *it, he,* and *was,* read each word to students and have students write the words. Give students the cards, and instruct students to look for any spelling mistakes. Students should correct the mistakes.

3. Gather all of the sight word cards students have worked on to date and a timer. Have students read all of the sight word cards as accurately and quickly as possible. Make note of the time, as well as any errors students have made. Use the Online Tile Kit or Paper Letter Tiles to review words read incorrectly.

4. Gather the cards for the sight words *it, he,* and *was,* and up to two additional sight words students have yet to master. Show the first card to students, and ask students to read the word. If students read the word correctly, place in one pile. If students read the word incorrectly, place in a separate pile. On the back of the cards that were read correctly, make a note of the date and put aside. (Once students have read the word correctly five consecutive days, you can remove the word from the pile of cards students are working on.) Review any words students read incorrectly, and keep the cards for next time.

5. Gather the two sets of sight word cards for the words *it, he,* and *was,* and place all of the cards face down. Have students choose a card, read the word aloud, and then choose a second card. After students read the second card aloud, if the two cards match, students should keep the cards. If they do not match, students should return them to the table. Continue until all cards are collected.

Word Work
Sound Work and Sight Words 5
Name:

Sight Words

the	on	it
in	and	he
is	it	in
was	to	and
on	the	was
to	he	is

Time for first round: _____

Time for second round: _____

16

Sound Work

Sounds: Short *i*, Short *u*, /ch/, and /y/

Print a copy of today's Sound Work activity and work through it with students. Answer any questions students may have about Sound Work. Then, move on to Grammar, Usage, and Mechanics.

Objectives
- Identify sounds, given letters.

Grammar, Usage, and Mechanics

Identifying Subjects

All sentences contain a subject. The subject is typically a noun that names the person, place, or thing that the sentence is about.

Work with students to complete pages 17 and 18 in *MARK¹²Reading Activity Book*. Read page 17, Get Ready, with students. Have students complete the Try It page. To complete the Try It page, you will need to dictate each sentence to students. Be sure to discuss students' answers when the page is completed.

Objectives

- Identify subjects.

Page 17

G U M Grammar, Usage, and Mechanics   Name:

Sound Work and Sight Words 5

Get Ready

☑ All sentences have **subjects**. Let's learn what subjects are.

A sentence is a group of words that expresses a complete thought. A sentence always starts with a *capital letter*. A sentence always ends with the appropriate *punctuation mark*. A sentence always contains a *subject*. The subject of a sentence tells the person, place, or thing the sentence is about.

☑ To identify the subject of the sentence, it may help to ask, "Who is this sentence about?" or, "What is the sentence about?"

Avery is late again! *Who* is the sentence about? Avery. The subject of the sentence is *Avery*.

The capital of the United States of America is Washington, DC. *What* is the sentence about? The capital. The subject of the sentence is *capital*.

Remember: All sentences have a subject. The subject identifies the person, place, or thing that the sentence is about.

17

Page 18

G U M Grammar, Usage, and Mechanics   Name:

Sound Work and Sight Words 5

Try It

Listen as each sentence is read to you. Underline the subject in each sentence. Remember, a subject names the person, place, or thing that the sentence is about.

1. The bluebird perched on the birdhouse.
2. Brady was sick yesterday.
3. Jasper is friends with me.
4. The firemen rushed to the burning building.
5. The troop leader said we would camp out next month.
6. Sarah helped Mom pack.
7. The bike has a flat tire.
8. That lamp needs a new light bulb.
9. Can I have a tissue, please?
10. Jake and I are going to the movies.
11. The waitress brought us our desserts.
12. Dad went to the library without me!

18

Sound Work and Sight Words 6

ONLINE	Student & Computer	**:60** minutes	
	Adult : *Check Performance Review*		
OFFLINE	Student & Adult : Review online work	**:30** minutes	
	• Reading Warm-Up		
	• Code Work		
	• Word Work		
	• Sound Work		
	Composition	**:30** minutes	
		Instructional Time **2:00** hours	

Materials

- Online Tile Kit or Paper Letter Tiles
- *MARK¹² Reading Activity Book*, pages 19–22
- *Just Write*

Tip

*In English, the letter **q** is always followed by a **u**. Together these letters make the sound **/kw/**. Later, students will learn the letters **qu** make the sound **/kw/**, but today they should focus on the sound **/kw/** and not the letters that make the sound.*

Goals

In this lesson, students will read about a girl who plays soccer. Students will also learn about the sounds /sh/, /aw/, and /kw/ before reviewing sight words.

Advance Preparation

Based on the Performance Review, if students need to complete Word Work activity 2, gather the sight word cards for the following words: *it, he,* and *was.* If students need to complete Word Work activity 3, you will need a timer and the Online Tile Kit or Paper Letter Tiles. If students need to complete Word Work activity 5, gather the second set of sight word cards for the words *it, he,* and *was.*

ONLINE — Student & Computer

Students will work online to complete Warm-Up, Code Work, Word Work, and Sound Work activities, and a Wrap-Up assessment on their own. Be sure to read the Performance Review before beginning the offline portion of today's lesson.

Today you will work with students to complete Code Work, Word Work, and Composition activities. Be sure to read the online Performance Review before beginning the Code Work and Word Work activities.

#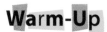

Sue Plays Soccer

Look at the Performance Review. If the student achieved a perfect score on today's Warm-Up, move on to Code Work. If the student scored 60 percent or 80 percent, print the story and review the comprehension questions with the student. If the student scored less than 60 percent, print the story, have the student read the story aloud, and then work through the comprehension questions together, before moving on to Code Work.

#

/sh/, /aw/, and /kw/

Look at the Performance Review. If the student achieved a perfect score on today's Code Work activities, complete the first two activities from the list below. If the student scored less than 100 percent but more than 85 percent, complete the first three activities from the list below. If the student scored 85 percent or less, complete all four of the activities listed below.

1. Have students complete page 19 in *MARK¹² Reading Activity Book*. Tell students to listen to each word that is read to them. Read each word shown in the answer key. If a word has the sound /kw/ in it, tell students to mark the column with the picture of a queen. If a word has the sound /sh/, tell students to mark the column with a picture of a shoe. If a word has the sound /aw/, tell students to mark the column with a picture of a paw.

2. Have students complete page 20 in *MARK¹² Reading Activity Book*. Tell students to listen to the word that is read to them. Read the first word shown in the answer key. Tell students to count the number of sounds in the word, and mark a box in the first row for each sound in the word. Show students the example and explain that the word *August* contains five sounds, so five boxes have been marked. Continue for all words shown in the answer key.

3. Ask students to identify the individual sounds in the words used on page 19 of *MARK¹² Reading Activity Book*. For example, students should say, "Quilt. /kw/, /ĭ/, /l/, /t/. Quilt," and so on.

4. Have students listen as you say the individual sounds in words. Ask students to tell you the whole word. For example, say to students, /ch/, /aw/, /k/. Students should answer *chalk*.

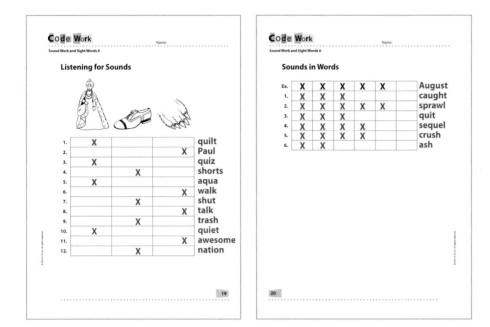

Code Work

Sound Work and Sight Words 6

Name:

Listening for Sounds

#				word
1.	X			quilt
2.			X	Paul
3.	X			quiz
4.		X		shorts
5.	X			aqua
6.			X	walk
7.		X		shut
8.			X	talk
9.		X		trash
10.	X			quiet
11.			X	awesome
12.		X		nation

19

Code Work

Sound Work and Sight Words 6

Name:

Sounds in Words

#						word
Ex.	X	X	X	X	X	August
1.	X	X	X			caught
2.	X	X	X	X	X	sprawl
3.	X	X	X			quit
4.	X	X	X			sequel
5.	X	X	X	X		crush
6.	X	X				ash

20

Word Work

Look at the Performance Review. If the student achieved a perfect score on today's Word Work activities, complete the first activity from the list below. If the student scored less than 100 percent but more than 85 percent, complete the first three activities from the list below. If the student scored 85 percent or less, complete all five of the activities listed below.

Objectives

- Read sight words.
- Increase reading vocabulary.

1. Have students complete pages 21 and 22 in *MARK¹² Reading Activity Book*. For page 21, tell students to find and circle each word from the word box in the word search. Words are written across and down. For page 22, tell students to unscramble each sight word and write the unscrambled words on the lines provided.

2. Using the sight word cards for *it, he,* and *was,* read each word to students and have students write the words. Give students the cards, and instruct students to look for any spelling mistakes. Students should correct the mistakes.

3. Gather all of the sight word cards students have worked on to date and a timer. Have students read all of the sight word cards as accurately and quickly as possible. Make note of the time, as well as any errors students have made. Use the Online Tile Kit or Paper Letter Tiles to review words read incorrectly.

4. Gather the cards for the sight words *it, he,* and *was,* and up to two additional sight words students have yet to master. Show the first card to students, and ask students to read the word. If students read the word correctly, place in one pile. If students read the word incorrectly, place in a separate pile. On the back of the cards that were read correctly, make a note of the date and put aside. (Once students have read the word correctly five consecutive days, you can remove the word from the pile of cards students are working on.) Review any words students read incorrectly, and keep the cards for next time.

5. Gather the two sets of sight word cards for the words *it, he,* and *was,* and place all of the cards face down. Have students choose a card, read the word aloud, and then choose a second card. After students read the second card aloud, if the two cards match, students should keep the cards. If they do not match, students should return them to the table. Continue until all cards are collected.

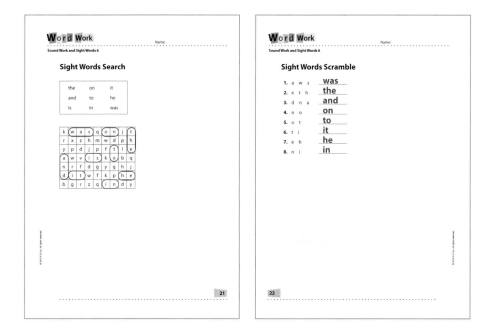

Sound Work

Sounds: /sh/, /aw/, and /kw/

Print a copy of today's Sound Work activity and work through it with students. Answer any questions students may have about Sound Work. Then, move on to Composition.

- Identify sounds, given letters.

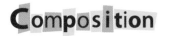omposition

Gather students' composition materials and begin where they left off.

Sound Work and Sight Words 7

ONLINE	Student & Computer	:60 minutes
	Adult : *Check Performance Review*	
OFFLINE	Student & Adult : Review online work	:30 minutes
	• Reading Warm-Up	
	• Code Work	
	• Word Work	
	• Speed Work	
	Classics Session 1	:30 minutes
	Instructional Time	**2:00** hours

Materials

- *MARK¹² Classics for Young Readers*
- Online Tile Kit or Paper Letter Tiles
- *MARK¹² Reading Activity Book*, pages 23–24
- "Mount Olympus and Its Inhabitants" MP3

Goals

In this lesson, students will read about a boy who moves to a new house. They will also work on the sounds /oi/, /ū/, and /ks/ before learning three new sight words: *says, have,* and *with.* In today's Classics activity, students will listen to a story about Greek gods.

Advance Preparation

Based on the Performance Review, if students need to complete Word Work activity 2, create sight word cards for the following words: *says, have,* and *with.* If students need to complete Word Work activity 3, you will need a timer and the Online Tile Kit or Paper Letter Tiles. If students need to complete Word Work activity 5, create a second set of sight word cards for the words *says, have,* and *with.*

ONLINE	Student & Computer

Students will work online to complete Warm-Up, Code Work, Word Work, and Sound Work activities, and a Wrap-Up assessment on their own. Be sure to read the Performance Review before beginning the offline portion of today's lesson.

Today you will work with students to complete Code Work, Word Work, and *MARK¹² Classics for Young Readers* activities. Be sure to read the online Performance Review before beginning the Code Work and Word Work activities.

Warm-Up • • • • • • • • • • • • • • • •

Moving

Look at the Performance Review. If the student achieved a perfect score on today's Warm-Up, move on to Code Work. If the student scored 60 percent or 80 percent, print the story and review the comprehension questions with the student. If the student scored less than 60 percent, print the story, have the student read the story aloud, and then work through the comprehension questions together, before moving on to Code Work.

Objectives

- Improve reading and comprehension skills.

Code Work • • • • • • • • • • • • • • • •

/oi/, /ū/, and /ks/

Look at the Performance Review. If the student achieved a perfect score on today's Code Work activities, complete the first activity from the list below. If the student scored less than 100 percent but more than 85 percent, complete the first two activities from the list below. If the student scored 85 percent or less, complete all three of the activities listed below.

Objectives

- Identify individual sounds in words.
- Identify same sounds in words.

1. Have students complete page 23 in *MARK¹² Reading Activity Book*. Tell students to listen to each pair of words. Read the word pairs in the answer key to students. If the vowel sounds in a word pair are the same, students should put a check in the *Same* column. If the vowel sounds are different, they should put a check in the *Different* column.

2. Have students tell you the words that individual sounds make. For example, if you say /l/ … /oi/ … /l/, students should answer *loyal*. Then, reverse the activity: say a word, and ask students for the individual sounds that make up the word.

3. Say the word *boil*. Tell students to change the first sound in *boil* to the sound /t/. Ask students to name the new word (*toil*). Ask students to change the middle sound in *toil* to the sound /ā/. Students should answer *tail*. Ask students to change the beginning sound in *tail* to /j/. Students should answer *jail*. Ask students to change the first sound in *jail* to /m/. Students should answer *mail*. Ask students to change the middle sound in *mail* to /aw/. Students should answer *mall*. Ask students to change the first sound in *mall* to the sound /t/. Students should answer *tall*. Ask students to change the middle sound in *tall* to /oi/. Students should answer *toil*. Finally, ask students to remove the last sound in *toil*. Students should answer *toy*.

Code Work   Name:

Sound Work and Sight Words 7

Same or Different?

	Same	Different	*Word Pairs*
1.		√	coil, fall
2.	√		shawl, ball
3.		√	meet, great
4.		√	stew, few
5.	√		edge, bet
6.	√		cut, sum
7.	√		fish, itch
8.		√	mug, beg
9.	√		joy, oil
10.		√	cute, cut

23

Word Work

Sight Words

Look at the Performance Review. If the student achieved a perfect score on today's Word Work activities, complete the first activity from the list below. If the student scored less than 100 percent but more than 85 percent, complete the first three activities from the list below. If the student scored 85 percent or less, complete all four of the activities listed below.

1. Have students complete page 24 in *MARK¹² Reading Activity Book*. Tell students to listen to the word that is read to them. Read the first word located in the answer key to students. Students should write the word in the first column and then read the word aloud. After they read the word, they should place a check mark in the second column. Students should then cover the word, and try to write it again in the third column. Finally, they should uncover the word and check their spelling. If they wrote the word correctly, students should place a check in the fourth column. Continue with each word shown in the answer key.

2. Using the sight word cards you created for *says, have,* and *with,* read each word to students and have students write the word on a piece of paper. Give students the sight words, and instruct students to look for any spelling mistakes they may have made. Students should correct the mistakes and then read the list of words aloud.

3. Gather all of the sight word cards students have worked on to date and a timer. Have students read all of the sight word cards as accurately and quickly as possible. Make note of the time, as well as any errors students have made. Use the Online Tile Kit or Paper Letter Tiles to review words read incorrectly.

4. Gather the cards for the sight words *says, have,* and *with,* and up to two additional sight words students have yet to master. Show the first card to students, and ask students to read the word. If students read the word correctly, place in one pile. If students read the word incorrectly, place in a separate pile. On the back of the cards that were read correctly, make a note of the date and put aside. (Once students have read the word correctly five consecutive days, you can remove the word from the pile of cards students are working on.) Review any words students read incorrectly, and keep the cards for next time.

Word Work

Name: _____

Sound Work and Sight Words 7

Sight Words: Spell and Check

Listen and Write	Read	Cover and Write	Check
the	✓	the	✓
and	✓	and	✓
is	✓	is	✓
on	✓	on	✓
to	✓	to	✓
in	✓	in	✓
it	✓	it	✓
he	✓	he	✓
is	✓	is	✓
was	✓	was	✓
says	✓	says	✓
have	✓	have	✓
with	✓	with	✓

24

Sound Work

Sounds: /oi/, Long *u*, and /ks/

Print a copy of today's Sound Work activity and work through it with students. Answer any questions students may have about Sound Work. Then, move on to Classics Session 1.

Classics Session 1

Mount Olympus and Its Inhabitants

Today's story, "Mount Olympus and Its Inhabitants," tells about a variety of Greek gods. Download the story. Have students listen to the story while following along in *MARK[12] Classics for Young Readers*. Have students listen to the story again before writing a summary of the story.

Students should write a summary of the story to complete today's Classics activity.

Sound Work and Sight Words 8

ONLINE	Student & Computer	:60	minutes
	Adult : *Check Performance Review*		
OFFLINE	Student & Adult : Review online work	:30	minutes
	• Reading Warm-Up		
	• Sound Work		
	• Assessment		
	Classics Session 2	:30	minutes
	Instructional Time **2:00** hours		

Materials

- *MARK¹² Classics for Young Readers*
- *MARK¹² Reading Activity Book*, pages 25–28

Goals

In this lesson, students will read about a soap box derby. Students will learn about the sounds /oi/, /j/, and /ks/ before reviewing sight words. After taking a Unit Assessment, students will answer questions about the reading in *MARK¹² Classics for Young Readers*.

ONLINE   Student & Computer

Students will work online to complete Warm-Up, Code Work, Word Work, and Sound Work activities, and a review game on their own. Be sure to read the Performance Review before beginning the offline portion of today's lesson.

Today you will administer a Unit Assessment and work with students to complete *MARK¹² Classics for Young Readers* activities.

Warm-Up

Soap Box Derby

Look at the Performance Review. If the student achieved a perfect score on today's Warm-Up, move on to Sound Work. If the student scored 60 percent or 80 percent, print the story and review the comprehension questions with the student. If the student scored less than 60 percent, print the story, have the student read the story aloud, and then work through the comprehension questions together, before moving on to Sound Work.

Objectives

• Improve reading and comprehension skills.

Sound Work

Sounds: Long Double *o* and /ow/

Print a copy of today's Sound Work activity and work through it with students. Answer any questions students may have about Sound Work. Then, move on to the Assessment.

Objectives

• Identify sounds, given letters.

☼ Assessment

Sound Work and Sight Words

Today's Unit Assessment covers all content found in Unit 1. Carefully read the instructions on the student pages before administering the test to the student. If necessary, read the directions to the student. After you have scored the student's assessment, be sure to go online and enter student performance scores in the assessment entry tool.

Part 1. Tell students to read each sight word aloud.

Part 2. Read the following word pairs to students. If the words rhyme, tell students to write *Y* for *yes* on the line provided. If the words do not rhyme, tell students to write *N* for *no* on the line provided: *few/cue; cut/cute; house/mouse; joy/jump; make/bake; beet/bat; plan/man;* and *bean/teen.*

Part 3. Read the following words to students. Tell students to write the number of syllables in each word on the lines provided: *television; instructor; understand; shrimp; wonderful; summer; January;* and *brisk.*

Part 4. Read the following syllable groups to students. Have students tell you the whole word for each group of syllables: *ant...ler; al...pha...bet; bub...ble; fence...post; arch...i...tect; re...spect; un...cle;* and *af...ter.*

Part 5. Read the following word pairs to students: *play/gas; bugle/mule; gem/get; flip/skit; bug/mat; flag/stack; blue/stew; soil/soy; pet/Pete; light/lit; plow/plot;* and *mood/might.* If the words have the same vowel sound, have students put a check mark in the column marked *Same.* If words have different vowel sounds, have students put a check mark in the column marked *Different.*

Part 6. Dictate the following words to students and have students write each word on the lines provided: *it, he, to, in, on, was, is, says, and, have, the,* and *with.*

Assessment
Sound Work and Sight Words

Unit 1 Assessment

Part 1.

1.	the	7.	it
2.	and	8.	he
3.	is	9.	was
4.	on	10.	says
5.	to	11.	have
6.	in	12.	with

Part 2.

13. Y
14. N
15. Y
16. N
17. Y
18. N
19. Y
20. Y

25

Assessment
Sound Work and Sight Words

Part 3.

21. 4
22. 3
23. 3
24. 1
25. 3
26. 2
27. 4
28. 1

Part 4.

29. antler
30. alphabet
31. bubble
32. fencepost
33. architect
34. respect
35. uncle
36. after

26

Assessment
Sound Work and Sight Words

Part 5.

	Same	Different
37.		✓
38.	✓	
39.	✓	
40.	✓	
41.		✓
42.	✓	
43.	✓	
44.	✓	
45.		✓
46.		✓
47.		✓
48.		✓

27

Assessment
Sound Work and Sight Words

Part 6.

49. it
50. he
51. to
52. in
53. on
54. was
55. is
56. says
57. and
58. have
59. the
60. with

28

Mount Olympus and Its Inhabitants

Have students listen to the story again while following along in *MARK¹² Classics for Young Readers*. Afterward, students should complete the comprehension questions in *MARK¹² Classics for Young Readers* on their own.

Write

Mount Olympus and Its Inhabitants

1. Which sea is closest to the country of Greece?
   A. Red Sea
   B. Caspian Sea
   C. Caribbean Sea
   D. Mediterranean Sea ✓

2. What did ancient Greeks enjoy telling stories about?
   A. children
   B. gods ✓
   C. education
   D. travels

3. Where did the ancient Greeks believe many of their greatest gods and goddesses lived?
   Ancient Greeks believed many of their greatest gods and goddesses lived on Mount Olympus.

Mount Olympus and Its Inhabitants 13

---

4. According to the story, which of the following is **not** a magical power of the gods?
   A. They could change into animals.
   B. They could predict the future. ✓
   C. They could fly through the air.
   D. They could hurl thunderbolts.

5. What was Zeus's wife named?
   Zeus's wife was named Hera.

6. Who was the goddess of wisdom?
   A. Artemis
   B. Apollo
   C. Aphrodite
   D. Athena ✓

7. What was the name of the food eaten by the gods and goddesses?
   The name of the food eaten by the gods and goddesses was ambrosia.

8. Who rose to power after the Greeks?
   A. French
   B. Chinese
   C. Romans ✓
   D. Turks

14 *Mount Olympus and Its Inhabitants*

---

9. Why were the banquets **not** always pleasant?
   The banquets were not always pleasant because the gods and goddesses often quarreled.

10. What is the Roman name for the Greek god, Hades?
    The Roman name for the Greek god, Hades, is Pluto.

Mount Olympus and Its Inhabitants 15

Sounds for Letters and Sight Words 1

ONLINE	Student & Computer	**:60** minutes	
	Adult : *Check Performance Review*		
OFFLINE	Student & Adult : Review online work	**:30** minutes	
	• Reading Warm-Up		
	• Code Work		
	• Word Work		
	• Sound Work		
	Grammar, Usage, and Mechanics (GUM)	**:30** minutes	
	Instructional Time **2:00** hours		

Materials

- Online Tile Kit or Paper Letter Tiles
- *MARK¹² Reading Activity Book*, pages 29–32

Tip

*It is important that students can differentiate between a letter and a sound. For example, when shown this: **B**, students should understand that the name of the letter is **B** but the sound of the letter is /**b**/.*

Goals

In this lesson, students will read about a child who goes kayaking. Students will also learn the sounds for the letters *a, b, f, m, s,* and *t* before learning the sight words *where, from,* and *there.* In today's *MARK¹² Reading Activity Book,* you will work with students to reinforce their understanding of the sounds and sight words from the lesson. Afterward, you will work with students to complete activities on predicates.

Advance Preparation

Based on the Performance Review, if students need to complete Code Work activities 2, 3, or 4, you will need the Online Tile Kit or Paper Letter Tiles. If students need to complete Word Work activity 2, create sight word cards for the following words: *where, from,* and *there.* If students need to complete Word Work activity 3, you will need a timer and the Online Tile Kit or Paper Letter Tiles. If students need to complete Word Work activity 5, create a second set of sight word cards for the words *where, from,* and *there.*

ONLINE   Student & Computer

Students will work online to complete Warm-Up, Code Work, Word Work, and Sound Work activities, and a Wrap-Up assessment on their own. Be sure to read the Performance Review before beginning the offline portion of today's lesson.

Today you will work with students to complete Code Work, Word Work, and GUM activities. Be sure to read the online Performance Review before beginning the Code Work and Word Work activities.

Warm-Up

Kayaking

Look at the Performance Review. If the student achieved a perfect score on today's Warm-Up, move on to Code Work. If the student scored 60 percent or 80 percent, print the story and review the comprehension questions with the student. If the student scored less than 60 percent, print the story, have the student read the story aloud, and then work through the comprehension questions together, before moving on to Code Work.

Objectives

- Improve reading and comprehension skills.

Code Work

Sounds for Letters: *a, b, f, m, s,* and *t*

Look at the Performance Review. If the student achieved a perfect score on today's Code Work activities, complete the first activity from the list below. If the student scored less than 100 percent but more than 85 percent, complete the first three activities from the list below. If the student scored 85 percent or less, complete all four of the activities listed below.

Objectives

- Identify the sounds, given the letters *a, b, f, m, s,* and *t.*
- Identify the letters, given the sounds /ă/, /b/, /f/, /m/, /s/, and /t/.

1. Have students complete page 29 in *MARK¹² Reading Activity Book.* For items 1–12, dictate the following words to students: *turn, act, surf, back, mud, far, fuzz, by, mail, safe, add,* and *take.* For items 13–16, dictate the following words to students: *at, bat, mat,* and *sat.*

2. Using the Online Tile Kit or Paper Letter Tiles, give students the letter *a.* Have them say the sound. Repeat with the letters *b, f, m, s,* and *t.*

3. Using the Online Tile Kit or Paper Letter Tiles, give students the letters *a, t,* and *s.* Have students tell you the first *sound* in *sat.* Then have students choose the letter that makes the sound /s/. Continue the procedure for the rest of the word, adding on to the word with each tile. Then repeat the procedure with the letters to build the words *mat, bat,* and *fat,* only pulling the letters for one word at a time.

4. Using the Online Tile Kit or Paper Letter Tiles, give students the letters *a, b, f, m, s,* and *t.* Build the word *sat* for students and say the sound for each letter in *sat* before reading the whole word. Tell students the next word is *mat.* Have students tell you what sound changes and choose the letter that makes the sound. Then have students point to each letter while making the sound for that letter, and then read the whole word. Continue with this procedure to make the words *fat, bat, sat, at,* and *am.*

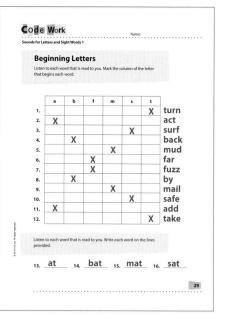

Word Work

Sight Words

Look at the Performance Review. If the student achieved a perfect score on today's Word Work activities, complete the first activity from the list below. If the student scored less than 100 percent but more than 85 percent, complete the first three activities from the list below. If the student scored 85 percent or less, complete all five of the activities listed below.

1. Have students complete page 30 in *MARK¹² Reading Activity Book*. For items 1–6, dictate the following words to students: *from, where, have, says, there,* and *with.*

2. Using the sight word cards for *where, from,* and *there,* read each word to students and have students write the word on a piece of paper. Give students the sight words, and instruct students to look for any spelling mistakes they may have made. Students should correct the mistakes and then read the list of words aloud.

3. Gather all of the sight word cards students have worked on to date and a timer. Have students read all of the sight word cards as accurately and quickly as possible. Make note of the time, as well as any errors students have made. Use the Online Tile Kit or Paper Letter Tiles to review words read incorrectly.

4. Gather the cards for the sight words *where, from,* and *there,* and up to two additional sight words students have yet to master. Show the first card to students, and ask students to read the word. If students read the word correctly, place in one pile. If students read the word incorrectly, place in a separate pile. On the back of the cards that were read correctly, make a note of the date and put aside. (Once students have read the word correctly five consecutive days, you can remove the word from the pile of cards students are working on.) Review any words students read incorrectly, and keep the cards for next time.

5. Gather the two sets of sight word cards for the words *where, from,* and *there,* and place all of the cards face down on the table or another flat surface. Have students choose a card, read the word aloud, and then choose a second card. After students read the second card aloud, if the two cards match, students should keep the cards. If they do not match, students should return them to the table. Continue until all of the cards have been collected.

Word Work Name: ____

Sounds for Letters and Sight Words 1

Sight Words

Listen to each word that is read to you. Write each word on the lines provided.

1. from
2. where
3. have
4. says
5. there
6. with

Unscramble each sight word. Write each unscrambled sight word on the lines provided.

7. a, s, w — was
8. e, h — he
9. t, i — it
10. e, e, h, r, t — there
11. o, f, m, r — from
12. e, e, h, r, w — where

Read each word aloud. Say each word in a sentence.

Sentences will vary.

13. in
14. there
15. to
16. from
17. on
18. where

30

Sound Work

Sounds for Letters: *a, b, f, m, s,* and *t*

Print a copy of today's Sound Work activity. Ask students to identify the sound for each letter. If time permits, have students go through the sounds a second time. Answer any questions students may have about Sound Work. Then, move on to Grammar, Usage, and Mechanics.

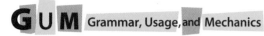

GUM Grammar, Usage, and Mechanics ·

Identifying Predicates

Objectives

• **Identify predicates.**

The predicate of a sentence contains the verb and tells more about what the subject is or does.

> Mrs. Jones knows everyone on our street.

The subject is Mrs. Jones. To find the predicate, ask, "What does the sentence tell about the subject?"

The predicate is *knows everyone on our street.*

Work with students to complete pages 31 and 32 in *MARK¹² Reading Activity Book*. Read page 31, Get Ready, with students. Have students complete the Try It page. Be sure to discuss students' answers when the page is completed.

GUM Grammar, Usage, and Mechanics   Name:

Sounds for Letters and Sight Words 1

Get Ready

▪ A sentence is a group of words that expresses a complete thought and contains both a subject and a predicate. The **predicate** of a sentence contains the verb and tells more about what the subject is or does. Look at this sentence:

  Mrs. Jones knows everyone on our street.

In this sentence, the subject is *Mrs. Jones.* To find the predicate, ask, "What does the sentence tell about the subject?"

  The predicate is *knows everyone on our street.*

Remember: All sentences have a predicate. The predicate of a sentence contains the verb and tells more about what the subject is or does.

31

GUM Grammar, Usage, and Mechanics   Name:

Sounds for Letters and Sight Words 1

Try It

Read each sentence. Underline the predicate in each sentence.

1. Matt threw the ball.
2. Mom drove to work.
3. That shirt fits Sam perfectly.
4. The taxi driver honked the horn.
5. My little brother draws very well.
6. The black cat jumped onto the bed.
7. My big sister likes to sing and dance.
8. My father plays the clarinet in a jazz band.
9. The big old branch cracked in the ice storm.
10. My friend runs faster than anyone else I know.

32

Sounds for Letters and Sight Words 2

ONLINE	Student & Computer	:60 minutes
	Adult : *Check Performance Review*	
OFFLINE	Student & Adult : Review online work	:30 minutes
	• Reading Warm-Up	
	• Code Work	
	• Word Work	
	• Sound Work	
	Composition	:30 minutes

Instructional Time **2:00** hours

Materials

- **Online Tile Kit or Paper Letter Tiles**
- *MARK¹² Reading Activity Book*, pages 33–36
- *Just Write*

Tip

*The letter **c** can make two sounds: /**k**/ as in **cat** or /**s**/ as in **city**. In this lesson, students focus on the sound /**k**/ for the letter **c**. In later units, students will learn about the sound /**s**/ for the letter **c**.*

Goals

In this lesson, students will read about a boy who leaves Earth to explore space. Students will also learn sounds for the letters *c, h, j, l, n,* and *r* before working with the sight words *where, from,* and *there*. In today's *MARK¹² Reading Activity Book*, you will work with students to reinforce their understanding of the sounds and sight words from the lesson. Afterward, students will spend 30 minutes working on composition.

Advance Preparation

Based on the Performance Review, if students need to complete Code Work activities 3 and 4, you will need the Online Tile Kit or Paper Letter Tiles. If students need to complete Word Work activity 2, gather the sight word cards for the following words: *where, from,* and *there.* If students need to complete Word Work activity 3, you will need a timer and the Online Tile Kit or Paper Letter Tiles. If students need to complete Word Work activity 5, gather the second set of sight word cards for the words *where, from,* and *there.*

ONLINE   Student & Computer

Students will work online to complete Warm-Up, Code Work, Word Work, and Sound Work activities, and a Wrap-Up assessment on their own. Be sure to read the Performance Review before beginning the offline portion of today's lesson.

Today you will work with students to complete Code Work, Word Work, and Composition activities. Be sure to read the online Performance Review before beginning the Code Work and Word Work activities.

Warm-Up ·

Space Monster

Look at the Performance Review. If the student achieved a perfect score on today's Warm-Up, move on to Code Work. If the student scored 60 percent or 80 percent, print the story and review the comprehension questions with the student. If the student scored less than 60 percent, print the story, have the student read the story aloud, and then work through the comprehension questions together, before moving on to Code Work.

Objectives

- Improve reading and comprehension skills.

Code Work ·

Sounds for Letters: *c, h, j, l, n,* and *p*

Look at the Performance Review. If the student achieved a perfect score on today's Code Work activities, complete the first two activities from the list below. If the student scored less than 100 percent but more than 85 percent, complete the first three activities from the list below. If the student scored 85 percent or less, complete all four of the activities listed below.

Objectives

- Identify sounds given the letters *c, h, j, l, n,* and *p.*
- Identify letters given the sounds /k/, /h/, /j/, /l/, /n/, and /p/.

1. Have students complete page 33 in *MARK¹² Reading Activity Book.* To complete the page, dictate the following sounds to students: /ă/, /n/, /b/, /m/, /k/, /l/, /f/, /j/, /h/, /p/, /n/, /l/, /j/, /h/, /k/, /t/, /s/, and /p/.

2. Have students complete page 34 in *MARK¹² Reading Activity Book.* To complete the page, dictate the following words to students: *cab, pal, jam, cat, can, hat, lap, pan, nap,* and *cap.*

3. Using the Online Tile Kit or Paper Letter Tiles, give students the letter c. Have students say the sound the letter makes. Repeat with the letters *h, j, l, n,* and *p.* Then have students listen to you say the sound of one of the letters. Have students repeat the sound and then touch its letter.

4. Using the Online Tile Kit or Paper Letter Tiles, give students the letters *a, b,* and *c.* Tell students they will build the word *cab.* Have students tell you the first sound in *cab.* Then have students choose the letter that makes the sound /k/. Continue the procedure for the rest of the word, adding on to the word with each tile. Then repeat the procedure with the letters to build the words *can, hat, jam, lab, man,* and *pan,* only pulling the letters for one word at a time.

Code Work   Name:

Sounds for Letters and Sight Words 2

Sounds and Letters

Listen to each sound that is read to you. On the lines provided, write the letter that makes each sound.

1. a
2. n
3. b
4. m
5. c
6. l
7. f
8. j
9. h

10. p
11. n
12. l
13. j
14. h
15. c
16. t
17. s
18. p

33

Code Work   Name:

Sounds for Letters and Sight Words 2

Complete the Word

Listen to each word that is read to you. On the lines provided, write the missing letter in each word.

1. c__ab
2. pa__l
3. j__am
4. c__at
5. ca__n
6. h__at
7. l__ap
8. pa__n
9. na__p
10. ca__p

34

Word Work ●

Sight Words

Look at the Performance Review. If the student achieved a perfect score on today's Word Work activities, complete the first activity from the list below. If the student scored less than 100 percent but more than 85 percent, complete the first three activities from the list below. If the student scored 85 percent or less, complete all five of the activities listed below.

Objectives

- **Read sight words.**
- **Increase reading vocabulary.**

1. Have students complete pages 35 and 36 in *MARK¹² Reading Activity Book*. On page 36, dictate the underlined words on the Answer Key to students.

2. Using the sight word cards you created for *where, from,* and *there,* read each word to students and have students write the word on a piece of paper. Give students the sight words, and instruct students to look for any spelling mistakes they may have made. Students should correct the mistakes and then read the list of words aloud.

3. Gather all of the sight word cards students have worked on to date and a timer. Have students read all of the sight word cards as accurately and quickly as possible. Make note of the time, as well as any errors students have made. Use the Online Tile Kit or Paper Letter Tiles to review words read incorrectly.

4. Gather the cards for the sight words *where, from,* and *there,* and up to two additional sight words students have yet to master. Show the first card to students, and ask students to read the word. If students read the word correctly, place in one pile. If students read the word incorrectly, place in a separate pile. On the back of the cards that were read correctly, make a note of the date and put aside. (Once students have read the word correctly five consecutive days, you can remove the word from the pile of cards students are working on.) Review any words students read incorrectly, and keep the cards for next time.

5. Gather the two sets of sight word cards for the words *where, from,* and *there,* and place all of the cards face down on the table or another flat surface. Have students choose a card, read the word aloud, and then choose a second card. After students read the second card aloud, if the two cards match, students should keep the cards. If they do not match, students should return them to the table. Continue until all of the cards have been collected.

Word Work

Name: _____

Sounds for Letters and Sight Words 2

Sight Words

In each row, underline the word that is read to you.

1. and | from | <u>with</u>
2. <u>he</u> | on | says
3. in | is | <u>it</u>
4. <u>on</u> | says | and
5. the | there | <u>to</u>
6. was | <u>where</u> | with
7. <u>from</u> | have | on
8. he | <u>says</u> | and
9. <u>is</u> | it | in
10. <u>there</u> | to | the
11. where | with | <u>was</u>
12. <u>have</u> | on | says
13. he | <u>and</u> | from
14. it | <u>in</u> | is
15. to | <u>the</u> | there

35

Word Work

Name: _____

Sounds for Letters and Sight Words 2

Word Search

Read each word in the box aloud. Circle each word from the box in the word search below. Words may appear left to right or up and down.

| from | have | in | on | says | there |
| was | with | he | and | to | where |

36

Sound Work

Sounds for Letters: *c, h, j, l, n,* and *p*

Print a copy of today's Sound Work activity. Ask students to identify the sound for each letter. If time permits, have students go through the sounds a second time. Answer any questions students may have about Sound Work. Then, move on to Composition.

Objectives

- Identify sounds, given letters.

Sounds for Letters and Sight Words 2

47

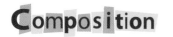Composition

Gather students' composition materials and begin where they left off.

Sounds for Letters and Sight Words 3

ONLINE	Student & Computer	**:60** minutes
	Adult : *Check Performance Review*	
OFFLINE	Student & Adult : Review online work	**:30** minutes
	• Reading Warm-Up	
	• Code Work	
	• Word Work	
	• Sound Work	
	Grammar, Usage, and Mechanics (GUM)	**:30** minutes
	Instructional Time	**2:00** hours

Materials

- Online Tile Kit or Paper Letter Tiles
- *MARK¹² Reading Activity Book*, pages 37–40

Goals

In this lesson, students will read about two children who decide to race. Students will also learn the sounds for the letters *d, g, o, r,* and *v* before learning the sight words *that, of,* and *put.* In today's *MARK¹² Reading Activity Book,* you will work with students to reinforce their understanding of the sounds and sight words from the lesson. Afterward, you will work with students to complete activities on punctuation.

Advance Preparation

Based on the Performance Review, if students need to complete Word Work activity 2, create sight word cards for the following words: *that, of,* and *put.* If students need to complete Word Work activity 3, you will need a timer and the Online Tile Kit or Paper Letter Tiles. If students need to complete Word Work activity 5, create a second set of sight word cards for the words *that, of,* and *put.*

ONLINE   Student & Computer

Students will work online to complete Warm-Up, Code Work, Word Work, and Sound Work activities, and a Wrap-Up assessment on their own. Be sure to read the Performance Review before beginning the offline portion of today's lesson.

OFFLINE | **Student & Adult**

Today you will work with students to complete Code Work, Word Work, and GUM activities. Be sure to read the online Performance Review before beginning the Code Work and Word Work activities.

Warm-Up

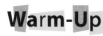

The Race

Look at the Performance Review. If the student achieved a perfect score on today's Warm-Up, move on to Code Work. If the student scored 60 percent or 80 percent, print the story and review the comprehension questions with the student. If the student scored less than 60 percent, print the story, have the student read the story aloud, and then work through the comprehension questions together, before moving on to Code Work.

Objectives

- **Improve reading and comprehension skills.**

Code Work

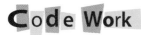

Sounds for Letters: *d, g, o, r,* and *v*

Look at the Performance Review. If the student achieved a perfect score on today's Code Work activities, complete the first activity from the list below. If the student scored less than 100 percent but more than 85 percent, complete the first three activities from the list below. If the student scored 85 percent or less, complete all four of the activities listed below.

Objectives

- **Identify the sounds, given the letters *d, g, o, r,* and *v*.**
- **Identify the letters, given the sounds /d/, /g/, /ŏ/, /r/, and /v/.**

1. Have students complete page 37 in *MARK*[12] *Reading Activity Book* for more practice on the sounds for the letters *d, g, o, r,* and *v.*
2. Using the Online Tile Kit or Paper Letter Tiles, give students the letter *d*. Have students touch the letter and say the sound. Repeat the procedure with the letters *g, o, r,* and *v*. Then have students listen to you say the sound of one of the letters. Have students repeat the sound and then touch its letter.
3. Using the Online Tile Kit or Paper Letter Tiles, give students the letters *o, j,* and *b*. Tell students they are going to build the word *job*. Have students tell you the first sound (not letter) in *job*. Then have students choose the letter that makes the sound /j/. Continue the procedure for the rest of the word, adding on to the word with each tile. Then repeat the procedure with the letters to build the words *cap, dog, fog, got, jog,* and *pot,* only pulling the letters for one word at a time.
4. Dictate the following sentences to students and have them write each one:
   The hog is fat.
   Jan ran to the van.
   The man is in the lab.
   Sam and the cat sat on the mat.

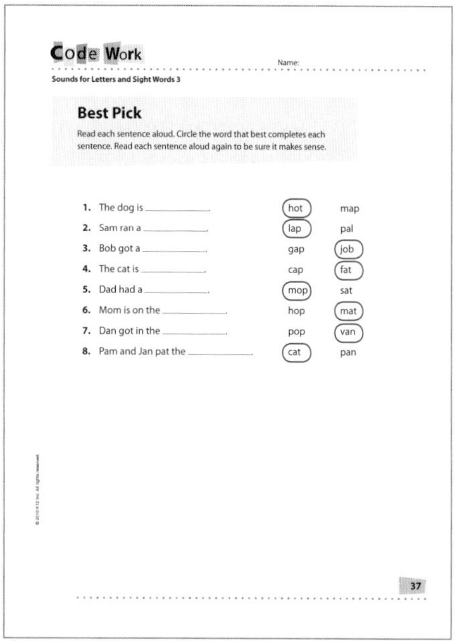
Code Work Name:
Sounds for Letters and Sight Words 3

Best Pick

Read each sentence aloud. Circle the word that best completes each sentence. Read each sentence aloud again to be sure it makes sense.

1. The dog is ______. hot map
2. Sam ran a ______. lap pal
3. Bob got a ______. gap job
4. The cat is ______. cap fat
5. Dad had a ______. mop sat
6. Mom is on the ______. hop mat
7. Dan got in the ______. pop van
8. Pam and Jan pat the ______. cat pan

37

Word Work

Sight Words

Look at the Performance Review. If the student achieved a perfect score on today's Word Work activities, complete the first activity from the list below. If the student scored less than 100 percent but more than 85 percent, complete the first three activities from the list below. If the student scored 85 percent or less, complete all five of the activities listed below.

1. Have students complete page 38 in *MARK¹² Reading Activity Book* for more practice on sight words.

2. Using the sight word cards you created for *that, of,* and *put,* read each word to students and have students write the word on a piece of paper. Give students the sight words, and instruct students to look for any spelling mistakes they may have made. Students should correct the mistakes and then read the list of words aloud.

3. Gather all of the sight word cards students have worked on to date and a timer. Have students read all of the sight word cards as accurately and quickly as possible. Make note of the time, as well as any errors students have made. Use the Online Tile Kit or Paper Letter Tiles to review words read incorrectly.

4. Gather the cards for the sight words *that, of,* and *put,* and up to two additional sight words students have yet to master. Show the first card to students, and ask students to read the word. If students read the word correctly, place in one pile. If students read the word incorrectly, place in a separate pile. On the back of the cards that were read correctly, make a note of the date and put aside. (Once students have read the word correctly five consecutive days, you can remove the word from the pile of cards students are working on.) Review any words students read incorrectly, and keep the cards for next time.

5. Gather the two sets of sight word cards for the words *that, of,* and *put,* and place all of the cards face down on the table or another flat surface. Have students choose a card, read the word aloud, and then choose a second card. After students read the second card aloud, if the two cards match, students should keep the cards. If they do not match, students should return them to the table. Continue until all of the cards have been collected.

Word Work

Name:

Sounds for Letters and Sight Words 3

By Sight

See how many words you can read correctly in one minute. Read aloud across the rows. When you get to the bottom of the page, start over. Try to read more words the second time.

and	from	have	in
of	put	says	that
was	of	put	that
he	is	on	the
where	it	there	with

Number of words read correctly: _____

38

Sound Work

Sounds for Letters: *d, g, o, r,* and *v*

Print a copy of today's Sound Work activity. Ask students to identify the sound for each letter. If time permits, have students go through the sounds a second time. Answer any questions students may have about Sound Work. Then, move on to Grammar, Usage, and Mechanics.

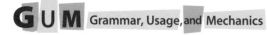

Using Punctuation

There are four kinds of sentences: statements, questions, commands, and exclamations.

- *Statements* tell something. They end in a period.
- *Questions* ask for information. They end in a question mark.
- *Commands* give an order or an instruction. They usually end in a period,but if they express strong emotion, they might also and in an exclamation mark.
- *Exclamations* express strong emotion. They end in an exclamation point.

Work with students to complete pages 39 and 40 in *MARK¹² Reading Activity Book*. Read page 39, Get Ready, with students. Have students complete the Try It page. Be sure to discuss students' answers when the page is completed.

GUM Grammar, Usage, and Mechanics   Name: _____

Sounds for Letters and Sight Words 3

Get Ready

■ What **punctuation mark** is used at the end of a sentence? It depends on what kind of sentence it is. There are four kinds of sentences:

 statements
 questions
 commands
 exclamations

Statements tell something. They end in a period.

 I am in my room.

Questions ask for information. They end in a question mark.

 What are you doing?

Commands give an order or an instruction. They usually end in a period, but if they express strong emotion, they might also end in an exclamation point.

 Hurry up. or Hurry up!

Exclamations express strong emotion. They end in an exclamation point.

 That spider is huge!

39

GUM Grammar, Usage, and Mechanics   Name: _____

Sounds for Letters and Sight Words 3

Try It

Each sentence below is missing its end punctuation. Decide if each sentence is a statement, command, question, or exclamation. Write the missing punctuation marks on the lines provided.

1. Is this your cat **?** ____
2. Where did you find her **?** ____
3. I found her in my yard • ____
4. She is so cute • **or !** ____
5. Pick her up • ____

On the lines provided below, write one statement, one command, one question, and one exclamation. Remember to end each sentence with the correct punctuation mark.

6. _____
7. _____
8. _____
9. _____

40

Sounds for Letters and Sight Words 4

ONLINE	Student & Computer	**:60**	minutes
	Adult : *Check Performance Review*		
OFFLINE	Student & Adult : Review online work	**:30**	minutes
	• Reading Warm-Up		
	• Code Work		
	• Word Work		
	• Sound Work		
	Classics Session 1	**:30**	minutes

Instructional Time **2:00** hours

Materials

- *MARK¹² Classics for Young Readers*
- Online Tile Kit or Paper Letter Tiles
- *MARK¹² Reading Activity Book*, pages 41–44

Goals

In this lesson, students will read about a good dog that always gets in trouble. Students will also learn the sounds for the letters *i, k, qu,* and *z* before working with the sight words *that, of,* and *put.* In today's *MARK¹² Reading Activity Book*, you will work with students to reinforce their understanding of the sounds and sight words from the lesson. You will also work with students to complete Classics activities.

Tip *In the English language, the letter **q** is always followed by the letter **u**. Together, the letters **qu** make the sound /**kw**/. For this reason, students will learn about the letters **qu** together rather than just the letter **q**.*

Advance Preparation

Based on the Performance Review, if students need to complete Code Work activities 3 and 4, you will need the Online Tile Kit or Paper Letter Tiles. If students need to complete Word Work activity 2, gather the sight word cards for the following words: *that, of,* and *put.* If students need to complete Word Work activity 3, you will need a timer and the Online Tile Kit or Paper Letter Tiles. If students need to complete Word Work activity 5, gather the second set of sight word cards for the words *that, of,* and *put.*

ONLINE   Student & Computer

Students will work online to complete Warm-Up, Code Work, Word Work, and Sound Work activities, and a Wrap-Up assessment on their own. Be sure to read the Performance Review before beginning the offline portion of today's lesson.

Today you will work with students to complete Code Work, Word Work, and *MARK¹² Classics for Young Readers* activities. Be sure to read the online Performance Review before beginning the Code Work and Word Work activities.

Warm-Up 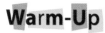 •

The Good Dog

Look at the Performance Review. If the student achieved a perfect score on today's Warm-Up, move on to Code Work. If the student scored 60 percent or 80 percent, print the story and review the comprehension questions with the student. If the student scored less than 60 percent, print the story, have the student read the story aloud, and then work through the comprehension questions together, before moving on to Code Work.

Objectives

- Improve reading and comprehension skills.

Code Work •

Sounds for Letters: *i, k, qu,* and *z*

Look at the Performance Review. If the student achieved a perfect score on today's Code Work activities, complete the first two activities from the list below. If the student scored less than 100 percent but more than 85 percent, complete the first three activities from the list below. If the student scored 85 percent or less, complete all five of the activities listed below.

Objectives

- Identify the sounds, given the letters *i, k, qu,* and *z*.
- Identify the letters, given the sounds /i/, /k/, /kw/, and /z/.

1. Have students complete page 41 in *MARK¹² Reading Activity Book* for more practice on letters and their sounds.

2. Have students complete page 42 in *MARK¹² Reading Activity Book*. Dictate the following words for students: *dog, got, kid, pig, quit, van, zap, kit, quiz,* and *zip.*

3. Using the Online Tile Kit or Paper Letter Tiles, give students the letter *i.* Have students touch the letter and say the sound. Repeat the procedure with the letters *k, qu,* and *z.* Then have students listen to you say the sound of one of the letters. Have students repeat the sound and touch its letter.

4. Using the Online Tile Kit or Paper Letter Tiles, give students the letters *n, p,* and *i.* Tell students they are going to build the word *pin.* Have students tell you the first sound (not letter) in *pin.* Then have students choose the letter that makes the sound /p/. Continue the procedure for the rest of the word, adding on to the word with each tile. Repeat the procedure with the letters to build the words *fit, kid, lip, quit,* and *zip,* only pulling the letters for one word at a time.

5. Dictate the following sentences to students and have them write each one:

Is the lid on the pot?

Kim did not quit her job.

Sam is not a kid.

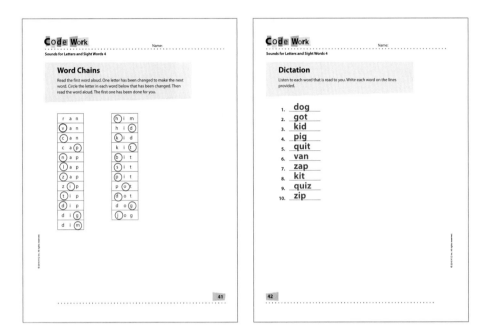

Word Work ·

Sight Words

Look at the Performance Review. If the student achieved a perfect score on today's Word Work activities, complete the first activity from the list below. If the student scored less than 100 percent but more than 85 percent, complete the first three activities from the list below. If the student scored 85 percent or less, complete all five of the activities listed below.

1. Have students complete pages 43 and 44 in *MARK¹² Reading Activity Book* for more practice on sight words. For page 43 you will need to dictate the words shown on the Answer Key.

2. Using the sight word cards you created for *that, of,* and *put,* read each word to students and have students write the word on a piece of paper. Give students the sight words, and instruct students to look for any spelling mistakes they may have made. Students should correct the mistakes and then read the list of words aloud.

3. Gather all of the sight word cards students have worked on to date and a timer. Have students read all of the sight word cards as accurately and quickly as possible. Make note of the time, as well as any errors students have made. Use the Online Tile Kit or Paper Letter Tiles to review words read incorrectly.

4. Gather the cards for the sight words *that, of,* and *put,* and up to two additional sight words students have yet to master. Show the first card to students, and ask students to read the word. If students read the word correctly, place in one pile. If students read the word incorrectly, place in a separate pile. On the back of the cards that were read correctly, make a note of the date and put aside. (Once students have read the word correctly five consecutive days, you can remove the word from the pile of cards students are working on.) Review any words students read incorrectly, and keep the cards for next time.

5. Gather the two sets of sight word cards for the words *that, of,* and *put,* and place all of the cards face down on the table or another flat surface. Have students choose a card, read the word aloud, and then choose a second card. After students read the second card aloud, if the two cards match, students should keep the cards. If they do not match, students should return them to the table. Continue until all of the cards have been collected.

Word Work Name:

Sounds for Letters and Sight Words 4

Sight Words

Listen as each word is read to you. Write the word in the first column. Read the word aloud. After you read the word, place a check mark in the second column. Cover the word, and try to write it again in the third column. Uncover the word and check your spelling. If you wrote it correctly, place a check in the fourth column.

Listen and Write	Read	Cover and Write	Check
from	✓	from	✓
have	✓	have	✓
it	✓	it	✓
of	✓	of	✓
put	✓	put	✓
says	✓	says	✓
that	✓	that	✓
was	✓	was	✓
he	✓	he	✓
in	✓	in	✓
there	✓	there	✓
where	✓	where	✓
with	✓	with	✓

43

Word Work Name:

Sounds for Letters and Sight Words 4

Word Search

Read each word in the box aloud. Circle each word in the word search below. Words may appear left to right or up and down.

and	have	from	is	of	put
says	that	was	on	the	to

```
s o w y a z x v t
a n d p h a v e k
b d f h i g e c s
f r o m z i s   a
j l f p q o m k y
a c e g p u t d s
s u w y z x h t r
t h a t q o e k i
b d s h t o e c a
```

44

Sound Work

Sounds for Letters: *i*, *k*, *qu*, and *z*

Print a copy of today's Sound Work activity. Ask students to identify the sound for each letter. If time permits, have students go through the sounds a second time. Answer any questions students may have about Sound Work. Then, move on to Classics Session 1.

Classics Session 1 ·

The Stone in the Road

Today's story, "The Stone in the Road," is about a king's test for the people in his kingdom. Review the keywords with students. Read the story with students, and then use the Discussion Questions below as a guide to share ideas about the story. Have students read the story again before writing a summary of the story.

Keywords

nimble, adj. – quick and light in motion
Her **nimble** fingers moved quickly over the piano keys.

scold, v. – to speak sternly and find fault with
Mother **scolded** me for playing instead of finishing my chores.

grumble, v. – to mutter, usually in an unhappy manner
"I don't want to get up. I'm too tired," the little girl **grumbled**.

fault, n. – responsibility for a wrong doing
I did not wake up on time, so it was my **fault** for being late.

Discussion Questions

1. What do you think the king was trying to teach the people? Answers may include that when you see a problem that needs to be fixed, do it yourself whenever possible.

2. How do you think the people felt after listening to the king? Answers may include that the people may have felt embarrassed. The fact that they said nothing means that they were probably thinking carefully about the king's words.

3. What do you think the people will do the next time they come across a stone in the road? Answers may include that they will most likely remember the king's message and move the stone.

4. *Responsibility* means "doing your part or doing your duty." Responsible people don't leave all the work for someone else. They don't just complain about problems without helping fix them. Responsible people do their part to make things better. Whose responsibility was it to move the stone? Why do you think so? Answers will vary.

5. In the story, whoever moved the stone would have had the ring and coins for his or her reward. But helping others is rewarding in many ways. What other rewards would the person who moved the stone receive? Answers may include that the person who moved the stone would feel good about having done the right thing. He or she may have received thanks and praise from others.

Students should write a summary of the story to complete today's Classics activity.

Sounds for Letters and Sight Words 5

ONLINE	Student & Computer	**:60**	minutes
	Adult : *Check Performance Review*		
OFFLINE	Student & Adult : Review online work	**:30**	minutes
	• Reading Warm-Up		
	• Code Work		
	• Word Work		
	• Sound Work		
	Classics Session 2	**:30**	minutes
	Instructional Time	**2:00**	hours

Materials

- *MARK¹² Classics for Young Readers*
- Online Tile Kit or Paper Letter Tiles
- *MARK¹² Reading Activity Book*, pages 45–46

Goals

In this lesson, students will read about a thief who steals a ring from a queen. Students will also learn the sounds for the letters *u, w,* and *x* before learning the sight words *both, they,* and *two*. In today's *MARK¹² Reading Activity Book*, you will work with students to reinforce their understanding of the sounds and sight words from the lesson. You will also work with students to complete Classics activities.

Advance Preparation

Based on the Performance Review, if students need to complete Code Work activities 2, 3, and 4, you will need the Online Tile Kit or Paper Letter Tiles. If students need to complete Word Work activity 2, create sight word cards for the following words: *both, they,* and *two*. If students need to complete Word Work activity 3, you will need a timer and the Online Tile Kit or Paper Letter Tiles. If students need to complete Word Work activity 5, create a second set of sight word cards for the words *both, they,* and *two*.

ONLINE   Student & Computer

Students will work online to complete Warm-Up, Code Work, Word Work, and Sound Work activities, and a Wrap-Up assessment on their own. Be sure to read the Performance Review before beginning the offline portion of today's lesson.

Today you will work with students to complete Code Work, Word Work, and *MARK¹² Classics for Young Readers* activities. Be sure to read the online Performance Review before beginning the Code Work and Word Work activities.

Warm-Up ·

Bell and the Queen

Look at the Performance Review. If the student achieved a perfect score on today's Warm-Up, move on to Code Work. If the student scored 60 percent or 80 percent, print the story and review the comprehension questions with the student. If the student scored less than 60 percent, print the story, have the student read the story aloud, and then work through the comprehension questions together, before moving on to Code Work.

Objectives

- Improve reading and comprehension skills.

Code Work ·

Sounds for Letters *u, w,* and *x*

Look at the Performance Review. If the student achieved a perfect score on today's Code Work activities, complete the first activity from the list below. If the student scored less than 100 percent but more than 85 percent, complete the first three activities from the list below. If the student scored 85 percent or less, complete all four of the activities listed below.

Objectives

- Identify the sounds, given the letters *u, w,* and *x.*
- Identify the letters, given the sounds /ŭ/, /w/, and /ks/.

1. Have students complete page 45 in *MARK¹² Reading Activity Book* for more practice on letters and their sounds.

2. Using the Online Tile Kit or Paper Letter Tiles, give students the letter *u.* Have students touch the letter and say the sound. Repeat the procedure with the letters *w* and *x.* Then have students listen to you say the sound of one of the letters. Have students repeat the sound and then touch its letter.

3. Using the Online Tile Kit or Paper Letter Tiles, give students the letters *u, b,* and *g.* Tell students they are going to build the word *bug.* Have students tell you the first sound (not letter) in *bug.* Then have students choose the letter that makes the sound /b/. Continue the procedure for the rest of the word, adding on to the word with each tile. Then repeat the procedure with the letters to build the words *tax, sun, wax, wig,* and *wet,* only pulling the letters for one word at a time.

4. Dictate the following sentences to students and have them write each one:
    The wax is hot.
    The bug is in the cup.
    The wig is in the box.
    The dog sat in the tub.

Code Work | Name:
Sounds for Letters and Sight Words 5

Best Pick

Read each sentence aloud. Circle the word that best completes each sentence. Read each sentence aloud again to be sure it makes sense.

1. The _____ is hot.   (wax) wet
2. The _____ has a lid.   (box) bun
3. I can _____ to the van. rat (run)
4. The dog is in the _____. map (mud)
5. The _____ has six kids in it. bat (bus)

Word Scramble

Unscramble the letters to create a word. Write each word on the lines provided. Then read the words aloud.

6. x f o   fox
7. n f u   fun
8. n t u   nut
9. g m u   mug or gum
10. i n w   win

45

Word Work ·

Sight Words

Look at the Performance Review. If the student achieved a perfect score on today's Word Work activities, complete the first activity from the list below. If the student scored less than 100 percent but more than 85 percent, complete the first three activities from the list below. If the student scored 85 percent or less, complete all five of the activities listed below.

1. Have students complete page 46 in *MARK¹² Reading Activity Book.* Dictate the following words to students: *both, they, two, put, that,* and *of.*

2. Using the sight word cards you created for *both, they,* and *two,* read each word to students and have students write the word on a piece of paper. Give students the sight words, and instruct students to look for any spelling mistakes they may have made. Students should correct the mistakes and then read the list of words aloud.

3. Gather all of the sight word cards students have worked on to date and a timer. Have students read all of the sight word cards as accurately and quickly as possible. Make note of the time, as well as any errors students have made. Use the Online Tile Kit or Paper Letter Tiles to review words read incorrectly.

4. Gather the cards for the sight words *both, they,* and *two,* and up to two additional sight words students have yet to master. Show the first card to students, and ask students to read the word. If students read the word correctly, place in one pile. If students read the word incorrectly, place in a separate pile. On the back of the cards that were read correctly, make a note of the date and put aside. (Once students have read the word correctly five consecutive days, you can remove the word from the pile of cards students are working on.) Review any words students read incorrectly, and keep the cards for next time.

5. Gather the two sets of sight word cards for the words *both, they,* and *two,* and place all of the cards face down on the table or another flat surface. Have students choose a card, read the word aloud, and then choose a second card. After students read the second card aloud, if the two cards match, students should keep the cards. If they do not match, students should return them to the table. Continue until all of the cards have been collected.

Word Work Name: ___

Sounds for Letters and Sight Words 5

Sight Words

Listen to each word that is read to you. Write each word on the lines provided.

1. both   4. put
2. they   5. that
3. two   6. of

Unscramble each sight word. Write each unscrambled sight word on the lines provided.

7. e, h, y, t **they**   10. e, e, h, r, t **there**
8. t, h, b, o **both**   11. o, f, m, r **from**
9. p, t, u **put**   12. o, t, w **two**

Read each word aloud. Say each word in a sentence.

Sentences will vary.

13. both   16. they
14. he   17. two
15. says   18. with

46

Sound Work ·

Sounds for Letters: *u, x,* and *w*

Print a copy of today's Sound Work activity. Ask students to identify the sound for each letter. If time permits, have students go through the sounds a second time. Answer any questions students may have about Sound Work. Then, move on to Classics Session 2.

Classics Session 2

The Stone in the Road

Review the keywords with students. Have students reread the story on their own. After rereading the story, students should complete the comprehension questions in *MARK^{12} Classics for Young Readers* on their own. Afterward, if time allows, have students read the story aloud to you.

Objectives

- Improve reading and comprehension questions.

Write

The Stone in the Road

1. According to the story, who was the first person to see the stone in the road?

    A. maid
    B. soldier
    C. doctor
    D. farmer

2. What did each character do instead of moving the stone?

    Each character walked past the stone and complained that others did not move it.

3. What did the farmer have in his cart?

    A. ears of corn
    B. jugs of milk
    C. bushels of hay
    D. crates of apples

4. Why didn't the soldier see the stone?

    The soldier did not see the stone because he was walking proudly, with his head high in the air.

The Stone in the Road **19**

---

5. How many men on horses rode by the stone?

    A. 4
    B. 5
    C. 6
    D. 7

6. What was under the stone?

    Under the stone was a box with these words on a piece of paper: *for the person who moves the stone.* **The box contained a gold ring and ten coins.**

7. How many weeks did the king wait before calling all of the people together?

    A. 2
    B. 3
    C. 4
    D. 5

8. Who put the stone in the road?

    A. soldier
    B. maid
    C. doctor
    D. king

20 *The Stone in the Road*

---

y

b

Classics Session 2

The Stone in the Road

Review the keywords with students. Have students reread the story on their own. After rereading the story, students should complete the comprehension questions in *MARK^{12} Classics for Young Readers* on their own. Afterward, if time allows, have students read the story aloud to you.

Sounds for Letters and Sight Words 6

ONLINE	Student & Computer	**:60** minutes	
	Adult : *Check Performance Review*		
OFFLINE	Student & Adult : Review online work	**:30** minutes	
	• Reading Warm-Up		
	• Sound Work		
	• Assessment		
	Composition	**:30** minutes	
		Instructional Time **2:00** hours	

Materials

- *MARK[12] Reading Activity Book*, pages 47–50
- *Just Write*

Goals

In this lesson, students will read about Paul Bunyan and Babe the blue ox. Students will also learn sounds for the letters *e* and *y* before working with the sight words *both, they,* and *two*. In today's Unit Assessment, you will administer a test covering all content from Unit 2. Afterward, students will spend 30 minutes working on composition.

Advance Preparation

For the offline portion of today's lesson, gather students' composition materials.

ONLINE	**Student & Computer**

Students will work online to complete Warm-Up, Code Work, Word Work, and Sound Work activities, and a review game on their own. Be sure to read the Performance Review before beginning the offline portion of today's lesson.

Today you will administer a Unit Assessment and work with students to complete a Composition activity.

Warm-Up ·

Paul Bunyan

Look at the Performance Review. If the student achieved a perfect score on today's Warm-Up, move on to Sound Work. If the student scored 60 percent or 80 percent, print the story and review the comprehension questions with the student. If the student scored less than 60 percent, print the story, have the student read the story aloud, and then work through the comprehension questions together, before moving on to Sound Work.

Objectives

- Improve reading and comprehension skills.

Sound Work ·

Sounds for Letters: *y* and *e*

Print a copy of today's Sound Work activity. Ask students to identify the sound for each letter. If time permits, have students go through the sounds a second time. Answer any questions students may have about Sound Work. Then, move on to the Assessment.

Objectives

- Identify sounds, given letters.

☼ Assessment ·

Sounds for Letters and Sight Words

Today's Unit Assessment covers all content found in Unit 2. Carefully read the instructions on the student pages before administering the test to the student. If necessary, read the directions to the student. After you have scored the student's assessment, be sure to go online and input student performance scores in the assessment entry tool.

Part 2. Read aloud the following sounds to students: /ĕ/, /y/, /k/, /b/, /ŭ/, /r/, /w/, /ĭ/, /ks/, /z/, /kw/, /v/, /s/, /ă/, /k/, /g/, /d/, /h/, /p/, /n/, /l/, /j/, /f/, /m/, /t/, and /ŏ/.

Part 3. Read aloud the following words to students: *am, jet, big, dog, it, hit, box, red, us,* and *van.*

Part 4. Read aloud the following sounds to students: /ă/, /z/, /ĕ/, /y/, /ŭ/, /ks/, /ŏ/, /w/, /kw/, and /ĭ/.

Part 5. Dictate the following words to students: *bat, yet, hot, zip, jog, lip, mud, on, fox,* and *up.*

Part 7. Read aloud the following words to students: *they, where, that, put, of, there, from, both,* and *two.*

Assessment
Name: _____

Sounds for Letters and Sight Words

Unit 2 Assessment

Part 1.
Say the sound each letter or letters make.

1. y /y/
2. v /v/
3. p /p/
4. c /k/
5. t /t/
6. w /w/
7. k /k/
8. n /n/
9. f /f/
10. w /w/
11. x /ks/
12. g /g/
13. l /l/
14. b /b/
15. z /z/
16. z /z/
17. d /d/
18. h /h/
19. m /m/
20. x /ks/
21. qu /kw/
22. r /r/
23. p /p/
24. s /s/
25. y /y/

Part 2.
Listen to each sound that is read to you. Circle the letter that makes each sound.

26. a (e) i o u
27. v w x (y) z
28. (c) d qu s x
29. (b) c f g h
30. a e i o (u)
31. p qu (r) s t
32. v (w) x y z
33. a e (i) o u
34. c k qu s (x)
35. v w x y (z)
36. c k (qu) s x
37. r s t (v) w
38. (s) t v w x
39. (a) e i o u
40. f (k) qu s x
41. c d f (g) h
42. (d) j k l m
43. f g (h) j k
44. n (p) qu r s
45. l m (n) p qu
46. g h j k (l)
47. d f g h (j)
48. b c d (f) g
49. k l (m) n p
50. s (t) v w x
51. a e i (o) u

47

Assessment
Name: _____

Sounds for Letters and Sight Words

Part 3.
Listen to each word that is read to you. Write the letter that is missing from each word in the blank space.

52. **a** m
53. j **e** t
54. bi **g**
55. **d** og
56. **i** t
57. **h** it
58. b. **o** x
59. **r** ed
60. **u** s
61. **v** an

Part 4.
Listen to each sound that is read to you. Say the letter that makes each sound. Write each letter on the lines provided.

62. **a**
63. **z**
64. **e**
65. **y**
66. **u**
67. **x**
68. **o**
69. **w**
70. **qu**
71. **i**

48

Assessment
Name: _____

Sounds for Letters and Sight Words

Part 5.
Listen to each word that is read to you. Write each word on the lines provided.

72. **bat**
73. **yet**
74. **hot**
75. **zip**
76. **jog**
77. **lip**
78. **mud**
79. **on**
80. **fox**
81. **up**

Part 6.
Read each word aloud.

82. two
83. both
84. they
85. from
86. there
87. of
88. put
89. that
90. where

49

Assessment
Name: _____

Sounds for Letters and Sight Words

Part 7.
In each row, underline the word that is read to you.

91. the — there — <u>they</u>
92. <u>where</u> — was — wet
93. <u>that</u> — the — there
94. pat — <u>put</u> — pet
95. at — in — <u>of</u>
96. the — <u>there</u> — they
97. fan — fit — <u>from</u>
98. bat — <u>both</u> — bit
99. <u>two</u> — ten — top

50

Objectives

- Identify letters, given sounds.
- Identify sounds, given letters.
- Read words.

Sounds for Letters and Sight Words 6   **65**

Composition

Gather students' composition materials and begin where they left off.

Short Vowels and Sight Words 1

ONLINE	**Student & Computer**	**:60** minutes	
	Adult : *Check Performance Review*		
OFFLINE	**Student & Adult :** Review online work	**:30** minutes	
	• Reading Warm-Up		
	• Code Work		
	• Word Work		
	• Speed Work		
	Grammar, Usage, and Mechanics (GUM)	**:30** minutes	
	Instructional Time **2:00** hours		

Materials

- **Online Tile Kit or Paper Letter Tiles**
- ***MARK¹² Reading Activity Book*, pages 51–54**

> **Tip**
>
> *The short vowel sounds /ĕ/ and /ĭ/ are very similar (for example, ten vs. tin). This can make it hard for students to distinguish one from the other. Use care when pronouncing words with these short vowel sounds during activities.*

Goals

In this lesson, students will read about a boy who finds a treasure map. Students will also work with the short vowel sounds /ă/, /ĕ/, and /ĭ/, as well as be introduced to the sight words *you, we,* and *went.* In today's *MARK¹² Reading Activity Book* pages, you will work with students to complete activities that use words with short vowel sounds and sight words.

Advance Preparation

Based on the Performance Review, if students need to complete Code Work activity 4, gather nine index cards and write each of the following words on the cards: *bag, rid, tap, fit, ten, sip, pan, pet,* and *hen.* If students need to complete Word Work activity 2, create sight word cards for the following words: *you, we,* and *went.* If students need to complete Word Work activity 3, you will need a timer and the Online Tile Kit or Paper Letter Tiles. If students need to complete Word Work activity 5, create a second set of sight word cards for the words *you, we,* and *went.*

ONLINE Student & Computer

Students will work online to complete Warm-Up, Code Work, Word Work, and Speed Work activities, and a Wrap-Up assessment on their own. Be sure to read the Performance Review before beginning the offline portion of today's lesson.

Today you will work with students to complete Code Work, Word Work, and GUM activities. Be sure to read the online Performance Review before beginning the Code Work and Word Work activities.

Warm-Up

Treasure!

Look at the Performance Review. If the student achieved a perfect score on today's Warm-Up, move on to Code Work. If the student scored 60 percent or 80 percent, print the story and review the comprehension questions with the student. If the student scored less than 60 percent, print the story, have the student read the story aloud, and then work through the comprehension questions together, before moving on to Code Work.

Objectives

- Improve reading and comprehension skills.

Code Work

Short Vowels

Look at the Performance Review. If the student achieved a perfect score on today's Code Work activities, complete the first two activities from the list below. If the student scored less than 100 percent but more than 85 percent, complete the first three activities from the list below. If the student scored 85 percent or less, complete all five of the activities listed below.

Objectives

- Identify and use /ǎ/, /ě/, and /ǐ/.

1. Have students complete page 51 in *MARK¹² Reading Activity Book* for more practice on words with the short vowel sounds /ǎ/, /ě/, and /ǐ/.

2. Using the Online Tile Kit or Paper Letter Tiles, have students build the following words: *bat, red, tip, cap, rag, big, man, net, bad,* and *sit.* Ask students to identify the short vowel sound in each word.

3. Read aloud one of the words listed in activity 2. Have students say a new word by changing the first letter of the word you read (possible answers in parentheses): *bat* (cat, hat), *red* (bed, Ted), *tip* (rip, sip), *cap* (map, tap), *rag* (bag, tag), *big* (dig, fig), *man* (can, fan), *net* (get, set), *bad* (dad, sad), and *sit* (bit, fit). Discuss how the new word also has a short vowel sound and therefore rhymes with the first word. Repeat for all words.

4. Gather the nine index cards you previously prepared. Choose a card and show the card to the students. Say the word aloud and exaggerate the short vowel sound (example: *baaag*). Have students spell and then say the word aloud. Put the used card aside. Continue until all cards have been read.

5. Gather the cards from activity 4. Hold up a card randomly. Have students say the word aloud, and then use it in a sentence.

Code Work   Name:

Short Vowels and Sight Words 1

Words with Short Vowels

Add or subtract a letter to make a new word. Write the new word on the line provided.

Example: f + at = ___fat___

1. c + at = **cat**
2. t + ax = **tax**
3. pad – p = **ad**
4. r + an = **ran**
5. kit – k = **it**
6. can – c = **an**
7. p + in = **pin**
8. hat – h = **at**
9. p + it = **pit**
10. ram – r = **am**

Choose the word from the box that best completes each sentence. Write the word on the line provided.

| fed | tin | pig | sad | hat | bed |

11. Deb has a **tin** can.
12. Pam has a red **hat**.
13. Tim sat on the **bed**.
14. Ted is **sad**.
15. The **pig** had a nap.
16. Wes **fed** the cat.

51

Word Work

Sight Words

Look at the Performance Review. If the student achieved a perfect score on today's Word Work activities, complete the first activity from the list below. If the student scored less than 100 percent but more than 85 percent, complete the first three activities from the list below. If the student scored 85 percent or less, complete all five of the activities listed below.

1. Have students complete page 54 in *MARK¹² Reading Activity Book* for more practice on sight words.

2. Using the sight word cards you created for *you, went,* and *we,* read each word to students and have students write the words on a piece of paper. Give students the sight word cards, and instruct students to look for any spelling mistakes they may have made. Students should correct the mistakes and then read the list of words aloud.

3. Gather all of the sight word cards students have worked on to date and a timer. Have students read all of the sight word cards as accurately and quickly as possible. Make note of the time, as well as any errors students have made. Use the Online Tile Kit or Paper Letter Tiles to review words read incorrectly.

4. Gather the cards for the sight words *you, went,* and *we,* and up to two additional sight words students have yet to master. Show the first card to students, and ask students to read the word. If students read the word correctly, place in one pile. If students read the word incorrectly, place in a separate pile. On the back of the cards that were read correctly, make a note of the date and put aside. (Once students have read the word correctly five consecutive days, you can remove the word from the pile of cards students are working on.) Review any words students read incorrectly, and keep the cards for next time.

5. Gather the two sets of sight word cards for the words *you, went,* and *we,* and place all of the cards face down on the table or another flat surface. Have students choose a card, read the word aloud, and then choose a second card. After students read the second card aloud, if the two cards match, students should keep the cards. If they do not match, students should return them to the table. Continue until all of the cards have been collected.

Speed Work

Sit a Bit

Look at the Performance Review, or check the student's fluency chart. Fluency scores (words read per minute) should not fall below 80. If the student scored below 80 words per minute, print a copy of the Speed Work story and have the student read the story silently before reading it aloud. Otherwise, move on to Grammar, Usage, and Mechanics.

Identifying Punctuation

When we include a speaker's exact words in a quotation, it is called a *direct quotation*. Quotation marks enclose not only the speaker's words, but also the end punctuation.

Work with students to complete pages 53 and 54 in *MARK¹² Reading Activity Book*. Read page 53, Get Ready, with students. Have students complete the Try It page. Be sure to discuss students' answers when the page is completed.

Dictate the following two sentences to students for the first part of the Try It:

> *"Put that bag in the shed," Pat says to Gus.*
>
> *Jan says, "I have a big dog."*

GUM Grammar, Usage, and Mechanics   Name: _____

Short Vowels and Sight Words 1

Get Ready

Direct Quotations and Quotation Marks

When you quote a speaker's words exactly, it is called a **direct quotation**. The two sentences below have direct quotations.

> Henry asked, "Can you come over today, Jeff?"
>
> "Yes, I can!" said Jeff.

Notice that each sentence contains Henry's and Jeff's exact words, and their words are inside **quotation marks**. Remember that punctuation marks are like road signs for readers. Here, they signal someone's exact words are inside the quotation marks. Notice that the quotation marks enclose the end punctuation, too.

Commas in Direct Quotations

If the direct quotation comes at the end of the sentence, introduce it with a comma before the first set of quotation marks. End the direct quotation with the punctuation mark that fits the kind of sentence quoted. Put the punctuation mark before the second set of quotation marks.

> Henry said to Jeff, "Let's play football."

But if the direct quotation *starts a sentence*, you usually use a comma instead of a period at the end of it. Compare the sentence above to the sentence below. Notice how the punctuation changes from a period to a comma when the direct quotation is moved from the end to the beginning of the sentence.

> "Let's play football," Henry said to Jeff.

Some direct quotations use question marks or exclamation points, whether the quotation starts or ends the sentence.

> Jeff replied, "Can't we do something else?"
>
> "Sure! I'm sick of football, anyway!" Henry exclaimed.

53

GUM Grammar, Usage, and Mechanics   Name: _____

Short Vowels and Sight Words 1

Try It

Listen as two sentences with direct quotations are read to you. Write each sentence on the line provided. Be sure to use correct punctuation.

1. **"Put that bag in the shed," Pat says to Gus.**

2. **Jan says, "I have a big dog."**

Underline the punctuation that shows Ned is asking a question in the following sentence.

3. Ben had to ask me, "Where is the cat?"

Underline the punctuation that shows Dad is shouting in the following sentence.

4. "Do not do that!" Dad says.

54

Short Vowels and Sight Words 2

ONLINE	**Student & Computer**	**:60** minutes	
	Adult : *Check Performance Review*		
OFFLINE	**Student & Adult : Review online work**	**:30** minutes	
	• Reading Warm-Up		
	• Speed Work		
	• Assessment		
	Composition	**:30** minutes	
		Instructional Time **2:00** hours	

Materials

- *MARK[12] Reading Activity Book*, pages 55–58
- *Just Write*

Goals

In this lesson, students will read about a boy who finds an unusual item in a shed. Students will also work with the short vowel sounds /ŏ/ and /ŭ/ before reviewing the sight words *you, went,* and *we.* In today's Unit Assessment, you will administer a test covering all content from Unit 3.

Advance Preparation

For the offline portion of today's lesson, gather students' composition materials.

ONLINE   Student & Computer

Students will work online to complete Warm-Up, Code Work, Word Work, and Speed Work activities, and a review game on their own. Be sure to read the Performance Review before beginning the offline portion of today's lesson.

Today you will administer a Unit Assessment and work with students to complete a Composition activity.

Warm-Up

The Carpet

Look at the Performance Review. If the student achieved a perfect score on today's Warm-Up, move on to Speed Work. If the student scored 60 percent or 80 percent, print the story and review the comprehension questions with the student. If the student scored less than 60 percent, print the story, have the student read the story aloud, and then work through the comprehension questions together, before moving on to Speed Work.

Speed Work

Where Are They?

Look at the Performance Review, or check the student's fluency chart. Fluency scores (words read per minute) should not fall below 80. If the student scored below 80 words per minute, print a copy of the Speed Work story and have the student read the story silently before reading it aloud to you. Otherwise, move on to the Assessment.

☼ Assessment

Short Vowels and Sight Words

Today's Unit Assessment covers all content found in Unit 3. Carefully read the instructions on the student pages before administering the test to the student. If necessary, read the directions to the student. After you have scored the student's assessment, be sure to go online and enter student performance scores in the assessment entry tool.

Part 1. Dictate the following words to students: *hen, mug, top, went, tan, hot, bed, you, cup, pin, we, rib, map,* and *red.*

Part 4. Dictate the following words to students: *you, went,* and *we.*

Part 6. Dictate the following words to students: *went, we,* and *you.*

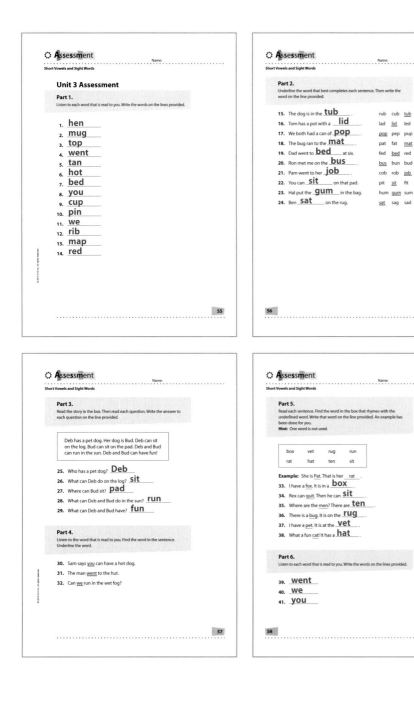

Unit 3 Assessment

Part 1.
Listen to each word that is read to you. Write the words on the lines provided.

1. hen
2. mug
3. top
4. went
5. tan
6. hot
7. bed
8. you
9. cup
10. pin
11. we
12. rib
13. map
14. red

55

Part 2.
Underline the word that best completes each sentence. Then write the word on the line provided.

15. The dog is in the **tub** _____.   rub   cub   <u>tub</u>
16. Tom has a pot with a ___**lid**___.   lad   <u>lid</u>   led
17. We both had a can of **pop** _____.   <u>pop</u>   pep   pup
18. The bug ran to the **mat** _____.   pat   fat   <u>mat</u>
19. Dad went to **bed** _____ at six.   fed   <u>bed</u>   red
20. Ron met me on the **bus** _____.   <u>bus</u>   bun   bud
21. Pam went to her **job** _____.   cob   rob   <u>job</u>
22. You can __**sit**___ on that pad.   pit   <u>sit</u>   fit
23. Hal put the **gum** _____ in the bag.   hum   <u>gum</u>   sum
24. Ben __**sat**___ on the rug.   <u>sat</u>   sag   sad

56

Part 3.
Read the story in the box. Then read each question. Write the answer to each question on the line provided.

> Deb has a pet dog. Her dog is Bud. Deb can sit on the log. Bud can sit on the pad. Deb and Bud can run in the sun. Deb and Bud can have fun!

25. Who has a pet dog? **Deb**
26. What can Deb do on the log? **sit**
27. Where can Bud sit? **pad**
28. What can Deb and Bud do in the sun? **run**
29. What can Deb and Bud have? **fun**

Part 4.
Listen to the word that is read to you. Find the word in the sentence. Underline the word.

30. Sam says <u>you</u> can have a hot dog.
31. The man <u>went</u> to the hut.
32. Can <u>we</u> run in the wet fog?

57

Part 5.
Read each sentence. Find the word in the box that rhymes with the underlined word. Write that word on the line provided. An example has been done for you.
Hint: One word is not used.

box	vet	rug	run
rat	hat	ten	sit

Example: She is <u>Pat</u>. That is her ___rat___.

33. I have a <u>fox</u>. It is in a **box**
34. Rex can <u>quit</u>. Then he can **sit**
35. Where are the <u>men</u>? There are **ten**
36. There is a <u>bug</u>. It is on the **rug**
37. I have a <u>pet</u>. It is at the **vet**
38. What a fun <u>cat</u>! It has a **hat**

Part 6.
Listen to each word that is read to you. Write the words on the lines provided.

39. went
40. we
41. you

58

Objectives

- Identify and use /ă/.
- Identify and use /ĕ/.
- Identify and use /ĭ/.
- Identify and use /ŏ/.
- Identify and use /ŭ/.
- Increase reading vocabulary.
- Read sight words.

Gather students' composition materials and begin where they left off.

Digraphs and Sight Words 1

ONLINE	Student & Computer	:60 minutes
	Adult : *Check Performance Review*	
OFFLINE	Student & Adult : Review online work	:30 minutes
	• Reading Warm-Up	
	• Code Work	
	• Word Work	
	• Speed Work	
	Classics Session 1	:30 minutes
	Instructional Time **2:00** hours	

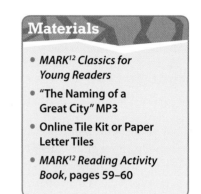

Materials

- *MARK¹² Classics for Young Readers*
- "The Naming of a Great City" MP3
- Online Tile Kit or Paper Letter Tiles
- *MARK¹² Reading Activity Book*, pages 59–60

Goals

In this lesson, students will read about a girl and her puppy named Flash. Students will also be introduced to the digraphs *sh* and *th,* as well the sight words *said, your,* and *so.* In today's *MARK¹² Reading Activity Book* pages, you will work with students to sort and use words with the digraphs *sh* and *th,* as well as work on sight words. You will also work with students to complete Classics activities.

Advance Preparation

For the offline portion of today's lesson, download this story: "The Naming of a Great City." Based on the Performance Review, if students need to complete Word Work activity 2, create sight word cards for the following words: *said, your,* and *so.* If students need to complete Word Work activity 3, you will need a timer and the Online Tile Kit or Paper Letter Tiles. If students need to complete Word Work activity 5, create a second set of sight word cards for the words *said, your,* and *so.*

ONLINE	**Student & Computer**

Students will work online to complete Warm-Up, Code Work, Word Work, and Speed Work activities, and a Wrap-Up assessment on their own. Be sure to read the Performance Review before beginning the offline portion of today's lesson.

Today you will work with students to complete Code Work, Word Work, and *MARK¹² Classics for Young Readers* activities. Be sure to read the online Performance Review before beginning the Code Work and Word Work activities.

Warm-Up ·

Flash

Look at the Performance Review. If the student achieved a perfect score on today's Warm-Up, move on to Code Work. If the student scored 60 percent or 80 percent, print the story and review the comprehension questions with the student. If the student scored less than 60 percent, print the story, have the student read the story aloud, and then work through the comprehension questions together, before moving on to Code Work.

Code Work ·

Digraphs *sh* & *th*

Look at the Performance Review. If the student achieved a perfect score on today's Code Work activities, complete the first two activities from the list below. If the student scored less than 100 percent but more than 85 percent, complete the first three activities from the list below. If the student scored 85 percent or less, complete all four of the activities listed below.

1. Have students complete page 59 in *MARK¹² Reading Activity Book* for more practice on words with the digraphs *sh* and *th*.

2. Using the Online Tile Kit or Paper Letter Tiles, have students build these words: *shag, path, wish, bath, this, dash,* and *that*. Have students say each word aloud. Pay particular attention to the pronunciation of words with a voiced <u>th</u> (*this, that*). Then have them identify the digraph that is contained in each word.

3. Have students fold a piece of paper in half lengthwise, and write the digraph *sh* over the left column and the digraph *th* over the right column. Say the following words aloud: *ship, thin, moth, rash, math, shut, fish, wash,* and *thug*. Have students write the words in the corresponding columns (*sh: ship, rash, shut, fish,* and *wash; th: thin, moth, math,* and *thug*). Have students underline all digraphs.

4. Have students fold another piece of paper in half lengthwise, and write the digraph *th* over the left column and the digraph <u>th</u> (with an underline to represent the voiced *th*) over the right column. Say the following words aloud: *that, this, thin, path, with,* and *the*. Have students write the words in the corresponding columns (*th: thin, path,* and *with;* <u>th</u>: *that, this,* and *the*). Have students underline all digraphs.

Code Work Name: _____

Digraphs and Sight Words 1

Practice Digraphs

Write each word in the correct column below, according to the digraph found in each word.

| sash | moth | ship | fish | thin | this |
| then | that | than | bath | path | shop |

sh	*th*	*th*
sash	moth	then
ship	bath	that
fish	thin	than
shop	path	this

Choose the word from the box that best completes each sentence. Write the word on the line provided.

| the | shot | wish | math | thug | dash |

1. Tim had to get a **shot** from Doctor Nash.
2. The **thug** ran from the cop.
3. I **wish** I had a pet dog.
4. This **math** is fun!
5. Don had to **dash** to the bus.
6. Bob has **the** mug.

59

Word Work

Sight Words

Look at the Performance Review. If the student achieved a perfect score on today's Word Work activities, complete the first activity from the list below. If the student scored less than 100 percent but more than 85 percent, complete the first three activities from the list below. If the student scored 85 percent or less, complete all five of the activities listed below.

Objectives

- Read sight words.
- Increase reading vocabulary.

1. Have students complete page 60 in *MARK¹² Reading Activity Book* for more practice on sight words.

2. Using the sight word cards you created for *said, your,* and *so,* read each word to students and have students write the words on a piece of paper. Give students the sight word cards, and instruct students to look for any spelling mistakes they may have made. Students should correct the mistakes and then read the list of words aloud.

3. Gather all of the sight word cards students have worked on to date and a timer. Have students read all of the sight word cards as accurately and quickly as possible. Make note of the time, as well as any errors students have made. Use the Online Tile Kit or Paper Letter Tiles to review words read incorrectly.

4. Gather the cards for the sight words *said, your,* and *so,* and up to two additional sight words students have yet to master. Show the first card to students, and ask students to read the word. If students read the word correctly, place in one pile. If students read the word incorrectly, place in a separate pile. On the back of the cards that were read correctly, make a note of the date and put aside. (Once students have read the word correctly five consecutive days, you can remove the word from the pile of cards students are working on.) Review any words students read incorrectly, and keep the cards for next time.

5. Gather the two sets of sight word cards for the words *said, your,* and *so,* and place all of the cards face down on the table or another flat surface. Have students choose a card, read the word aloud, and then choose a second card. After students read the second card aloud, if the two cards match, students should keep the cards. If they do not match, students should return them to the table. Continue until all of the cards have been collected.

Speed Work

Yes!

Objectives

- Increase reading fluency rate.

Look at the Performance Review, or check the student's fluency chart. Fluency scores (words read per minute) should not fall below 80. If the student scored below 80 words per minute, print a copy of the Speed Work story and have the student read the story silently before reading it aloud. Otherwise, move on to Classics Session 1.

Classics Session 1

Today's story, "The Naming of a Great City," is about the naming of the city of Athens. Download the story. Have students listen to the story while following along in *MARK¹² Classics for Young Readers*. Have students listen to the story again before writing a summary of the story.

Students should write a summary of the story to complete today's Classics activity.

Digraphs and Sight Words 2

ONLINE	Student & Computer	**:60** minutes	
	Adult : *Check Performance Review*		
OFFLINE	Student & Adult : Review online work	**:30** minutes	
	• Reading Warm-Up		
	• Code Work		
	• Word Work		
	• Speed Work		
	Classics Session 2	**:30** minutes	

Instructional Time **2:00** hours

Materials

- *MARK[12] Classics for Young Readers*
- **"The Naming of a Great City"** MP3
- *MARK[12] Reading Activity Book*, pages 61–64

Tip

Remind students that a digraph is made up of two letters that work together to make one sound.

Goals

In this lesson, students will read about children eating ice cream. Students will also be introduced to the digraphs *ch* and *wh*, as well as continue to work with the sight words *said, your,* and *so.* In today's *MARK[12] Reading Activity Book* pages, you will work with students to sort and use words with the digraphs *ch* and *wh*, as well as practice sight words.

Advance Preparation

For the offline portion of today's lesson, download this story: "The Naming of a Great City." Based on the Performance Review, if students need to complete Word Work activity 2, gather the sight word cards for the following words: *said, your,* and *so.* If students need to complete Word Work activity 3, you will need a timer and the Online Tile Kit or Paper Letter Tiles. If students need to complete Word Work activity 5, gather the second set of sight word cards for the words *said, your,* and *so.*

ONLINE Student & Computer

Students will work online to complete Warm-Up, Code Work, Word Work, and Speed Work activities, and a Wrap-Up assessment on their own. Be sure to read the Performance Review before beginning the offline portion of today's lesson.

Today you will work with students to complete Code Work, Word Work, and *MARK¹² Classics for Young Readers* activities. Be sure to read the online Performance Review before beginning the Code Work and Word Work activities.

Warm-Up ·

Brain Freeze

Look at the Performance Review. If the student achieved a perfect score on today's Warm-Up, move on to Code Work. If the student scored 60 percent or 80 percent, print the story and review the comprehension questions with the student. If the student scored less than 60 percent, print the story, have the student read the story aloud, and then work through the comprehension questions together, before moving on to Code Work.

Code Work ·

Digraphs *ch & wh*

Look at the Performance Review. If the student achieved a perfect score on today's Code Work activities, complete the first two activities from the list below. If the student scored less than 100 percent but more than 85 percent, complete the first three activities from the list below. If the student scored 85 percent or less, complete all four of the activities listed below.

1. Have students complete page 61 in *MARK¹² Reading Activity Book* for more practice on words with the digraphs *ch* and *wh*.

2. Remove the "Chip and Chad" story from *MARK¹² Reading Activity Book*. Fold the pages in half to create a small booklet. Review the following words with students: *look* and *good*. Have students read the story silently once or twice before reading the story aloud. When students read aloud, make note of any errors, and review those words with students.

3. Using the Online Tile Kit or Paper Letter Tiles, have students build the following words: *chop, much, when, chat, what,* and *whip*. Have students say each word aloud. Then have them identify the digraph that is contained in each word.

4. Give students clues for words with the digraph *ch*. Tell students the word begins with *ch*, and then describe characteristics of the mystery word. Example: I'm thinking of a word that begins with the digraph *ch*. This word is part of your face. It is below your mouth and sticks out. Answer: *chin*. Words to use: *chin, chop, chat,* and *chip*. Have students spell each word aloud once it is guessed.

Code Work   Name: _____
Digraphs and Sight Words 2

Digraphs *ch* and *wh*
Read each sentence. Underline each word that has the digraph *ch* or the digraph *wh*.

1. Dan and <u>Chad</u> were on the bus.
2. Tom hit the can with a <u>whip</u>.
3. The van can <u>chug</u> up the path.
4. We went to the pet shop on a <u>whim</u>.
5. The ball hit <u>Chip</u> on the <u>chin</u>.
6. We can <u>chat</u> <u>when</u> I get there.

Choose the correct diagraph from the box and write the digraph on the line to make a word. Then say the word aloud.

ch	wh

Example: ch in
7. ri__**ch**__
8. __**ch/wh**__op
9. __**wh**__en
10. mu__**ch**__
11. __**wh**__iz
12. __**ch**__um
13. su__**ch**__
14. __**wh**__ere

61

Word Work · · · · · · · · · · · · · · · · · ·

Sight Words

Look at the Performance Review. If the student achieved a perfect score on today's Word Work activities, complete the first activity from the list below. If the student scored less than 100 percent but more than 85 percent, complete the first three activities from the list below. If the student scored 85 percent or less, complete all five of the activities listed below.

1. Have students complete page 62 in *MARK¹² Reading Activity Book* for more practice on sight words.

2. Using the sight word cards you created for *said, your,* and *so,* read each word to students and have students write the word on a piece of paper. Give students the sight words, and instruct students to look for any spelling mistakes they may have made. Students should correct the mistakes and then read the list of words aloud.

3. Gather all of the sight word cards students have worked on to date and a timer. Have students read all of the sight word cards as accurately and quickly as possible. Make note of the time, as well as any errors students have made. Use the Online Tile Kit or Paper Letter Tiles to review words read incorrectly.

4. Gather the cards for the sight words *said, your,* and *so,* and up to two additional sight words students have yet to master. Show the first card to students, and ask students to read the word. If students read the word correctly, place in one pile. If students read the word incorrectly, place in a separate pile. On the back of the cards that were read correctly, make a note of the date and put aside. (Once students have read the word correctly five consecutive days, you can remove the word from the pile of cards students are working on.) Review any words students read incorrectly, and keep the cards for next time.

5. Gather the two sets of sight word cards for the words *said, your,* and *so,* and place all of the cards face down on the table or another flat surface. Have students choose a card, read the word aloud, and then choose a second card. After students read the second card aloud, if the two cards match, students should keep the cards. If they do not match, students should return them to the table. Continue until all of the cards have been collected.

Speed Work · · · · · · · · · · · · · · · · · ·

I Wish!

Look at the Performance Review, or check the student's fluency chart. Fluency scores (words read per minute) should not fall below 80. If the student scored below 80 words per minute, print a copy of the Speed Work story and have the student read the story silently before reading it aloud. Otherwise, move on to Classics Session 2.

Have students listen to the story again while following along in *MARK¹² Classics for Young Readers*. Afterward, students should complete the comprehension questions in *MARK¹² Classics for Young Readers* on their own.

Objectives

- Improve reading and comprehension skills.

✏️ Ⓦ **Write**

The Naming of a Great City

1. Why does Poseidon think the people should name their city for him?

Poseidon thinks the people should name their city for him because he believes he can make it a stronger city than any other on earth.

2. What is Athena the goddess of?
   - A. happiness
   - B. peace
   - Ⓒ. wisdom
   - D. kindness

3. The people want help deciding for whom they should name their city. From whom do they seek advice?

The people seek Zeus's advice.

4. How will the judgment be made as to whether the city is named for Athena or Poseidon?

Zeus will be the judge, and he will decide whether Athena or Poseidon present the better gift. The one with the better gift "may claim the city."

The Naming of a Great City 23

---

5. What gift does Poseidon bring the people?

Poseidon brings the people a shining warhorse.

6. What do the people do when they see Poseidon's gift?
   - A. hide
   - Ⓑ. cheer
   - C. cry
   - D. laugh

7. What kind of tree did Athena give the people?
   - A. apple
   - Ⓑ. olive
   - C. plum
   - D. banana

8. For whom is the city named—Poseidon or Athena?

The city is named Athens, after Athena.

24 The Naming of a Great City

Digraphs and Sight Words 3

ONLINE	Student & Computer	:60 minutes
	Adult : *Check Performance Review*	
OFFLINE	Student & Adult : Review online work	:30 minutes
	• Reading Warm-Up	
	• Speed Work	
	• Assessment	
	Grammar, Usage, and Mechanics (GUM)	:30 minutes
	Instructional Time **2:00** hours	

Materials

• *MARK¹² Reading Activity Book*, pages 65–70

Goals

In this lesson, students will read about a boy who loves to paint. Students will also be introduced to the digraph *ck* and the trigraph *tch* before working with the sight words *what, their,* and *want.* In today's Unit Assessment, you will administer a test covering all content from Unit 4. Afterward, you will work with students to complete activities on nouns.

ONLINE Student & Computer

Students will work online to complete Warm-Up, Code Work, Word Work, and Speed Work activities, and a review game on their own. Be sure to read the Performance Review before beginning the offline portion of today's lesson.

Today you will administer a Unit Assessment and work with students to complete a GUM activity.

Warm-Up ·

Painting

Look at the Performance Review. If the student achieved a perfect score on today's Warm-Up, move on to Speed Work. If the student scored 60 percent or 80 percent, print the story and review the comprehension questions with the student. If the student scored less than 60 percent, print the story, have the student read the story aloud, and then work through the comprehension questions together, before moving on to Speed Work.

Objectives

- Improve reading and comprehension skills.

Speed Work ·

Can They?

Look at the Performance Review, or check the student's fluency chart. Fluency scores (words read per minute) should not fall below 80. If the student scored below 80 words per minute, print a copy of the Speed Work story and have the student read the story silently before reading it aloud to you. Otherwise, move on to the Assessment.

Objectives

- Increase reading fluency rate.

☼ Assessment ·

Digraphs and Sight Words

Today's Unit Assessment covers all content found in Unit 4. Carefully read the instructions on the student pages before administering the test to the student. If necessary, read the directions to the student. After you have scored the student's assessment, be sure to go online and enter student performance scores in the assessment entry tool.

Part 1. Dictate the following words to students: *shut, math, chip, tuck, whim, pitch, this, mush, tack, thin, such, whap, notch,* and *that.*

Part 4. Dictate the following words to students: *their, what, so, said, want,* and *your.*

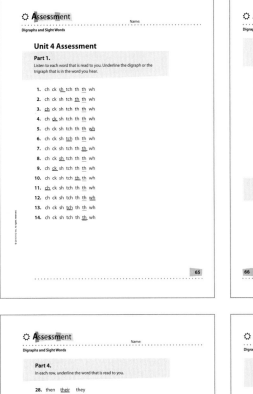

☼ **Assessment**   Name:

Digraphs and Sight Words

Unit 4 Assessment

Part 1.
Listen to each word that is read to you. Underline the digraph or the trigraph that is in the word you hear.

1. ch ck <u>sh</u> tch th <u>th</u> wh
2. ch ck sh tch <u>th</u> th wh
3. <u>ch</u> ck sh tch th <u>th</u> wh
4. ch <u>ck</u> sh tch th th wh
5. ch ck sh tch th th <u>wh</u>
6. ch ck sh <u>tch</u> th <u>th</u> wh
7. ch ck sh tch th <u>th</u> wh
8. ch ck <u>sh</u> tch th <u>th</u> wh
9. ch <u>ck</u> sh tch th <u>th</u> wh
10. ch ck sh tch <u>th</u> th wh
11. <u>ch</u> ck sh tch th th wh
12. ch ck sh tch th <u>th</u> wh
13. ch ck sh <u>tch</u> th <u>th</u> wh
14. ch ck sh tch th <u>th</u> wh

65

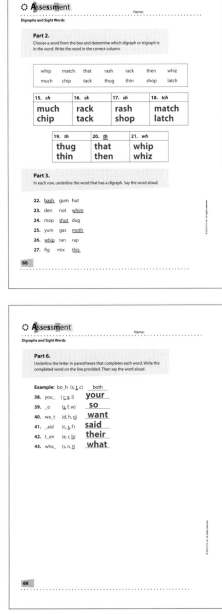

☼ **Assessment**   Name:

Digraphs and Sight Words

Part 2.
Choose a word from the box and determine which digraph or trigraph is in the word. Write the word in the correct column.

| whip | match | that | rash | rack | then | whiz |
| much | chip | tack | thug | thin | shop | latch |

15. *ch*	16. *ck*	17. *sh*	18. *tch*
much	rack	rash	match
chip	tack	shop	latch

19. *th*	20. *th*	21. *wh*
thug	that	whip
thin	then	whiz

Part 3.
In each row, underline the word that has a digraph. Say the word aloud.

22. <u>bash</u> gum hut
23. den not <u>whim</u>
24. mop <u>shut</u> dug
25. yum gas <u>moth</u>
26. <u>whip</u> tan rap
27. fig mix <u>this</u>

66

☼ **Assessment**   Name:

Digraphs and Sight Words

Part 4.
In each row, underline the word that is read to you.

28. then <u>their</u> they
29. <u>what</u> was when
30. son <u>so</u> shop
31. sad <u>said</u> some
32. went win <u>want</u>
33. <u>your</u> or you

Part 5.
Choose the word from the box that best completes each sentence. Write the word on the line provided.
Hint: Two words in the box are not used.

| went | so | both | want | what | your |

34. Is that **your** cup?
35. Tad **went** to the pet shop.
36. I **want** a red truck.
37. That cat is **so** big!

67

☼ **Assessment**   Name:

Digraphs and Sight Words

Part 6.
Underline the letter in parentheses that completes each word. Write the completed word on the line provided. Then say the word aloud.

Example: bo_h (s, <u>t</u>, c) ___both___

38. you_   (<u>r</u>, g, l)   **your**
39. _o   (<u>s</u>, f, w)   **so**
40. wa_t   (d, h, <u>n</u>)   **want**
41. _aid   (c, <u>s</u>, f)   **said**
42. t_eir   (e, r, <u>h</u>)   **their**
43. wha_   (s, n, <u>t</u>)   **what**

68

Objectives

- Identify the letters, given the sound /sh/, /th/, /<u>th</u>/, /ch/, /wh/, /ck/, and /tch/.
- Identify and use the digraphs *sh, th, <u>th</u>, ch, wh,* and *ck*.
- Identify and use the trigraph *tch*.
- Read sight words.

Nouns

A noun names a *person, place, thing,* or *idea.*

> *Persons:* baker, dad, captain, waiter, doctor, astronaut
>
> *Places:* library, home, pond, store, gym, beach
>
> *Things:* plate, cat, window, ant, finger, doll
>
> *Ideas:* freedom, sadness, love, hate, trust, truth

Work with students to complete pages 69 and 70 in *MARK¹²Reading Activity Book.* Read page 69, Get Ready, with students. Have students complete the Try It page. Be sure to discuss students' answers when the page is completed.

<table>
<tr><td>

GUM Grammar, Usage, and Mechanics   Name: ....

Digraphs and Sight Words 3

Get Ready

▪ **Nouns**

A **noun** names a *person, place, thing,* or *idea.*

Here are some examples of nouns.

Persons: baker, dad, captain
Places: library, home, pond
Things: plate, cat, window
Ideas: freedom, sadness, love

A noun can tell *who* or *what.*

Who: man, baby, friend, kid, clown
What: garden, city, pencil, dog, happiness

Read the sentence below. Each underlined word is a noun.

The <u>boy</u> went to the <u>zoo</u> to watch the <u>monkey</u> for <u>fun</u>.

The <u>boy</u> is a *person.* The <u>zoo</u> is a *place.* The <u>monkey</u> is a *thing.* Having <u>fun</u> is an *idea.*

Interesting to know: The word **noun** is a noun! It names a *thing.*

69

</td><td>

GUM Grammar, Usage, and Mechanics   Name: ....

Digraphs and Sight Words 3

Try It

Read each word in the box. Underline the word if it is a noun.

<u>dog</u>	run	they	when	<u>sun</u>
quick	<u>shack</u>	fetch	<u>sash</u>	where
<u>tent</u>	rich	<u>cup</u>	both	what

Read each sentence. Underline the noun or nouns in each sentence.

1. The <u>girl</u> found a pink <u>shell</u> on the <u>sand</u>.
2. She put it in her big <u>bucket</u>.
3. Suddenly the <u>shell</u> began to move!
4. There was a <u>crab</u> inside the <u>shell</u>!
5. The <u>girl</u> put the <u>shell</u> with the <u>crab</u> back on the <u>sand</u>.

70

</td></tr>
</table>

Objectives

• Identify nouns.

Long Vowels and Sight Words 1

ONLINE	Student & Computer	**:60**	minutes
	Adult : *Check Performance Review*		
OFFLINE	Student & Adult : Review online work	**:30**	minutes
	• Reading Warm-Up		
	• Code Work		
	• Word Work		
	• Speed Work		
	Composition	**:30**	minutes
	Instructional Time	**2:00**	hours

Materials

- *MARK¹² Reading Activity Book*, pages 71–74
- *Just Write*

Tip

Diacritical marks tell us how to read a sound. The short vowel sounds are noted by a breve: /ă/, /ĕ/, /ĭ/, /ŏ/, and /ŭ/. Long vowel sounds are noted by a macron: /ā/, /ē/, /ī/, /ō/, and /ū/.

Goals

In this lesson, students will read about a boy who dreams he becomes a snail. Students will also work with the long vowel sounds /ā/ and /ē/ before reviewing the sight words *what, their,* and *want*. In today's *MARK¹² Reading Activity Book* pages, you will work with students to reinforce their understanding of the long vowel sounds /ā/ and /ē/ and to reinforce their correct use of the sight words *what, their,* and *want*. Afterward, students will spend 30 minutes working on composition.

Advance Preparation

For the offline portion of today's lesson, gather the students' composition materials. Based on the Performance Review, if students need to complete Code Work activity 3, you will need the Online Tile Kit or Paper Letter Tiles. If students need to complete Code Work activity 4, gather the following Paper Letter Tiles: *a, d, e, e, f, m, t,* and *th*. If students need to complete Word Work activity 2, create sight word cards for the following words: *what, their,* and *want*. If students need to complete Word Work activity 3, you will need a timer and the Online Tile Kit or Paper Letter Tiles. If students must complete Word Work activity 5, create a second set of sight word cards for the words *what, their,* and *want*.

ONLINE Student & Computer

Students will work online to complete Warm-Up, Code Work, Word Work, and Speed Work activities, and a Wrap-Up assessment on their own. Be sure to read the Performance Review before beginning the offline portion of today's lesson.

Today you will work with students to complete Code Work, Word Work, and Composition activities. Be sure to read the online Performance Review before beginning the Code Work and Word Work activities.

Life as a Snail

Look at the Performance Review. If the student achieved a perfect score on today's Warm-Up, move on to Code Work. If the student scored 60 percent or 80 percent, print the story and review the comprehension questions with the student. If the student scored less than 60 percent, print the story, have the student read the story aloud, and then work through the comprehension questions together, before moving on to Code Work.

Objectives

- Improve reading and comprehension skills.

Long Vowels

Look at the Performance Review. If the student achieved a perfect score on today's Code Work activities, complete the first two activities from the list below. If the student scored less than 100 percent but more than 85 percent, complete the first three activities from the list below. If the student scored 85 percent or less, complete all four of the activities listed below.

Objectives

- Identify and use silent *e*.
- Identify and use /ā/ and /ē/ spelling patterns.

1. Have students complete page 71 in *MARK¹² Reading Activity Book* for more practice on the long vowel sounds /ā/ and /ē/. To complete the activity, you will need to dictate the following words to students: *at, Beth, Chad, chase, dash, deck, Eve, Pete, Shane, tape, theme,* and *yet.*

2. Remove "The Date" story from *MARK¹² Reading Activity Book.* Fold the pages in half to create a small booklet. Review the following word with students: *off.* Have students read the story silently once or twice before reading the story aloud. When students read aloud, make note of any pronunciation errors, and review those words with students.

3. Have students use the Online Tile Kit or Paper Letter Tiles to build the following words: *at, can, Jan, mad,* and *pet.* Students should read the words aloud and then point to the letter that makes the vowel sound in each word. Then have students add an *e* to the end of each word and read the new words aloud. Ask students to point to the letters that make the long *a* or long *e* sound in each word.

4. Gather the Paper Letter Tiles for the letters *a, d, e, e, f, m, t,* and *th.* Have students use the tiles to build words as time permits. Some words students may create include: *fade, fame, made, tame,* and *theme.*

Code Work   Name: _____

Long Vowels and Sight Words 1

Sorting Words by Vowel Sounds

Repeat each word after it is read to you. Listen for the vowel sound and write each word under the correct column for the vowel sound that you hear. Then write two more words for each vowel sound.

Short *a*	Long *a*	Short *e*	Long *e*
at	chase	Beth	Eve
Chad	Shane	deck	Pete
dash	tape	yet	theme

Additional words chosen by student will vary.

71

Word Work · · · · · · · · · · · · · · ·

Sight Words

Look at the Performance Review. If the student achieved a perfect score on today's Word Work activities, complete the first activity from the list below. If the student scored less than 100 percent but more than 85 percent, complete the first three activities from the list below. If the student scored 85 percent or less, complete all five of the activities listed below.

1. Have students complete page 72 in *MARK¹² Reading Activity Book* for more practice on the sight words *what, their,* and *want.*

2. Using the sight word cards you created for *what, their,* and *want,* read each word to students and have students write the word on a piece of paper. Give students the sight words, and instruct students to look for any spelling mistakes they may have made. Students should correct the mistakes and then read the list of words aloud.

3. Gather all of the sight word cards students have worked on to date and a timer. Have students read all of the sight word cards as accurately and quickly as possible. Make note of the time, as well as any errors students have made. Use the Online Tile Kit or Paper Letter Tiles to review words read incorrectly.

4. Gather the cards for the sight words *what, their,* and *want,* and up to two additional sight words students have yet to master. Show the first card to students, and ask students to read the word. If students read the word correctly, place in one pile. If students read the word incorrectly, place in a separate pile. On the back of the cards that were read correctly, make a note of the date and put aside. (Once students have read the word correctly five consecutive days, you can remove the word from the pile of cards students are working on.) Review any words students read incorrectly, and keep the cards for next time.

5. Gather the two sets of sight word cards for the words *what, their,* and *want,* and place all of the cards face down on the table or another flat surface. Have students choose a card, read the word aloud, and then choose a second card. After students read the second card aloud, if the two cards match, students should keep the cards. If they do not match, students should return them to the table. Continue until all of the cards have been collected.

Speed Work · · · · · · · · · · · · · · ·

A Fish Cake

Look at the Performance Review, or check the student's fluency chart. Fluency scores (words read per minute) should not fall below 80. If the student scored below 80 words per minute, print a copy of the Speed Work story and have the student read the story silently before reading it aloud. Otherwise, move on to Composition.

Composition

Gather students' composition materials and begin where they left off.

Long Vowels and Sight Words 2

ONLINE	Student & Computer	**:60** minutes	
	Adult : *Check Performance Review*		
OFFLINE	Student & Adult : Review online work	**:30** minutes	
	• Reading Warm-Up		
	• Speed Work		
	• Assessment		
	Grammar, Usage, and Mechanics (GUM)	**:30** minutes	
	Instructional Time **2:00** hours		

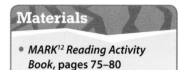

Materials

• *MARK¹² Reading Activity Book*, pages 75–80

Goals

In this lesson, students will read about the human heart. Students will also work with the long vowel sounds /ī/, /ō/, and /ū/ before learning the sight words *who, see,* and *or*. In today's Unit Assessment, you will administer a test covering all content from Unit 5. Afterward, you will work with students to complete activities on common and proper nouns.

ONLINE   Student & Computer

Students will work online to complete Warm-Up, Code Work, Word Work, and Speed Work activities, and a review game on their own. Be sure to read the Performance Review before beginning the offline portion of today's lesson.

Today you will administer a Unit Assessment and work with students to complete a GUM activity.

Warm-Up ·

Your Heart

Look at the Performance Review. If the student achieved a perfect score on today's Warm-Up, move on to Speed Work. If the student scored 60 percent or 80 percent, print the story and review the comprehension questions with the student. If the student scored less than 60 percent, print the story, have the student read the story aloud, and then work through the comprehension questions together, before moving on to Speed Work.

Objectives
- Improve reading and comprehension skills.

Speed Work ·

The Robe

Look at the Performance Review, or check the student's fluency chart. Fluency scores (words read per minute) should not fall below 80. If the student scored below 80 words per minute, print a copy of the Speed Work story and have the student read the story silently before reading it aloud to you. Otherwise, move on to the Assessment.

Objectives
- Increase reading fluency rate.

☼ Assessment ·

Long Vowels and Sight Words

Today's Unit Assessment covers all content found in Unit 5. Carefully read the instructions on the student pages before administering the test to the student. If necessary, read the directions to the student. After you have scored the student's assessment, be sure to go online and enter student performance scores in the assessment entry tool.

Part 2. Dictate the following words to students: *ape, bite, cave, mute, theme, white, code, tape, woke,* and *cute.*

Part 4. Dictate the following words to students: *or, said, who, so, see, so, or, said, who, your, see,* and *your.*

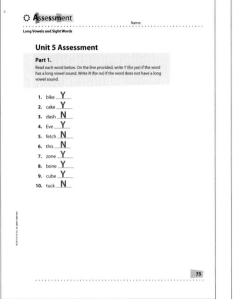

☼ **A**ssessment

Name: _____

Long Vowels and Sight Words

Unit 5 Assessment

Part 1.

Read each word below. On the line provided, write *Y* (for yes) if the word has a long vowel sound. Write *N* (for no) if the word does not have a long vowel sound.

1. bike __Y__
2. cake __Y__
3. dash __N__
4. Eve __Y__
5. fetch __N__
6. this __N__
7. zone __Y__
8. bone __Y__
9. cube __Y__
10. tuck __N__

75

☼ **A**ssessment

Name: _____

Long Vowels and Sight Words

Part 2.

Listen to each word that is read to you. Write the word on the line provided.

11. __ape__
12. __bite__
13. __cave__
14. __mute__
15. __theme__
16. __white__
17. __code__
18. __tape__
19. __woke__
20. __cute__

76

☼ **A**ssessment

Name: _____

Long Vowels and Sight Words

Part 3.

In each row, underline the word that contains a long vowel sound.

21. chop — <u>chase</u> — check
22. den — <u>dive</u> — dog
23. <u>fume</u> — fan — fed
24. mash — met — <u>mute</u>
25. <u>Pete</u> — Pam — Peg
26. thick — top — <u>take</u>
27. <u>whole</u> — wax — wet
28. cash — <u>cone</u> — cup
29. that — thin — <u>these</u>
30. <u>time</u> — tag — ten

77

☼ **A**ssessment

Name: _____

Long Vowels and Sight Words

Part 4.

In each row, underline the word that is read to you.

31. said — so — <u>or</u>
32. <u>said</u> — your — so
33. <u>who</u> — see — or
34. your — <u>so</u> — see
35. said — <u>see</u> — or
36. who — see — <u>so</u>
37. said — who — <u>or</u>
38. <u>said</u> — your — so
39. <u>who</u> — see — or
40. so — who — <u>your</u>
41. said — <u>see</u> — or
42. <u>your</u> — so — who

Part 5.

Read each word aloud.

43. said   47. see   51. or
44. your   48. or   52. who
45. so   49. so   53. your
46. who   50. said   54. see

78

Objectives

- Identify and use silent *e* and /ā/, /ē/, /ī/, /ō/, and /ū/ spelling patterns.
- Identify and read sight words.

Long Vowels and Sight Words 2   **93**

Proper and Common Nouns

A noun is a *person, place, thing,* or *idea*. A common noun is a general group or kind of person, place, or thing. A proper noun names a particular person, place, or thing.

Common Nouns	Proper Nouns
boy	Ethan
city	Dallas
state	California

Work with students to complete pages 79 and 80 in *MARK¹²Reading Activity Book*. Read page 79, Get Ready, with students. Have students complete the Try It page. Be sure to discuss students' answers when the page is completed.

Objectives

- Identify and use proper and common nouns.

G U M Grammar, Usage, and Mechanics   Name:

Long Vowels and Sight Words 2

Get Ready

▢ A **noun** is a *person, place, thing,* or *idea*. Here are some examples of nouns:

Persons: carpenter, parent, Mayor Ruiz
Places: library, New York, pond
Things: plate, Statue of Liberty, window
Ideas: freedom, sadness, liberty

▢ Take a look at these two nouns:

city
Chicago

We call *city* a **common noun**. Common nouns tell about a *general* group or kind of person, place, or thing.

Chicago names a particular city. We call *Chicago* a **proper noun**. Proper nouns name a *particular* person, place, or thing. Proper nouns are *capitalized*.

Common Nouns	Proper Nouns
man	Mr. Davis
city	Jacksonville
team	Lakers
state	Kansas
holiday	Thanksgiving
ocean	Pacific Ocean
author	E.B. White

79

G U M Grammar, Usage, and Mechanics   Name:

Long Vowels and Sight Words 2

Try It

Underline the common nouns in the box. Circle the proper nouns.

run	bag	Dan
fade	gave	hat
Denver	sadness	sit
rock	bake	Sarah
freedom	made	Boston

Write each noun from the box above in the correct column below. Then write one more word of your own in each column.

Person	Place	Thing	Idea
Dan Sarah	Denver Boston	bag hat rock	sadness freedom

Additional words from student will vary.

80

Ending Blends and Sight Words 1

ONLINE	Student & Computer	:60 minutes
	Adult : *Check Performance Review*	
OFFLINE	Student & Adult : Review online work	:30 minutes
	• Reading Warm-Up	
	• Code Work	
	• Word Work	
	• Speed Work	
	Classics Session 1	:30 minutes
	Instructional Time **2:00** hours	

Materials

- *MARK¹² Classics for Young Readers*
- *MARK¹² Reading Activity Book*, pages 81–84

Tip

*In a blend, each letter keeps its own sound. Note the words **talk** and **walk** are not examples of the ending blend –**lk**. **Walk** and **talk** are examples of **al** working together to say /aw/, and are taught later in the MARK¹² program.*

Goals

In this lesson, students will read about human teeth. Students will also work with the ending blends –*nd*, –*ft*, –*lk*, and –*ct* before working with the sight words *who, see,* and *or*. In today's *MARK¹² Reading Activity Book* pages, you will work with students to reinforce their understanding of the ending blends –*nd*, –*ft*, –*lk*, and –*ct* and to reinforce their correct use of the sight words *who, see,* and *or*. You will also work with students to complete Classics activities.

Advance Preparation

Based on the Performance Review, if students need to complete Code Work activity 3, you will need to gather eight index cards. Write one of the following words on each card: *bond, end, soft, left, bulk, elk, fact,* and *pact*. If students need to complete Word Work activity 2, create sight word cards for the following words: *who, see,* and *or*. If students need to complete Word Work activity 3, you will need a timer and the Online Tile Kit or Paper Letter Tiles. If students need to complete Word Work activity 5, create a second set of sight word cards for the words *who, see,* and *or*.

ONLINE	Student & Computer

Students will work online to complete Warm-Up, Code Work, Word Work, and Speed Work activities, and a Wrap-Up assessment on their own. Be sure to read the Performance Review before beginning the offline portion of today's lesson.

Today you will work with students to complete Code Work, Word Work, and *MARK¹² Classics for Young Readers* activities. Be sure to read the online Performance Review before beginning the Code Work and Word Work activities.

Warm-Up •••••••••••••••••••••••••••••••••••••••

Your Teeth

Look at the Performance Review. If the student achieved a perfect score on today's Warm-Up, move on to Code Work. If the student scored 60 percent or 80 percent, print the story and review the comprehension questions with the student. If the student scored less than 60 percent, print the story, have the student read the story aloud, and then work through the comprehension questions together, before moving on to Code Work.

Objectives

• **Improve reading and comprehension skills.**

Code Work •••••••••••••••••••••••••••••••••••

Ending Blends: *–nd, –ft, –lk, & –ct*

Look at the Performance Review. If the student achieved a perfect score on today's Code Work activities, complete the first two activities from the list below. If the student scored less than 100 percent but more than 85 percent, complete the first three activities from the list below. If the student scored 85 percent or less, complete all five of the activities listed below.

Objectives

• **Identify and use the blends *–nd, –ft, –lk,* and *–ct.***

1. Have students complete page 81 in *MARK¹² Reading Activity Book* for more practice on the ending blends *–nd, –ft, –lk,* and *–ct.*

2. Remove the "Bug! Bug! Bug!" poem from *MARK¹² Reading Activity Book.* Fold the pages in half to create a small booklet. Have students read the poem silently once or twice before reading the poem aloud. When students read aloud, make note of any errors, and review those words with the students.

3. Gather the eight index cards you created (*bond, end, soft, left, bulk, elk, fact,* and *pact*) and place cards face down. Have students flip one card over and read it, and then flip another card over and read it. If the two cards contain words with the same ending blend, students may keep them. If the ending blends do not match, students should replace the cards where they were. Continue until all cards are picked up.

4. On a piece of paper, make four columns. Label the columns as follows: *–nd, –ft, –lk,* and *–ct.* Have students think of two or three words that end with those blends, and write the words in the corresponding columns.

5. Have students use the Online Tile Kit or the Paper Letter Tiles to spell the following words: *act, and, bend, bulk, fact, lift, raft,* and *silk.*

Code Work Name _____
Ending Blends and Sight Words 1

Ending Blends

Draw a line from two beginning letters to an ending blend to make a word. Write the word on the line. Then read each word aloud. The first one has been done for you.

1. ra ___ ct   raft
2. bu ___ ft   **bulk**
3. fa ___ nd   **fact**
4. be ___ lk   **bend**

Add beginning letters to each ending blend to create a word.

Example: se nd   **Answers will vary.**
5. _____ct
6. _____ft
7. _____nd
8. _____lk

81

Word Work ·

Sight Words

Look at the Performance Review. If the student achieved a perfect score on today's Word Work activities, complete the first activity from the list below. If the student scored less than 100 percent but more than 85 percent, complete the first three activities from the list below. If the student scored 85 percent or less, complete all five of the activities listed below.

- **Read sight words.**
- **Increase reading vocabulary.**

1. Have students complete page 82 in *MARK¹² Reading Activity Book* for more practice on sight words.

2. Using the sight word cards you created for *who, see,* and *or,* read each word to students and have students write the word on a piece of paper. Give students the sight words, and instruct students to look for any spelling mistakes they may have made. Students should correct the mistakes and then read the list of words aloud.

3. Gather all of the sight word cards students have worked on to date and a timer. Have students read all of the sight word cards as accurately and quickly as possible. Make note of the time, as well as any errors students have made. Use the Online Tile Kit or Paper Letter Tiles to review words read incorrectly.

4. Gather the cards for the sight words *who, see,* and *or,* and up to two additional sight words students have yet to master. Show the first card to students, and ask students to read the word. If students read the word correctly, place in one pile. If students read the word incorrectly, place in a separate pile. On the back of the cards that were read correctly, make a note of the date and put aside. (Once students have read the word correctly five consecutive days, you can remove the word from the pile of cards students are working on.) Review any words students read incorrectly, and keep the cards for next time.

5. Gather the two sets of sight word cards for the words *who, see,* and *or,* and place all of the cards face down on the table or another flat surface. Have students choose a card, read the word aloud, and then choose a second card. After students read the second card aloud, if the two cards match, students should keep the cards. If they do not match, students should return them to the table. Continue until all of the cards have been collected.

Speed Work ·

The Raft

Look at the Performance Review, or check the student's fluency chart. Fluency scores (words read per minute) should not fall below 80. If the student scored below 80 words per minute, print a copy of the Speed Work story and have the student read the story silently before reading it aloud. Otherwise, move on to Classics Session 1.

- **Increase reading fluency rate.**

Classics Session 1 ·

Bruce and the Spider

Today's story, "Bruce and the Spider," is about a king inspired by a spider. Review the keywords with students. Read the story with students, and then use the Discussion Questions below as a guide to share ideas about the story. Have students read the story again before writing a summary of the story.

Keywords

foe, n. – an enemy
The brave soldier knew he was stronger than his **foe** and believed he could win the battle.

head, n. – a place of leadership; a place of command
The general rode at the **head** of his troops, ready to battle the enemy.

thread, n. – a very thin cord of twisted fibers
She used red **thread** to stitch the rip in her satin dress.

Discussion Questions

1. Think about the reasons Robert Bruce is in hiding. How do you think he feels about what has happened to him?
   Answers may include that Robert Bruce is hiding from his enemies. He is likely scared and discouraged. He may feel bad that soldiers died under his command. He may also be embarrassed that he lost so many battles.

2. There is an old saying: "If at first you don't succeed, try, try again." What do you think this means? Do you think this is good advice? Why?
   Answers will vary.

3. Characters in a story often change as a result of trying to solve their problems. For example, a character may become braver or wiser, or may be asked to solve an even harder problem. Think about a problem you have had. How did you solve it? How did it change you?
   Answers will vary.

4. How is Robert Bruce like the spider? What did Bruce learn from watching the spider?
   Answers may include that Robert Bruce, like the spider, is trying to accomplish something. The spider teaches Bruce not to give up.

5. Think of a time when you saw something that changed how you felt or what you did. Describe the situation. What about it made you change your thinking or actions?
   Answers will vary.

Students should write a summary of the story to complete today's Classics activity.

Ending Blends and Sight Words 2

ONLINE	Student & Computer	:60 minutes
	Adult : *Check Performance Review*	
OFFLINE	Student & Adult : Review online work	:30 minutes
	• Reading Warm-Up	
	• Code Work	
	• Word Work	
	• Speed Work	
	Classics Session 2	:30 minutes
	Instructional Time **2:00** hours	

Materials

- *MARK¹² Classics for Young Readers*
- *MARK¹² Reading Activity Book*, pages 85–86

Tip

In a blend, each letter keeps its own sound. In this lesson, students will work with four ending blends: –lp, –lt, –mp, and –sp. Help, belt, lump, and gasp contain the ending blends from today's lesson.

Goals

In this lesson, students will read about the parts of the ear. Students will also work with the ending blends *–lp, –lt, –mp,* and *–sp* before learning the sight words *for, she,* and *her.* In today's *MARK¹² Reading Activity Book* pages, you will work with students to reinforce their understanding of the ending blends *–lp, –lt, –mp,* and *–sp* and to reinforce their correct use of the sight words *for, she,* and *her.* You will also work with students to complete Classics activities.

Advance Preparation

Based on the Performance Review, if students need to complete Code Work activity 2, you will need to gather 11 index cards. Write one of the following words on each card: *bump, chimp, felt, gasp, help, kelp, melt, pulp, stump, tilt,* and *wisp.* If students need to complete Word Work activity 2, create sight word cards for the following words: *for, she,* and *her.* If students need to complete Word Work activity 3, you will need a timer and the Online Tile Kit or Paper Letter Tiles. If students need to complete Word Work activity 5, you will need to create a second set of sight word cards for the words *for, she,* and *her.*

ONLINE Student & Computer

Students will work online to complete Warm-Up, Code Work, Word Work, and Speed Work activities, and a Wrap-Up assessment on their own. Be sure to read the Performance Review before beginning the offline portion of today's lesson.

Today you will work with students to complete Code Work, Word Work, and *MARK¹² Classics for Young Readers* activities. Be sure to read the online Performance Review before beginning the Code Work and Word Work activities.

Warm-Up

Your Ears

Look at the Performance Review. If the student achieved a perfect score on today's Warm-Up, move on to Code Work. If the student scored 60 percent or 80 percent, print the story and review the comprehension questions with the student. If the student scored less than 60 percent, print the story, have the student read the story aloud, and then work through the comprehension questions together, before moving on to Code Work.

Code Work

Ending Blends : *–lp, –lt, –mp, & –sp*

Look at the Performance Review. If the student achieved a perfect score on today's Code Work activities, complete the first two activities from the list below. If the student scored less than 100 percent but more than 85 percent, complete the first three activities from the list below. If the student scored 85 percent or less, complete all four of the activities listed below.

1. Have students complete page 85 in *MARK¹² Reading Activity Book* for more practice on the ending blends *–lp, –lt, –mp,* and *–sp.*

2. Gather the 11 index cards you created (*bump, chimp, felt, gasp, help, kelp, melt, pulp, stump, tilt,* and *wisp*) and place cards face down. Have students flip one card over and read it, and then flip another card over and read it. If the two cards contain words with the same ending blend, students may keep them. If the two ending blends do not match, students replace the cards exactly where they were. Continue until all cards are picked up.

3. Have students write the following words on a piece of paper: *belt, champ, gasp, gulp, help, lamp, quilt, wilt,* and *yelp.*Ask students to read the words aloud and underline the ending blend in each word.

4. Take turns with students thinking of words containing the ending blend *–lp.* Start by giving students a word (example: *scalp*). Have students think of a different word containing the ending blend *–lp.* Take turns for one minute or until you run out of words. Repeat the procedure with words that contain the ending blends *–lt, –mp,* and *–sp.*

Code Work   Name:

Ending Blends and Sight Words 2

Find the Blends

Read each word aloud. Underline the words that have an ending blend. Remember, you must be able to hear both sounds separately in an ending blend.

wish	felt	help	rush	bump
gasp	rash	melt	pulp	hatch
chomp	dish	quilt	catch	yelp
lump	tilt	quick	thump	bath

85

Word Work ·

Sight Words

Look at the Performance Review. If the student achieved a perfect score on today's Word Work activities, complete the first activity from the list below. If the student scored less than 100 percent but more than 85 percent, complete the first three activities from the list below. If the student scored 85 percent or less, complete all five of the activities listed below.

1. Have students complete page 86 in *MARK¹² Reading Activity Book* for more practice on the sight words *for, she,* and *her*. To complete the page, you will need a timer. As students read the sight words, keep track of how many are read correctly.

2. Using the sight word cards you created for *for, she,* and *her,* read each word to students and have students write the word on a piece of paper. Give students the sight words, and instruct students to look for any spelling mistakes. Students should correct the mistakes and then read the list of words aloud.

3. Gather all of the sight word cards students have worked on to date and a timer. Have students read all of the sight word cards as accurately and quickly as possible. Make note of the time, as well as any errors students have made. Use the Online Tile Kit or Paper Letter Tiles to review words read incorrectly.

4. Gather the cards for the sight words *for, she,* and *her,* and up to two additional sight words students have yet to master. Show the first card to students, and ask students to read the word. If students read the word correctly, place in one pile. If students read the word incorrectly, place in a separate pile. On the back of the cards that were read correctly, make a note of the date and put aside. (Once students have read the word correctly five consecutive days, you can remove the word from the pile of cards students are working on.) Review any words students read incorrectly, and keep the cards for next time.

5. Gather the two sets of sight word cards for the words *for, she,* and *her,* and place the cards face down. Have students choose a card, read the word aloud, and then choose a second card. After students read the second card aloud, if the two cards match, students should keep the cards. If they do not match, students should return them to the table. Continue until all cards have been collected.

Speed Work ·

Milk

Look at the Performance Review, or check the student's fluency chart. Fluency scores (words read per minute) should not fall below 80. If the student scored below 80 words per minute, print a copy of the Speed Work story and have the student read the story silently before reading it aloud. Otherwise, move on to Classics Session 2.

Bruce and the Spider

Review the keywords with students. Have students reread the story on their own. After rereading the story, students should complete the comprehension questions in *MARK¹² Classics for Young Readers* on their own. Afterward, if time allows, have students read the story aloud to you.

Objectives

- Improve reading and comprehension skills.

"I learned a lesson," Bruce said. "Thank you. I won't give up yet. I will get my army, and I will try once more. Perhaps I can beat our enemies."

The king kept his word. He stood again at the **head** of his army. He fought bravely and proudly. This time, he won! Scotland was free.

W Write

Bruce and the Spider

1. What country is Robert Bruce from?
   Robert Bruce is from the country of Scotland.

2. Where does Robert Bruce go to hide?
   Robert Bruce goes to a small hut in the forest to hide.

3. Which word best describes Robert Bruce at the end of the story?
   (A) proud
   B. joyful
   C. unafraid
   D. disappointed

26   Bruce and the Spider

---

4. How many times does Robert Bruce watch the spider swing from beam to beam?
   A. three times
   B. five times
   (C) seven times
   D. ten times

5. Why is Robert Bruce in hiding?
   Robert Bruce lost many battles against Scotland's enemies. He and many of his soldiers were chased into hiding.

6. Why was Robert Bruce impressed by the spider?
   Robert Bruce was impressed by the spider because it never gave up.

7. What did Robert Bruce decide to do after watching the spider?
   A. stay in hiding
   B. give up his kingship
   C. surrender to his enemies
   (D) go to battle one more time

8. What happens at the end of the story?
   At the end of story, Robert Bruce defeats his enemies and Scotland is free.

Bruce and the Spider   27

Ending Blends and Sight Words 3

ONLINE	Student & Computer	:60 minutes
	Adult : *Check Performance Review*	
OFFLINE	Student & Adult : Review online work	:30 minutes
	• Reading Warm-Up	
	• Code Work	
	• Word Work	
	• Speed Work	
	Composition	:30 minutes
	Instructional Time **2:00** hours	

Materials

- *MARK[12] Reading Activity Book*, pages 87–90
- *Just Write*

Goals

In this lesson, students will read about the parts of the eye. Students will also work with the ending sounds *–ng* and *–nk* before working with the sight words *for, she,* and *her*. In today's *MARK[12] Reading Activity Book* pages, you will work with students to reinforce their understanding of the ending sounds *–ng* and *–nk* and to reinforce their correct use of the sight words *for, she,* and *her*. Afterward, students will spend 30 minutes working on composition.

Advance Preparation

For the offline portion of today's lesson, gather the students' composition materials. Based on the Performance Review, if students need to complete Code Work activity 4, gather a newspaper or magazine. If students need to complete Word Work activity 2, gather the sight word cards for the following words: *for, she,* and *her*. If students need to complete Word Work activity 3, you will need a timer and the Online Tile Kit or Paper Letter Tiles. If students need to complete Word Work activity 5, gather the second set of sight word cards for the words *for, she,* and *her*.

ONLINE Student & Computer

Students will work online to complete Warm-Up, Code Work, Word Work, and Speed Work activities, and a Wrap-Up assessment on their own. Be sure to read the Performance Review before beginning the offline portion of today's lesson.

Today you will work with students to complete Code Work, Word Work, and Composition activities. Be sure to read the online Performance Review before beginning the Code Work and Word Work activities.

Warm-Up ·

Your Eyes

Look at the Performance Review. If the student achieved a perfect score on today's Warm-Up, move on to Code Work. If the student scored 60 percent or 80 percent, print the story and review the comprehension questions with the student. If the student scored less than 60 percent, print the story, have the student read the story aloud, and then work through the comprehension questions together, before moving on to Code Work.

Objectives
- Improve reading and comprehension skills.

Code Work ·

Ending Blends: –ng & –nk

Look at the Performance Review. If the student achieved a perfect score on today's Code Work activities, complete the first two activities from the list below. If the student scored less than 100 percent but more than 85 percent, complete the first three activities from the list below. If the student scored less than 85 percent, complete all five of the activities listed below.

Objectives
- Identify and use the blend –ng.
- Identify and use the blend –nk.

1. Have students complete page 87 in *MARK¹² Reading Activity Book* for more practice on the ending blends –ng and –nk.

2. Remove the "Champ the Chimp Can Camp" story from *MARK¹² Reading Activity Book*. Fold the pages in half to create a small booklet. Review the following words with students: *alone, bear,* and *forest.* Have students read the story silently once or twice before reading the story aloud. When students read aloud, make note of any pronunciation errors, and review those words with students.

3. Have students write the following five words on a piece of paper: *chunk, long, thank, thing,* and *think.* Have students read the words aloud and underline the three letters that make the ending sound in each word.

4. Have students look through a newspaper or magazine, and circle as many words with the ending sounds –ng or –nk as they can find in two minutes. Have students read the words aloud. Help students with pronunciations, if necessary.

5. Have students come up with five words that contain the endings –ng or –nk (the words should differ from those used in activity 3). Have students write a sentence for each word and read the sentences aloud.

Wor**d** **W**ork ·

Sight Words

Look at the Performance Review. If the student achieved a perfect score on today's Word Work activities, complete the first activity from the list below. If the student scored less than 100 percent but more than 85 percent, complete the first three activities from the list below. If the student scored 85 percent or less, complete all five of the activities listed below.

1. Have students complete page 88 in *MARK¹² Reading Activity Book* for more practice on sight words. To complete the page, you will need a timer. As students read the sight words, keep track of how many are read correctly.

2. Using the sight word cards you created for *for, she,* and *her,* read each word to students and have students write each word. Give students the sight words, and instruct students to look for any spelling mistakes. Students should correct the mistakes and then read the list of words aloud.

3. Gather all of the sight word cards students have worked on to date and a timer. Have students read all of the sight word cards as accurately and quickly as possible. Make note of the time, as well as any errors students have made. Use the Online Tile Kit or Paper Letter Tiles to review words read incorrectly.

4. Gather the cards for the sight words *for, she,* and *her,* and up to two additional sight words students have yet to master. Show the first card to students, and ask students to read the word. If students read the word correctly, place in one pile. If students read the word incorrectly, place in a separate pile. On the back of the cards that were read correctly, make a note of the date and put aside. (Once students have read the word correctly five consecutive days, you can remove the word from the pile of cards students are working on.) Review any words students read incorrectly, and keep the cards for next time.

5. Gather the two sets of sight word cards for the words *for, she,* and *her,* and place the cards face down. Have students choose a card, read the word aloud, and then choose a second card. After students read the second card aloud, if the two cards match, students should keep the cards. If they do not match, students should return them to the table. Continue until all cards are collected.

Wor**d** Work

Ending Blends and Sight Words 3   Name: _____

By Sight

See how many words you can read correctly in one minute. Read aloud across the rows. When you get to the bottom of the page, start over. Try to read more words the second time.

who	for	her	of	put
said	their	want	you	or
see	they	we	your	she
two	went	so	what	both

Number of words read correctly: _____

88

Speed **W**ork ·

This and That

Look at the Performance Review, or check the student's fluency chart. Fluency scores (words read per minute) should not fall below 80. If the student scored below 80 words per minute, print a copy of the Speed Work story and have the student read the story silently before reading it aloud. Otherwise, move on to Composition.

Composition

Gather students' composition materials and begin where they left off.

Ending Blends and Sight Words 4

ONLINE	Student & Computer	**:60** minutes	
	Adult : *Check Performance Review*		
OFFLINE	Student & Adult : Review online work	**:30** minutes	
	• Reading Warm-Up		
	• Speed Work		
	• Assessment		
	Grammar, Usage, and Mechanics (GUM)	**:30** minutes	
	Instructional Time **2:00** hours		

Materials

• *MARK¹² Reading Activity Book*, pages 91–96

Goals

In this lesson, students will read about Helen Keller. Students will also work with the ending blends *–sk, –st, –nt,* and *–nch* before working with the sight words *does, why,* and *one.* In today's Unit Assessment, you will administer a test covering all content from Unit 6. Afterward, you will work with students to complete activities on capitalization.

ONLINE	**Student & Computer**

Students will work online to complete Warm-Up, Code Work, Word Work, and Speed Work activities, and a review game on their own. Be sure to read the Performance Review before beginning the offline portion of today's lesson.

Today you will administer a Unit Assessment and work with students to complete a GUM activity.

Warm-Up ·

Helen Keller

Look at the Performance Review. If the student achieved a perfect score on today's Warm-Up, move on to Speed Work. If the student scored 60 percent or 80 percent, print the story and review the comprehension questions with the student. If the student scored less than 60 percent, print the story, have the student read the story aloud, and then work through the comprehension questions together.

Speed Work ·

The Ranch

Look at the Performance Review, or check the student's fluency chart. Fluency scores (words read per minute) should not fall below 80. If the student scored below 80 words per minute, print a copy of the Speed Work story and have the student read the story silently before reading it aloud to you. Otherwise, move on to the Assessment.

☼ Assessment ·

Ending Blends and Sight Words

Today's Unit Assessment covers all content found in Unit 6. Carefully read the instructions on the student pages before administering the test to the student. If necessary, read the directions to the student. After you have scored the student's assessment, be sure to go online and enter student performance scores in the assessment entry tool.

Part 1. Dictate the following words to students: *and, raft, elk, long, act, help, belt, camp, pink, wisp, ask,* and *cast.*

Part 2. Dictate the following words to students: *bent, bang, lunch, honk, rust, mask, gasp, thump, tilt,* and *gulp.*

Part 3. Dictate the following sentences to students:
> *The sand is wet at the pond.*
> *Help Pat shift the raft.*
> *The elk ran and hid.*
> *Did you bump the lamp?*
> *I left the milk in the cup.*
> *The king sank in the mud.*

Part 4. Dictate the following words to students: *for, one, who, does, she, see, why, or, her, does, for, one, she, why,* and *her.*

☼ **A**ssessment Name:

Ending Blends and Sight Words

Unit 6 Assessment

Part 1.
Listen to each word that is read to you. Write the blend heard at the end of each word on the lines provided.

1. nd
2. ft
3. lk
4. ng
5. ct
6. lp
7. lt
8. mp
9. nk
10. sp
11. sk
12. st

91

☼ **A**ssessment Name:

Ending Blends and Sight Words

Part 2.
Listen to each word that is read to you. Write each word on the lines provided. Underline the blend at the end of each word.

13. bent
14. bang
15. lunch
16. honk
17. rust

18. mask
19. gasp
20. thump
21. tilt
22. gulp

Part 3.
Listen to each sentence that is read to you. Write each sentence on the lines provided.

23. The sand is wet at the pond.
24. Help Pat shift the raft.
25. The elk ran and hid.
26. Did you bump the lamp?
27. I left the milk in the cup.
28. The king sank in the mud.

92

☼ **A**ssessment Name:

Ending Blends and Sight Words

Part 4.
In each row, underline the word that is read to you.

29. does — <u>for</u> — her
30. <u>one</u> — or — see
31. she — <u>who</u> — why
32. <u>does</u> — why — for
33. who — her — <u>she</u>
34. one — <u>see</u> — or
35. <u>why</u> — who — she
36. see — <u>or</u> — one
37. <u>her</u> — for — does
38. why — <u>does</u> — who
39. <u>for</u> — she — her
40. see — or — <u>one</u>
41. does — see — <u>she</u>
42. for — or — <u>why</u>
43. <u>her</u> — one — who

93

☼ **A**ssessment Name:

Ending Blends and Sight Words

Part 5.
Read each word aloud.

44. why
45. does
46. for
47. who
48. she
49. her
50. one
51. see
52. or
53. for
54. she
55. her
56. does
57. why
58. one

94

Objectives

- Identify and use the blends –nd, –ft, –lk, –ct, –lp, –lt, –mp, –sp, –sk, –st, –nt, and –nch.
- Increase reading vocabulary.
- Read sight words.

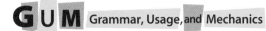
Capitalization

Most nouns are *common nouns*. Common nouns are written with lowercase first letters. *Proper nouns* name a particular person, place, or thing. Proper nouns begin with capital letters. First words in sentences and the pronoun "I" should also be capitalized.

Capitalize	Example
proper nouns	Mary
first words in sentences	My sister's name is Mary.
pronoun "I"	She was born when I was five years old.

Work with students to complete pages 95 and 96 in *MARK¹² Reading Activity Book*. Read page 96, Get Ready, with students. Have students complete the Try It page. Be sure to discuss students' answers when the page is completed.

GUM Grammar, Usage, and Mechanics   Name:

Ending Blends and Sight Words 4

Get Ready

Capital Letters

■ **Common nouns** tell about a *general* group or kind of person, place, or thing. Common nouns are written with *lowercase* first letters. For example, *boy* and *street* are common nouns, so they are not capitalized.

■ **Proper nouns** name a *particular* person, place, or thing. Proper nouns are *capitalized*. For example, *Alan* and *Riverside Road* are proper nouns, so they are capitalized.

Proper nouns include:

■ Names of people and pets:

Jeff   Ms. White   Fluffy

■ Names of streets, cities, states, and countries:

Forest Lane   Mexico City   Kansas   England

■ Names of holidays:

New Year's Day   Memorial Day   Labor Day

■ Names of days and months:

Saturday   November

■ Names of buildings and bridges:

Tower of London   Brooklyn Bridge

95

GUM Grammar, Usage, and Mechanics   Name:

Ending Blends and Sight Words 4

Try It

In the paragraph below, six common nouns are mistakenly capitalized. Draw a slash mark (/) through the first letters of these six common nouns to show that they should be lowercase.
Example: /oy

Also, four proper nouns are not capitalized and should be. Use the proofreading symbol (≡) to show which letters should be capitalized.
Example: jane
                  ≡

My friend ellen and I like to walk into /own together. First we walk
          ≡

down Heidi Drive, then we cross the Second Street Bridge, and then we

turn onto main Street. On the Fourth of july, our town is decorated with
        ≡   ≡

/ed, /hite, and /lue everywhere. On saturdays, different shop owners
                                      ≡

tie colorful /alloons to lampposts. Yet, the best place to visit is the First

National Bank, because they give away free /ollipops!

96

Beginning Blends and Sight Words 1

ONLINE	Student & Computer	**:60** minutes	
	Adult : *Check Performance Review*		
OFFLINE	Student & Adult : Review online work	**:30** minutes	
	• Reading Warm-Up		
	• Code Work		
	• Word Work		
	• Speed Work		
	Composition	**:30** minutes	

Instructional Time **2:00** hours

Materials

- Online Tile Kit or Paper Letter Tiles
- *MARK¹² Reading Activity Book*, pages 97–98
- *Just Write*

Tip

*Inform students that the blends **bl–**, **cl–**, **fl–**, **gl–**, **pl–**, and **sl–** are called "consonant blends" because they are formed by two consonants.*

Goals

In this lesson, students will read about badgers. Students will also learn about the blends *bl–*, *cl–*, *fl–*, *gl–*, *pl–*, and *sl–*, before exploring the sight words *does*, *why*, and *one*. In today's *MARK¹² Reading Activity Book*, you will work with students to complete words using the blends *bl–*, *cl–*, *fl–*, *gl–*, *pl–*, and *sl–*.

Advance Preparation

For the offline portion of today's lesson, gather the students' composition materials. Based on the Performance Review, if students need to complete Code Work activity 3, write the following 12 words on index cards (one word per card): *black, blot, clap, clock, flash, flat, glad, glum, plan, plug, sled,* and *slam*. If students need to complete Word Work activity 2, create the sight word cards for the following words: *does, why,* and *one*. If students need to complete Word Work activity 3, you will need a timer and the Online Tile Kit or Paper Letter Tiles. If students need to complete Word Work activity 5, create a second set of sight word cards for the words *does, why,* and *one*.

ONLINE   Student & Computer

Students will work online to complete Warm-Up, Code Work, Word Work, and Speed Work activities, and a Wrap-Up assessment on their own. Be sure to read the Performance Review before beginning the offline portion of today's lesson.

Today you will work with students to complete Code Work, Word Work, and Composition activities. Be sure to read the online Performance Review before beginning the Code Work and Word Work activities.

Warm-Up

Badgers

Look at the Performance Review. If the student achieved a perfect score on today's Warm-Up, move on to Code Work. If the student scored 60 percent or 80 percent, print the story and review the comprehension questions with the student. If the student scored less than 60 percent, print the story, have the student read the story aloud, and then work through the comprehension questions together, before moving on to Code Work.

Objectives

- Improve reading and comprehension skills.

Code Work

Beginning Blends: *bl–, cl–, fl–, gl–, pl–, & sl–*

Look at the Performance Review. If the student achieved a perfect score on today's Code Work activities, complete the first two activities from the list below. If the student scored less than 100 percent but more than 85 percent, complete the first three activities from the list below. If the student scored 85 percent or less, complete all five of the activities listed below.

Objectives

- Identify and use the blends *bl–, cl–, fl–, gl–, pl–,* and *sl–*.

1. Have students complete page 97 in *MARK¹² Reading Activity Book* for more practice on the blends *bl–, cl–, fl–, gl–, pl–,* and *sl–*.

2. Have students use the Online Tile Kit or the Paper Tile Kit to spell the following words: *blob, clot, flip, glad, plot,* and *slap.* Have students say each word aloud after spelling it. Remind students that both letters in a blend keep their sound.

3. Gather the 12 index cards that you created. Hold up a card at random and have students read it aloud. Continue for all 12 cards.

4. Shuffle the index cards from activity 3. Have students sort the cards into six groups—one for each blend (*bl–, cl–, fl–, gl–, pl–,* and *sl–*). Have students read aloud the words as they sort them. Ask students to think of at least one more word that could go in each blend group.

5. Gather and shuffle the index cards from activity 4. Hold up a card at random and have students say the word in a sentence. Help students with definitions when necessary.

Code Work
Name: _____
Beginning Blends and Sight Words 1

Choose the Blend
Underline the blend that completes the word. Write the word on the line provided.

Example: ____ush   bl   gl   cl   **blush**

1. ____an   sl   pl   gl   **plan**
2. ____ap   gl   fl   bl   **flap**
3. ____ock   sl   pl   cl   **clock**
4. ____ad   bl   gl   fl   **glad**
5. ____ed   sl   gl   cl   **sled**
6. ____ack   pl   bl   gl   **black**
7. ____ug   pl   cl   bl   **plug**
8. ____ap   gl   bl   sl   **slap**
9. ____ock   sl   bl   pl   **block**
10. ____am   bl   cl   pl   **clam**
11. ____ob   gl   fl   cl   **glob**
12. ____ag   bl   pl   fl   **flag**

97

Word Work ·····································

Sight Words

Look at the Performance Review. If the student achieved a perfect score on today's Word Work activities, complete the first activity from the list below. If the student scored less than 100 percent but more than 85 percent, complete the first three activities from the list below. If the student scored 85 percent or less, complete all five of the activities listed below.

1. Have students complete page 98 in *MARK¹² Reading Activity Book* for more practice on sight words.

2. Using the sight word cards you created for *does, why,* and *one,* read each word to students and have students write the word on a piece of paper. Give students the sight words, and instruct students to look for any spelling mistakes they may have made. Students should correct the mistakes and then read the list of words aloud.

3. Gather all of the sight word cards students have worked on to date and a timer. Have students read all of the sight word cards as accurately and quickly as possible. Make note of the time, as well as any errors students have made. Use the Online Tile Kit or Paper Letter Tiles to review words read incorrectly.

4. Gather the cards for the sight words *does, why,* and *one,* and up to two additional sight words students have yet to master. Show the first card to students, and ask students to read the word. If students read the word correctly, place in one pile. If students read the word incorrectly, place in a separate pile. On the back of the cards that were read correctly, make a note of the date and put aside. (Once students have read the word correctly five consecutive days, you can remove the word from the pile of cards students are working on.) Review any words students read incorrectly, and keep the cards for next time.

5. Gather the two sets of sight word cards for the words *does, why,* and *one,* and place all of the cards face down on the table or another flat surface. Have students choose a card, read the word aloud, and then choose a second card. After students read the second card aloud, if the two cards match, students should keep the cards. If they do not match, students should return them to the table. Continue until all of the cards have been collected.

Speed Work ·····································

The Big Blast

Look at the Performance Review, or check the student's fluency chart. Fluency scores (words read per minute) should not fall below 80. If the student scored below 80 words per minute, print a copy of the Speed Work story and have the student read the story silently before reading it aloud. Otherwise, move on to Composition.

Composition

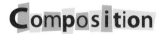

Gather students' composition materials and begin where they left off.

Objectives

- Develop composition skills.

Beginning Blends and Sight Words 2

ONLINE	Student & Computer	**:60** minutes	
	Adult : *Check Performance Review*		
OFFLINE	Student & Adult : Review online work	**:30** minutes	
	• Reading Warm-Up		
	• Code Work		
	• Word Work		
	• Speed Work		
	Classics Session 1	**:30** minutes	
	Instructional Time	**2:00** hours	

Materials

- *MARK¹² Classics for Young Readers*
- "The Story of Arachne" MP3
- Online Tile Kit or Paper Letter Tiles
- *MARK¹² Reading Activity Book*, pages 99–100

Tip

Beginning blends are often difficult for students to distinguish aurally; be sure to enunciate activity words clearly.

Goals

In this lesson, students will read facts about owls. Students will also be introduced to the beginning blends *br–, cr–, dr–, fr–, gr–, pr–,* and *tr–* before learning the sight words *were, my,* and *are*. In today's *MARK¹² Reading Activity Book*, you will work with students to complete words using the blends *br–, cr–, dr–, fr–, gr–, pr–,* and *tr–* and to practice recognizing sight words.

Advance Preparation

For the offline portion of today's lesson, download this story: "The Story of Arachne." Based on the Performance Review, if students must complete Word Work activity 2, create sight word cards for the following words: *were, my,* and *are*. If students need to complete Word Work activity 3, you will need a timer and the Online Tile Kit or Paper Letter Tiles. If students need to complete Word Work activity 5, create a second set of sight word cards for the words *were, my,* and *are*.

 ONLINE | **Student & Computer**

Students will work online to complete Warm-Up, Code Work, Word Work, and Speed Work activities, and a Wrap-Up assessment on their own. Be sure to read the Performance Review before beginning the offline portion of today's lesson.

Today you will work with students to complete Code Work, Word Work, and *MARK¹² Classics for Young Readers* activities. Be sure to read the online Performance Review before beginning the Code Work and Word Work activities.

Warm-Up

Owls

Look at the Performance Review. If the student achieved a perfect score on today's Warm-Up, move on to Code Work. If the student scored 60 percent or 80 percent, print the story and review the comprehension questions with the student. If the student scored less than 60 percent, print the story, have the student read the story aloud, and then work through the comprehension questions together, before moving on to Code Work.

Code Work

Beginning Blends: *br–, cr–, dr–, fr–, gr–, pr–, & tr–*

Look at the Performance Review. If the student achieved a perfect score on today's Code Work activities, complete the first two activities from the list below. If the student scored less than 100 percent but more than 85 percent, complete the first three activities from the list below. If the student scored 85 percent or less, complete all five of the activities listed below.

1. Have students complete page 99 in *MARK¹² Reading Activity Book* for more practice on words with the beginning blends *br–, cr–, dr–, fr–, gr–, pr–,* and *tr–*.

2. Have students use the Online Tile Kit or the Paper Tile Kit to spell the following words: *brag, crisp, drip, frog, grand, print,* and *trap*. Have students say each word aloud after spelling it. Remind students that each letter in a blend keeps its sound.

3. Using the words listed in activity 2, say a word aloud, and then have students verbally use the word in a sentence.

4. Dictate the following sentences to students and have them write each one on a piece of paper:
   Brad sat on a drab bench.
   Glen can have a fresh fig for lunch.
   Help me grab that black cat.
   Review any spelling errors with students.

5. Say a word with one of the beginning blends from this lesson (example words: *crib, drag, front, grin, prune,* and *trip*). Challenge students to think of as many words as they can in one minute that begin with that particular blend. Continue for three of the blends, or more if time permits.

Code Work

Beginning Blends and Sight Words 2

Name: _____

Choose the Blend

Underline the blend that completes the word given. Then, write the word on the line provided. Say each word aloud when done. An example has been done for you.

Example:	pr	fr	br	___ ag	brag
1.	fr	cr	tr	___ og	frog
2.	pr	gr	tr	___ ab	grab
3.	cr	pr	br	___ int	print
4.	dr	fr	cr	___ ash	crash
5.	dr	fr	pr	___ um	drum
6.	tr	pr	gr	___ ash	trash
7.	fr	dr	cr	___ ib	crib
8.	pr	gr	dr	___ and	grand
9.	fr	tr	br	___ ip	trip
10.	gr	cr	fr	___ ame	frame
11.	pr	tr	gr	___ une	prune
12.	tr	fr	dr	___ ag	drag
13.	br	dr	gr	___ ick	brick

99

Word Work •

Sight Words

Look at the Performance Review. If the student achieved a perfect score on today's Word Work activities, complete the first activity from the list below. If the student scored less than 100 percent but more than 85 percent, complete the first three activities from the list below. If the student scored 85 percent or less, complete all five of the activities listed below.

1. Have students complete page 100 in *MARK¹² Reading Activity Book* for more practice on sight words.

2. Using the sight word cards you created for *were, my,* and *are,* read each word to students and have students write the word on a piece of paper. Give students the sight words, and instruct students to look for any spelling mistakes they may have made. Students should correct the mistakes and then read the list of words aloud.

3. Gather all of the sight word cards students have worked on to date and a timer. Have students read all of the sight word cards as accurately and quickly as possible. Make note of the time, as well as any errors students have made. Use the Online Tile Kit or Paper Letter Tiles to review words read incorrectly.

4. Gather the cards for the sight words *were, my,* and *are,* and up to two additional sight words students have yet to master. Show the first card to students, and ask students to read the word. If students read the word correctly, place in one pile. If students read the word incorrectly, place in a separate pile. On the back of the cards that were read correctly, make a note of the date and put aside. (Once students have read the word correctly five consecutive days, you can remove the word from the pile of cards students are working on.) Review any words students read incorrectly, and keep the cards for next time.

5. Gather the two sets of sight word cards for the words *were, my,* and *are,* and place all of the cards face down on the table or another flat surface. Have students choose a card, read the word aloud, and then choose a second card. After students read the second card aloud, if the two cards match, students should keep the cards. If they do not match, students should return them to the table. Continue until all of the cards have been collected.

Speed Work • • • • • • • • • • • • • • • • • • •

Fred

Look at the Performance Review, or check the student's fluency chart. Fluency scores (words read per minute) should not fall below 80. If the student scored below 80 words per minute, print a copy of the Speed Work story and have the student read the story silently before reading it aloud. Otherwise, move on to Classics Session 1.

Classics Session 1 ·

The Story of Arachne

Today's story, "The Story of Arachne," is a Greek myth about a young girl who spins and weaves cloth. Download the story. Have students listen to the story while following along in *MARK*[12] *Classics for Young Readers*. Have students listen to the story again before writing a summary of the story.

Students should write a summary of the story to complete today's Classics activity.

Objectives

- Improve reading and comprehension skills.

Beginning Blends and Sight Words 3

ONLINE	Student & Computer	**:60** minutes
	Adult : *Check Performance Review*	
OFFLINE	Student & Adult : Review online work	**:30** minutes
	• Reading Warm-Up	
	• Code Work	
	• Word Work	
	• Speed Work	
	Classics Session 2	**:30** minutes
	Instructional Time **2:00** hours	

Materials

- *MARK¹² Classics for Young Readers*
- "The Story of Arachne" MP3
- *MARK¹² Reading Activity Book*, pages 101–104

Tip

*A digraph consists of two consonants that form one sound. The beginning blend **shr–** consists of the digraph **sh** followed by the consonant **r**. The beginning blend **thr–** consists of the digraph **th** followed by the consonant **r**.*

Goals

In this lesson, students will read about the game of chess. Students will also learn about the beginning blends *shr–* and *thr–* before reviewing the sight words *were, my,* and *are*. In today's Activity Book pages, Tear Out Reader story, and *MARK¹² Classics for Young Readers* activities, you will work with students to reinforce their learning of the beginning blends *shr–* and *thr–* and sight words *were, my,* and *are*.

Advance Preparation

For the offline portion of today's lesson, download this story: "The Story of Arachne." Based on the Performance Review, if students need to complete Code Work activity 4, gather 16 index cards and write each of the following words on two cards: *shrub, shrimp, shrug, shred, throb, thrush, thrift,* and *thrust*. If students must complete Code Work activity 5, access the Online Tile Kit or Paper Letter Tiles. If students must complete Word Work activity 2, gather the sight word cards for the following words: *were, my,* and *are*. If students must complete Word Work activity 3, gather a timer and access the Online Tile Kit or Paper Letter Tiles. If students must complete Word Work activity 5, gather the second set of sight word cards for the words *were, my,* and *are*.

ONLINE	**Student & Computer**

Students will work online to complete Warm-Up, Code Work, Word Work, and Speed Work activities, and a Wrap-Up assessment on their own. Be sure to read the Performance Review before beginning the offline portion of today's lesson.

Today you will work with students to complete Code Work, Word Work, and *MARK¹² Classics for Young Readers* activities. Be sure to read the online Performance Review before beginning the Code Work and Word Work activities.

Warm-Up ·

Chess

Look at the Performance Review. If the student achieved a perfect score on today's Warm-Up, move on to Code Work. If the student scored 60 percent or 80 percent, print the story and review the comprehension questions with the student. If the student scored less than 60 percent, print the story, have the student read the story aloud, and then work through the comprehension questions together, before moving on to Code Work.

Objectives

* Improve reading and comprehension skills.

Code Work ·

Beginning Blends: *shr & thr*

Look at the Performance Review. If the student achieved a perfect score on today's Code Work activities, complete the first two activities from the list below. If the student scored less than 100 percent but more than 85 percent, complete the first three activities from the list below. If the student scored 85 percent or less, complete all five of the activities listed below.

Objectives

* Identify and use the blend *shr*.
* Identify and use the blend *thr*.

1. Have students complete page 101 in *MARK¹² Reading Activity Book* for more practice on the beginning blends *shr–* and *thr–*.

2. Remove "The Shrimp Shack" story from the *MARK¹² Reading Activity Book*. Fold the pages in half to create a small booklet. Review the following words with students: *chuckle, lucky,* and *those*. Have students read the story silently once or twice before reading the story aloud. Make note of any errors, and review with the students.

3. Take turns with students thinking of words with the beginning blends *shr–* and *thr–*. Start by giving students a word beginning with either blend. Students should think of a different word with the same beginning blend. Continue taking turns for one minute for each blend.

4. Gather the index cards with words beginning with *shr–* and *thr–*. Place all of the cards face down. Have students choose a card, read the word aloud, and then choose a second card. After students read the second card aloud, if the two cards match, students should keep the cards. If they do not match, students should return them to the table. Continue until all of the cards have been collected.

5. Have students use the Online Tile Kit or Paper Letter Tiles to spell the following words: *shrub, shrimp, shrug, shred, throb, thrush, thrift,* and *thrust*.

Code Work
Name
Beginning Blends and Sight Words 3

Find the Word
Read each sentence. Find the word that begins with the beginning blend *shr* or *thr*. Write the word on the line. Then say the word aloud.

1. See the nest in the shrub.
    shrub
2. Thrift means to save cash.
    thrift
3. Socks can shrink in the wash.
    shrink
4. We watch the thrush.
    thrush
5. The dog thrust his nose in the dish.
    thrust
6. Mom and Dad like shrimp for lunch.
    shrimp
7. Tom felt a throb in his hand.
    throb
8. That bad cat shred the cloth!
    shred

101

Word Work

Sight Words

Look at the Performance Review. If the student achieved a perfect score on today's Word Work activities, complete the first activity from the list below. If the student scored less than 100 percent but more than 85 percent, complete the first three activities from the list below. If the student scored 85 percent or less, complete all five of the activities listed below.

1. Have students complete page 110 in *MARK¹² Reading Activity Book* for more practice on sight words.

2. Using the sight word cards you created for *were, my,* and *are,* read each word to students and have students write the word on a piece of paper. Give students the sight words, and instruct students to look for any spelling mistakes they may have made. Students should correct the mistakes and then read the list of words aloud.

3. Gather all of the sight word cards students have worked on to date and a timer. Have students read all of the sight word cards as accurately and quickly as possible. Make note of the time, as well as any errors students have made. Use the Online Tile Kit or Paper Letter Tiles to review words read incorrectly.

4. Gather the cards for the sight words *were, my,* and *are,* and up to two additional sight words students have yet to master. Show the first card to students, and ask students to read the word. If students read the word correctly, place in one pile. If students read the word incorrectly, place in a separate pile. On the back of the cards that were read correctly, make a note of the date and put aside. (Once students have read the word correctly five consecutive days, you can remove the word from the pile of cards students are working on.) Review any words students read incorrectly, and keep the cards for next time.

5. Gather the two sets of sight word cards for the words *were, my,* and *are,* and place all of the cards face down on the table or another flat surface. Have students choose a card, read the word aloud, and then choose a second card. After students read the second card aloud, if the two cards match, students should keep the cards. If they do not match, students should return them to the table. Continue until all of the cards have been collected.

Speed Work

Gus and the Thrush

Look at the Performance Review, or check the student's fluency chart. Fluency scores (words read per minute) should not fall below 80. If the student scored below 80 words per minute, print a copy of the Speed Work story and have the student read the story silently before reading it aloud. Otherwise, move on to Classics Session 2.

The Story of Arachne

Have students listen to the story again while following along in *MARK¹² Classics for Young Readers*. Afterward, students should complete the comprehension questions in *MARK¹² Classics for Young Readers* on their own.

Objectives

- Improve reading and comprehension skills.

W Write

The Story of Arachne

1. What was Arachne skilled at?
   A. baking
   B. hunting
   C. weaving
   D. gardening

2. The people of Athens warn Arachne that her _____ might anger the goddess Athena.
   A. boasting
   B. great skill
   C. intelligence
   D. selfishness

3. Who is the stranger, dressed as an old woman, who approaches Arachne?
   Athena is the stranger, dressed as an old woman, who approaches Arachne.

4. What agreement do Athena and Arachne make before they begin to work at their looms?
   Athena and Arachne agree that the one whose cloth is best may continue to weave. The other may never weave again.

The Story of Arachne   **31**

---

5. What did Athena weave pictures of into her cloth?
   A. fruit trees
   B. wild animals
   C. sun and moon
   D. gods and goddesses

6. How does Arachne feel when she sees that Athena's cloth is much more beautiful than hers?
   Arachne feels grief and anger when she sees that Athena's cloth is much more beautiful than hers.

7. How does Arachne feel about weaving?
   A. It is her life.
   B. It is a fun hobby.
   C. It is something anyone can do well.
   D. It is nothing more than a silly pastime.

8. What does Athena do to Arachne at the end of the story?
   At the end of the story, Athena turns Arachne into a spider.

32   The Story of Arachne

Beginning Blends and Sight Words 4

ONLINE	Student & Computer	**:60** minutes
	Adult : *Check Performance Review*	
OFFLINE	Student & Adult : Review online work	**:30** minutes
	• Reading Warm-Up	
	• Code Work	
	• Word Work	
	• Speed Work	
	Grammar, Usage, and Mechanics (GUM)	**:30** minutes
	Instructional Time	**2:00** hours

Materials

- Online Tile Kit or Paper Letter Tiles
- *MARK¹² Reading Activity Book*, pages 105–108

Tip *Because all of today's blends begin with the letter **s**, give particular attention to the clear and proper enunciation of words during today's activities.*

Goals

In this lesson, students will read about flying squirrels. Students will also be introduced to the beginning blends *sc–, sp–, st–, sw–, sk–, sm–,* and *sn–* as well as the titles *Dr., Mr.,* and *Mrs.* In today's *MARK¹² Reading Activity Book* pages, you will work with students to unscramble words with the beginning blends they just learned as well as practice sight words.

Advance Preparation

Based on the Performance Review, if students need to complete Word Work activity 2, create sight word cards for the following words: *Dr., Mr.,* and *Mrs.* If students need to complete Word Work activity 3, you will need a timer and the Online Tile Kit or Paper Letter Tiles. If students need to complete Word Work activity 5, create a second set of sight word cards for the words *Dr., Mr.,* and *Mrs.*

ONLINE	Student & Computer

Students will work online to complete Warm-Up, Code Work, Word Work, and Speed Work activities, and a Wrap-Up assessment on their own. Be sure to read the Performance Review before beginning the offline portion of today's lesson.

Today you will work with students to complete Code Work, Word Work, and GUM activities. Be sure to read the online Performance Review before beginning the Code Work and Word Work activities.

Warm-Up ·

Flying Squirrels

Look at the Performance Review. If the student achieved a perfect score on today's Warm-Up, move on to Code Work. If the student scored 60 percent or 80 percent, print the story and review the comprehension questions with the student. If the student scored less than 60 percent, print the story, have the student read the story aloud, and then work through the comprehension questions together, before moving on to Code Work.

Objectives

* Improve reading and comprehension skills.

Code Work ·

Beginning Blends: *sc–, sp–, st–, sw–, sk–, sm–,* & *sn–*

Look at the Performance Review. If the student achieved a perfect score on today's Code Work activities, complete the first two activities from the list below. If the student scored less than 100 percent but more than 85 percent, complete the first three activities from the list below. If the student scored 85 percent or less, complete all five of the activities listed below.

Objectives

* Identify and use the blends *sc–, sk–, sm–, sn–, sp–, st–,* and *sw–*.

1. Have students complete page 105 in *MARK¹² Reading Activity Book* for more practice on the beginning blends *sc–, sk–, sm–, sn–, sp–, st–,* and *sw–*.

2. Using the Online Tile Kit or Paper Letter Tiles, have students build the following words: *scan, skin, smack, snag, spin, stick,* and *swim.* Have students identify the beginning blend in each word.

3. Using the list of words from activity 2, have students verbally use each word in a sentence.

4. Dictate the following sentences to students, and have students circle each word that contains a beginning blend that begins with the letter *s*:
   Mom says not to pick at your <u>scab</u>.
   Mr. <u>Smith</u> <u>snuck</u> up on the thug.
   Ted <u>spat</u> out the bad <u>skim</u> milk.
   <u>Stan</u> had a fresh fig for a <u>snack</u>.
   We can <u>skip</u> to the hot dog <u>stand</u>.

5. Using the list of words from activity 2, say a word aloud and then have students think of another word that begins with the same blend. Pay particular attention to the words students say for the blends *sc–* and *sk–*, because these two blends have the same sounds and can be easily confused (e.g., *scam, scat, scab; skid, skip,* and *skit*).

Code Work   Name: _____

Beginning Blends and Sight Words 4

Blend Scramble

Unscramble the letters to make a word. Write the word on the line provided.
Hint: Each word begins with a blend.

Example: wgis   _swig_

1. psit   **spit**
2. wipse   **swipe**
3. shast   **stash**
4. kisp   **skip**
5. anps   **snap or span**
6. msgo   **smog**
7. canks   **snack**
8. tosp   **spot or stop**
9. tasdn   **stand**
10. mwis   **swim**
11. dkis   **skid**
12. nacs   **scan**
13. ekoms   **smoke**
14. sacb   **scab**

105

Word Work •

Sight Words

Look at the Performance Review. If the student achieved a perfect score on today's Word Work activities, complete the first activity from the list below. If the student scored less than 100 percent but more than 85 percent, complete the first three activities from the list below. If the student scored 85 percent or less, complete all five of the activities listed below.

1. Have students complete page 106 in *MARK¹² Reading Activity Book* for more practice on the sight words *Dr., Mr.,* and *Mrs.*

2. Using the sight word cards you created for *Dr., Mr.,* and *Mrs.,* read each word to students and have students write the word on a piece of paper. Give students the sight words, and instruct students to look for any spelling mistakes they may have made. Students should correct the mistakes and then read the list of words aloud.

3. Gather all of the sight word cards students have worked on to date and a timer. Have students read all of the sight word cards as accurately and quickly as possible. Make note of the time, as well as any errors students have made. Use the Online Tile Kit or Paper Letter Tiles to review words read incorrectly.

4. Gather the cards for the sight words *Dr., Mr.,* and *Mrs.,* and up to two additional sight words students have yet to master. Show the first card to students, and ask students to read the word. If students read the word correctly, place in one pile. If students read the word incorrectly, place in a separate pile. On the back of the cards that were read correctly, make a note of the date and put aside. (Once students have read the word correctly five consecutive days, you can remove the word from the pile of cards students are working on.) Review any words students read incorrectly, and keep the cards for next time.

5. Gather the two sets of sight word cards for the words *Dr., Mr.,* and *Mrs.,* and place all of the cards face down on the table or another flat surface. Have students choose a card, read the word aloud, and then choose a second card. After students read the second card aloud, if the two cards match, students should keep the cards. If they do not match, students should return them to the table. Continue until all of the cards have been collected.

Word Work
Beginning Blends and Sight Words 4

Name:

Sight Word Sentences

Choose the word from the box that best completes each sentence. Write the words on the lines provided.

| were | my | Dr. | are | Mr. | Mrs. |

1. My mom is called **Mrs.** Smith.
2. My shoes **are** too tight.
3. My dad is called **Mr.** Smith.
4. Tom and Joe **were** gone yesterday.
5. We went to see **Dr.** Sam when I hurt my leg.
6. He took **my** coat.

106

Speed Work •

Lost

Look at the Performance Review, or check the student's fluency chart. Fluency scores (words read per minute) should not fall below 80. If the student scored below 80 words per minute, print a copy of the Speed Work story and have the student read the story silently before reading it aloud. Otherwise, move on to Grammar, Usage, and Mechanics.

Singular and Plural Possessives

If you possess something, you own it. Possessive nouns show *ownership*.

A *singular* possessive noun shows that *one* person, place, thing, or idea has ownership.

Bill's cat (the cat owned by Bill)

A *plural* possessive noun shows that *more than one* person, place, thing, or idea has ownership.

the Romanovs' car (the car owned by the Romanov family)

Work with students to complete pages 107 and 108 in *MARK¹² Reading Activity Book*. Read page 107, Get Ready, with students. Have students complete the Try It page. Be sure to discuss students' answers when the page is completed.

GUM Grammar, Usage, and Mechanics   Name: _____

Beginning Blends and Sight Words 4

Get Ready

Singular and Plural Possessive Nouns
If you possess something, you own it. **Possessive nouns** show *ownership*.

A **singular** possessive noun shows that *one* person, place, thing, or idea has ownership.

| Fred's dog | the dog owned by Fred |
| a day's work | the work of one day |

A **plural** possessive noun shows that *more than one* person, place, thing, or idea has ownership.

| the Chens' party | the party that the Chen family had |
| kids' fingerprints | the fingerprints made by many kids |

Singular Possessive Nouns
To form the singular possessive, add an apostrophe and an –s to the singular noun.

Singular	Singular Possessive
Tom	Tom's notebook
cat	cat's paw

Plural Possessive Nouns
To form a plural possessive noun, usually you just add an apostrophe to the end of the plural noun. You can use this rule for any plural noun that ends in –s.

Singular	Plural	Plural Possessive
pig	pigs	pigs' pens
fox	foxes	foxes' tails

107

GUM Grammar, Usage, and Mechanics   Name: _____

Beginning Blends and Sight Words 4

Try It

Read each word. Write the singular possessive, the plural form, and the plural possessive for each word on the lines provided.

	Singular Noun	Singular Possessive	Plural Noun	Plural Possessive
Example:	cub	cub's	cubs	cubs'
	dish	dish's	dishes	dishes'
	pit	pit's	pits	pits'
	kite	kite's	kites	kites'
	box	box's	boxes	boxes'
	bunch	bunch's	bunches	bunches'
	nest	nest's	nests	nests'
	fact	fact's	facts	facts'
	truth	truth's	truths	truths'

108

Beginning Blends and Sight Words 5

ONLINE	Student & Computer	:60 minutes
	Adult : *Check Performance Review*	
OFFLINE	Student & Adult : Review online work	:30 minutes
	• Reading Warm-Up	
	• Code Work	
	• Word Work	
	• Speed Work	
	Composition	:30 minutes
	Instructional Time **2:00** hours	

Materials

- *MARK¹² Reading Activity Book*, pages 109–112
- *Just Write*

Tip *The sounds for the blend* **squ–** *are* **/skw/**, *not* */skwuh/.*

Goals

In this lesson, students will read about a trip to Carlsbad Caverns. Students will also be introduced to the beginning blends *tw–, spr–, str–, squ–, scr–,* and *sp–* before continuing to work with the sight words *Dr., Mr.,* and *Mrs.* In today's *MARK¹² Reading Activity Book* pages, you will work with students to match beginning blends and identify words with blends, as well as work with *Dr., Mr.,* and *Mrs.*

Advance Preparation

For the offline portion of today's lesson, gather the students' composition materials. Based on the Performance Review, if students need to complete Word Work activity 2, gather the sight word cards for the following words: *Dr., Mr.,* and *Mrs.* If students need to complete Word Work activity 3, you will need a timer and the Online Tile Kit or Paper Letter Tiles. If students need to complete Word Work activity 5, gather the second set of sight word cards for the words *Dr., Mr.,* and *Mrs.*

ONLINE	Student & Computer

Students will work online to complete Warm-Up, Code Work, Word Work, and Speed Work activities, and a Wrap-Up assessment on their own. Be sure to read the Performance Review before beginning the offline portion of today's lesson.

Today you will work with students to complete Code Work, Word Work, and Composition activities. Be sure to read the online Performance Review before beginning the Code Work and Word Work activities.

Warm-Up •

A Trip to Carlsbad Caverns

Look at the Performance Review. If the student achieved a perfect score on today's Warm-Up, move on to Code Work. If the student scored 60 percent or 80 percent, print the story and review the comprehension questions with the student. If the student scored less than 60 percent, print the story, have the student read the story aloud, and then work through the comprehension questions together, before moving on to Code Work.

Objectives

• Improve reading and comprehension skills.

Code Work •

Beginning Blends: *tw–, spr–, str–, squ–, scr–,* & *spl–*

Look at the Performance Review. If the student achieved a perfect score on today's Code Work activities, complete the first two activities from the list below. If the student scored less than 100 percent but more than 85 percent, complete the first three activities from the list below. If the student scored 85 percent or less, complete all five of the activities listed below.

Objectives

• Identify and use the blends *tw–, spr–, str–, squ–, scr–,* and *spl–*.

1. Have students complete page 109 in *MARK¹² Reading Activity Book* for more practice on the beginning blends *tw–, spr–, str–, squ–, scr–,* and *spl–*.

2. Remove the "Max Takes a Bath" story from *MARK¹² Reading Activity Book*. Fold the pages in half to create a small booklet. Review the following words with students: *fur, soap,* and *bubbles.* Have students read the story silently once or twice before reading the story aloud. When students read aloud, make note of any errors, and review those words with the students.

3. Using the Online Tile Kit or Paper Letter Tiles, have students build the following words: *twin, spring, strip, squash, scrap,* and *splat.* Have students identify the beginning blend in each word.

4. Using the list of words from activity 3, have students verbally use each word in a sentence.

5. Using the list of words from activity 3, say a word aloud and then have students write another word that begins with the same blend (possible answers are in parentheses): twin (*twig, twist, twitch*), spring (*sprig, sprang, sprung*), strip (*strap, stretch, string*), squash (*squat, squid*), scrap (*scram, scratch*), and splat (*splish, splash, splat*). Have students verbally use each of their words in a sentence, if time allows.

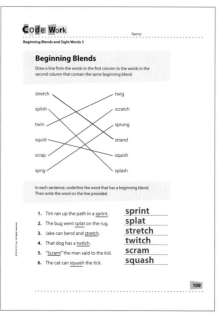

Word Work

Sight Words

Look at the Performance Review. If the student achieved a perfect score on today's Word Work activities, complete the first activity from the list below. If the student scored less than 100 percent but more than 85 percent, complete the first three activities from the list below. If the student scored 85 percent or less, complete all five of the activities listed below.

1. Have students complete page 110 in *MARK¹² Reading Activity Book* for more practice on sight words.

2. Using the sight word cards students are currently working on, read each word to students and have students write the word on a piece of paper. Give students the sight words, and instruct students to look for any spelling mistakes they may have made. Students should correct the mistakes and then read the list of words aloud.

3. Gather all of the sight word cards students have worked on to date and a timer. Have students read all of the sight word cards as accurately and quickly as possible. Make note of the time, as well as any errors students have made. Use the Online Tile Kit or Paper Letter Tiles to review words read incorrectly.

4. Gather the cards for the sight words *Dr., Mr.,* and *Mrs.,* and up to two additional sight words students have yet to master. Show the first card to students, and ask students to read the word. If students read the word correctly, place in one pile. If students read the word incorrectly, place in a separate pile. On the back of the cards that were read correctly, make a note of the date and put aside. (Once students have read the word correctly five consecutive days, you can remove the word from the pile of cards students are working on.) Review any words students read incorrectly, and keep the cards for next time.

5. Gather the two sets of sight word cards for the words *Dr., Mr.,* and *Mrs.,* and place all of the cards face down on the table or another flat surface. Have students choose a card, read the word aloud, and then choose a second card. After students read the second card aloud, if the two cards match, students should keep the cards. If they do not match, students should return them to the table. Continue until all of the cards have been collected.

Speed Work

Flip Flop

Look at the Performance Review, or check the student's fluency chart. Fluency scores (words read per minute) should not fall below 80. If the student scored below 80 words per minute, print a copy of the Speed Work story and have the student read the story silently before reading it aloud. Otherwise, move on to Composition.

Composition

Gather students' composition materials and begin where they left off.

Beginning Blends and Sight Words 6

ONLINE	Student & Computer	:60 minutes
	Adult : *Check Performance Review*	
OFFLINE	Student & Adult : Review online work	:30 minutes
	• Reading Warm-Up	
	• Speed Work	
	• Assessment	
	Grammar, Usage, and Mechanics (GUM)	:30 minutes
	Instructional Time **2:00** hours	

Materials

- *MARK¹² Reading Activity Book*, pages 113–118

Goals

In this lesson, students will read about Venus flytraps. Students will also review beginning blends before working with sight words. In today's Unit Assessment, you will administer a test covering all content from Unit 7. Afterward, you will work with students to complete activities on verbs.

ONLINE   **Student & Computer**

Students will work online to complete Warm-Up, Code Work, Word Work, and Speed Work activities, and a review game on their own. Be sure to read the Performance Review before beginning the offline portion of today's lesson.

Today you will administer a Unit Assessment and work with students to complete a GUM activity.

Warm-Up •

Venus Flytraps

Look at the Performance Review. If the student achieved a perfect score on today's Warm-Up, move on to Speed Work. If the student scored 60 percent or 80 percent, print the story and review the comprehension questions with the student. If the student scored less than 60 percent, print the story, have the student read the story aloud, and then work through the comprehension questions together, before moving on to Speed Work.

Objectives

• Improve reading and comprehension skills.

Speed Work •

Blend Trend

Look at the Performance Review, or check the student's fluency chart. Fluency scores (words read per minute) should not fall below 80. If the student scored below 80 words per minute, print a copy of the Speed Work story and have the student read the story silently before reading it aloud to you. Otherwise, move on to the Assessment.

Objectives

• Increase reading fluency rate.

 Assessment •

Beginning Blends and Sight Words

Today's Unit Assessment covers all content found in Unit 7. Carefully read the instructions on the student pages before administering the test to the student. If necessary, read the directions to the student. After you have scored the student's assessment, be sure to go online and enter student performance scores in the assessment entry tool.

Part 1. Dictate the following words to students: *brag, my, twist, grin, sled, clock, scrap, crab, thrush,* and *were.*

Part 3. Dictate the following words to students: *slot, span, skip, swam,* and *squint.*

Part 4. Dictate the following words to students: *clap, trim, snug, does, scan, grab, drift, crush, why,* and *are.*

Part 5. Dictate the following words to students: *sprint, walk, flash, print, smug, splat, talk, twin, Mr., stamp, squash, too, frog, one,* and *shred.*

Unit 7 Assessment

Part 1.
Listen to each word that is read to you. Write each word on the lines provided.

1. brag
2. my
3. twist
4. grin
5. sled
6. clock
7. scrap
8. crab
9. thrush
10. were

113

Part 2.
Read each sentence. Underline the word that best completes each sentence.

11. "I want some milk, _____," said Tom. (<u>too</u>, two)
12. Grant has a _____ cat. (brick, <u>black</u>)
13. Trent broke the _____ to his backpack. (<u>strap</u>, scrap)
14. I am _____ that you won the game! (<u>glad</u>, grand)
15. Sam put the _____ in the bin. (twist, <u>trash</u>)

Part 3.
Listen to each word that is read to you. Underline the beginning blend that is contained in each word.

16. sk   <u>sl</u>   sm   sp   spr   st   str
17. sl   sm   sn   <u>sp</u>   squ   st   sw
18. <u>sk</u>   sl   sp   spr   squ   st   str
19. sl   sm   sn   sp   st   str   <u>sw</u>
20. sc   sl   sp   spr   <u>squ</u>   st   str

114

Part 4.
Listen to each word that is read to you. Write each word on the lines provided.

21. clap
22. trim
23. snug
24. does
25. scan
26. grab
27. drift
28. crush
29. why
30. are

115

Part 5.
In each row, underline the word that is read to you.

31. split   <u>sprint</u>   spit
32. wink   work   <u>walk</u>
33. <u>flash</u>   fresh   flesh
34. prim   plan   <u>print</u>
35. stung   <u>smug</u>   slug
36. <u>splat</u>   spat   slap
37. take   <u>talk</u>   tack
38. <u>twin</u>   tin   trim
39. Mrs.   Dr.   <u>Mr.</u>
40. skimp   <u>stamp</u>   strand
41. stash   slash   <u>squash</u>
42. you   <u>too</u>   who
43. fog   <u>frog</u>   flog
44. <u>one</u>   win   on
45. sled   shed   <u>shred</u>

116

Objectives

- Identify and use the blends *bl–*, *cl–*, *fl–*, *gl–*, *pl–*, *sl–*, *br–*, *cr–*, *dr–*, *fr–*, *gr–*, *pr–*, *tr–*, *shr–*, *thr–*, *sc–*, *sp–*, *st–*, *sw–*, *sk–*, *sm–*, *sn–*, *tw–*, *spr–*, *str–*, *squ–*, *scr–*, and *spl–*.

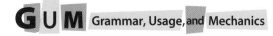

Action Verbs and Being Verbs

Action verbs tell what the subject *does*.

    Andrew *eats* pizza for supper every Tuesday.

    I *remember* that book very well.

Being verbs tell what someone or something *is* or *is like*.

    That motorcycle *was* very fast.

    subject = *motorcycle*

    being verb = *was*

    more about the subject = *very fast*

Work with students to complete pages 117 and 118 in *MARK¹² Reading Activity Book*. Read page 117, Get Ready, with students. Have students complete the Try It page. Be sure to discuss students' answers when the page is completed.

Objectives

• **Identify and use action verbs and being verbs.**

GUM Grammar, Usage, and Mechanics   Name:

Beginning Blends and Sight Words 6

   Get Ready

▪ Verbs in sentences tell what the subject does or is. **Action verbs** tell what the subject *does*. Read the following sentences with action verbs:

    Andrew *eats* pizza for supper every Tuesday.
    The cheetah *ran* across the plain.
    Squirrels *climb* to the tops of trees.
    I *remember* that book very well.

Sometimes the action of a verb is *physical* and easy to see.

    hit, dig, drag, kick

Sometimes the action of a verb is *mental* (in your head) and not as easy to see.

    think, like, hope, enjoy

Being verbs tell what someone or something *is or is like*. It makes a connection between the subject and other words that tell more about the subject.

    That motorcycle was very fast.

    subject = *motorcycle*
    being verb = *was*
    more about the subject = *very fast*

Being verbs are different forms of the verb *to be*. Study the list of common being verbs below.

| is | was | am | has been | have been |
| are | were | be | had been | will be |

117

GUM Grammar, Usage, and Mechanics   Name:

Beginning Blends and Sight Words 6

   Try It

Choose the *action verb* from the box below that best completes each sentence. Write each verb on the lines provided.

| dug | like | shut | think |

1. Jan and Dan **like** to watch TV.
2. Tom **dug** a hole in the dirt.
3. Gus **shut** the lid to the box.
4. Do you **think** you can help me wash my car?

Choose the *being verb* from the box below that best completes each sentence. Write each verb on the lines provided.

| is | were | be | was |

5. Mark **is/was** my best pal.
6. That game **was/is** fun!
7. Can you **be** at the park by six o'clock?
8. Pat and Mike **were** too late to catch the bus.

118

Word Endings and Sight Words 1

ONLINE	Student & Computer	**:60** minutes	
	Adult : *Check Performance Review*		
OFFLINE	Student & Adult : Review online work	**:30** minutes	
	• Reading Warm-Up		
	• Code Work		
	• Word Work		
	• Speed Work		
	Classics Session 1	**:30** minutes	
	Instructional Time **2:00** hours		

Materials

- *MARK[12] Classics for Young Readers*
- *MARK[12] Reading Activity Book,* pages 119–122

Goals

In this lesson, students will read about Mount Fuji in Japan. Students will also practice reading words with double consonant endings (*–ff, –ll, –ss, –zz*) before learning the sight words *too, talk,* and *walk.* In today's Activity Book pages, Tear Out Reader story, and *MARK[12] Classics for Young Readers* activities, you will work with students to reinforce their learning about double consonant endings (*–ff, –ll, –ss, –zz*) and the sight words *too, talk,* and *walk.*

Advance Preparation

Based on the Performance Review, if students must complete Code Work activity 4, you will need to access the Online Tile Kit or Paper Letter Tiles. If students must complete Word Work activity 2, create the sight word cards for the following words: *too, talk,* and *walk.* If students need to complete Word Work activity 3, you will need a timer and the Online Tile Kit or Paper Letter Tiles. If students need to complete Word Work activity 5, create a second set of sight word cards for the words *too, talk,* and *walk.*

ONLINE Student & Computer

Students will work online to complete Warm-Up, Code Work, Word Work, and Speed Work activities, and a Wrap-Up assessment on their own. Be sure to read the Performance Review before beginning the offline portion of today's lesson.

Today you will work with students to complete Code Work, Word Work, and *MARK¹² Classics for Young Readers* activities. Be sure to read the online Performance Review before beginning the Code Work and Word Work activities.

Warm-Up ·

Mt. Fuji

Look at the Performance Review. If the student achieved a perfect score on today's Warm-Up, move on to Code Work. If the student scored 60 percent or 80 percent, print the story and review the comprehension questions with the student. If the student scored less than 60 percent, print the story, have the student read the story aloud, and then work through the comprehension questions together, before moving on to Code Work.

Objectives

- Improve reading and comprehension skills.

Code Work ·

Double Trouble Endings: –ff, –ll, –ss, & –zz

Look at the Performance Review. If the student achieved a perfect score on today's Code Work activities, complete the first two activities from the list below. If the student scored less than 100 percent but more than 85 percent, complete the first three activities from the list below. If the student scored 85 percent or less, complete all five of the activities listed below.

Objectives

- Identify words with double consonant endings that have only one sound.

1. Have students complete page 119 in *MARK¹² Reading Activity Book* for more practice on double consonant endings.

2. Remove the "Fun on the Grass" story from *MARK¹² Reading Activity Book*. Fold the pages in half to create a small booklet. Review the following words with students: *our, ring,* and *ding*. Have students read the story silently once or twice before reading the story aloud. Make note of any errors, and review those words with the students.

3. Take turns with students thinking of words with double consonant endings –*ff, –ll, –ss,* and –*zz*. On a piece of paper, create four columns with each double consonant ending as a column heading. Write an example word in each column. Have students suggest other words. Students should write them in the correct columns.

4. Have students use the Online Tile Kit or Paper Letter Tiles to spell the following words: *puff, hill, dress, buzz, stuff, chill, grass,* and *fizz*.

5. Divide a paper into four columns with the double consonant endings –*ff, –ll, –ss, –zz* as column headings. Write two to four example words in each column (try to use words not used in activities 3 or 4). Have students say the words aloud, then circle the double consonant ending, and finally write the word on another piece of paper.

<table>
<tr><td colspan="2">Code Work   Name:</td></tr>
<tr><td colspan="2">Word Endings and Sight Words 1</td></tr>
<tr><td colspan="2">**Double Trouble Endings**
Underline the double letter ending in each word. Then say the words aloud and write each word on the lines provided.</td></tr>
<tr><td colspan="2">**Example:** shell   shell</td></tr>
<tr><td>1. fuzz</td><td>fuzz</td></tr>
<tr><td>2. grass</td><td>grass</td></tr>
<tr><td>3. stuff</td><td>stuff</td></tr>
<tr><td>4. well</td><td>well</td></tr>
<tr><td>5. pass</td><td>pass</td></tr>
<tr><td>6. sniff</td><td>sniff</td></tr>
<tr><td>7. brass</td><td>brass</td></tr>
<tr><td>8. buzz</td><td>buzz</td></tr>
<tr><td>9. spill</td><td>spill</td></tr>
<tr><td>10. mess</td><td>mess</td></tr>
<tr><td>11. chill</td><td>chill</td></tr>
<tr><td colspan="2" align="right">119</td></tr>
</table>

Word Work

Sight Words

Look at the Performance Review. If the student achieved a perfect score on today's Word Work activities, complete the first activity from the list below. If the student scored less than 100 percent but more than 85 percent, complete the first three activities from the list below. If the student scored 85 percent or less, complete all five of the activities listed below.

1. Have students complete page 120 in *MARK¹² Reading Activity Book* for more practice on sight words.

2. Using the sight word cards you created for *too, walk,* and *talk,* read each word to students and have students write the word on a piece of paper. Give students the sight words, and instruct students to look for any spelling mistakes they may have made. Students should correct the mistakes and then read the list of words aloud.

3. Gather all of the sight word cards students have worked on to date and a timer. Have students read all of the sight word cards as accurately and quickly as possible. Make note of the time, as well as any errors students have made. Use the Online Tile Kit or Paper Letter Tiles to review words read incorrectly.

4. Gather the cards for the sight words *too, walk,* and *talk* and up to two additional sight words students have yet to master. Show the first card to students, and ask students to read the word. If students read the word correctly, place in one pile. If students read the word incorrectly, place in a separate pile. On the back of the cards that were read correctly, make a note of the date and put aside. (Once students have read the word correctly five consecutive days, you can remove the word from the pile of cards students are working on.) Review any words students read incorrectly, and keep the cards for next time.

5. Gather the two sets of sight word cards for the words *too, walk,* and *talk,* and place all of the cards face down on the table or another flat surface. Have students choose a card, read the word aloud, and then choose a second card. After students read the second card aloud, if the two cards match, students should keep the cards. If they do not match, students should return them to the table. Continue until all of the cards have been collected.

Speed Work

A Walk and a Talk

Look at the Performance Review, or check the student's fluency chart. Fluency scores (words read per minute) should not fall below 80. If the student scored below 80 words per minute, print a copy of the Speed Work story and have the student read the story silently before reading it aloud. Otherwise, move on to Classics Session 1.

Classics Session 1 ·

Columbus at the Court of Spain

Today's story, "Columbus at the Court of Spain," is a play about Christopher Columbus and Queen Isabella of Spain. Review the keywords with students. Read the play with students, and then use the Discussion Questions below as a guide to share ideas about the play. Have students read the play again, before writing a summary of the play.

Keywords

folly, n. – a foolish idea
"What **folly**!" the sailor said to one of his crew. "Do you really think I would set sail in such awful winds?"

vast, adj. – large in size
I could not believe how **vast** the great plains of Africa were.

jeer, v. – to mock
The teacher scolded the class for **jeering** a student who gave an incorrect answer to a seemingly easy question.

earnest, adj. – having a serious attitude
I might not have believed your story, had you not told it in such an **earnest** manner.

Discussion Questions

1. Don Gomez describes himself as a plain, matter-of-fact man many times throughout the play. What do you think he means by this? Answers may include that Don Gomez believes in only what he knows to be true. He believes that others' visions, such as Columbus's, are silly and a waste of time and money.

2. Pretend you are Isabella, and Columbus has come to you for help. What would you do? Would you make the same decision she made, or would you take Don Gomez's side? Answers will vary.

3. How would you describe Columbus's reaction when Isabella says she will help him finance his voyage? Answers may include that Columbus is most grateful for the opportunity as he promises not to let Isabella down and to bring her "a jewel as has never been worn by any queen."

4. How do you think Don Gomez will feel when Columbus proves that he did indeed travel to a distant land? Answers may include that Don Gomez may feel embarrassed for not having more faith in Columbus.

5. Do you think Columbus believed the stories about monsters that swallow ships in single mouthfuls or waters that could burn a ship? Why or why not? Answers will vary.

Students should write a summary of the play to complete today's Classics activity.

Word Endings and Sight Words 2

ONLINE	Student & Computer	:60 minutes
	Adult : *Check Performance Review*	
OFFLINE	Student & Adult : Review online work	:30 minutes
	• Reading Warm-Up	
	• Code Work	
	• Word Work	
	• Speed Work	
	Classics Session 2	:30 minutes
	Instructional Time **2:00** hours	

Materials

- *MARK¹² Classics for Young Readers*
- *MARK¹² Reading Activity Book*, pages 123–124

Tip

Display the rules for adding endings –s and –es to nouns and verbs on poster board or a chart. Include examples and encourage students to add to the list as they encounter new words.

Goals

In this lesson, students will read about lions. Students will also practice adding the word endings –s and –es before practicing the sight words, *again, out,* and *pull*. In today's Activity Book pages and *MARK¹² Classics for Young Readers* activities, you will work with students to reinforce their learning about the word endings –s and –es and sight words.

Advance Preparation

Based on the Performance Review, if students need to complete Code Work activity 4, gather two index cards and label one with –s and the other with –es. Gather 20 more index cards and, on each card, write one noun. At least 10 of these nouns should end in –sh, –x, –z, –s, –ss, or –ch. If students must complete Code Work activity 5, gather a magazine. If students must complete Word Work activity 2, create sight word cards for the following words: *again, out,* and *pull*. If students need to complete Word Work activity 3, you will need a timer and the Online Tile Kit or Paper Letter Tiles. If students need to complete Word Work activity 5, create a second set of sight word cards for the words *again, out,* and *pull*.

ONLINE	Student & Computer

Students will work online to complete Warm-Up, Code Work, Word Work, and Speed Work activities, and a Wrap-Up assessment on their own. Be sure to read the Performance Review before beginning the offline portion of today's lesson.

Today you will work with students to complete Code Work, Word Work, and *MARK¹² Classics for Young Readers* activities. Be sure to read the online Performance Review before beginning the Code Work and Word Work activities.

Warm-Up ·

Lions

Look at the Performance Review. If the student achieved a perfect score on today's Warm-Up, move on to Code Work. If the student scored 60 percent or 80 percent, print the story and review the comprehension questions with the student. If the student scored less than 60 percent, print the story, have the student read the story aloud, and then work through the comprehension questions together, before moving on to Code Work.

Objectives

● Improve reading and comprehension skills.

Code Work ·

Endings –s & –es

Look at the Performance Review. If the student achieved a perfect score on today's Code Work activities, complete the first two activities from the list below. If the student scored less than 100 percent but more than 85 percent, complete the first three activities from the list below. If the student scored 85 percent or less, complete all five of the activities listed below.

Objectives

● Identify and use endings –s and –es.

1. Have students complete page 125 in *MARK¹² Reading Activity Book* for more practice on the word endings –s and –es.

2. Ask students to pick a letter of the alphabet. Both you and the students should write down as many words that begin with the chosen letter and end in –es as you can think of in one minute. Then read your lists to each other.

3. Using the Online Tile Kit or Paper Letter Tiles, have students build the following words: *buzz, glass, rock, match, fox, dress, bus, dash, lamp,* and *bag.* After students build a word, have them add the ending –s or –es. Then have students build five other words of their choosing that end in –es.

4. Gather the 20 index cards on which you previously wrote nouns. Give the –s and –es index cards you created to the students. Place the word cards face down. Have students draw cards and match each word with the correct ending card (–s or –es). If correct, they keep the card. Play until students have collected all word cards.

5. Using the magazine you gathered, have students identify words that take an –es ending. Write the base word and correct ending for students to see.

Code Work   Name: ____

Word Endings and Sight Words 2

More Than One

Read the base words in the first column. Some take the ending, –s, when becoming plural. Others take the ending, –es. Decide which plural ending each base word takes. Then write the new words on the lines provided.
Hint: Base words ending in s, sh, ch, x, or z take the –es ending.

Base Word	Base Word + Plural Ending
Example: box	boxes
1. cat	cats
2. nut	nuts
3. dish	dishes
4. buzz	buzzes
5. watch	watches
6. bat	bats
7. dress	dresses
8. hip	hips
9. glass	glasses
10. bus	buses
11. snack	snacks

123

Word Work · ·

Sight Words

Look at the Performance Review. If the student achieved a perfect score on today's Word Work activities, complete the first activity from the list below. If the student scored less than 100 percent but more than 85 percent, complete the first three activities from the list below. If the student scored 85 percent or less, complete all five of the activities listed below.

1. Have students complete page 126 in *MARK¹² Reading Activity Book* for more practice on sight words.

2. Using the sight word cards you created for *again, out,* and *pull,* read each word to students and have students write the word on a piece of paper. Give students the sight words, and instruct students to look for any spelling mistakes they may have made. Students should correct the mistakes and then read the list of words aloud.

3. Gather all of the sight word cards students have worked on to date and a timer. Have students read all of the sight word cards as accurately and quickly as possible. Make note of the time, as well as any errors students have made. Use the Online Tile Kit or Paper Letter Tiles to review words read incorrectly.

4. Gather the cards for the sight words *again, out,* and *pull* and up to two additional sight words students have yet to master. Show the first card to students, and ask students to read the word. If students read the word correctly, place in one pile. If students read the word incorrectly, place in a separate pile. On the back of the cards that were read correctly, make a note of the date and put aside. (Once students have read the word correctly five consecutive days, you can remove the word from the pile of cards students are working on.) Review any words students read incorrectly, and keep the cards for next time.

5. Gather the two sets of sight word cards for the words *again, out,* and *pull,* and place all of the cards face down on the table or another flat surface. Have students choose a card, read the word aloud, and then choose a second card. After students read the second card aloud, if the two cards match, students should keep the cards. If they do not match, students should return them to the table. Continue until all of the cards have been collected.

Word Work
Word Endings and Sight Words 2

Name: _____

Sight Words Scramble
Unscramble each sight word and write it on the line provided.

1. lupl — **pull**
2. oto — **too**
3. uto — **out**
4. lakw — **walk**
5. aaing — **again**
6. klat — **talk**

Which Word?
Choose the words from the box that best complete each sentence. Write the words on the lines provided.

| again | out | pull |

7. Can we do that **again** ?
8. Do not **pull** on that string.
9. I will take the dog **out** .

124

Speed Work · ·

Snacks for Brett and Mitch

Look at the Performance Review, or check the student's fluency chart. Fluency scores (words read per minute) should not fall below 80. If the student scored below 80 words per minute, print a copy of the Speed Work story and have the student read the story silently before reading it aloud. Otherwise, move on to Classics Session 2.

Classics Session 2

Columbus at the Court of Spain

Review the keywords with students. Have students reread the story on their own. After rereading the story, students should complete the comprehension questions in *MARK¹² Classics for Young Readers* book on their own. Afterward, if time allows, have students read the story aloud to you.

Objectives

- Improve reading and comprehension questions.

Write

Columbus at the Court of Spain

1. What is the setting of the play in Scene 1?
   - A. ship
   - **B.** palace
   - C. Columbus's house
   - D. Don Gomez's office

2. What does Columbus wish to do?
   Columbus wishes to reach India by sailing west—something no one had done before.

3. What will Isabella use to raise money for Columbus's voyage?
   - A. ships
   - B. palace
   - **C.** jewels
   - D. clothes

4. What does Don Gomez think will happen once Isabella gives Columbus the requested money?
   Don Gomez thinks Columbus will take Isabella's money and disappear. He does not think they will see Columbus again.

5. What is Don Gomez's reaction to the news that Columbus has returned?
   Don Gomez does not believe the news is true. He thinks it is a trick.

6. What does Don Gomez believe happened on Columbus's trip?
   Don Gomez thinks Columbus sailed south instead of west. He believes anything Columbus claims as proof of his trip is only a trick.

7. How does Don Gomez's secretary think the people of Spain will react to the news that Columbus has returned?
   - **A.** They will be filled with excitement.
   - B. They will be bored by Columbus's stories.
   - C. They will be fearful of what Columbus has to say.
   - D. They will be disappointed by what Columbus brought back.

8. What is the meaning of the underlined portion of the following sentence?
   The fact is, even if the sea monsters do not swallow Columbus's ships, we know that where the sun sinks into the ocean, the boiling waters will burn a ship like a dry leaf in a flame.
   - A. No part of a ship would burn.
   - B. A ship would burn very slowly.
   - **C.** A ship would burn very quickly.
   - D. Only a portion of a ship would burn.

Columbus at the Court of Spain **39**

40 Columbus at the Court of Spain

Columbus at the Court of Spain **41**

Word Endings and Sight Words 3

ONLINE	Student & Computer	:60 minutes	
	Adult : *Check Performance Review*		
OFFLINE	Student & Adult : Review online work	:30 minutes	
	• Reading Warm-Up		
	• Code Work		
	• Word Work		
	• Speed Work		
	Composition	:30 minutes	

Instructional Time **2:00** hours

Materials

- *MARK¹² Reading Activity Book*, pages 125–128
- *Just Write*

Tip *The ending –**ed** typically forms the past tense of words. The letters –**ed** can make three different sounds: /**ed**/ as in **landed**; /**d**/ as in **slammed**; and /**t**/ as in **jumped**.*

Goals

In this lesson, students will read about the sport of skateboarding. Students will also learn and practice the rules for adding *–ed* to a word to indicate past tense before reviewing the sight words, *again, out,* and *pull.* In today's Activity Book pages and Tear Out Reader story, you will work with students to reinforce their learning about adding *–ed* to words for past tense and the sight words, *again, out,* and *pull.*

Advance Preparation

For the offline portion of the lesson, gather the students' composition materials. Based on the Performance Review, if students need to complete Word Work activity 2, gather the sight word cards for the following words: *again, out,* and *pull.* If students need to complete Word Work activity 3, you will need a timer and the Online Tile Kit or Paper Letter Tiles. If students need to complete Word Work activity 5, gather the second set of sight word cards for the words *again, out,* and *pull.*

ONLINE	Student & Computer

Students will work online to complete Warm-Up, Code Work, Word Work, and Speed Work activities, and a Wrap-Up assessment on their own. Be sure to read the Performance Review before beginning the offline portion of today's lesson.

Today you will work with students to complete Code Work, Word Work, and Composition activities. Be sure to read the online Performance Review before beginning the Code Work and Word Work activities.

Warm-Up ·

Skateboarding

Look at the Performance Review. If the student achieved a perfect score on today's Warm-Up, move on to Code Work. If the student scored 60 percent or 80 percent, print the story and review the comprehension questions with the student. If the student scored less than 60 percent, print the story, have the student read the story aloud, and then work through the comprehension questions together, before moving on to Code Work.

Objectives

- Improve reading and comprehension skills.

Code Work ·

Ending –ed

Look at the Performance Review. If the student achieved a perfect score on today's Code Work activities, complete the first two activities from the list below. If the student scored less than 100 percent but more than 85 percent, complete the first three activities from the list below. If the student scored 85 percent or less, complete all four of the activities listed below.

Objectives

- Identify and use ending –ed for /ed/, /d/, and /t/.

1. Have students complete page 125 in *MARK¹² Reading Activity Book* for more practice on adding the ending –ed to form the past tense of words.

2. Remove the story "The Hike" from *MARK¹² Reading Activity Book*. Fold the pages in half to create a small booklet. Review the following words with students: *looked, lucky,* and *any.* Have students read the story silently once or twice before reading the story aloud. When students read aloud, make note of any errors, and review those words with the students.

3. Make a chart with three columns with these three headings: Just add –ed; Drop silent e before adding –ed; Double final consonant before adding –ed. Write a base word in each column and have students write the word with –ed added. Then take turns with students finding new words for each column. Have students write the past tense for all words.

4. Have students use the Online Tile Kit or Paper Letter Tiles to build the following words: *hike, blast, wipe, pop, spot, flinch, shrug, plan,* and *like.* Ask students to pick two of the words and use them in oral sentences.

Code Work   Name:
Word Endings and Sight Words 3

Ending –ed

Read the rule above each table. Add the ending –ed to each base word in the table by following the rule given. Write the new word in the second column. Then say the sound the ending –ed makes in that word.

Rule: Double the single ending consonant of a one-syllable word. Then add –ed.

Base Word	Base Word with Ending –ed
nod	nodded
pat	patted
pop	popped
plan	planned

Rule: Drop the silent e, then add –ed.

Base Word	Base Word with Ending –ed
rake	raked
fade	faded
hope	hoped
pile	piled

Rule: Don't change anything; just add –ed.

Base Word	Base Word with Ending –ed
land	landed
last	lasted
rush	rushed
walk	walked

125

Word Work

Sight Words

Look at the Performance Review. If the student achieved a perfect score on today's Word Work activities, complete the first activity from the list below. If the student scored less than 100 percent but more than 85 percent, complete the first three activities from the list below. If the student scored 85 percent or less, complete all five of the activities listed below.

1. Have students complete page 126 in *MARK¹² Reading Activity Book* for more practice on sight words.

2. Using the sight word cards you created for *again, out,* and *pull,* read each word to students and have students write the word on a piece of paper. Give students the sight words, and instruct students to look for any spelling mistakes they may have made. Students should correct the mistakes and then read the list of words aloud.

3. Gather all of the sight word cards students have worked on to date and a timer. Have students read all of the sight word cards as accurately and quickly as possible. Make note of the time, as well as any errors students have made. Use the Online Tile Kit or Paper Letter Tiles to review words read incorrectly.

4. Gather the cards for the sight words *again, out,* and *pull,* and up to two additional sight words students have yet to master. Show the first card to students, and ask students to read the word. If students read the word correctly, place in one pile. If students read the word incorrectly, place in a separate pile. On the back of the cards that were read correctly, make a note of the date and put aside. (Once students have read the word correctly five consecutive days, you can remove the word from the pile of cards students are working on.) Review any words students read incorrectly, and keep the cards for next time.

5. Gather the two sets of sight word cards for the words *again, out,* and *pull* and place all of the cards face down on the table or another flat surface. Have students choose a card, read the word aloud, and then choose a second card. After students read the second card aloud, if the two cards match, students should keep the cards. If they do not match, students should return them to the table. Continue until all of the cards have been collected.

Speed Work

The Ring

Look at the Performance Review, or check the student's fluency chart. Fluency scores (words read per minute) should not fall below 80. If the student scored below 80 words per minute, print a copy of the Speed Work story and have the student read the story silently before reading it aloud. Otherwise, move on to Composition.

Composition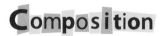

Gather students' composition materials and begin where they left off.

Word Endings and Sight Words 4

ONLINE	Student & Computer	**:60** minutes	
	Adult : *Check Performance Review*		
OFFLINE	Student & Adult : Review online work	**:30** minutes	
	• Reading Warm-Up		
	• Speed Work		
	• Assessment		
	Grammar, Usage, and Mechanics (GUM)	**:30** minutes	
	Instructional Time **2:00** hours		

Materials

- *MARK¹² Reading Activity Book*, pages 129–134

Goals

In this lesson, students will read about grizzly bears. Students will also review the word endings *–s, –es,* and *–ed* before reviewing the sight words *pull, out,* and *again* and practicing new sight words *next, my,* and *friend*. In today's Unit Assessment, you will administer a test covering all content from Unit 8. Afterward, you will work with students to complete activities on main and helping verbs.

ONLINE   Student & Computer

Students will work online to complete Warm-Up, Code Work, Word Work, and Speed Work activities, and a review game on their own. Be sure to read the Performance Review before beginning the offline portion of today's lesson.

Today you will administer a Unit Assessment and work with students to complete a GUM activity.

Warm-Up  . . . .

Grizzly Bears

Look at the Performance Review. If the student achieved a perfect score on today's Warm-Up, move on to Speed Work. If the student scored 60 percent or 80 percent, print the story and review the comprehension questions with student. If the student scored less than 60 percent, print the story, have the student read the story aloud, and then work through the comprehension questions together, before moving on to Speed Work.

Objectives

• Improve reading and comprehension skills.

Speed Work . . . .

Who Said That?

Look at the Performance Review, or check the student's fluency chart. Fluency scores (words read per minute) should not fall below 80. If the student scored below 80 words per minute, print a copy of the Speed Work story and have the student read the story silently before reading it aloud to you. Otherwise, move on to the Assessment.

Objectives

• Increase reading fluency rate.

☼ Assessment  . . . .

Word Endings and Sight Words

Today's Unit Assessment covers all content found in Unit 8. Carefully read the instructions on the student pages before administering the test to the student. If necessary, read the directions to the student. After you have scored the student's assessment, be sure to go online and enter student performance scores in the assessment entry tool.

Part 2. Dictate the following words to students: *less, puff, hands, foxes, glasses, bells, liked, granted, matches,* and *hugged.*

Part 3. Dictate the following sentences to students:
Ted walked in to the class.
Jan wishes for a bike.
I dropped the pop and it spilled.
We watched the dog do tricks.
Ling hiked with her friend.

Part 5. Dictate the following words to students: *too, pull, my, again, talk, out, next, friend, walk,* and *again.*

Assessment
Word Endings and Sight Words

Name:

Unit 8 Assessment

Part 1.
Read each word below. Then say it aloud. Decide which sound –ed makes at the end of the word. Underline the sound you hear.

1.	landed	_/ed/_	/d/	/t/
2.	fussed	/ed/	/d/	_/t/_
3.	filled	/ed/	_/d/_	/t/
4.	watched	/ed/	/d/	_/t/_
5.	boxed	/ed/	/d/	_/t/_
6.	kissed	/ed/	/d/	_/t/_
7.	grunted	_/ed/_	/d/	/t/
8.	buzzed	/ed/	_/d/_	/t/
9.	spotted	_/ed/_	/d/	/t/
10.	grabbed	/ed/	_/d/_	/t/

Assessment
Word Endings and Sight Words

Name:

Part 2.
Listen to each word that is read to you. Write each word on the lines provided.

11. less
12. puff
13. hands
14. foxes
15. glasses
16. bells
17. liked
18. granted
19. matches
20. hugged

Assessment
Word Endings and Sight Words

Name:

Part 3.
Listen to each sentence that is read to you. Write each sentence on the lines provided.

21. Ted walked in to the class.
22. Jan wishes for a bike.
23. I dropped the pop and it spilled.
24. We watched the dog do tricks.
25. Ling hiked with her friend.

Part 4.
Read each word and name aloud.

26. again
27. out
28. pull
29. Dr. Tell
30. friend
31. Mrs. Siff
32. out
33. too
34. next
35. Mr. Russ

Assessment
Word Endings and Sight Words

Name:

Part 5.
In each row, underline the word that is read to you.

36.	toe	_too_	do
37.	_pull_	put	see
38.	we	_my_	me
39.	pen	end	_again_
40.	_talk_	tan	tuck
41.	or	_out_	at
42.	_next_	net	nest
43.	find	end	_friend_
44.	want	_walk_	watch
45.	ask	_again_	are

Part 6.
Read each name aloud.

46. Dr. Will
47. Mrs. Friend
48. Mr. Cliff
49. Dr. Buzz
50. Mrs. Liss

Objectives

- Identify and use –ff, –ll, –ss, and –zz.
- Identify and use the ending –ed for /ed/, /d/, and /t/.
- Identify and use suffixes –s and –es.
- Read sight words.
- Increase reading vocabulary.

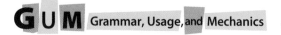

Main Verbs and Helping Verbs

Some tenses of verbs include a helping verb as well as a main verb. Here are examples of helping and main verbs:

Helping Verb	Main Verb
am	teaching
was	working
will	study
has	eaten

Work with students to complete pages 133 and 134 in the *MARK¹² Reading Activity Book*. Read page 133, Get Ready, with students. Have students complete the Try It page. Be sure to discuss students' answers with them after they complete the page.

G U M Grammar, Usage, and Mechanics   Name:
· ·
Word Endings and Sight Words 4

Get Ready

■ Many verbs need more than one word to express their meaning. For example:

  Jan *is going* to the shop.
  She *will get* a new dress.

■ This kind of verb has two parts: a **main verb** and a **helping verb**. The helping verb does exactly what the name says. It helps the main verb.

  I *am chatting* with my friend.
  Helping verb: *am*
  Main verb: *chatting*

■ Main verbs can have more than one helping verb.

  We *have been sitting* in the bus for a long time.
  Helping verbs: *have been*
  Main verb: *sitting*

■ Study the list of helping verbs below:

am	was	has	will	is
were	have	can	are	been
had	might	be		

133

G U M Grammar, Usage, and Mechanics   Name:
· ·
Word Endings and Sight Words 4

Try It

In the sentences below, write **M** over the main verb and **H** over the helping verb or verbs. Remember that a main verb can have more than one helping verb.

     H M
1. The fox is hiding in the grass.

    H H M
2. We have been watching the foxes all day.

    H M
3. I will talk to my friends about foxes.

134

Difficult Spellings & r-Controlled Vowels and Sight Words 1

ONLINE	Student & Computer	:60 minutes
	Adult : *Check Performance Review*	
OFFLINE	Student & Adult : Review online work	:30 minutes
	• Reading Warm-Up	
	• Code Work	
	• Word Work	
	• Speed Work	
	Composition	:30 minutes
	Instructional Time	**2:00** hours

Materials

- *MARK[12] Reading Activity Book*, pages 135–138
- *Just Write*

Tip

*The sound /f/ is usually spelled with the letter **f**, but it can also be spelled with the digraph **ph**. A digraph is two letters together that make one sound. **Alphabet** and **elephant** are two words that use the digraph **ph** to make the sound /f/.*

Goals

In this lesson, students will read about the Great Wall of China. Students will also work with the digraph *ph* before working with the sight words *next, my,* and *friend.* In today's *MARK[12] Reading Activity Book* pages, you will work with students to reinforce their understanding of the digraph *ph* and to reinforce their correct use of sight words. Afterward, students will spend 30 minutes working on composition.

Advance Preparation

For the offline portion of today's lesson, gather the students' composition materials. Based on the Performance Review, if students need to complete Word Work activity 2, create sight word cards for the following words: *next, laugh,* and *friend.* If students need to complete Word Work activity 3, you will need a timer and the Online Tile Kit or Paper Letter Tiles. If students need to complete Word Work activity 5, create a second set of sight word cards for the words *next, laugh,* and *friend.*

| ONLINE | **Student & Computer** |

Students will work online to complete Warm-Up, Code Work, Word Work, and Speed Work activities, and a Wrap-Up assessment on their own. Be sure to read the Performance Review before beginning the offline portion of today's lesson.

Today you will work with students to complete Code Work, Word Work, and Composition activities. Be sure to read the online Performance Review before beginning the Code Work and Word Work activities.

Warm-Up

The Great Wall of China

Look at the Performance Review. If the student achieved a perfect score on today's Warm-Up, move on to Code Work. If the student scored 60 percent or 80 percent, print the story and review the comprehension questions with the student. If the student scored less than 60 percent, print the story, have the student read the story aloud, and then work through the comprehension questions together, before moving on to Code Work.

Objectives

- Improve reading and comprehension skills.

Code Work

Difficult Spellings – /f/

Look at the Performance Review. If the student achieved a perfect score on today's Code Work activities, complete the first two activities from the list below. If the student scored less than 100 percent but more than 85 percent, complete the first three activities from the list below. If the student scored 85 percent or less, complete all four of the activities listed below.

Objectives

- Identify and use *ph* for the sound /f/.

1. Have students complete page 139 in *MARK¹² Reading Activity Book* for more practice on the digraph *ph*.

2. Remove the "Where Are We" story from *MARK¹² Reading Activity Book*. Fold the pages in half to create a small booklet. Review the following words with students: *voice, gizmo,* and *magic*. Have students read the story silently once or twice before reading the story aloud. When students read aloud, make note of any pronunciation errors, and review those words with students.

3. Ask students to secretly choose three of the following words: *alphabet, dolphin, elephant, graph,* or *phone*. Then have students draw each word for you, while you guess which word is being drawn. Students should not make any sounds or gestures to help you figure out the word.

4. Have students write the following 10 words on a piece of paper: *film, fish, graph, if, life, phase, Phil, phone, Ralph,* and *shelf*. Then ask students to read the words aloud and underline the letter or letters that make the sound /f/ in each word.

Code Work
Name:
Difficult Spellings & r-Controlled Vowels and Sight Words 1

The Sound /f/
Read each sentence aloud. Find the word in each sentence that contains the sound /f/. Write that word on the line provided. Read the sentence again.
Hint: One sentence contains more than one word with the sound /f/.

1. Pick up the phone. — **phone**
2. Ralph made a graph. — **Ralph, graph**
3. Steph threw the ball. — **Steph**
4. Phil smiled at the joke. — **Phil**
5. The dolphin swam and jumped. — **dolphin**

Write three sentences. In each sentence, use one word with the sound /f/ spelled with *ph*.

6. **Sentences will vary.**
7.
8.

135

Word **W**ork ·

Sight Words

Look at the Performance Review. If the student achieved a perfect score on today's Word Work activities, complete the first activity from the list below. If the student scored less than 100 percent but more than 85 percent, complete the first three activities from the list below. If the student scored 85 percent or less, complete all five of the activities listed below.

1. Have students complete page 144 in *MARK¹² Reading Activity Book* for more practice on sight words.

2. Using the sight word cards you created for *next, laugh,* and *friend,* read each word to students and have students write the word on a piece of paper. Give students the sight words, and instruct students to look for any spelling mistakes they may have made. Students should correct the mistakes and then read the list of words aloud.

3. Gather all of the sight word cards students have worked on to date and a timer. Have students read all of the sight word cards as accurately and quickly as possible. Make note of the time, as well as any errors students have made. Use the Online Tile Kit or Paper Letter Tiles to review words read incorrectly.

4. Gather the cards for the sight words *next, laugh,* and *friend,* and up to two additional sight words students have yet to master. Show the first card to students, and ask students to read the word. If students read the word correctly, place in one pile. If students read the word incorrectly, place in a separate pile. On the back of the cards that were read correctly, make a note of the date and put aside. (Once students have read the word correctly five consecutive days, you can remove the word from the pile of cards students are working on.) Review any words students read incorrectly, and keep the cards for next time.

5. Gather the two sets of sight word cards for the words *next, laugh,* and *friend,* and place all of the cards face down on the table or another flat surface. Have students choose a card, read the word aloud, and then choose a second card. After students read the second card aloud, if the two cards match, students should keep the cards. If they do not match, students should return them to the table. Continue until all of the cards have been collected.

Word Work
Name:
Difficult Spellings & r-Controlled Vowels and Sight Words 1

Sight Words Scramble
Unscramble each sight word and write it on the line provided.

1. fdnier — friend
2. naiag — again
3. ualhg — laugh
4. tou — out
5. xent — next
6. lulp — pull

Sentences
Choose the words from the box that best complete each sentence. Write each word on the lines provided.

next   laugh   friend

7. I will have some **next** time.
8. I had to **laugh** at the chimp!
9. My **friend** went with me to the game.

136

Speed **W**ork ·

Lance in a Trance

Look at the Performance Review, or check the student's fluency chart. Fluency scores (words read per minute) should not fall below 80. If the student scored below 80 words per minute, print a copy of the Speed Work story and have the student read the story silently before reading it aloud. Otherwise, move on to Composition.

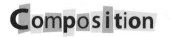# Composition

Gather students' composition materials and begin where they left off.

Difficult Spellings & r-Controlled Vowels and Sight Words 2

ONLINE	Student & Computer	:60 minutes
	Adult : *Check Performance Review*	
OFFLINE	Student & Adult : Review online work	:30 minutes
	• Reading Warm-Up	
	• Code Work	
	• Word Work	
	• Speed Work	
	Classics Session 1	:30 minutes
	Instructional Time **2:00** hours	

Materials

- *MARK¹² Classics for Young Readers*
- "The Story of Proserpina" MP3
- Online Tile Kit or Paper Letter Tiles
- *MARK¹² Reading Activity Book*, pages 139–140

> **Tip**
>
> *The letter **c** almost always makes the sound /**s**/ when followed by **e, i,** or **y**. **Cent, city,** and **cycle** are three examples. The letter **g** almost always makes the sound /**j**/ when followed by **e, i,** or **y**. **Age, giant,** and **gym** are three examples.*

Goals

In this lesson, students will read about the history of salt. Students will also work with the letter *c* making the sound /s/ and the letter *g* making the sound /j/, before working with the sight words *anything, goes,* and *begin.* In today's *MARK¹² Reading Activity Book* pages, you will work with students to reinforce the letter *c* making the sound /s/ and the letter *g* making the sound /j/, and to reinforce their correct use of sight words. You will also work with students to complete *MARK¹² Classics for Young Readers* activities.

Advance Preparation

For the offline portion of today's lesson, download this story: "The Story of Proserpina." Based on the Performance Review, if students need to complete Word Work activity 2, create sight word cards for the following words: *anything, goes,* and *begin.* If students need to complete Word Work activity 3, you will need a timer and the Online Tile Kit or Paper Letter Tiles. If students need to complete Word Work activity 5, create a second set of sight word cards for the words *anything, goes,* and *begin.*

 ONLINE | **Student & Computer**

Students will work online to complete Warm-Up, Code Work, Word Work, and Speed Work activities, and a Wrap-Up assessment on their own. Be sure to read the Performance Review before beginning the offline portion of today's lesson.

Today you will work with students to complete Code Work, Word Work, and *MARK¹² Classics for Young Readers* activities. Be sure to read the online Performance Review before beginning the Code Work and Word Work activities.

Warm-Up ·····

Salt

Look at the Performance Review. If the student achieved a perfect score on today's Warm-Up, move on to Code Work. If the student scored 60 percent or 80 percent, print the story and review the comprehension questions with the student. If the student scored less than 60 percent, print the story, have the student read the story aloud, and then work through the comprehension questions together, before moving on to Code Work.

Code Work ·····

Difficult Spellings – /s/ and /j/

Look at the Performance Review. If the student achieved a perfect score on today's Code Work activities, complete the first two activities from the list below. If the student scored less than 100 percent but more than 85 percent, complete the first three activities from the list below. If the student scored 85 percent or less, complete all five of the activities listed below.

1. Have students complete page 145 in *MARK¹² Reading Activity Book* for more practice on the soft *c* and soft *g* sounds.

2. Have students use the Online Tile Kit or Paper Letter Tiles to spell the following words: *age, gym, fence, ice, magic,* and *place.*

3. Have students fold a piece of paper in half and label the left half "Hard *c*" and the right half "Soft *c*." Remind students that when a *c* is pronounced /k/, it is called a hard *c*. When it is pronounced /s/, it is called a soft *c*. Read the following words aloud, and have students write the words in the correct columns: *rice, cab, cube, mice, clap, crust, slice,* and *space.*

4. Have students fold a piece of paper in half and label the left half "Hard *g*" and the right half "Soft *g*." Remind students that when a *g* is pronounced /g/, it is called a hard *g*. When it is pronounced /j/, it is called a soft *g*. Read the following words aloud, and have students write the words in the correct columns: *bulge, gripe, fringe, gap, huge,* and *gift.*

5. Have students choose two of the soft *c* words and two of the soft *g* words from activities 3 and 4 and use each word in a sentence.

Code Work — Difficult Spellings & r-Controlled Vowels and Sight Words 2

Words with Soft c and Soft g

Write each word with a soft c, as in *ace*, in the box below.
Hint: Seven words have a soft c.

twice	catch		words with a soft c
call	cinch		
came	place		twice, nice, chance, cinch, place, cell, since
nice	cash		
camp	cell		
chance	since		

Write each word with a soft g, as in *age*, in the box below.
Hint: Seven words have a soft g.

hinge	huge		words with a soft g
gym	goes		
bulge	gem		hinge, gym, bulge, page, huge, gem, stage
hug	gust		
page	stage		
begin	twig		

139

Word Work

Sight Words

Look at the Performance Review. If the student achieved a perfect score on today's Word Work activities, complete the first activity from the list below. If the student scored less than 100 percent but more than 85 percent, complete the first three activities from the list below. If the student scored 85 percent or less, complete all five of the activities listed below.

1. Have students complete page 146 in *MARK¹² Reading Activity Book* for more practice on sight words.

2. Using the sight word cards you created for *anything, goes,* and *begin,* read each word to students and have students write the word on a piece of paper. Give students the sight words, and instruct students to look for any spelling mistakes they may have made. Students should correct the mistakes and then read the list of words aloud.

3. Gather all of the sight word cards students have worked on to date and a timer. Have students read all of the sight word cards as accurately and quickly as possible. Make note of the time, as well as any errors students have made. Use the Online Tile Kit or Paper Letter Tiles to review words read incorrectly.

4. Gather the cards for the sight words *anything, goes,* and *begin,* and up to two additional sight words students have yet to master. Show the first card to students, and ask students to read the word. If students read the word correctly, place in one pile. If students read the word incorrectly, place in a separate pile. On the back of the cards that were read correctly, make a note of the date and put aside. (Once students have read the word correctly five consecutive days, you can remove the word from the pile of cards students are working on.) Review any words students read incorrectly, and keep the cards for next time.

5. Gather the two sets of sight word cards for the words *anything, goes,* and *begin,* and place all of the cards face down on the table or another flat surface. Have students choose a card, read the word aloud, and then choose a second card. After students read the second card aloud, if the two cards match, students should keep the cards. If they do not match, students should return them to the table. Continue until all of the cards have been collected.

Speed Work

Camp

Look at the Performance Review, or check the student's fluency chart. Fluency scores (words read per minute) should not fall below 80. If the student scored below 80 words per minute, print a copy of the Speed Work story and have the student read the story silently before reading it aloud. Otherwise, move on to Classics Session 1.

Classics Session 1 ·

The Story of Proserpina

Today's story, "The Story of Proserpina," is based on a Roman myth. Download the story. Have students listen to the story while following along in *MARK¹² Classics for Young Readers*. Have students listen to the story again before writing a summary of the story.

Students should write a summary of the story to complete today's Classics activity.

Difficult Spellings & r-Controlled Vowels and Sight Words 3

ONLINE	Student & Computer	**:60**	minutes
	Adult : *Check Performance Review*		
OFFLINE	Student & Adult : Review online work	**:30**	minutes
	• Reading Warm-Up		
	• Code Work		
	• Word Work		
	• Speed Work		
	Classics Session 2	**:30**	minutes
	Instructional Time	**2:00**	hours

Materials

- *MARK¹² Classics for Young Readers*
- "The Story of Proserpina" MP3
- *MARK¹² Reading Activity Book*, pages 141–144

Tip

When the letters e and r are together in a word, they make the sound /er/. The letters i and r together also make the sound /er/. After and bird are two words that use e and r together or i and r together to make the sound /er/.

Goals

In this lesson, students will read about Mahatma Gandhi. Students will also work with the sound /er/ before working with the sight words *anything, begin,* and *goes*. In today's *MARK¹² Reading Activity Book* pages, you will work with students to reinforce their understanding of the sound /er/ and to reinforce their correct use of the sight words *anything, begin,* and *goes*. You will also work with students to complete *MARK¹² Classics for Young Readers* activities.

Advance Preparation

For the offline portion of today's lesson, download this story: "The Story of Proserpina." Based on the Performance Review, if students need to complete Code Work activity 4, gather eight index cards. On each of the cards, write one of the following words: *clerk, crunch, first, fresh, girl, grill, perch,* and *press*. If students need to complete Word Work activity 2, gather the sight word cards for the following words: *anything, begin,* and *goes*. If students need to complete Word Work activity 3, you will need a timer and the Online Tile Kit or Paper Letter Tiles. If students need to complete Word Work activity 5, gather the second set of sight word cards for the words *anything, begin,* and *goes*.

ONLINE Student & Computer

Students will work online to complete Warm-Up, Code Work, Word Work, and Speed Work activities, and a Wrap-Up assessment on their own. Be sure to read the Performance Review before beginning the offline portion of today's lesson.

Today you will work with students to complete Code Work, Word Work, and *MARK¹² Classics for Young Readers* activities. Be sure to read the online Performance Review before beginning the Code Work and Word Work activities.

Warm-Up •

Mahatma Gandhi

Look at the Performance Review. If the student achieved a perfect score on today's Warm-Up, move on to Code Work. If the student scored 60 percent or 80 percent, print the story and review the comprehension questions with the student. If the student scored less than 60 percent, print the story, have the student read the story aloud, and then work through the comprehension questions together, before moving on to Code Work.

Objectives

- Improve reading and comprehension skills.

Code Work •

r-Controlled Vowels

Look at the Performance Review. If the student achieved a perfect score on today's Code Work activities, complete the first two activities from the list below. If the student scored less than 100 percent but more than 85 percent, complete the first three activities from the list below. If the student scored 85 percent or less, complete all five of the activities listed below.

Objectives

- Identify and use –er.
- Identify and use –ir.

1. Have students complete page 147 in *MARK¹² Reading Activity Book* for more practice on the sound /er/.

2. Remove the "Surf's Up!" story from *MARK¹² Reading Activity Book*. Fold the pages in half to create a small booklet. Review the following words with students: *surfboard* and *toes*. Have students read the story silently once or twice before reading the story aloud. When students read aloud, make note of any pronunciation errors, and review those words with students.

3. On a piece of paper, have students write down the following six words: *bird, her, squirm, term, third,* and *verb*. Have students read the words aloud, and then underline the letters that make the sound /er/ in each word.

4. Give students the index cards you previously prepared. Have them sort the cards into two piles: one pile for words that contain the sound /er/ (*clerk, first, girl,* and *perch*) and one pile for words that do not contain the sound /er/ (*crunch, fresh, grill,* and *press*).

5. Have students choose three of the /er/ sound words from activities 3 and 4 and use each word in a sentence.

Code Work
Name:
Difficult Spellings & r-Controlled Vowels and Sight Words 3

r-Controlled Vowels
Underline each word in the box that contains the sound /er/, as in *her*.

brush	squirm	shirt	term	trim
stir	fist	first	shrimp	stern
thrill	swirl	third	thirst	trip
trust	verb	gem	germs	twirl

Your Turn!
On the lines provided, write two words that contain the sound /er/ spelled *er*. (Choose words not shown in the box above.)

1. Answers will vary
2. _____

On the lines provided, write two words that contain the sound /er/ spelled *ir*. (Choose words *not shown* in the box above.)

3. _____
4. _____

141

Word Work

Sight Words

Look at the Performance Review. If the student achieved a perfect score on today's Word Work activities, complete the first activity from the list below. If the student scored less than 100 percent but more than 85 percent, complete the first three activities from the list below. If the student scored 85 percent or less, complete all five of the activities listed below.

1. Have students complete page 148 in *MARK¹² Reading Activity Book* for more practice on sight words.

2. Using the sight word cards you created for *anything, goes,* and *begin,* read each word to students and have students write the word on a piece of paper. Give students the sight words, and instruct students to look for any spelling mistakes they may have made. Students should correct the mistakes and then read the list of words aloud.

3. Gather all of the sight word cards students have worked on to date and a timer. Have students read all of the sight word cards as accurately and quickly as possible. Make note of the time, as well as any errors students have made. Use the Online Tile Kit or Paper Letter Tiles to review words read incorrectly.

4. Gather the cards for the sight words *anything, goes,* and *begin,* and up to two additional sight words students have yet to master. Show the first card to students, and ask students to read the word. If students read the word correctly, place in one pile. If students read the word incorrectly, place in a separate pile. On the back of the cards that were read correctly, make a note of the date and put aside. (Once students have read the word correctly five consecutive days, you can remove the word from the pile of cards students are working on.) Review any words students read incorrectly, and keep the cards for next time.

5. Gather the two sets of sight word cards for the words *anything, goes,* and *begin,* and place all of the cards face down on the table or another flat surface. Have students choose a card, read the word aloud, and then choose a second card. After students read the second card aloud, if the two cards match, students should keep the cards. If they do not match, students should return them to the table. Continue until all of the cards have been collected.

Speed Work

Fun with Mr. Chips

Look at the Performance Review, or check the student's fluency chart. Fluency scores (words read per minute) should not fall below 80. If the student scored below 80 words per minute, print a copy of the Speed Work story and have the student read the story silently before reading it aloud. Otherwise, move on to Classics Session 2.

Have students listen to the story again while following along in *MARK¹² Classics for Young Readers*. Afterward, students should complete the comprehension questions in *MARK¹² Classics for Young Readers* on their own.

Objectives

- Improve reading and comprehension skills.

Write

The Story of Proserpina

1. Which words best describe Pluto's home?
   - (A.) joyless and sad
   - B. calm and pleasant
   - C. bright and cheerful
   - D. noisy and crowded

2. Why does Proserpina sit down on a stone?
   Proserpina, tired from playing, sits down on a stone to rest.

3. How does Proserpina feel when she first sees Pluto and his horses?
   - A. sleepy
   - (B.) scared
   - C. excited
   - D. confused

4. Where does Ceres go to look for her daughter, Proserpina?
   Ceres "crossed the seas and went from land to land, and asked all that dwelt on the earth if they had seen her child."

The Story of Proserpina 47

5. For how long does Ceres search for Proserpina before going to Helios?
   - A. one day
   - B. one week
   - C. one month
   - (D.) one year

6. What message does Ceres send to Jupiter?
   Ceres sends a message to Jupiter telling him that no fruits or grain would grow while Pluto kept Proserpina.

7. According to the book from which Pluto reads, gods or people cannot return to earth if they do what in the land of Pluto?
   - (A.) eat
   - B. sing
   - C. sleep
   - D. dance

8. What was the bright red fruit that Proserpina plucked from a tree near the Styx?
   Proserpina plucked a pomegranate from a tree near the Styx.

48 *The Story of Proserpina*

Difficult Spellings & r-Controlled Vowels and Sight Words 4

ONLINE	Student & Computer	**:60** minutes
	Adult : *Check Performance Review*	
OFFLINE	Student & Adult : Review online work	**:30** minutes
	• Reading Warm-Up	
	• Code Work	
	• Word Work	
	• Speed Work	
	Grammar, Usage, and Mechanics (GUM)	**:30** minutes
	Instructional Time	**2:00** hours

Materials

- Online Tile Kit or Paper Letter Tiles
- *MARK¹² Reading Activity Book*, pages 145–148

Tip

*When the letters **u** and **r** are together in a word, they make the sound /**er**/. The letters **e, a,** and **r** together also make the sound /**er**/. **Burn** and **learn** are two words that use **u** and **r** together or **e, a,** and **r** together to make the sound /**er**/.*

Goals

In this lesson, students will read about bald eagles. Students will also work with the sound /er/ before learning the sight words *after, down,* and *know.* In today's *MARK¹² Reading Activity Book* pages, you will work with students to reinforce their understanding of the sound /er/ and to reinforce their correct use of sight words. Afterward, you will work with students to complete activities on past and past participle forms of regular and irregular verbs.

Advance Preparation

Based on the Performance Review, if students need to complete Code Work activity 3, gather a newspaper or magazine. If students need to complete Code Work activity 4, gather eight index cards. On each of the cards, write one of the following words: *burn, brunch, curl, crust, earth, elk, learn,* and *lashes.* If students must complete Word Work activity 2, create sight word cards for the following words: *after, down,* and *know.* If students need to complete Word Work activity 3, you will need a timer and the Online Tile Kit or Paper Letter Tiles. If students need to complete Word Work activity 5, create a second set of sight word cards for the words *after, down,* and *know.*

ONLINE	**Student & Computer**

Students will work online to complete Warm-Up, Code Work, Word Work, and Speed Work activities, and a Wrap-Up assessment on their own. Be sure to read the Performance Review before beginning the offline portion of today's lesson.

Today you will work with students to complete Code Work, Word Work, and GUM activities. Be sure to read the online Performance Review before beginning the Code Work and Word Work activities.

Warm-Up ·

Bald Eagles

Look at the Performance Review. If the student achieved a perfect score on today's Warm-Up, move on to Code Work. If the student scored 60 percent or 80 percent, print the story and review the comprehension questions with the student. If the student scored less than 60 percent, print the story, have the student read the story aloud, and then work through the comprehension questions together, before moving on to Code Work.

Objectives

- Improve reading and comprehension skills.

Code Work ·

r-Controlled Vowels

Look at the Performance Review. If the student achieved a perfect score on today's Code Work activities, complete the first two activities from the list below. If the student scored less than 100 percent but more than 85 percent, complete the first three activities from the list below. If the student scored 85 percent or less, complete all five of the activities listed below.

Objectives

- Identify and use –ur.
- Identify and use –ear.

1. Have students complete page 153 in *MARK¹² Reading Activity Book* for more practice on the sound /er/.

2. Have students use the Online Tile Kit or Paper Letter Tiles to spell the following words: *burst, churn, earn, heard, search,* and *surf*.

3. Have students look through the newspaper or magazine you gathered, and circle as many words with the sound /er/ as they can find in two minutes. The words can contain the *–er, –ir, –ur,* or *–ear* spellings. Have students read the words aloud. Help students with pronunciations, if necessary.

4. Give students the index cards you previously prepared. Have them sort the cards into two piles: one pile for words that contain the sound /er/ (*burn, curl, earth,* and *learn*) and one pile for words that do not contain the sound /er/ (*brunch, crust, elk,* and *lashes*).

5. Have students choose three of the /er/ words from activities 2 and 4 and use each word in a sentence.

Code Work Name:
Difficult Spellings & r-Controlled Vowels and Sight Words 4

r-Controlled Vowels

Sort the words in the box according to their spelling of the sound /er/. Write each word in the correct column.

after	burn	clerk	curb
fern	girl	heard	herd
learn	stir	third	thirst
yearn	earth	hurt	turn

er	ir	ur	ear
after	girl	burn	earth
clerk	stir	curb	heard
fern	third	hurt	learn
herd	thirst	turn	yearn

Choose the words from the box above that best complete each sentence below. Write each word on the lines provided. Then read each sentence aloud.

1. I would like to **learn** ____ to play baseball.
2. The **girl** ____ helped her brother fix his bike.
3. Please **stir** ____ the soup so it does not **burn** ____.
4. I **heard** ____ the duck quack as it swam in the pond.
5. The **herd** ____ of sheep moved together in the field.

145

Word **W**ork ·

Sight Words

Look at the Performance Review. If the student achieved a perfect score on today's Word Work activities, complete the first activity from the list below. If the student scored less than 100 percent but more than 85 percent, complete the first three activities from the list below. If the student scored 85 percent or less, complete all five of the activities listed below.

1. Have students complete page 154 in *MARK¹² Reading Activity Book* for more practice on sight words.

2. Using the sight word cards you created for *down, after,* and *know,* read each word to students and have students write the word on a piece of paper. Give students the sight words, and instruct students to look for any spelling mistakes they may have made. Students should correct the mistakes and then read the list of words aloud.

3. Gather all of the sight word cards students have worked on to date and a timer. Have students read all of the sight word cards as accurately and quickly as possible. Make note of the time, as well as any errors students have made. Use the Online Tile Kit or Paper Letter Tiles to review words read incorrectly.

4. Gather the cards for the sight words *down, after,* and *know,* and up to two additional sight words students have yet to master. Show the first card to students, and ask students to read the word. If students read the word correctly, place in one pile. If students read the word incorrectly, place in a separate pile. On the back of the cards that were read correctly, make a note of the date and put aside. (Once students have read the word correctly five consecutive days, you can remove the word from the pile of cards students are working on.) Review any words students read incorrectly, and keep the cards for next time.

5. Gather the two sets of sight word cards for the words *down, after,* and *know,* and place all of the cards face down on the table or another flat surface. Have students choose a card, read the word aloud, and then choose a second card. After students read the second card aloud, if the two cards match, students should keep the cards. If they do not match, students should return them to the table. Continue until all of the cards have been collected.

Word Work

Difficult Spellings & r-Controlled Vowels and Sight Words 4

Complete the Sentences

Use the sight words from the box to complete each sentence below.
Hint: One word will be used in two sentences. Then read each sentence aloud.

after	begin	down	goes	know	anything

1. Pat **goes** camping every summer.
2. Do you **know** how to play chess?
3. I went to bed **after** I brushed my teeth.
4. The cat did not want to climb **down** from the tree.
5. Eve played with her friends **after** she cleaned her room.
6. Can I help you with **anything** to get ready for the party?
7. We will **begin** planting the garden on Saturday morning.

146

Speed **W**ork ·

Pack It Up!

Look at the Performance Review, or check the student's fluency chart. Fluency scores (words read per minute) should not fall below 80. If the student scored below 80 words per minute, print a copy of the Speed Work story and have the student read the story silently before reading it aloud. Otherwise, move on to Grammar, Usage, and Mechanics.

Past and Past Participle Verb Forms

The regular ending for past and past participle verbs is *–d* or *–ed*. Past and past participle forms of irregular verbs do *not* end in *–d* or *–ed*. Irregular verbs are unpredictable, and they must be learned individually.

Present	Past	Past Participle
bring	brought	(has) brought
buy	bought	(have) bought
come	came	(has) come

Work with students to complete pages 155 and 156 in *MARK¹² Reading Activity Book*. Read page 155, Get Ready, with students. Have students complete the Try It page. Be sure to discuss students' answers when the page is completed.

GUM Grammar, Usage, and Mechanics   Name: _____

Difficult Spellings & r-Controlled Vowels and Sight Words 4

Get Ready

- The *regular* ending for **past** and **past participle verbs** is *–d* or *–ed*. Some verbs are irregular and don't follow the usual rules. Past and past participle forms of *irregular* verbs do *not* end in *–d* or *–ed*.

- Irregular verbs are unpredictable, so you must practice and learn them. Study the list of some irregular verbs below. Pick any three verbs from the list and make up sentences with the present, past, and past participle. For example, for *eat*:

  I *eat* my peas with honey.
  I *ate* peas with my marshmallow sandwich.
  I *have eaten* too many peas and marshmallows.

Present	Past	Past Participle
bring	brought	(has) brought
buy	bought	(have) bought
come	came	(has) come
cut	cut	(have) cut
do	did	(has) done
eat	ate	(have) eaten
feel	felt	(has) felt
give	gave	(have) given
go	went	(has) gone
is (am, are)	was (were)	(have) been
know	knew	(has) known
make	made	(have) made
run	ran	(has) run
see	saw	(have) seen
sit	sat	(has) sat
understand	understood	(have) understood
take	took	(has) taken
tear	tore	(have) torn

147

GUM Grammar, Usage, and Mechanics   Name: _____

Difficult Spellings & r-Controlled Vowels and Sight Words 4

Try It

Write the missing forms of each word on the lines provided.

	Present	Past	Past Participle
1.	drip	dripped	(has) **dripped**
2.	know	**knew**	(have) **known**
3.	**cut**	cut	(has) **cut**
4.	cry	**cried**	(have) cried
5.	give	**gave**	(has) given
6.	**go**	went	(have) **gone**

Choose one verb from above and write sentences using the present, past, and past participle forms of that verb. Then read your sentences aloud.

7. Present: **Sentences will vary.** _____

8. Past: _____

9. Past participle: _____

148

Difficult Spellings & r-Controlled Vowels and Sight Words 5

ONLINE	Student & Computer	**:60** minutes
	Adult : *Check Performance Review*	
OFFLINE	Student & Adult : Review online work	**:30** minutes
	• Reading Warm-Up	
	• Code Work	
	• Word Work	
	• Speed Work	
	Composition	**:30** minutes

Instructional Time **2:00** hours

Materials

- *MARK*[12] *Reading Activity Book*, pages 149–152
- *Just Write*

> **Tip**
>
> *When the letters **a** and **r** are together in a word, sometimes they make the sound /**ar**/. When the letters **o** and **r** are together in a word, sometimes they make the sound /**or**/. **Arch, yarn, cord,** and **worn** are four words that contain the sounds /**ar**/ and /**or**/.*

Goals

In this lesson, students will read about ladybugs. Students will also work with the sounds /ar/ and /or/ before working with the sight words *after, down,* and *know.* In today's *MARK*[12] *Reading Activity Book* pages, you will work with students to reinforce their understanding of the sounds /ar/ and /or/ and to reinforce their correct use of sight words. Afterward, students will spend 30 minutes working on composition.

Advance Preparation

For the offline portion of today's lesson, gather the students' composition materials. Based on the Performance Review, if students need to complete Code Work activity 3 you will need the Online Tile Kit or Paper Letter Tiles. If students need to complete Word Work activity 2, gather the sight word cards for the following words: *after, down,* and *know.* If students need to complete Word Work activity 3, you will need a timer and the Online Tile Kit or Paper Letter Tiles. If students need to complete Word Work activity 5, gather the second set of sight word cards for the words *after, down,* and *know.*

ONLINE   Student & Computer

Students will work online to complete Warm-Up, Code Work, Word Work, and Speed Work activities, and a Wrap-Up assessment on their own. Be sure to read the Performance Review before beginning the offline portion of today's lesson.

Today you will work with students to complete Code Work, Word Work, and Composition activities. Be sure to read the online Performance Review before beginning the Code Work and Word Work activities.

Warm-Up ·

Ladybugs

Look at the Performance Review. If the student achieved a perfect score on today's Warm-Up, move on to Code Work. If the student scored 60 percent or 80 percent, print the story and review the comprehension questions with the student. If the student scored less than 60 percent, print the story, have the student read the story aloud, and then work through the comprehension questions together, before moving on to Code Work.

Objectives

* Improve reading and comprehension skills.

Code Work ·

r-Controlled Vowels

Look at the Performance Review. If the student achieved a perfect score on today's Code Work activities, complete the first two activities from the list below. If the student scored less than 100 percent but more than 85 percent, complete the first three activities from the list below. If the student scored 85 percent or less, complete all four of the activities listed below.

Objectives

* Identify and use –ar.
* Identify and use –or.

1. Have students complete page 157 in MARK¹² Reading Activity Book for more practice on the sounds /ar/ and /or/.

2. Remove the "Mind Your Mother" story from MARK¹² Reading Activity Book. Fold the pages in half to create a small booklet. Review the following words with students: *against* and *outside*. Have students read the story silently once or twice before reading the story aloud. When students read aloud, make note of any errors, and review those words with the students

3. Have students use the Online Tile Kit or Paper Letter Tiles to spell the following words: *fork, harp, park, sort, star,* and *worn*.

4. Give students clues for words with the sounds /ar/ or /or/. Tell students which sound your word contains, and then describe characteristics about the mystery word. For example: "I'm thinking of a word with the sound /ar/. This word is a body part. You have two of them. They bend. You use them to hold things." Answer: *arm*. Give students three words using each sound. Words to consider: *farm, garden, shark, corn, porch,* and *storm*. Then, if time permits, ask students to come up with at least one example of a word containing the sound /ar/ and one example of a word containing the sound /or/, and give you clues to help you figure out the mystery words.

Difficult Spellings & r-Controlled Vowels and Sight Words

Word Work

Sight Words

Look at the Performance Review. If the student achieved a perfect score on today's Word Work activities, complete the first activity from the list below. If the student scored less than 100 percent but more than 85 percent, complete the first three activities from the list below. If the student scored 85 percent or less, complete all five of the activities listed below.

1. Have students complete page 158 in *MARK¹² Reading Activity Book* for more practice on sight words.

2. Using the sight word cards you created for *down, after,* and *know,* read each word to students and have students write the word on a piece of paper. Give students the sight words, and instruct students to look for any spelling mistakes they may have made. Students should correct the mistakes and then read the list of words aloud.

3. Gather all of the sight word cards students have worked on to date and a timer. Have students read all of the sight word cards as accurately and quickly as possible. Make note of the time, as well as any errors students have made. Use the Online Tile Kit or Paper Letter Tiles to review words read incorrectly.

4. Gather the cards for the sight words *down, after,* and *know,* and up to two additional sight words students have yet to master. Show the first card to students, and ask students to read the word. If students read the word correctly, place in one pile. If students read the word incorrectly, place in a separate pile. On the back of the cards that were read correctly, make a note of the date and put aside. (Once students have read the word correctly five consecutive days, you can remove the word from the pile of cards students are working on.) Review any words students read incorrectly, and keep the cards for next time.

5. Gather the two sets of sight word cards for the words *down, after,* and *know,* and place all of the cards face down on the table or another flat surface. Have students choose a card, read the word aloud, and then choose a second card. After students read the second card aloud, if the two cards match, students should keep the cards. If they do not match, students should return them to the table. Continue until all of the cards have been collected.

Speed Work

The Yard Sale

Look at the Performance Review, or check the student's fluency chart. Fluency scores (words read per minute) should not fall below 80. If the student scored below 80 words per minute, print a copy of the Speed Work story and have the student read the story silently before reading it aloud. Otherwise, move on to Composition.

Composition ·

Gather students' composition materials and begin where they left off.

Difficult Spellings & r-Controlled Vowels and Sight Words 6

ONLINE	Student & Computer	**:60**	minutes
	Adult : *Check Performance Review*		
OFFLINE	Student & Adult : Review online work	**:30**	minutes
	• Reading Warm-Up		
	• Code Work		
	• Word Work		
	• Speed Work		
	Grammar, Usage, and Mechanics (GUM)	**:30**	minutes
	Instructional Time	**2:00**	hours

Materials

- Online Tile Kit or Paper Letter Tiles
- *MARK¹² Reading Activity Book*, pages 153–156

> **Tip**
>
> *The sound /ĕ/ is usually spelled with the letter* **e***, but it can also be spelled with the letters* **ea***. Ahead, heavy,* and **weather** *are examples of words that use* **ea** *to make the sound /ĕ/.*

Goals

In this lesson, students will read about life in ancient Egypt. Students will also work with the letters *ea* making the sound /ĕ/ before learning the sight words *mother, father,* and *only*. In today's *MARK¹² Reading Activity Book* pages, you will work with students to reinforce their understanding of the letters *ea* making the sound /ĕ/ and to practice sight words. Afterward, you will work with students to complete activities on irregular verbs.

Advance Preparation

Based on the Performance Review, if students need to complete Word Work activity 2, create sight word cards for the following words: *mother, father,* and *only*. If students need to complete Word Work activity 3, you will need a timer and the Online Tile Kit or Paper Letter Tiles. If students need to complete Word Work activity 5, create a second set of sight word cards for the words *mother, father,* and *only*.

ONLINE   Student & Computer

Students will work online to complete Warm-Up, Code Work, Word Work, and Speed Work activities, and a Wrap-Up assessment on their own. Be sure to read the Performance Review before beginning the offline portion of today's lesson.

Today you will work with students to complete Code Work, Word Work, and GUM activities. Be sure to read the online Performance Review before beginning the Code Work and Word Work activities.

Warm-Up

Life in Ancient Egypt

Look at the Performance Review. If the student achieved a perfect score on today's Warm-Up, move on to Code Work. If the student scored 60 percent or 80 percent, print the story and review the comprehension questions with the student. If the student scored less than 60 percent, print the story, have the student read the story aloud, and then work through the comprehension questions together, before moving on to Code Work.

Code Work

ea Spells Short e

Look at the Performance Review. If the student achieved a perfect score on today's Code Work activities, complete the first two activities from the list below. If the student scored less than 100 percent but more than 85 percent, complete the first three activities from the list below. If the student scored 85 percent or less, complete all four of the activities listed below.

1. Have students complete page 153 in *MARK¹² Reading Activity Book* for more practice on the letters *ea* making the sound /ĕ/.

2. Have students use the Online Tile Kit or Paper Letter Tiles to spell the following words: *bread, dead, head, spread, thread,* and *wealth.*

3. Ask students to choose two of the words from activity 2 to draw for you. Students should neither tell you which word they are drawing, nor make any sounds or gestures to help you figure out the word. Once you guess the correct word, have students write that word under the picture. If time permits, switch roles.

4. On a piece of paper, have students write sentences using three words from activity 2. Then have students read the sentences aloud.

Code Work Name: _____

Difficult Spellings & r-Controlled Vowels and Sight Words 6

Complete the Sentence

Read each word in the box aloud. Choose the word from the box that best completes each sentence. Write each word on the lines provided. Then read each sentence aloud.
Hint: One word is used twice.

| bread | breath | dealt | head | meant | thread |

1. I can **thread** _____ the needle.
2. Mom **meant** _____ what she said.
3. I like peanut butter on my **bread** _____ .
4. This **thread** _____ is perfect for my shirt.
5. He **dealt** _____ the cards so we could play the game.
6. Dad stopped to catch his **breath** _____ during our jog.
7. She was careful not to hit her **head** _____ as she got into the car.

153

Word Work

Sight Words

Look at the Performance Review. If the student achieved a perfect score on today's Word Work activities, complete the first activity from the list below. If the student scored less than 100 percent but more than 85 percent, complete the first three activities from the list below. If the student scored less than 85 percent or less, complete all five of the activities listed below.

Objectives

- Read sight words.
- Increase reading vocabulary.

1. Have students complete page 154 in *MARK¹² Reading Activity Book* for more practice on sight words. As students read the sight words, keep track of how many are read correctly with a timer.

2. Using the sight word cards you created for *mother, father,* and *only,* read each word to students and have students write the word on a piece of paper. Give students the sight words, and instruct students to look for any spelling mistakes. Students should correct the mistakes and then read the list of words aloud.

3. Gather all of the sight word cards students have worked on to date and a timer. Have students read all of the sight word cards as accurately and quickly as possible. Make note of the time, as well as any errors students have made. Use the Online Tile Kit or Paper Letter Tiles to review words read incorrectly.

4. Gather the cards for the sight words *mother, father,* and *only,* and up to two additional sight words students have yet to master. Show the first card to students, and ask students to read the word. If students read the word correctly, place in one pile. If students read the word incorrectly, place in a separate pile. On the back of the cards that were read correctly, make a note of the date and put aside. (Once students have read the word correctly five consecutive days, you can remove the word from the pile of cards students are working on.) Review any words students read incorrectly, and keep the cards for next time.

5. Gather the two sets of cards for the sight words *mother, father,* and *only,* and place the cards face down. Have students choose a card, read the word aloud, and then choose a second card. After students read the second card aloud, if the two cards match, students should keep the cards. If they do not match, students should return them to the table. Continue until all cards are collected.

Speed Work

The Drip

Look at the Performance Review, or check the student's fluency chart. Fluency scores (words read per minute) should not fall below 80. If the student scored below 80 words per minute, print a copy of the Speed Work story and have the student read the story silently before reading it aloud. Otherwise, move on to Grammar, Usage, and Mechanics.

Objectives

- Increase reading fluency rate.

Bring, Buy, Come, Go, Eat, See, Sit, Take, and *Write*

Verbs in English have four principal forms: present, present participle, past, and past participle. The past and past participle forms of irregular verbs must be memorized because they do not follow any rules.

present:	bring	buy	come	eat
present participle:	bringing	buying	coming	eating
past:	brought	bought	came	ate
past participle:	brought	bought	come	eaten

Work with students to complete pages 155 and 156 in *MARK¹² Reading Activity Book.* Read page 155, Get Ready, with students. Have students complete the Try It page. Be sure to discuss students' answers with them after they complete the page.

Objectives

• Correctly use *bring, buy, come, go, eat, see, sit, take,* and *write.*

G U M Grammar, Usage, and Mechanics   Name:

Difficult Spellings & r-Controlled Vowels and Sight Words 6

Get Ready

☞ Verbs in English have four principal forms:

1. Present
2. Present participle (uses helping verbs *is, am, are, was, were*)
3. Past
4. Past participle (uses helping verbs *has, have, had*)

You form the past and past participle of a regular verb by adding *–d* or *–ed*. For example, *walk* becomes *walked*. However, you just have to learn the past and past participle forms of irregular verbs because—well, because they're not regular!

☞ Study the principal forms of the following *irregular* verbs:

Present	Present Participle	Past	Past Participle
bring	bringing	brought	brought
buy	buying	bought	bought
come	coming	came	come
eat	eating	ate	eaten
go	going	went	gone
see	seeing	saw	seen
sit	sitting	sat	sat
take	taking	took	taken
write	writing	wrote	written

Look at the present participle *bringing*. Read the sentence:

I bringing my dog to the beach.

What is missing in the sentence?

A helping verb is missing, such as *am, is, are, was,* or *were*. The sentence should say:

I *am* bringing my dog to the beach.

155

G U M Grammar, Usage, and Mechanics   Name:

Difficult Spellings & r-Controlled Vowels and Sight Words 6

Try It

On the lines provided, write the correct form of the irregular verbs to complete each sentence. Include the right kind of helping verb for participles. An example has been done for you.

Example: present, *sit*
   Jim __sits__ on the floor.

1. past, *bring*
   Anne __brought__ her dog to my house.

2. past, *buy*
   I __bought__ a sandwich for lunch.

3. present participle, come
   My grandparents __are coming__ to my soccer game today.

4. past participle, *eat*
   I __have eaten__ twice this afternoon but I am still hungry.

5. present, *go*
   Let's __go__ to the park.

6. past participle, *see*
   I know I __have seen__ that girl before, I just cannot remember where.

7. past participle, *take*
   It __has taken__ a long time to get here.

8. present participle, *write*
   The note __was written/__ in a secret code.
       __is written__

156

Difficult Spellings & r-Controlled Vowels and Sight Words 7

ONLINE	Student & Computer	:60 minutes
	Adult : *Check Performance Review*	
OFFLINE	Student & Adult : Review online work	:30 minutes
	• Reading Warm-Up	
	• Speed Work	
	• Assessment	
	Classics Session 1	:30 minutes
	Instructional Time **2:00** hours	

Materials

- *MARK¹² Classics for Young Readers*
- *MARK¹² Reading Activity Book*, pages 157–160

Goals

In this lesson, students will read about King Tut. Students will also work with the letters *ea* making the sound /ĕ/ before working with the sight words *mother, father,* and *only.* In today's Unit Assessment, you will administer a test covering all content from Unit 9. Afterward, you will also work with students to complete Classics activities.

ONLINE	Student & Computer

Students will work online to complete Warm-Up, Code Work, Word Work, and Speed Work activities, and a review game on their own. Be sure to read the Performance Review before beginning the offline portion of today's lesson.

Today you will administer a Unit Assessment and work with students to complete a *MARK¹² Classics for Young Readers* activity.

Warm-Up ·

King Tut

Look at the Performance Review. If the student achieved a perfect score on today's Warm-Up, move on to Speed Work. If the student scored 60 percent or 80 percent, print the story and review the comprehension questions with the student. If the student scored less than 60 percent, print the story, have the student read the story aloud, and then work through the comprehension questions together, before moving on to Speed Work.

Objectives

• Improve reading and comprehension skills.

Speed Work ·

Liz the Lizard

Look at the Performance Review, or check the student's fluency chart. Fluency scores (words read per minute) should not fall below 80. If the student scored below 80 words per minute, print a copy of the Speed Work story and have the student read the story silently before reading it aloud to you. Otherwise, move on to the Assessment.

Objectives

• Increase reading fluency rate.

☼ Assessment ·

Difficult Spellings & r-Controlled Vowels and Sight Words

Today's Unit Assessment covers all content found in Unit 9. Carefully read the instructions on the student pages before administering the test to the student. If necessary, read the directions to the student. After you have scored the student's assessment, be sure to go online and enter student performance scores in the assessment entry tool

Part 1. Dictate the following sounds to students: /er/, /ĕ/, /or/, /er/, /ar/, /er/, /f/, /er/, /ar/, and /ĕ/.

Part 2. Dictate the following words to students: *graph, porch, twice, smart, phone, weather, arch, age, storm,* and *bread.*

Part 5. Dictate the following words to students: *after, begin, down, father, goes, know, laugh, mother, next, only, anything,* and *friend.*

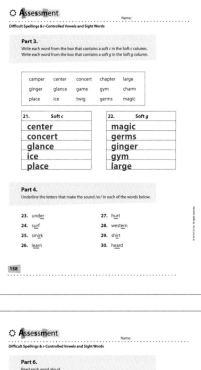

Assessment

Name: ....

Difficult Spellings & r-Controlled Vowels and Sight Words

Unit 9 Assessment

Part 1.
Listen to each sound that is read to you. Underline the letters that make each sound.
Hint: You will underline more than one pair of letters for some sounds.

1.	<u>ear</u>	<u>er</u>	<u>ir</u>	ph	6.	ea	ph	<u>ur</u>	<u>ear</u>
2.	<u>ea</u>	or	ph	ur	7.	er	ir	or	<u>ph</u>
3.	ar	<u>or</u>	er	ir	8.	<u>ur</u>	<u>er</u>	ea	<u>ir</u>
4.	ea	ear	<u>ur</u>	<u>ir</u>	9.	<u>ar</u>	ur	or	er
5.	ea	ear	ur	<u>ar</u>	10.	ar	<u>ea</u>	or	er

Part 2.
Listen to each word that is read to you. Write each word on the lines provided.

11. **graph**
12. **porch**
13. **twice**
14. **smart**
15. **phone**
16. **weather**
17. **arch**
18. **age**
19. **storm**
20. **bread**

157

Assessment

Name: ....

Difficult Spellings & r-Controlled Vowels and Sight Words

Part 3.
Write each word from the box that contains a soft c in the Soft c column.
Write each word from the box that contains a soft g in the Soft g column.

camper	center	concert	chapter	large
ginger	glance	game	gym	charm
place	ice	twig	germs	magic

21.	Soft c	22.	Soft g
center		magic	
concert		germs	
glance		ginger	
ice		gym	
place		large	

Part 4.
Underline the letters that make the sound /er/ in each of the words below.

23.	und<u>er</u>	27.	h<u>ur</u>t
24.	s<u>ur</u>f	28.	w<u>es</u>tern
25.	sm<u>ir</u>k	29.	sh<u>ir</u>t
26.	l<u>ear</u>n	30.	h<u>ear</u>d

158

Assessment

Name: ....

Difficult Spellings & r-Controlled Vowels and Sight Words

Part 5.
In each row, underline the word that is read to you.

31.	<u>after</u>	again	anything
32.	<u>begin</u>	both	breath
33.	dirt	does	<u>down</u>
34.	farm	<u>father</u>	friend
35.	gather	get	<u>goes</u>
36.	kept	kiss	<u>know</u>
37.	lace	lamp	<u>laugh</u>
38.	made	<u>mother</u>	my
39.	napkin	<u>next</u>	nut
40.	on	one	<u>only</u>
41.	again	<u>anything</u>	are
42.	frame	<u>friend</u>	from

159

Assessment

Name: ....

Difficult Spellings & r-Controlled Vowels and Sight Words

Part 6.
Read each word aloud.

43. anything
44. only
45. next
46. mother
47. laugh
48. know
49. goes
50. friend
51. father
52. down
53. begin
54. after

160

Objectives

- Identify and use *ph* for the sound /f/, *c* for the sound /s/, and *g* for the sound /j/.
- Identify and use *–ar, –er, –ir, –or, –ur,* and *–ear*.
- Identify and use *e* and *ea* for the sound of / ĕ/.

Classics Session 1 ....

Daniel Webster's First Case

Today's story, "Daniel Webster's First Case," is about the lawyer Daniel Webster's first case that took place when he was 10 years old. Review the keywords with students. Read the story with students, and then use the Discussion Questions below as a guide to share ideas about the story. Have students read the story again before writing a summary of the story.

Objectives

- Improve reading and comprehension skills.

Keywords

pity, n. – a feeling of sadness for the suffering of another person or creature
I feel **pity** for the cats and dogs at the animal shelter because they do not have special homes and humans of their own.

cruel, adj. – mean or hurtful
It's **cruel** to tease or make fun of others.

plenty, n. – a lot; more than enough
When I asked if my friend could join us for dinner, my mother replied, "Of course, we have **plenty** of food for everyone."

tremble, v. – to shake with fear
I **trembled** as the giant shadow came closer and closer.

Discussion Questions

1. What are the main points of Zeke's argument to kill the woodchuck? What are the main points of Daniel's argument to let the woodchuck go? Whose argument do you think is more convincing? Why? Answers may include that Zeke's argument was that the woodchuck would keep eating their vegetables. Skinning it may get back some of the money it cost the family. Daniel's argument was that the woodchuck ate only what it needed. It has a right to life, food, and freedom.

2. Daniel was scared for a moment because he thought his brother had won the case. What do you think made him feel this way? Answers may include that Zeke spoke well, and Mr. Webster thought Zeke was right.

3. What decision did Mr. Webster make about the woodchuck's fate? Do you think it was the right decision? Explain your answer. Answers may include that Mr. Webster decided to let the woodchuck go.

4. Daniel pitied the woodchuck. Have you ever pitied something? Describe the situation. What did you do about it? Answers will vary

5. Daniel Webster grew up to be a great lawyer and speaker. Do you think he remembered his first case? Do you think his first case affected his decision to become a lawyer? Explain your answer. Answers will vary.

Students should write a summary of the story to complete today's Classics activity.

oi/oy and Sight Words 1

ONLINE	Student & Computer	:60 minutes
	Adult : *Check Performance Review*	
OFFLINE	Student & Adult : Review online work	:30 minutes
	• Reading Warm-Up	
	• Code Work	
	• Word Work	
	• Speed Work	
	Classics Session 2	:30 minutes
	Instructional Time	**2:00** hours

Materials

- *MARK¹² Classics for Young Readers*
- **Magazine**
- *MARK¹² Reading Activity Book*, pages 161–162

Tip

*Explain to students that, even though the /oi/ sound is made up of two letters (**o-i** or **o-y**), the two vowels make one vowel sound. Typically, the letters **oi** are found in the middle of a word or syllable and the letters **oy** are found at the end of a word or syllable.*

Goals

In this lesson, students will read about life in ancient Greece. Students will also be introduced to two spellings of the vowel sound /oi/ (*oi* and *oy*) before learning the sight words *even, look,* and *gone.* In today's *MARK¹² Reading Activity Book* pages, you will work with students to spell words with the /oi/ sound and explore the sight words *even, look,* and *gone.*

Advance Preparation

Based on the Performance Review, if students need to complete Code Work Activity 3, gather six index cards and write each of the following words on the cards, one word per card: *coin, foil, point, boy, joy,* and *Roy.* If students need to complete Code Work activity 5, you will need the Online Tile Kit or Paper Letter Tiles. If students must complete Word Work activity 2, create sight word cards for the following words: *even, look,* and *gone.* If students need to complete Word Work activity 3, you will need a timer and the Online Tile Kit or Paper Letter Tiles. If students need to complete Word Work activity 5, create a second set of sight word cards for the words *even, look,* and *gone.*

ONLINE Student & Computer

Students will work online to complete Warm-Up, Code Work, Word Work, and Speed Work activities, and a Wrap-Up assessment on their own. Be sure to read the Performance Review before beginning the offline portion of today's lesson.

Today you will work with students to complete Code Work, Word Work, and *MARK¹² Classics for Young Readers* activities. Be sure to read the online Performance Review before beginning the Code Work and Word Work activities.

Warm-Up •

Life in Ancient Greece

Look at the Performance Review. If the student achieved a perfect score on today's Warm-Up, move on to Code Work. If the student scored 60 percent or 80 percent, print the story and review the comprehension questions with the student. If the student scored less than 60 percent, print the story, have the student read the story aloud, and then work through the comprehension questions together, before moving on to Code Work.

Code Work •

oi/oy

Look at the Performance Review. If the student achieved a perfect score on today's Code Work activities, complete the first two activities from the list below. If the student scored less than 100 percent but more than 85 percent, complete the first three activities from the list below. If the student scored 85 percent or less, complete all five of the activities listed below.

1. Have students complete page 161 in *MARK¹² Reading Activity Book* for more practice on the two spellings of the vowel sound /oi/.

2. Using the magazine you gathered, have students spend a few minutes searching for words that contain the /oi/ sound. Make a chart with two headings: *oi* and *oy*. As students suggest words, write them in the column under the correct heading. Keep this chart available to students after the lesson. Whenever students encounter a word with the sound /oi/ spelled *oi* or *oy*, have them write the word on the chart in the correct column.

3. Gather the six index cards you previously prepared. Randomly select and then read one card (do not show the card to students). Ask students to identify the spelling of the vowel sound /oi/ contained in the word (either *oi* or *oy*). Continue for all six cards.

4. Using the index cards from activity 3, randomly select and then hold up one card. Have students say the word and then verbally use it in a sentence. Continue for all six cards.

5. Have students use the Online Tile Kit or Paper Letter Tiles to build the following words: *boil, coin, foil, joy, oil, point,* and *toy*.

Code Work   Name: _____

oi/oy and Sight Words 1

Spell the Sound

Underline the letters that spell the vowel sound that completes each word. Then write each word on the lines provided. An example has been done for you.

Example: b___l	oi	oy	boil
1. t___	oi	oy	toy
2. f___l	oi	oy	foil
3. b___	oi	oy	boy
4. R___	oi	oy	Roy
5. c___n	oi	oy	coin
6. p___nt	oi	oy	point
7. j___	oi	oy	joy
8. ___l	oi	oy	oil

161

Word Work

・・・・・・・・・・・・・・・・・・・・・・・・

Sight Words

Look at the Performance Review. If the student achieved a perfect score on today's Word Work activities, complete the first activity from the list below. If the student scored less than 100 percent but more than 85 percent, complete the first three activities from the list below. If the student scored 85 percent or less, complete all five of the activities listed below.

1. Have students complete page 162 in *MARK¹² Reading Activity Book* for more practice on sight words.

2. Using the sight word cards you created for *even, look,* and *gone,* read each word to students and have students write the word on a piece of paper. Give students the sight words, and instruct students to look for any spelling mistakes they may have made. Students should correct the mistakes and then read the list of words aloud.

3. Gather all of the sight word cards students have worked on to date and a timer. Have students read all of the sight word cards as accurately and quickly as possible. Make note of the time, as well as any errors students have made. Use the Online Tile Kit or Paper Letter Tiles to review words read incorrectly.

4. Gather the cards for the sight words *even, look,* and *gone,* and up to two additional sight words students have yet to master. Show the first card to students, and ask students to read the word. If students read the word correctly, place in one pile. If students read the word incorrectly, place in a separate pile. On the back of the cards that were read correctly, make a note of the date and put aside. (Once students have read the word correctly five consecutive days, you can remove the word from the pile of cards students are working on.) Review any words students read incorrectly, and keep the cards for next time.

5. Gather the two sets of sight word cards for the words *even, look,* and *gone,* and place all of the cards face down on the table or another flat surface. Have students choose a card, read the word aloud, and then choose a second card. After students read the second card aloud, if the two cards match, students should keep the cards. If they do not match, students should return them to the table. Continue until all of the cards have been collected.

Word Work sample worksheet

Word Work   Name:

oi/oy and Sight Words 1

Complete the Sentence

Choose the sight words from the box that best complete each sentence. Write the words on the lines provided. Then read each sentence aloud.

| even | mother | gone | look | father | only |

1. There is **only** one hot dog left on the grill.
2. The number six is an **even** number.
3. My **mother** went to shop for a new skirt.
4. All the cake was **gone** by the time I got to the party.
5. Help me **look** for my lost cat!
6. Ted's **father** is a fireman.

Choose two words from the box above. On the lines provided, write each word in a sentence.

7. **Sentences will vary.**

8. _____

162

Speed Work

・・・・・・・・・・・・・・・・・・・・・・・・

Lunch with Dad

Look at the Performance Review, or check the student's fluency chart. Fluency scores (words read per minute) should not fall below 80. If the student scored below 80 words per minute, print a copy of the Speed Work story and have the student read the story silently before reading it aloud. Otherwise, move on to Classics Session 2.

Classics Session 2

Daniel Webster's First Case

Review the key words with students. Have students reread the story on their own. After rereading the story, students should complete the comprehension questions in *MARK¹² Classics for Young Readers* book on their own. Afterward, if time allows, have students read the story aloud to you.

Write

Daniel Webster's First Case

1. What was Daniel Webster's occupation?

   A. judge
   B. lawyer
   C. zookeeper
   D. veterinarian

2. Why does Zeke trap the woodchuck?

   A. Zeke wanted to keep the woodchuck as a pet.
   B. The woodchuck was making a mess in the garden.
   C. The woodchuck was stealing corn from the garden.
   D. Zeke wanted to bring the woodchuck to school for show-and-tell.

3. Zeke and Daniel cannot agree about what to do with the woodchuck. How is this problem solved?

   Their father acts as a judge and makes the final decision.

4. Based on information from the story, which words best describe Daniel?

   A. shy and weak
   B. bold and clever
   C. cruel and selfish
   D. kind and thoughtful

52   Daniel Webster's First Case

---

5. How does Zeke think the woodchuck should pay for what it's done?

   Zeke thinks the woodchuck should die and its skin should be sold.

6. List two rights that Daniel says the woodchuck has.

   Daniel says the woodchuck has the right to life, food, freedom, and sunshine.

7. What animal does Daniel compare the woodchuck to?

   A. dog
   B. fox
   C. wolf
   D. beaver

8. Why does Mr. Webster's voice shake when he tells his sons to let the woodchuck go?

   Mr. Webster is touched by Daniel's argument and is crying as he speaks.

Daniel Webster's First Case   53

---

oi/oy and Sight Words 2

ONLINE	Student & Computer	:60 minutes
	Adult : *Check Performance Review*	
OFFLINE	Student & Adult : Review online work	:30 minutes
	• Reading Warm-Up	
	• Speed Work	
	• Assessment	
	Composition	:30 minutes
	Instructional Time **2:00** hours	

Materials

- *MARK[12] Reading Activity Book*, pages 163–166
- *Just Write*

Goals

In this lesson, students will read about a child who lives in old Norway. Students will also continue learning about the vowel sound /oi/ before reviewing the sight words *even*, *look*, and *gone*. In today's Unit Assessment, you will administer a test covering all content from Unit 10. Afterward, you will work with students to complete composition activities.

Advance Preparation

For the offline portion of today's lesson, gather the students' composition materials.

ONLINE	Student & Computer

Students will work online to complete Warm-Up, Code Work, Word Work, and Speed Work activities, and a review game on their own. Be sure to read the Performance Review before beginning the offline portion of today's lesson.

Today you will administer a Unit Assessment and work with students to complete a Composition activity.

Warm-Up  •

Life in Old Norway

Look at the Performance Review. If the student achieved a perfect score on today's Warm-Up, move on to Speed Work. If the student scored 60 percent or 80 percent, print the story and review the comprehension questions with the student. If the student scored less than 60 percent, print the story, have the student read the story aloud, and then work through the comprehension questions together, before moving on to Speed Work.

Objectives

• Improve reading and comprehension skills.

Speed Work  •

Cowboy Roy

Look at the Performance Review, or check the student's fluency chart. Fluency scores (words read per minute) should not fall below 80. If the student scored below 80 words per minute, print a copy of the Speed Work story and have the student read the story silently before reading it aloud to you. Otherwise, move on to the Assessment.

Objectives

• Increase reading fluency rate.

☼ Assessment 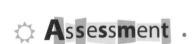 •

oi/oy and Sight Words

Today's Unit Assessment covers all content found in Unit 10. Carefully read the instructions on the student pages before administering the test to the student. If necessary, read the directions to the student. After you have scored the student's assessment, be sure to go online and enter student performance scores in the assessment entry tool.

Part 1. Dictate the following words to students: *coin, boy, look, join, gone, toy, boil, even, joy,* and *spoil.*

Part 2. Dictate the following words to students: *even, point, spoil, look, soil, gone, joint, voice, Roy,* and *coin.*

Part 3. Dictate the following words to students: *look, soil, even, gone, foil,* and *toy.*

Part 4. Dictate the following sentences to students:
> *There was an oyster on the sand.*
> *Hal dropped the oil can.*
> *I enjoy this song.*
> *Gus put a coin in the tin bank.*

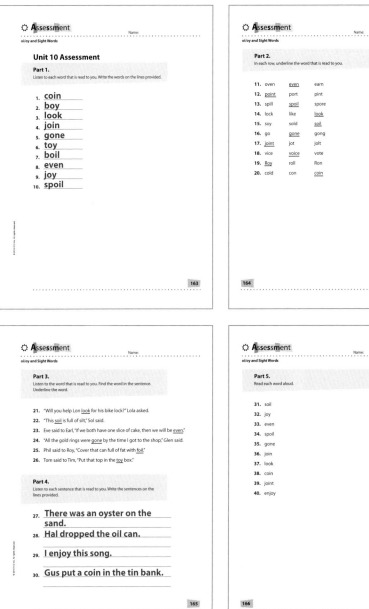

Unit 10 Assessment

Part 1.

Listen to each word that is read to you. Write the words on the lines provided.

1. coin
2. boy
3. look
4. join
5. gone
6. toy
7. boil
8. even
9. joy
10. spoil

163

Part 2.

In each row, underline the word that is read to you.

11.	oven	<u>even</u>	earn
12.	<u>point</u>	port	pint
13.	spill	<u>spoil</u>	spore
14.	lock	like	<u>look</u>
15.	soy	sold	<u>soil</u>
16.	go	<u>gone</u>	gong
17.	<u>joint</u>	jot	jolt
18.	vice	<u>voice</u>	vote
19.	<u>Roy</u>	roll	Ron
20.	cold	con	<u>coin</u>

164

Part 3.

Listen to the word that is read to you. Find the word in the sentence.
Underline the word.

21. "Will you help Lon <u>look</u> for his bike lock?" Lola asked.
22. "This <u>soil</u> is full of silt," Sol said.
23. Eve said to Earl, "If we both have one slice of cake, then we will be <u>even</u>."
24. "All the gold rings were <u>gone</u> by the time I got to the shop," Glen said.
25. Phil said to Roy, "Cover that can full of fat with <u>foil</u>."
26. Tom said to Tim, "Put that top in the <u>toy</u> box."

Part 4.

Listen to each sentence that is read to you. Write the sentences on the
lines provided.

27. There was an oyster on the sand.
28. Hal dropped the oil can.
29. I enjoy this song.
30. Gus put a coin in the tin bank.

165

Part 5.

Read each word aloud.

31. soil
32. joy
33. even
34. spoil
35. gone
36. join
37. look
38. coin
39. joint
40. enjoy

166

Objectives

- Identify and use *oi* and *oy* spelling patterns.
- Increase reading vocabulary.
- Read sight words.

....

Gather students' composition materials and begin where they left off.

au/aw and Sight Words 1

ONLINE	Student & Computer	**:60** minutes	
	Adult : *Check Performance Review*		
OFFLINE	Student & Adult : Review online work	**:30** minutes	
	• Reading Warm-Up		
	• Code Work		
	• Word Work		
	• Speed Work		
	Grammar, Usage, and Mechanics (GUM)	**:30** minutes	
	Instructional Time **2:00** hours		

Materials

- **Online Tile Kit or Paper Letter Tiles**
- *MARK[12] Reading Activity Book*, pages 167–170
- **Magazine**

Goals

In this lesson, students will read about family life in Mexico 500 years ago. Students will also be introduced to the spellings *au* and *aw* for the vowel sound /aw/ before learning the sight words *love, very,* and *some*. In today's *MARK[12] Reading Activity Book* pages, you will work with students to sort words with *au* and *aw* spelling patterns as well as to identify the missing letter in sight words.

Advance Preparation

Based on the Performance Review, if students need to complete Code Work activity 4, you will need to gather 10 index cards. On each card, write one of the following words: *fault, haul, sauce, taunt, taut, crawl, lawn, paw, straw,* and *yawn*. If students must complete Word Work activity 2, create sight word cards for the following words: *love, very,* and *some*. If students need to complete Word Work activity 3, you will need a timer and the Online Tile Kit or Paper Letter Tiles. If students need to complete Word Work activity 5, create a second set of sight word cards for the words *love, very,* and *some*.

(Tip) *Explain to students that the vowel sound /**aw**/ (**saw**) is similar to, but not quite the same as, the sound of the short o (**sob**). Use this as an example of how knowing the correct spelling of a word is essential to reading and writing.*

ONLINE	**Student & Computer**

Students will work online to complete Warm-Up, Code Work, Word Work, and Speed Work activities, and a Wrap-Up assessment on their own. Be sure to read the Performance Review before beginning the offline portion of today's lesson.

Today you will work with students to complete Code Work, Word Work, and GUM activities. Be sure to read the online Performance Review before beginning the Code Work and Word Work activities.

Warm-Up  •

Mexico Long Ago

Look at the Performance Review. If the student achieved a perfect score on today's Warm-Up, move on to Code Work. If the student scored 60 percent or 80 percent, print the story and review the comprehension questions with the student. If the student scored less than 60 percent, print the story, have the student read the story aloud, and then work through the comprehension questions together, before moving on to Code Work.

Code Work  • • • • • • • • • • • • • • • • • •

au/aw

Look at the Performance Review. If the student achieved a perfect score on today's Code Work activities, complete the first two activities from the list below. If the student scored less than 100 percent but more than 85 percent, complete the first three activities from the list below. If the student scored 85 percent or less, complete all five of the activities listed below.

1. Have students complete page 167 in *MARK¹² Reading Activity Book* for more practice on words with *au* and *aw* spelling patterns.

2. Using the magazine you gathered, have students spend a few minutes searching for words that contain the /aw/ sound. Make a chart with two headings: *au, aw*. As students suggest words, write them in the column under the correct heading. Keep this chart available to students after the lesson. Whenever students encounter a word with the sound /aw/ spelled *au* or *aw,* have them write the word on the chart.

3. Using the Online Tile Kit or Paper Letter Tiles, have students build the following words: *haunted, sauce, launch, awful, caw,* and *lawn.*

4. Gather and shuffle the 10 index cards that you prepared previously and spread them out face down. Have students randomly flip over one card and read it aloud, and then flip over a second card and do the same. If the two cards contain words with the same spelling of the vowel sound /aw/, students collect the cards. If they do not match, students replace the cards exactly where they were. Continue until all cards are collected.

5. Gather the 10 index cards from activity 4. Hold up a card and have students verbally use the word in a sentence. Continue with all cards.

Code Work   Name:

au/aw and Sight Words 1

Sort the Words

The vowel sound /aw/ can be spelled *au* or *aw*. Write the words from the box in the correct columns below according to how the sound /aw/ is spelled.

taut	lawn	August	awful	launch
author	sauce	yawn	straw	claw
fawn	crawl	haul	hawk	haunted

au	aw
taut	fawn
author	lawn
sauce	crawl
August	yawn
haul	awful
launch	straw
haunted	hawk
	claw

Choose one *au* word and one *aw* word from the box above. On the lines provided, write each word in a sentence.

1. Sentences will vary _____
2. _____

167

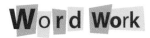ord Work

Sight Words

Look at the Performance Review. If the student achieved a perfect score on today's Word Work activities, complete the first activity from the list below. If the student scored less than 100 percent but more than 85 percent, complete the first three activities from the list below. If the student scored 85 percent or less, complete all five of the activities listed below.

1. Have students complete page 168 in *MARK¹² Reading Activity Book* for more practice on sight words.

2. Using the sight word cards you created for *love, very,* and *some,* read each word to students and have students write the word on a piece of paper. Give students the sight words, and instruct students to look for any spelling mistakes they may have made. Students should correct the mistakes and then read the list of words aloud.

3. Gather all of the sight word cards students have worked on to date and a timer. Have students read all of the sight word cards as accurately and quickly as possible. Make note of the time, as well as any errors students have made. Use the Online Tile Kit or Paper Letter Tiles to review words read incorrectly.

4. Gather the cards for the sight words *love, very,* and *some,* and up to two additional sight words students have yet to master. Show the first card to students, and ask students to read the word. If students read the word correctly, place in one pile. If students read the word incorrectly, place in a separate pile. On the back of the cards that were read correctly, make a note of the date and put aside. (Once students have read the word correctly five consecutive days, you can remove the word from the pile of cards students are working on.) Review any words students read incorrectly, and keep the cards for next time.

5. Gather the two sets of sight word cards for the words *love, very,* and *some,* and place all of the cards face down on the table or another flat surface. Have students choose a card, read the word aloud, and then choose a second card. After students read the second card aloud, if the two cards match, students should keep the cards. If they do not match, students should return them to the table. Continue until all of the cards have been collected.

Word Work — *au/aw and Sight Words 1*   Name: _____

Spell It!
In each row, underline the letter that completes the word. Write the full word on the line provided. Then read each word aloud.

1. d_es	e	o	a	**does**
2. ver_	t	e	y	**very**
3. do_n	w	r	l	**down**
4. f_ther	o	a	e	**father**
5. so_e	m	s	n	**some**
6. b_gin	i	a	e	**begin**
7. _ove	h	b	l	**love**
8. a_ter	n	f	r	**after**
9. lo_k	o	i	n	**look**
10. _nly	a	o	e	**only**

168

Speed Work

Pets

Look at the Performance Review, or check the student's fluency chart. Fluency scores (words read per minute) should not fall below 80. If the student scored below 80 words per minute, print a copy of the Speed Work story and have the student read the story silently before reading it aloud. Otherwise, move on to Grammar, Usage, and Mechanics.

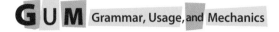

GUM Grammar, Usage, and Mechanics •

Regular and Irregular Verbs

The past and past participle forms of *regular* verbs are *–d* or *–ed*.

> I *love*. I *loved*. I *have loved*.
> I *walk* home. I *walked* home. I *have walked* home.

The past and past participle forms of *irregular* verbs do **not** end in *–d* or *–ed*.

> I *sing*. I *sang*. I *have sung*.
> I *am* sad. I *was* sad. I *have been* sad.

Work with students to complete pages 169 and 170 in *MARK¹² Reading Activity Book*. Read page 169, Get Ready, with students. Have students complete the Try It page. Be sure to discuss students' answers when the page is completed.

GUM Grammar, Usage, and Mechanics   Name:
au/aw and Sight Words 1

Get Ready

■ The regular ending for past and past participle verbs is -d or -ed. For example:

  I *fill* the glass. (present)
  I *filled* the glass. (past)
  I *have filled* the glass. (past participle)

■ Past and past participle forms of *irregular* verbs do not end in -d or -ed. For example:

  I *eat* an apple. (present)
  I *ate* an apple. (past)
  I *have eaten* an apple. (past participle)

■ Below is a list of common irregular verbs and their present, past, and past participle forms.

Present	Past	Past Participle
bring	brought	(have) brought
come	came	(have) come
do	did	(have) done
eat	ate	(have) eaten
give	gave	(have) given
go	went	(have) gone
is (am, are)	was (were)	(have) been
make	made	(have) made
see	saw	(have) seen
sit	sat	(have) sat
take	took	(have) taken
sing	sang	(have) sung

169

GUM Grammar, Usage, and Mechanics   Name:
au/aw and Sight Words 1

Try It

Write the missing forms of each regular or irregular verb on the lines provided.

	Present	Past	Past Participle
1.	walk	**walked**	(have) walked
2.	drip	dripped	(have) **dripped**
3.	see	**saw**	(have) seen
4.	**bake**	baked	(have) baked
5.	come	came	(have) **come**
6.	**sit**	sat	(have) sat
7.	give	**gave**	(have) given
8.	work	worked	(have) **worked**
9.	**take**	took	(have) taken
10.	walk	**walked**	(have) walked

170

---

au/aw and Sight Words 2

ONLINE	Student & Computer	**:60** minutes	
	Adult : *Check Performance Review*		
OFFLINE	Student & Adult : Review online work	**:30** minutes	
	• Reading Warm-Up		
	• Speed Work		
	• Assessment		
	Composition	**:30** minutes	
	Instructional Time **2:00** hours		

Materials

- *MARK[12] Reading Activity Book*, pages 171–174
- *Just Write*

Goals

In this lesson, students will read how the Lost Colony of Roanoke Island got its name. Students will also continue exploring the vowel spellings *a-u* and *a-w* before reviewing the sight words *love, very,* and *some.* In today's Unit Assessment, you will administer a test covering all content from Unit 11. Afterward, you will work with students on composition.

ONLINE	**Student & Computer**

Students will work online to complete Warm-Up, Code Work, Word Work, and Speed Work activities, and a review game on their own. Be sure to read the Performance Review before beginning the offline portion of today's lesson.

Today you will administer a Unit Assessment and work with students to complete a Composition activity.

Warm-Up

The Lost Colony

Look at the Performance Review. If the student achieved a perfect score on today's Warm-Up, move on to Speed Work. If the student scored 60 percent or 80 percent, print the story and review the comprehension questions with the student. If the student scored less than 60 percent, print the story, have the student read the story aloud, and then work through the comprehension questions together, before moving on to Speed Work.

Objectives

- Improve reading and comprehension skills.

Speed Work

Let's Draw!

Look at the Performance Review, or check the student's fluency chart. Fluency scores (words read per minute) should not fall below 80. If the student scored below 80 words per minute, print a copy of the Speed Work story and have the student read the story silently before reading it aloud to you. Otherwise, move on to the Assessment.

Objectives

- Increase reading fluency rate.

☼ Assessment

au/aw and Sight Words

Today's Unit Assessment covers all content found in Unit 11. Carefully read the instructions on the student pages before administering the test to the student. If necessary, read the directions to the student. After you have scored the student's assessment, be sure to go online and enter student performance scores in the assessment entry tool.

Part 1. Dictate the following words to students: *launch, claw, love, lawn, very, sauce, some, haul, awful,* and *paw.*

Part 2. Dictate the following words to students: *fault, law, awful, sauce,* and *yawn.*

Part 4. Dictate the following words to students: *straw, launch, love, awful, taut, haunted, very, crawl, hawk,* and *some.*

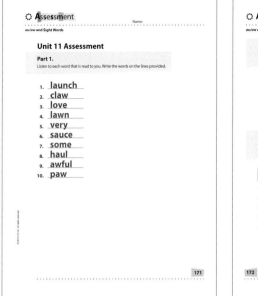

Unit 11 Assessment

Part 1.
Listen to each word that is read to you. Write the words on the lines provided.

1. launch
2. claw
3. love
4. lawn
5. very
6. sauce
7. some
8. haul
9. awful
10. paw

171

Part 2.
Listen to each word that is read to you. In each word, underline the letters that make the vowel sound in that word.

11. <u>au</u>   aw
12. <u>au</u>   aw
13. au   <u>aw</u>
14. <u>au</u>   aw
15. au   <u>aw</u>

Part 3.
Choose the word from the box that best completes each sentence. Write the words on the lines provided. Then read each sentence aloud.

| haunted | love | very | draw | fawn |

16. Jess likes to **draw** with a black ink pen.
17. "I **love** you so much!" the mother said to her child.
18. They say that the old cabin by the lake is **haunted**.
19. "That is a **very** old coin," the bank clerk said.
20. The **fawn** got lost in the forest.

172

Part 4.
In each row, underline the word that is read to you.

21. stall   <u>straw</u>   strong
22. lawn   lunch   <u>launch</u>
23. <u>love</u>   have   live
24. away   awning   <u>awful</u>
25. top   <u>taut</u>   trot
26. <u>haunted</u>   handed   hunted
27. ever   <u>very</u>   were
28. <u>crawl</u>   call   caw
29. hack   honk   <u>hawk</u>
30. Sam   <u>some</u>   sin

173

Part 5.
In each row, underline the letters that complete the word. Write the full word on the line provided. Then say the word aloud.

31. y__n   au   <u>aw</u>   **yawn**
32. cl__   au   <u>aw</u>   **claw**
33. f__lt   <u>au</u>   aw   **fault**
34. __ful   au   <u>aw</u>   **awful**
35. h__l   <u>au</u>   aw   **haul**
36. str__   au   <u>aw</u>   **straw**
37. __thor   <u>au</u>   aw   **author**
38. s__ce   <u>au</u>   aw   **sauce**
39. h__k   au   <u>aw</u>   **hawk**
40. __gust   <u>Au</u>   Aw   **August**

174

Objectives

- Identify and use *au* and *aw* spelling patterns.
- Increase reading vocabulary.
- Read sight words.

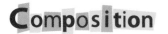omposition

Gather students' composition materials and begin where they left off.

ow/ou and Sight Words 1

ONLINE	Student & Computer	:60 minutes	
	Adult : *Check Performance Review*		
OFFLINE	Student & Adult : Review online work	:30 minutes	
	• Reading Warm-Up		
	• Code Work		
	• Word Work		
	• Speed Work		
	Classics Session 1	:30 minutes	

Instructional Time **2:00** hours

Materials

- *MARK¹² Classics for Young Readers*
- **"Flight Through the Sky"** MP3
- **Magazine**
- *MARK¹² Reading Activity Book*, pages 175–176

Goals

In this lesson, students will read about the colonial settlers in Jamestown, Virginia. Students will also learn about words that use the *ow* and *ou* spellings for the sound /ou/ before learning the sight words, *none, more,* and *held.* In today's *MARK¹² Reading Activity Book* pages, you will work with students on the *ou* and *ow* spellings of the sound /ou/, as well as sight words.

Advance Preparation

For the offline portion of today's lesson, download this story: "Flight Through the Sky." Based on the Performance Review, if students need to complete Code Work activity 3, access the Online Tile Kit or Paper Letter Tiles. If students must complete Word Work activity 2, create sight word cards for the following words: *none, more,* and *held.* If students need to complete Word Work activity 3, you will need a timer and the Online Tile Kit or Paper Letter Tiles. If students need to complete Word Work activity 5, create a second set of sight word cards for the words *none, more,* and *held.*

ONLINE   Student & Computer

Students will work online to complete Warm-Up, Code Work, Word Work, and Speed Work activities, and a Wrap-Up assessment on their own. Be sure to read the Performance Review before beginning the offline portion of today's lesson.

Today you will work with students to complete Code Work, Word Work, and *MARK¹² Classics for Young Readers* activities. Be sure to read the online Performance Review before beginning the Code Work and Word Work activities.

Warm-Up

A Jamestown Journal: The First Months

Look at the Performance Review. If the student achieved a perfect score on today's Warm-Up, move on to Code Work. If the student scored 60 percent or 80 percent, print the story and review the comprehension questions with the student. If the student scored less than 60 percent, print the story, have the student read the story aloud, and then work through the comprehension questions together, before moving on to Code Work.

Code Work

ow/ou

Look at the Performance Review. If the student achieved a perfect score on today's Code Work activities, complete the first two activities from the list below. If the student scored less than 100 percent but more than 85 percent, complete the first three activities from the list below. If the student scored 85 percent or less, complete all four of the activities listed below.

1. Have students complete page 175 in *MARK¹² Reading Activity Book* for more practice on reading and spelling the sound /ou/ with the letters *ow* and *ou*.

2. Using the magazine you gathered, have students spend a few minutes searching for words that contain the /ou/ sound. Make a chart with two headings: *ow* and *ou*. As students suggest words, write them in the column under the correct heading. Keep this chart available to students after the lesson. Whenever students encounter a word with the sound /ou/ spelled *ow* or *ou*, have them write the word on the chart in the correct column.

3. Have students use the Online Tile Kit or Paper Letter Tiles to spell the following words: *found, frown, brown, round, sound, down, shout, loud, aloud, around, ground,* and *towel.*

4. Have students choose two *ow* words and two *ou* words from activity 2 and say each word in a sentence.

Code Work   Name:
ow/ou and Sight Words 1

Spell It!

Write each word from the box in the correct column below according to how the sound /ou/ is spelled — *ow* or *ou*.

brown	round	mound	gown	frown
sound	plow	proud	aloud	how
cow	crouch	now	crowd	cloud
town	couch	found	towel	down
slouch	drown	clown	loud	grouch

ow		ou	
gown	town	mound	cloud
how	drown	aloud	couch
crowd	plow	loud	found
down	now	sound	slouch
brown	towel	crouch	round
frown	clown	grouch	
cow		proud	

175

Word Work ∙∙∙∙∙∙∙∙∙∙∙∙∙∙∙∙∙∙∙∙∙∙∙∙∙∙∙∙∙∙∙∙∙∙∙

Sight Words

Look at the Performance Review. If the student achieved a perfect score on today's Word Work activities, complete the first activity from the list below. If the student scored less than 100 percent but more than 85 percent, complete the first three activities from the list below. If the student scored 85 percent or less, complete all five of the activities listed below.

1. Have students complete page 176 in *MARK¹² Reading Activity Book* for more practice on sight words.

2. Using the sight word cards you created for *none, more,* and *held,* read each word to students and have students write the word on a piece of paper. Give students the sight words, and instruct students to look for any spelling mistakes they may have made. Students should correct the mistakes and then read the list of words aloud.

3. Gather all of the sight word cards students have worked on to date and a timer. Have students read all of the sight word cards as accurately and quickly as possible. Make note of the time, as well as any errors students have made. Use the Online Tile Kit or Paper Letter Tiles to review words read incorrectly.

4. Gather the cards for the sight words *none, more,* and *held,* and up to two additional sight words students have yet to master. Show the first card to students, and ask students to read the word. If students read the word correctly, place in one pile. If students read the word incorrectly, place in a separate pile. On the back of the cards that were read correctly, make a note of the date and put aside. (Once students have read the word correctly five consecutive days, you can remove the word from the pile of cards students are working on.) Review any words students read incorrectly, and keep the cards for next time.

5. Gather the two sets of sight word cards for the words *none, more,* and *held,* and place all of the cards face down on the table or another flat surface. Have students choose a card, read the word aloud, and then choose a second card. After students read the second card aloud, if the two cards match, students should keep the cards. If they do not match, students should return them to the table. Continue until all of the cards have been collected.

Speed Work ∙∙∙∙∙∙∙∙∙∙∙∙∙∙∙∙∙∙∙∙∙∙∙∙∙∙∙∙∙∙∙∙∙∙∙

What Is That Sound?

Look at the Performance Review, or check the student's fluency chart. Fluency scores (words read per minute) should not fall below 80. If the student scored below 80 words per minute, print a copy of the Speed Work story and have the student read the story silently before reading it aloud. Otherwise, move on to Classics Session 1.

Classics Session 1 ·

A Flight Through the Sky

Today's story, "A Flight Through the Sky," is an ancient Greek legend of Daedalus and his son Icarus who attempts to fly. Download the story. Have students listen to the story while following along in *MARK¹² Classics for Young Readers*. Have students listen to the story again before writing a summary of the story to complete the lesson.

ow/ou and Sight Words 2

ONLINE	Student & Computer	**:60** minutes	
	Adult : *Check Performance Review*		
OFFLINE	**Student & Adult : Review online work**	**:30** minutes	
	• Reading Warm-Up		
	• Code Work		
	• Word Work		
	• Speed Work		
	Classics Session 2	**:30** minutes	
	Instructional Time	**2:00** hours	

Materials

- *MARK¹² Classics for Young Readers*
- "A Flight Through The Sky" MP3
- Online Tile Kit or Paper Letter Tiles
- *MARK¹² Reading Activity Book,* pages 177–178

Goals

In this lesson, students will read about the colonial settlers in Jamestown, Virginia. Students will also review and practice the *ow* and *ou* spellings for the sound /ou/ before working with the sight words, *none, more,* and *held.* In today's *MARK¹² Reading Activity Book* pages, you will work with students to further practice the *ow* and *ou* spellings of the sound /ou/ and to practice sight words.

Advance Preparation

For the offline portion of today's lesson, download this story: "Flight Through the Sky." Based on the Performance Review, if students need to complete Code Work activity 3, gather eight index cards and write one of the following on each card: *do_n, clo_n, o_l, to_el, ro_nd, gro_nd, mo_se,* and *clo_d.* If students must complete Word Work activity 2, gather the sight word cards for the following words: *none, more,* and *held.* If students need to complete Word Work activity 3, you will need a timer and the Online Tile Kit or Paper Letter Tiles. If students need to complete Word Work activity 5, gather the second set of sight word cards for the words *none, more,* and *held.*

ONLINE   Student & Computer

Students will work online to complete Warm-Up, Code Work, Word Work, and Speed Work activities, and a Wrap-Up assessment on their own. Be sure to read the Performance Review before beginning the offline portion of today's lesson.

Today you will work with students to complete Code Work, Word Work, and *MARK¹² Classics for Young Readers* activities. Be sure to read the online Performance Review before beginning the Code Work and Word Work activities.

Warm-Up ·

A Jamestown Journal: Time Passes

Look at the Performance Review. If the student achieved a perfect score on today's Warm-Up, move on to Code Work. If the student scored 60 percent or 80 percent, print the story and review the comprehension questions with the student. If the student scored less than 60 percent, print the story, have the student read the story aloud, and then work through the comprehension questions together, before moving on to Code Work.

Objectives

- Improve reading and comprehension skills.

Code Work ·

ow/ou

Look at the Performance Review. If the student achieved a perfect score on today's Code Work activities, complete the first two activities from the list below. If the student scored less than 100 percent but more than 85 percent, complete the first three activities from the list below. If the student scored 85 percent or less, complete all five of the activities listed below.

Objectives

- Identify and use *ow* to spell the /ou/ sound.
- Identify and use *ou* to spell the /ou/ sound.

1. Have students complete page 177 in *MARK¹² Reading Activity Book* for more practice on recognizing and spelling the sound /ou/ with the letters *ow* and *ou*.

2. Have students use the Online Tile Kit or Paper LetterTiles to spell the following words: *cloud, mouse, down, drown, aloud, ouch, scowled, towel, clown, growl,* and *plow*.

3. Gather the eight index cards you previously prepared and spread them out face down. Have students turn over a card, supply the the correct letter that completes the word (*u* or *w*), and say the word aloud. If the student supplies the correct missing letter, the student keeps the card. If not, the card should be replaced. Play until all cards are collected.

4. Have students say as many words that contain the *ou* spelling of the sound /ou/ as they can in one minute. Repeat with words that contain the *ow* spelling of the sound /ou/.

5. Ask students to choose two *ou* words and two *ow* words from activity 3 and say each word in a sentence.

Code Work   Name: ____

ou/ow and Sight Words 2

Find the /ou/ Word

Read the sentences aloud. In each sentence, find the word that contains the sound /ou/. Write the word on the line provided. Then read the sentences aloud again.

1. There is a brand new park in my town.
   town

2. "Do not be a grouch or we will not be friends!"
   grouch

3. Let us be proud of our grand land!
   proud

4. Mr. Neff plants on his farm with a plow.
   plow

5. The crowd loved the rock band and its fun songs.
   crowd

6. The cat crouched near the bird that fell from its nest.
   crouched

7. Did the wedding gown have lots of lace?
   gown

8. At sunset, the clouds looked pink and red.
   clouds

177

Word Work

Sight Words

Look at the Performance Review. If the student achieved a perfect score on today's Word Work activities, complete the first activity from the list below. If the student scored less than 100 percent but more than 85 percent, complete the first three activities from the list below. If the student scored 85 percent or less, complete all five of the activities listed below.

1. Have students complete page 178 in *MARK¹² Reading Activity Book* for more practice on sight words.

2. Using the sight word cards you created for *none, more,* and *held,* read each word to students and have students write the word on a piece of paper. Give students the sight words, and instruct students to look for any spelling mistakes they may have made. Students should correct the mistakes and then read the list of words aloud.

3. Gather all of the sight word cards students have worked on to date and a timer. Have students read all of the sight word cards as accurately and quickly as possible. Make note of the time, as well as any errors students have made. Use the Online Tile Kit or Paper Letter Tiles to review words read incorrectly.

4. Gather the cards for the sight words *none, more,* and *held,* and up to two additional sight words students have yet to master. Show the first card to students, and ask students to read the word. If students read the word correctly, place in one pile. If students read the word incorrectly, place in a separate pile. On the back of the cards that were read correctly, make a note of the date and put aside. (Once students have read the word correctly five consecutive days, you can remove the word from the pile of cards students are working on.) Review any words students read incorrectly, and keep the cards for next time.

5. Gather the two sets of sight word cards for the words *none, more,* and *held* and place all of the cards face down on the table or another flat surface. Have students choose a card, read the word aloud, and then choose a second card. After students read the second card aloud, if the two cards match, students should keep the cards. If they do not match, students should return them to the table. Continue until all of the cards have been collected.

Word Work
Name:
ou/ow and Sight Words 2

Study, Cover, and Spell: Sight Words

Read each word and then cover it up so that you cannot see it. Spell the word out loud, and then write the word on the line provided. Uncover the word and check your spelling. If it does not match, erase the word and write it again.

1. none — none
2. very — very
3. some — some
4. held — held
5. even — even
6. love — love
7. more — more
8. only — only
9. know — know

178

Speed Work

Cloud Watching

Look at the Performance Review, or check the student's fluency chart. Fluency scores (words read per minute) should not fall below 80. If the student scored below 80 words per minute, print a copy of the Speed Work story and have the student read the story silently before reading it aloud. Otherwise, move on to Classics Session 2.

A Flight Through the Sky

Have students listen to the story again while following along in *MARK¹² Classics for Young Readers*. Afterward, students should complete the comprehension questions in *MARK¹² Classics for Young Readers* on their own.

- Improve reading and comprehension skills.

Write

A Flight Through the Sky

1. What was Daedalus excellent at?

A. mining
B. hunting
C. farming
D. building *(circled)*

2. Why is Daedalus unable to get off the island by sea?

Daedalus is unable to get off the island by sea because the king's ships kept watch and would capture him if he tried to escape.

3. Why does Daedalus make two sets of wings?

Daedalus makes two sets of wings— one for himself and one for his son, Icarus, so they can fly away.

4. What did Daedalus secretly teach Icarus to do?

A. fly *(circled)*
B. sail
C. sing
D. dance

5. What materials did Daedalus use to make the wings?

Daedalus used wood, cloth, feathers, and wax to make the wings.

6. Why does Daedalus say to Icarus, "Do not fly too close to the sun"?

Daedalus says to Icarus, "Do not fly too close to the sun" because the heat of the sun would melt the wax on the wings. If that happened, Icarus would no longer be able to fly and would fall into the sea.

7. How does Icarus feel as he soars through the air?

A. dizzy
B. thrilled *(circled)*
C. unhappy
D. frightened

8. At the end of the story, why does Daedalus never use his wings again?

Daedalus never uses his wings again because he is so saddened by the loss of his son.

A Flight Through the Sky **57**

58 A Flight Through the Sky

---

ow/ou and Sight Words 3

ONLINE	Student & Computer	**:60** minutes	
	Adult : *Check Performance Review*		
OFFLINE	Student & Adult : Review online work	**:30** minutes	
	• Reading Warm-Up		
	• Speed Work		
	• Assessment		
	Grammar, Usage, and Mechanics (GUM)	**:30** minutes	
	Instructional Time **2:00** hours		

Materials

● *MARK¹² Reading Activity Book*, pages 179–184

Goals

In this lesson, students will read about colonial children in America. Students will also learn and practice the sound /ō/ for the letters *ow* before reviewing the sight words, *none, more,* and *help* and practicing new sight words *would, could,* and *should.* In today's Unit Assessment, you will administer a test covering all content from Unit 12. Afterward, you will work with students to complete grammar activities.

ONLINE	**Student & Computer**

Students will work online to complete Warm-Up, Code Work, Word Work, and Speed Work activities, and a review game on their own. Be sure to read the Performance Review before beginning the offline portion of today's lesson.

Today you will administer a Unit Assessment and work with students to complete a GUM activity.

Warm-Up ·

Colonial Children

Look at the Performance Review. If the student achieved a perfect score on today's Warm-Up, move on to Speed Work. If the student scored 60 percent or 80 percent, print the story and review the comprehension questions with the student. If the student scored less than 60 percent, print the story, have the student read the story aloud, and then work through the comprehension questions together, before moving on to Speed Work.

Objectives

• **Improve reading and comprehension skills.**

Speed Work ·

The Missing Mittens

Look at the Performance Review, or check the student's fluency chart. Fluency scores (words read per minute) should not fall below 80. If the student scored below 80 words per minute, print a copy of the Speed Work story and have the student read the story silently before reading it aloud to you. Otherwise, move on to the Assessment.

Objectives

• **Increase reading fluency rate.**

☼ Assessment ·

ow/ou and Sight Words

Today's Unit Assessment covers all content found in Unit 12. Carefully read the instructions on the student pages before administering the test to the student. If necessary, read the directions to the student. After you have scored the student's assessment, be sure to go online and enter student performance scores in the assessment entry tool.

Part 2. Dictate the following words to students: *slow, clown, mouse, mow, ouch, blow, mouth, window, frown,* and *snowball*.

Part 4. Dictate the following words to students: *could, held, more, should, very, would, should, none, held, could, would,* and *more*.

☼ **A**ssessment

Name: _____

ow/ou and Sight Words

Unit 12 Assessment

Part 1.

Say each word below aloud. Underline the sound *ow* or *ou* makes in each word.

1. grow   /ou/   <u>/ō/</u>
2. plow   <u>/ou/</u>   /ō/
3. cloud   <u>/ou/</u>   /ō/
4. slow   /ou/   <u>/ō/</u>
5. brown   <u>/ou/</u>   /ō/
6. mound   <u>/ou/</u>   /ō/
7. town   <u>/ou/</u>   /ō/
8. row   /ou/   <u>/ō/</u>
9. house   <u>/ou/</u>   /ō/
10. flow   /ou/   <u>/ō/</u>

179

☼ **A**ssessment

Name: _____

ow/ou and Sight Words

Part 2.

Listen to each word that is read to you. Write each word on the lines provided.

11. <u>slow</u>
12. <u>clown</u>
13. <u>mouse</u>
14. <u>mow</u>
15. <u>ouch</u>
16. <u>blow</u>
17. <u>mouth</u>
18. <u>window</u>
19. <u>frown</u>
20. <u>snowball</u>

180

☼ **A**ssessment

Name: _____

ow/ou and Sight Words

Part 3.

In each row, underline the word that contains the long *o* sound.

21. sled   <u>slow</u>   slot
22. <u>glow</u>   gown   grade
23. <u>crow</u>   clown   cross
24. flag   <u>flow</u>   flower
25. ship   sound   <u>show</u>
26. brick   brown   <u>blown</u>
27. <u>shadow</u>   shade   should
28. take   <u>throw</u>   three
29. wound   <u>window</u>   where
30. <u>snow</u>   stand   shot

181

☼ **A**ssessment

Name: _____

ow/ou and Sight Words

Part 4.

In each row, underline the word that is read to you.

31. would   should   <u>could</u>
32. <u>held</u>   hand   hop
33. mouse   mow   <u>more</u>
34. would   <u>should</u>   could
35. vet   <u>very</u>   vow
36. <u>would</u>   should   could
37. shout   <u>should</u>   shed
38. now   <u>none</u>   no
39. hill   hole   <u>held</u>
40. <u>could</u>   cloud   cloth
41. where   what   <u>would</u>
42. mouth   <u>more</u>   saw

Part 5.

Read each word aloud.

43. none   47. more   51. some
44. would   48. could   52. would
45. held   49. even   53. should
46. should   50. love   54. could

182

Objectives

- Identify and use *ow/ou* spelling patterns.
- Identify and use *ow* for /ō/.
- Read sight words.

Principal Forms of Verbs

The principal forms of verbs are the present, the present participle, the past, and the past participle.

Work with students to complete pages 183 and 184 in *MARK¹²Reading Activity Book*. Read page 183, Get Ready, with students. Remind students that some forms of verbs have two parts: a main verb and a helping verb. Explain that when they use the present participle or past participle of a verb, they must add a helping verb. Go over the forms of participles and helping verbs used to describe events in the past and present. After this review, have students complete the Try It page. Be sure to discuss students' answers when the page is completed.

GUM Grammar, Usage, and Mechanics　　Name: _____
Principal Parts of Verbs

Get Ready

- There are four principal forms of verbs:

  1. present　**2.** present participle　**3.** past　**4.** past participle

- These four sentences show the principal forms of the verb, *play*.

  Present: I *play* softball.
  Present Participle: I *am playing* softball now.
  Past: I *played* softball yesterday.
  Past Participle: I *have played* softball all my life.

- For the *present tense*, just use a main verb.

  I *jump*.

- For the *present participle*, add *–ing* to the main verb. Add a helping verb such as *am, are, was,* or *were.*

  I *am jumping* now.

- For the *past*, just add the ending *–ed* to the main verb.

  I *jumped* yesterday.

- For the *past participle* of regular verbs, add the ending *–ed* to the main verb. Add a helping verb such as *has, have,* or *had.*
  Remember: Helping verbs go before a main verb.

  I *have jumped* for a long time.

183

GUM Grammar, Usage, and Mechanics　　Name: _____
Principal Parts of Verbs

Try It
On the line provided in each sentence, write the correct form of the *main verb* in parentheses.

1. Tess fell and (land) **landed** _____ on the ground.
2. Jeff has (live) **lived** _____ in his house for ten months.
3. The frog was (hop) **hopping** _____ into and out of the pond.
4. I had (hope) **hoped** _____ for a new bike for my birthday.

Read each sentence below. Write the correct verb on the line provided.
Hint: When you see the word *participle*, add a helping verb to the main verb of the sentence.

5. Mom (past of *frown*) **frowned** _____ when she saw the mess.
6. The band (present participle of *play*) **is playing** _____ right now, so let's dance.
7. The cat (past participle of *drag*) **has dragged or had dragged** _____ a mouse into the house.
8. We (present of *plow*) **plow** _____ the land to grow corn.
9. It (past participle of *snow*) **has snowed or had snowed** _____ for many months.
10. The wind (present participle of *blow*) **is blowing** _____ and it is very cold.

184

Long a and Sight Words 1

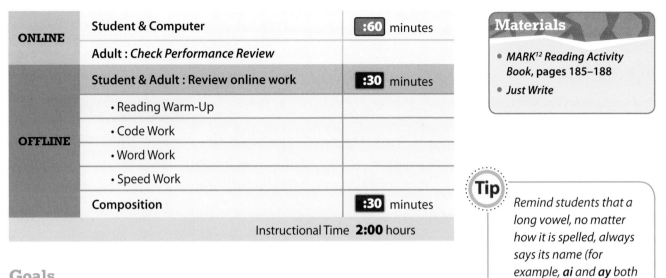

ONLINE	Student & Computer	:60 minutes
	Adult : *Check Performance Review*	
OFFLINE	Student & Adult : Review online work	:30 minutes
	• Reading Warm-Up	
	• Code Work	
	• Word Work	
	• Speed Work	
	Composition	:30 minutes
	Instructional Time **2:00** hours	

Materials

- *MARK¹² Reading Activity Book*, pages 185–188
- *Just Write*

Tip *Remind students that a long vowel, no matter how it is spelled, always says its name (for example, **ai** and **ay** both "say" /ā/).*

Goals

In this lesson, students will read about how people felt about being taxed by the British in colonial America. Students will also be introduced to the *ai* and *ay* spellings of the long *a* sound before reinforcing the sight words *would, could,* and *should*. In today's *MARK¹² Reading Activity Book* pages, you will work with students to practice using the *ai* and *ay* spellings for the long *a* sound in addition to reading sight words.

Advance Preparation

For the offline portion of today's lesson, gather the students' composition materials. Based on the Performance Review, if students need to complete Code Work activity 3, you will need the Online Tile Kit or Paper Letter Tiles. If students must complete Word Work activity 2, create sight word cards for the following words: *would, could,* and *should*. If students need to complete Word Work activity 3, you will need a timer and the Online Tile Kit or Paper Letter Tiles. If students need to complete Word Work activity 5, create a second set of sight word cards for the words *would, could,* and *should*.

| ONLINE | **Student & Computer** |

Students will work online to complete Warm-Up, Code Work, Word Work, and Speed Work activities, and a Wrap-Up assessment on their own. Be sure to read the Performance Review before beginning the offline portion of today's lesson.

Today you will work with students to complete Code Work, Word Work, and Composition activities. Be sure to read the online Performance Review before beginning the Code Work and Word Work activities.

Warm-Up ·····································

1765: Changes for the Colonists

Look at the Performance Review. If the student achieved a perfect score on today's Warm-Up, move on to Code Work. If the student scored 60 percent or 80 percent, print the story and review the comprehension questions with the student. If the student scored less than 60 percent, print the story, have the student read the story aloud, and then work through the comprehension questions together, before moving on to Code Work.

> **Objectives**
> • Improve reading and comprehension skills.

Code Work ·····································

Long *a*

Look at the Performance Review. If the student achieved a perfect score on today's Code Work activities, complete the first two activities from the list below. If the student scored less than 100 percent but more than 85 percent, complete the first three activities from the list below. If the student scored 85 percent or less, complete all five of the activities listed below.

> **Objectives**
> • Identify the letters, given the sound /ā/.
> • Identify and use /ā/ spelling patterns.

1. Have students complete page 185 in *Reading Activity Book* for more practice on the long *a* spellings a*i* and *ay*.

2. Remove the "Wet Paint" story from *MARK¹² Reading Activity Book*. Fold the pages in half to create a small booklet. Review the following words with students: *room, money,* and *floor*. Have students read the story silently once or twice before reading the story aloud. When students read aloud, make note of any errors, and review those words with the students.

3. Using the Online Tile Kit or Paper Letter Tiles, have students build the following words: *chain, nail, paint, rain, stain, clay, day, gray, pay,* and *clay*. Have students identify the letters that make the long *a* sound in each word.

4. Say the word *day*. Have students say as many new words as they can think of by changing the first letter (examples: *hay, jay, Kay, lay, may, pay, ray, say*). Continue for one minute. Point out to students that all these words rhyme because they end with the same sound, long *a*.

5. Have students verbally use each word from activity 3 in a sentence. Verify students' understanding of each word is correct. If time allows, continue this activity with the words listed in parentheses in activity 4.

Code Work   Name: _____

Long *a* and Sight Words 1

Choose the Spelling

Underline the long *a* spelling that completes each word. Write the full word on the line provided. Then say the words aloud.

1. cl___   ai   <u>ay</u>   clay
2. p___nt   <u>ai</u>   ay   paint
3. tr___   ai   <u>ay</u>   tray
4. ch___n   <u>ai</u>   ay   chain
5. r___n   <u>ai</u>   ay   rain
6. s___   ai   <u>ay</u>   say
7. gr___   ai   <u>ay</u>   gray
8. st___n   <u>ai</u>   ay   stain

Choose the words from above that best complete each sentence below. Write the words on the lines provided.

9. The red **paint** dripped off the brush onto the rug.
10. Grace wears a gold **chain**.
11. The **rain** came down all **day**.

185

Word Work

Sight Words

Look at the Performance Review. If the student achieved a perfect score on today's Word Work activities, complete the first activity from the list below. If the student scored less than 100 percent but more than 85 percent, complete the first three activities from the list below. If the student scored 85 percent or less, complete all five of the activities listed below.

1. Have students complete page 186 in *MARK¹² Reading Activity Book* for more practice on sight words. To complete the page, you will need a timer. As students read the sight words, keep track of how many are read correctly.

2. Using the sight word cards you created for *would, could,* and *should,* read each word to students and have students write the word on a piece of paper. Give students the sight words, and instruct students to correct any spelling mistakes. Students should correct the mistakes and then read the list of words aloud.

3. Gather all of the sight word cards students have worked on to date and a timer. Have students read all of the sight word cards as accurately and quickly as possible. Make note of the time, as well as any errors students have made. Use the Online Tile Kit or Paper Letter Tiles to review words read incorrectly.

4. Gather the cards for the sight words *would, could,* and *should,* and up to two additional sight words students have yet to master. Show the first card to students, and ask students to read the word. If students read the word correctly, place in one pile. If students read the word incorrectly, place in a separate pile. On the back of the cards that were read correctly, make a note of the date and put aside. (Once students have read the word correctly five consecutive days, you can remove the word from the pile of cards students are working on.) Review any words students read incorrectly, and keep the cards for next time.

5. Gather the two sets of sight word cards for *would, could,* and *should,* and place the cards face down. Have students choose a card, read the word aloud, and then choose a second card. After students read the second card aloud, if the two cards match, students should keep the cards. If they do not match, students should return them to the table. Continue until all of the cards are collected.

Speed Work

The Rain in Spain

Look at the Performance Review, or check the student's fluency chart. Fluency scores (words read per minute) should not fall below 80. If the student scored below 80 words per minute, print a copy of the Speed Work story and have the student read the story silently before reading it aloud. Otherwise, move on to Composition.

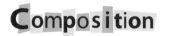omposition

Gather students' composition materials and begin where they left off.

Long a and Sight Words 2

ONLINE	**Student & Computer**	**:60** minutes	
	Adult : *Check Performance Review*		
OFFLINE	**Student & Adult :** Review online work	**:30** minutes	
	• Reading Warm-Up		
	• Code Work		
	• Word Work		
	• Speed Work		
	Grammar, Usage, and Mechanics (GUM)	**:30** minutes	
	Instructional Time	**2:00** hours	

Tip

*Remind students that the silent **e** makes the vowel **a** say its name. Show the difference between a word with a short **a** and a word with an **a-consonant-e** by using words such as **tap/tape**, **hat/hate**, and **can/cane**.*

Goals

In this lesson, students will read about events that led to the Boston Massacre. Students will also be introduced to the *a* and *a-consonant-e* spellings of the long *a* sound before learning the sight words *brother, sister,* and *baby*. In today's *MARK¹² Reading Activity Book* pages, you will work with students to recognize the *a* and *a-consonant-e* spellings for the long *a* sound and read sight words.

Advance Preparation

Based on the Performance Review, if students need to complete Word Work activity 2, create sight word cards for the following words: *brother, sister,* and *baby*. If students need to complete Word Work activity 3, you will need a timer and the Online Tile Kit or Paper Letter Tiles. If students need to complete Word Work activity 5, create a second set of sight word cards for the words *brother, sister,* and *baby*.

ONLINE Student & Computer

Students will work online to complete Warm-Up, Code Work, Word Work, and Speed Work activities, and a Wrap-Up assessment on their own. Be sure to read the Performance Review before beginning the offline portion of today's lesson.

Today you will work with students to complete Code Work, Word Work, and GUM activities. Be sure to read the online Performance Review before beginning the Code Work and Word Work activities.

Warm-Up • • • • • • • • • • • • • • •

1770: The Boston Massacre

Look at the Performance Review. If the student achieved a perfect score on today's Warm-Up, move on to Code Work. If the student scored 60 percent or 80 percent, print the story and review the comprehension questions with the student. If the student scored less than 60 percent, print the story, have the student read the story aloud, and then work through the comprehension questions together, before moving on to Code Work.

Code Work • • • • • • • • • • • • • •

Long *a*

Look at the Performance Review. If the student achieved a perfect score on today's Code Work activities, complete the first two activities from the list below. If the student scored less than 100 percent but more than 85 percent, complete the first three activities from the list below. If the student scored 85 percent or less, complete all five of the activities listed below.

1. Have students complete page 189 in *MARK¹² Reading Activity Book* for more practice on the long *a* spellings and *a-consonant-e*.

2. Using the Online Tile Kit or Paper Letter Tiles, have students build the following words: *apron, able, acorn, cake, gate, rake,* and *skate*. Have students identify the letters that make the long *a* sound in each word.

3. Say the word *cake*. Have students say as many new words as they can think of by changing the first letter (examples: *bake, fake, Jake, lake, make, rake, stake,* and *take*). Continue for one minute. Point out to students that all these words rhyme because they end with the same sound (*long a-consonant k-silent e*).

4. Have students verbally use each word from activity 2 in a sentence. Verify students' understanding of each word is correct.

5. Dictate the following sentences to students, have them tell you which word or words in each sentence contain the long *a* sound, and ask students to spell the long *a* word(s) aloud:
   This fence has no gate.
   That cake is for me!
   My apron has a big stain on it.
   April can skate to the park.

Code Work   Name:
Long *a* and Sight Words 2

Give Me an A!
In each sentence, find the word that has the long *a* sound. Then write the word on the line provided.

1. The man had to rake the sand.
   rake
2. That apron has a tan band at the top.
   apron
3. Fran saw the flame of a candle in the dark.
   flame
4. Brad asked if he could have some cake.
   cake
5. Tad planted an acorn in the backyard.
   acorn
6. My pal, April, has a bad cold.
   April
7. Jack slammed the backyard gate shut.
   gate
8. Matt can help Jan, but he is not able to help Mark.
   able

189

Word Work ··

Sight Words

Look at the Performance Review. If the student achieved a perfect score on today's Word Work activities, complete the first activity from the list below. If the student scored less than 100 percent but more than 85 percent, complete the first three activities from the list below. If the student scored 85 percent or less, complete all five of the activities listed below.

1. Have students complete page 190 in *MARK¹² Reading Activity Book* for more practice on sight words.

2. Using the sight word cards you created for *brother, sister,* and *baby* read each word to students and have students write the word on a piece of paper. Give students the sight words, and instruct students to look for any spelling mistakes they may have made. Students should correct the mistakes and then read the list of words aloud.

3. Gather all of the sight word cards students have worked on to date and a timer. Have students read all of the sight word cards as accurately and quickly as possible. Make note of the time, as well as any errors students have made. Use the Online Tile Kit or Paper Letter Tiles to review words read incorrectly.

4. Gather the cards for the sight words *brother, sister,* and *baby,* and up to two additional sight words students have yet to master. Show the first card to students, and ask students to read the word. If students read the word correctly, place in one pile. If students read the word incorrectly, place in a separate pile. On the back of the cards that were read correctly, make a note of the date and put aside. (Once students have read the word correctly five consecutive days, you can remove the word from the pile of cards students are working on.) Review any words students read incorrectly, and keep the cards for next time.

5. Gather the two sets of sight word cards for the words *brother, sister,* and *baby,* and place all of the cards face down on the table or another flat surface. Have students choose a card, read the word aloud, and then choose a second card. After students read the second card aloud, if the two cards match, students should keep the cards. If they do not match, students should return them to the table. Continue until all of the cards have been collected.

Word Work

Name: ____

Long *a* and Sight Words 2

Can You See Them?

Underline the sight word listed as many times as it appears in each row. An example has been done for you.

Example:	brother	other	brother	mother	bother	brother
1. could	could	cold	would	could	cold
2. sister	sitter	silver	sister	sitter	sister
3. none	gone	none	some	none	some
4. baby	baby	maybe	only	barb	baby
5. would	should	would	should	could	would
6. brother	other	brother	brother	bother	other
7. more	more	none	mare	more	mine
8. should	shout	shock	should	shout	should
9. held	help	held	held	helm	help

190

Speed Work ··

The Essay Contest

Look at the Performance Review, or check the student's fluency chart. Fluency scores (words read per minute) should not fall below 80. If the student scored below 80 words per minute, print a copy of the Speed Work story and have the student read the story silently before reading it aloud. Otherwise, move on to Grammar, Usage, and Mechanics.

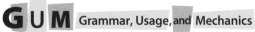

Correct Tense

The time of a verb's action or being is called its tense. Verb tenses include present, past, future, present progressive, and past progressive.

> The man *walks* home. (*present*)
>
> The man *walked* home. (*past*)
>
> The man *will walk* home. (*future*)
>
> The man *is walking* home. (*present progressive*)
>
> The man *was walking* home. (*past progressive*)

Work with students to complete pages 191 and 192 in *MARK¹² Reading Activity Book*. Read page 191, Get Ready, with students. Have students complete the Try It page. Be sure to discuss students' answers when the page is completed.

G U M Grammar, Usage, and Mechanics   Name: _____

Long a and Sight Words 2

Get Ready

■ The time of a verb's action or being is called its *tense*. The basic verb tenses are *present*, *past*, and *future*.

Present singular:	The cow *jumps* over the moon.
Present plural:	The cows *jump* over the moon.
Past singular:	The cow *jumped* over the moon.
Past plural:	The cows *jumped* over the moon.
Future singular:	The cow *will jump* over the moon.
Future plural:	The cows *will jump* over the moon

Note that the past form of an *irregular* verb does **not** end in *-d* or *-ed*.

Past singular:	I *saw* the cow jump over the moon.
Past plural:	We *saw* the cow jump over the moon.

■ The *present* or *past progressive* tense shows *continuous action or being.*

We make the present progressive tense by adding a present tense helping verb (*am, is, or are*) to the present participle of a verb.

Present progressive singular:	The cow *is jumping* over the moon.
Present progressive plural:	The cows *are jumping* over the moon.

We make the past progressive tense by adding a past tense helping verb (*was or were*) to the present participle of a verb.

Past progressive singular:	The cow *was jumping* over the moon.
Past progressive plural:	The cows *were jumping* over the moon.

191

G U M Grammar, Usage, and Mechanics   Name: _____

Long a and Sight Words 2

Try It

Underline the correct verb tense that completes each sentence.

1. Yesterday I (go, <u>went</u>) to the hat shop.
2. Bob (<u>has</u> , have) a pet pig.
3. Brent was (<u>running</u> , runs) in the big race when it started to rain.
4. Jack (taken, <u>took</u>) my sister to the dance.
5. The cat is (plays, <u>playing</u>) with the ball of string.
6. Don and I (was, <u>were</u>) the first two kids in line for the show.

Choose the verb from the box that best completes each sentence. Write each verb on the lines provided.
Hint: Not all the words in the box are used.

trips	says	flip	sitting	ate
sits	eat	sat	were	tripped
eaten	are	was	trip	am

7. Jake **tripped** _____ over that rock yesterday. Be careful that you don't **trip** _____ over it today!
8. Chuck **ate** _____ cake today, but I will **eat** _____ cake tomorrow.
9. Marla **sits** _____ in the van. I am **sitting** _____ next to her.
10. We ___**were**___ singing while Pat ___**was**___ dancing.

192

Long a and Sight Words 3

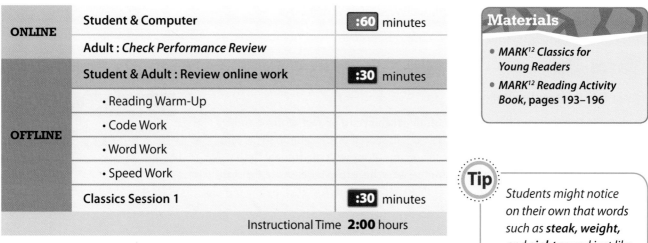

ONLINE	Student & Computer	:60 minutes
	Adult : *Check Performance Review*	
OFFLINE	Student & Adult : Review online work	:30 minutes
	• Reading Warm-Up	
	• Code Work	
	• Word Work	
	• Speed Work	
	Classics Session 1	:30 minutes
	Instructional Time	**2:00** hours

Materials

- *MARK¹² Classics for Young Readers*
- *MARK¹² Reading Activity Book*, pages 193–196

> **Tip**
>
> *Students might notice on their own that words such as **steak, weight,** and **eight** sound just like other words (**stake, wait, ate**). Explain that words that sound alike but have different spellings and meanings are called **homophones**.*

Goals

In this lesson, students will read about events that led to the Boston Tea Party. Students will also be introduced to the *ea* and *eigh* spellings of the long *a* sound before reviewing the sight words *brother, sister,* and *baby.* In today's *MARK¹² Reading Activity Book* pages, you will work with students to complete sentences with words that have the spellings *ea* and *eigh* and to practice sight words.

Advance Preparation

Based on the Performance Review, if students need to complete Code Work activity 3, you will need the Online Tile Kit or Paper Letter Tiles. If students need to complete Word Work activity 2, gather the sight word cards for the following words: *brother, sister,* and *baby.* If students need to complete Word Work activity 3, you will need a timer and the Online Tile Kit or Paper Letter Tiles. If students need to complete Word Work activity 5, gather the second set of sight word cards for the words *brother, sister,* and *baby.*

ONLINE   Student & Computer

Students will work online to complete Warm-Up, Code Work, Word Work, and Speed Work activities, and a Wrap-Up assessment on their own. Be sure to read the Performance Review before beginning the offline portion of today's lesson.

Today you will work with students to complete Code Work, Word Work, and *MARK¹² Classics for Young Readers* activities. Be sure to read the online Performance Review before beginning the Code Work and Word Work activities.

Warm-Up ••••••••••••••••••••••••••••••••••••••

1773: The Boston Tea Party

Look at the Performance Review. If the student achieved a perfect score on today's Warm-Up, move on to Code Work. If the student scored 60 percent or 80 percent, print the story and review the comprehension questions with the student. If the student scored less than 60 percent, print the story, have the student read the story aloud, and then work through the comprehension questions together, before moving on to Code Work.

Code Work ••••••••••••••••••••••••••••••••••••

Long *a*

Look at the Performance Review. If the student achieved a perfect score on today's Code Work activities, complete the first two activities from the list below. If the student scored less than 100 percent but more than 85 percent, complete the first three activities from the list below. If the student scored 85 percent or less, complete all five of the activities listed below.

1. Have students complete page 193 in *MARK¹² Reading Activity Book* for more practice on the long *a* spellings *ea* and *eigh*.

2. Remove "The Race" story from *MARK¹² Reading Activity Book*. Review the following words with students: *deserve* and *sneaker*. Fold the pages in half to create a small booklet. Have students read the story silently once or twice before reading the story aloud. When students read aloud, make note of any errors, and review those words with the students.

3. Using the Online Tile Kit or Paper Letter Tiles, have students build the following words: *break, steak, great, weigh, sleigh,* and *eight*. Have students identify the letters that make the long *a* sound in each word.

4. Have students verbally use each word from activity 3 in a sentence.

5. Dictate each sentence below to students. Have students identify the word or words in each sentence that contain the long *a* sound and write the word(s) on a piece of paper. Then have students underline the letters that make the long *a* sound in each word.
   How much does this can of corn w<u>eigh</u>?
   That was a gr<u>ea</u>t show!
   The baby has <u>eigh</u>t toys in her crib.

Code Work　　　　　　Name:

Long a and Sight Words 3

Which Word?

Choose the word from the box that best completes each sentence below. Write the words on the lines provided.

weight	sleigh	great	eight
break	freight	steak	weigh

1. How much does that box of crackers **weigh** ?
2. Pete wants to grill a **steak** for dinner.
3. "When will the **freight** train be here?" Greg asked the clerk.
4. Let's take a **break** from this hard work!
5. Those dogs will pull the **sleigh** .
6. "I have a **great** idea!" Carlos shouted to his sister.
7. Frank has six toy cars and Elvis has **eight** .
8. Alan used the scale to check the **weight** of the box.

193

Word Work ∙

Sight Words

Look at the Performance Review. If the student achieved a perfect score on today's Word Work activities, complete the first activity from the list below. If the student scored less than 100 percent but more than 85 percent, complete the first three activities from the list below. If the student scored 85 percent or less, complete all five of the activities listed below.

1. Have students complete page 194 in *MARK¹² Reading Activity Book* for more practice on sight words.

2. Using the sight word cards you created for *brother, sister,* and *baby* read each word to students and have students write the word on a piece of paper. Give students the sight words, and instruct students to look for any spelling mistakes they may have made. Students should correct the mistakes and then read the list of words aloud.

3. Gather all of the sight word cards students have worked on to date and a timer. Have students read all of the sight word cards as accurately and quickly as possible. Make note of the time, as well as any errors students have made. Use the Online Tile Kit or Paper Letter Tiles to review words read incorrectly.

4. Gather the cards for the sight words *brother, sister,* and *baby,* and up to two additional sight words students have yet to master. Show the first card to students, and ask students to read the word. If students read the word correctly, place in one pile. If students read the word incorrectly, place in a separate pile. On the back of the cards that were read correctly, make a note of the date and put aside. (Once students have read the word correctly five consecutive days, you can remove the word from the pile of cards students are working on.) Review any words students read incorrectly, and keep the cards for next time.

5. Gather the two sets of sight word cards for the words *brother, sister,* and *baby,* and place all of the cards face down on the table or another flat surface. Have students choose a card, read the word aloud, and then choose a second card. After students read the second card aloud, if the two cards match, students should keep the cards. If they do not match, students should return them to the table. Continue until all of the cards have been collected.

Speed Work ∙

Whale Tales

Look at the Performance Review, or check the student's fluency chart. Fluency scores (words read per minute) should not fall below 80. If the student scored below 80 words per minute, print a copy of the Speed Work story and have the student read the story silently before reading it aloud. Otherwise, move on to Classics Session 1.

Classics Session 1 ·

The Leak in the Dike

Today's story, "The Leak in the Dike," is an old story from Holland about a young boy who saves the country from flooding. Review the keywords with students. Read the story with students, and then use the Discussion Questions below as a guide to share ideas about the story. Have students read the story again before writing a summary of the story.

Objectives

- Improve reading and comprehension skills.

Keywords

canal, n. – a man-made waterway
The men dug a **canal** from the lake to the sea so ships could sail in and out.

thrust, v. – to push with great force
After defeating the enemy, the general **thrust** his sword into the ground and declared victory.

numb, adj. – without feeling, especially from the cold
After playing in the snow for several hours, I was so cold even my nose felt **numb**.

scold, v. – to speak angrily to someone
The babysitter **scolded** the twins for running through the house and knocking over the plant.

Discussion Questions

1. Think about a time when you acted bravely. Describe the situation. What did you do? How did you feel? Answers will vary.

2. Peter says that his father calls the waters "the angry waters." What does this description mean? Describe what you think the waters look like. Answers may include that the waters push against the dike; they act like they are mad.

3. Why is Peter able to save his country even though he is so young? What is he willing to do? Answers may include that Peter is able to stop the hole from getting bigger. He is willing to stay, with his finger in the hole, as long as necessary, even though he knew his mother would be mad.

4. What might have happened if Peter ran for help instead of sticking his finger in the dike? Answers may include that the hole could have gotten bigger and Holland may have started to flood.

5. What are some ways you can do small things that make a difference to others? Answers may include visiting an elderly or ill neighbor or picking up trash.

Students should write a summary of the story to complete today's Classics activity.

Long a and Sight Words 4

ONLINE	Student & Computer	:60 minutes
	Adult : *Check Performance Review*	
OFFLINE	Student & Adult : Review online work	:30 minutes
	• Reading Warm-Up	
	• Code Work	
	• Word Work	
	• Speed Work	
	Classics Session 2	:30 minutes
	Instructional Time **2:00** hours	

Materials

- *MARK¹² Classics for Young Readers*
- *MARK¹² Reading Activity Book*, pages 197–198

Goals

In this lesson, students will read about the Intolerable Acts—Britain's response to the Boston Tea Party. Students will also review the long *a* spellings *ai, ay,* and *a* before being introduced to the sight words *many, animals,* and *while.* In today's *MARK¹² Reading Activity Book* pages, you will work with students to identify and sort words with long *a* spellings and to spell sight words.

Advance Preparation

Based on the Performance Review, if students need to complete Word Work activity 2, create sight word cards for the following words: *many, animals,* and *while.* If students need to complete Word Work activity 3, you will need a timer and the Online Tile Kit or Paper Letter Tiles. If students need to complete Word Work activity 5, create a second set of sight word cards for the words *many, animals,* and *while.*

ONLINE   Student & Computer

Students will work online to complete Warm-Up, Code Work, Word Work, and Speed Work activities, and a Wrap-Up assessment on their own. Be sure to read the Performance Review before beginning the offline portion of today's lesson.

Today you will work with students to complete Code Work, Word Work, and *MARK¹² Classics for Young Readers* activities. Be sure to read the online Performance Review before beginning the Code Work and Word Work activities.

 Warm-Up •••••••••••••••••••••••••••••••••

1774: The Intolerable Acts

Look at the Performance Review. If the student achieved a perfect score on today's Warm-Up, move on to Code Work. If the student scored 60 percent or 80 percent, print the story and review the comprehension questions with the student. If the student scored less than 60 percent, print the story, have the student read the story aloud, and then work through the comprehension questions together, before moving on to Code Work.

Objectives

- Improve reading and comprehension skills.

Code Work •••••••••••••••••••••••••••••••••

Long *a*

Look at the Performance Review. If the student achieved a perfect score on today's Code Work activities, complete the first two activities from the list below. If the student scored less than 100 percent but more than 85 percent, complete the first three activities from the list below. If the student scored 85 percent or less, complete all five of the activities listed below.

Objectives

- Identify the letters, given the sound /ā/.
- Identify and use /ā/ spelling patterns.

1. Have students complete page 197 in *MARK¹² Reading Activity Book* for more practice on the long *a* spellings *ai, ay,* and *a.*

2. Say the word *ail.* Have students write that word and then as many new words as they can think of by adding a letter to the beginning of the word (examples: *bail, fail, hail, jail, mail,* and *nail*). If students accidentally include a misspelled word (such as *stail* instead of *stale*), correct their work and discuss the various spellings of the long *a* sound.

3. Using the Online Tile Kit or Paper Letter Tiles, have students build the following words: *able, acorn, apron, mail, paint, sprain, gray, play,* and *sway.* Have students identify the letter or letters that make the long *a* vowel sound in each word.

4. Have students verbally use each word from activity 3 in a sentence. Verify students' understanding of each word is correct.

5. Dictate the sentences below to students. Have students write down the word or words in each sentence that contain the long *a* sound, and underline the letters that spell the long *a* sound in each word.
    Kay has an apron with pink and gray dots on it.
    April showers bring May flowers.
    We had a fun day sailing on the bay.

Code Work Name: _____

Long a and Sight Words 4

Find the Sound

Read aloud the words in the box. Underline the letter or letters that make the long a sound in each word.

trail	tray	mail	able
April	Kay	payday	haystack
stain	acorn	apron	strain

Read and Sort

Write the words from the box above in the correct columns below according to how the long a sound is spelled in each word.

a	ai	ay
April	trail	tray
acorn	stain	Kay
able	mail	payday
apron	strain	haystack

197

Word Work ··························

Sight Words

Look at the Performance Review. If the student achieved a perfect score on today's Word Work activities, complete the first activity from the list below. If the student scored less than 100 percent but more than 85 percent, complete the first three activities from the list below. If the student scored 85 percent or less, complete all five of the activities listed below.

1. Have students complete page 198 in *MARK¹² Reading Activity Book* for more practice on sight words.

2. Using the sight word cards you created for *many, animals,* and *while,* read each word to students and have students write the word on a piece of paper. Give students the sight words, and instruct students to look for any spelling mistakes they may have made. Students should correct the mistakes and then read the list of words aloud.

3. Gather all of the sight word cards students have worked on to date and a timer. Have students read all of the sight word cards as accurately and quickly as possible. Make note of the time, as well as any errors students have made. Use the Online Tile Kit or Paper Letter Tiles to review words read incorrectly.

4. Gather the cards for the sight words *many, animals,* and *while,* and up to two additional sight words students have yet to master. Show the first card to students, and ask students to read the word. If students read the word correctly, place in one pile. If students read the word incorrectly, place in a separate pile. On the back of the cards that were read correctly, make a note of the date and put aside. (Once students have read the word correctly five consecutive days, you can remove the word from the pile of cards students are working on.) Review any words students read incorrectly, and keep the cards for next time.

5. Gather the two sets of sight word cards for the words *many, animals,* and *while,* and place all of the cards face down on the table or another flat surface. Have students choose a card, read the word aloud, and then choose a second card. After students read the second card aloud, if the two cards match, students should keep the cards. If they do not match, students should return them to the table. Continue until all of the cards have been collected.

Word Work
Name: _____

Long a and Sight Words 4

Spell It!

In each row, circle the letter that completes the word. Write the full word on the line provided. Then say each word aloud.

#					
1.	br_ther	<u>o</u>	u	e	brother
2.	anim_ls	i	<u>a</u>	e	animals
3.	ma_y	t	<u>n</u>	v	many
4.	hel__	b	t	<u>d</u>	held
5.	si_ter	<u>s</u>	n	a	sister
6.	n_ne	e	a	<u>o</u>	none
7.	w_ile	a	<u>h</u>	o	while
8.	_ome	<u>s</u>	t	k	some
9.	_aby	m	l	<u>b</u>	baby
10.	co_ld	<u>u</u>	o	i	could

198

Speed Work ··························

A Picnic on Pillows

Look at the Performance Review, or check the student's fluency chart. Fluency scores (words read per minute) should not fall below 80. If the student scored below 80 words per minute, print a copy of the Speed Work story and have the student read the story silently before reading it aloud. Otherwise, move on to Classics Session 2.

The Leak in the Dike

Review the key words with students. Have students reread the story on their own. After rereading the story, students should complete the comprehension questions in *MARK¹² Classics for Young Readers* book on their own. Afterward, if time allows, have students read the story aloud to you.

W Write

The Leak in the Dike

1. How old is Peter?

   A. seven years old
   B. eight years old *(B circled)*
   C. nine years old
   D. ten years old

2. Peter lives in the Netherlands. What else is the Netherlands known as?

   A. France
   B. Europe
   C. Holland *(C circled)*
   D. North Sea

3. What job does Peter's mother have for him?

   Peter's mother asks him to take cakes to his friend, the blind man.

4. Why might the blind man enjoy Peter's visits?

   The blind man may enjoy Peter's visits because Peter is able to describe things the blind man cannot see for himself, such as birds and ships.

The Leak in the Dike **63**

---

5. Why do people fear a hole in the dike?

   People fear a hole in the dike because water could run through the hole, make it bigger, and eventually break the dike.

6. How long does Peter stay with his finger in the dike?

   A. all day
   B. all night *(B circled)*
   C. one hour
   D. two hours

7. Why doesn't Peter's mother go looking for him after dark?

   A. She is sure he will be home soon.
   B. He is always out later than he should be.
   C. She thinks he chose to stay the night with his friend. *(C circled)*
   D. He told her he was going to take his time getting home.

8. Why does the man who finds Peter call him a hero?

   The man who finds Peter calls him a hero because he knows that Peter saved Holland from a possible break in the dike.

64 *The Leak in the Dike*

Long *a* and Sight Words 5

ONLINE	Student & Computer	:60 minutes
	Adult : *Check Performance Review*	
OFFLINE	Student & Adult : Review online work	:30 minutes
	• Reading Warm-Up	
	• Speed Work	
	• Assessment	
	Composition	:30 minutes
	Instructional Time **2:00** hours	

Materials

- *MARK^{12} Reading Activity Book,* pages 199–202
- *Just Write*

Goals

In this lesson, students will read a summary of how the American colonies became free from British rule. Students will also review the long *a* spellings *a-consonant-e, ea,* and *eigh* before reviewing the sight words *many, animals,* and *while.* In today's Unit Assessment, you will administer a test covering all content from Unit 13. Afterward, you will work with students to complete Composition activities.

Advance Preparation

For the offline portion of today's lesson, gather the students' composition materials.

ONLINE	**Student & Computer**

Students will work online to complete Warm-Up, Code Work, Word Work, and Speed Work activities, and a review game on their own. Be sure to read the Performance Review before beginning the offline portion of today's lesson.

Today you will administer a Unit Assessment and work with students to complete a Composition activity.

Warm-Up ·

1784: The End of the Colonies

Look at the Performance Review. If the student achieved a perfect score on today's Warm-Up, move on to Speed Work. If the student scored 60 percent or 80 percent, print the story and review the comprehension questions with the student. If the student scored less than 60 percent, print the story, have the student read the story aloud, and then work through the comprehension questions together, before moving on to Speed Work.

Objectives

- Improve reading and comprehension skills.

Speed Work ·

Saturday

Look at the Performance Review, or check the student's fluency chart. Fluency scores (words read per minute) should not fall below 80. If the student scored below 80 words per minute, print a copy of the Speed Work story and have the student read the story silently before reading it aloud. Otherwise, move on to the Assessment.

Objectives

- Increase reading fluency rate.

☼ Assessment ·

Long *a* and Sight Words

Today's Unit Assessment covers all content found in Unit 13. Carefully read the instructions on the student pages before administering the test to the student. If necessary, read the directions to the student. After you have scored the student's assessment, be sure to go online and enter student performance scores in the assessment entry tool.

Part 1. Dictate the following words to students: *apron, flame, train, tray, eight,* and *steak.*

Part 5. Dictate the following words to students: *brother, would, weigh, sister, should, while, many, able, baby, animals, bail,* and *could.*

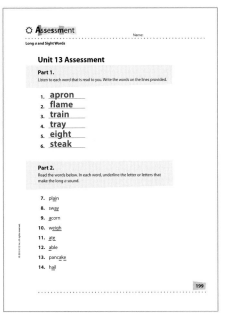

Unit 13 Assessment

Part 1.
Listen to each word that is read to you. Write the words on the lines provided.

1. **apron** ____
2. **flame** ____
3. **train** ____
4. **tray** ____
5. **eight** ____
6. **steak** ____

Part 2.
Read the words below. In each word, underline the letter or letters that make the long *a* sound.

7. plain
8. sway
9. acorn
10. weigh
11. ate
12. able
13. pancake
14. hail

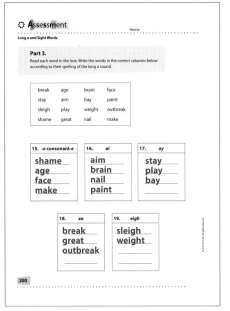

Part 3.
Read each word in the box. Write the words in the correct columns below according to their spelling of the long *a* sound.

break	age	brain	face
stay	aim	bay	paint
sleigh	play	weight	outbreak
shame	great	nail	make

15. *a-consonant-e*
shame
age
face
make

16. *ai*
aim
brain
nail
paint

17. *ay*
stay
play
bay

18. *ea*
break
great
outbreak

19. *eigh*
sleigh
weight

Part 4.
Choose the word from the box that best completes each sentence. Write the words on the lines provided.

| while | should | many | would |
| sleigh | baby | brother | animals |

20. Brent held his cat **while** ____ the vet gave it a shot.
21. What **would** ____ you like for lunch?
22. The **baby** ____ played in her crib.
23. There are **many** ____ kinds of rocks in this display.
24. It is fun to ride in a **sleigh** ____ through the snow.
25. My **brother** ____ likes to hike down this trail.
26. There are lots of **animals** ____ in the forest.
27. You **should** ____ never walk across this path without checking for cars.

Part 5.
In each row, underline the word that is read to you.

28. brother | both | bother
29. wand | world | would
30. weigh | wade | wane
31. sits | sister | sitter
32. shod | shoulder | should
33. wide | while | whine
34. many | mane | manner
35. above | able | about
36. baby | bade | babble
37. anvils | anyone | animals
38. ball | bail | bell
39. cold | cud | could

Objectives

- Identify the letters, given the sound /ā/.
- Identify and use /ā/ spelling patterns.
- Identify and use silent *e*.

Long a and Sight Words 5   225

Composition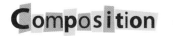

Gather students' composition materials and begin where they left off.

Long *i* and Sight Words 1

ONLINE	Student & Computer	:60 minutes
	Adult : *Check Performance Review*	
OFFLINE	Student & Adult : Review online work	:30 minutes
	• Reading Warm-Up	
	• Code Work	
	• Word Work	
	• Speed Work	
	Grammar, Usage, and Mechanics (GUM)	:30 minutes
	Instructional Time	**2:00** hours

Materials

- *MARK¹² Reading Activity Book*, pages 203–206

Tip

*The long i sound can be spelled many ways. One way is with the letter **i** alone. **Blind, climb**, and **grind** are three words that use the letter **i** alone to make the long i sound.*

Goals

In this lesson, students will read about a family preparing to take a wagon trip west. Students will also work with the long *i* sound before learning the sight words *other, together,* and *people.* In today's *MARK¹² Reading Activity Book* pages, you will work with students to reinforce their understanding of the long *i* sound and to reinforce their correct use of sight words. Afterward, you will work with students to complete activities on verbs.

Advance Preparation

Based on the Performance Review, if students must complete Word Work activity 2, create sight word cards for the following words: *other, together,* and *people.* If students need to complete Word Work activity 3, you will need a timer and the Online Tile Kit or Paper Letter Tiles. If students need to complete Word Work activity 5, create a second set of sight word cards for the words *other, together,* and *people.*

ONLINE | Student & Computer

Students will work online to complete Warm-Up, Code Work, Word Work, and Speed Work activities, and a Wrap-Up assessment on their own. Be sure to read the Performance Review before beginning the offline portion of today's lesson.

Today you will work with students to complete Code Work, Word Work, and GUM activities. Be sure to read the online Performance Review before beginning the Code Work and Word Work activities.

Warm-Up

A Wagon Full of Change

Look at the Performance Review. If the student achieved a perfect score on today's Warm-Up, move on to Code Work. If the student scored 60 percent or 80 percent, print the story and review the comprehension questions with the student. If the student scored less than 60 percent, print the story, have the student read the story aloud, and then work through the comprehension questions together, before moving on to Code Work.

Objectives

- Improve reading and comprehension skills.

Code Work

Long *i*

Look at the Performance Review. If the student achieved a perfect score on today's Code Work activities, complete the first activity from the list below. If the student scored less than 100 percent but more than 85 percent, complete the first three activities from the list below. If the student scored 85 percent or less, complete all five of the activities listed below.

Objectives

- Identify the letters, given the sound /ī/.
- Identify and use /ī/ spelling patterns.

1. Have students complete page 203 in *MARK¹² Reading Activity Book* for more practice on the long *i* sound.

2. Using the Online Tile Kit or Paper Letter Tiles, ask students to spell the following words: *child, find, grind, kind, mind,* and *wild.*

3. Have students secretly choose three of the words from activity 2. Then have students give you clues for each word while you guess which word is being described. Example: *A person is one of these before he or she becomes an adult.* Answer: *child.*

4. On a piece of paper, ask students to write sentences for three words from activity 2 and read the sentences aloud.

5. Have students write as many words with the long *i* sound spelled *i* as they think of in one minute. Words may include *child, mild, wild, climb, bind, find, hind, kind, mind, rind, wind, blind* and *grind.* Review the list with students. If students write the word *wind,* discuss the two ways it can be read: *I had to wind up the toy soldier to make it go. The wind blew the toy soldier over.* Use this as an opportunity to point out that reading words in context (in a sentence) helps readers understand the meaning of the word and therefore the pronunciation of the word.

Code Work   Name: _____

Long *i* and Sight Words 1

Practice Long *i*

Choose the word from the box that best completes each sentence. Write each word on the lines provided.

| child | find | hind | kind | wild |

1. Another word for nice is **kind** _____.
2. A lion is an example of a **wild** _____ animal.
3. An animal's back legs are called its **hind** _____ legs.
4. Can you help me **find** _____ my book?
5. A person is a **child** _____ before he or she becomes an adult.

Choose two words from the box above. Write each word in a sentence on the lines provided below.

6. _____

7. _____

203

ord Work ·

Sight Words

Look at the Performance Review. If the student achieved a perfect score on today's Word Work activities, complete the first activity from the list below. If the student scored less than 100 percent but more than 85 percent, complete the first three activities from the list below. If the student scored 85 percent or less, complete all of the activities listed below.

1. Have students complete page 204 in *MARK¹² Reading Activity Book* for more practice on sight words.

2. Using the sight word cards you created for *other, together,* and *people,* read each word to students and have students write the word on a piece of paper. Give students the sight words, and instruct students to look for any spelling mistakes they may have made. Students should correct the mistakes and then read the list of words aloud.

3. Gather all of the sight word cards students have worked on to date and a timer. Have students read all of the sight word cards as accurately and quickly as possible. Make note of the time, as well as any errors students have made. Use the Online Tile Kit or Paper Letter Tiles to review words read incorrectly.

4. Gather the cards for the sight words *other, together,* and *people,* and up to two additional sight words students have yet to master. Show the first card to students, and ask students to read the word. If students read the word correctly, place in one pile. If students read the word incorrectly, place in a separate pile. On the back of the cards that were read correctly, make a note of the date and put aside. (Once students have read the word correctly five consecutive days, you can remove the word from the pile of cards students are working on.) Review any words students read incorrectly, and keep the cards for next time.

5. Gather the two sets of sight word cards for the words *other, together,* and *people,* and place all of the cards face down on the table or another flat surface. Have students choose a card, read the word aloud, and then choose a second card. After students read the second card aloud, if the two cards match, students should keep the cards. If they do not match, students should return them to the table. Continue until all of the cards have been collected.

Code Work

Name: _____

Long *i* and Sight Words 1

Practice Long *i*

Choose the word from the box that best completes each sentence. Write each word on the lines provided.

| child | find | hind | kind | wild |

1. Another word for nice is __kind__
2. A lion is an example of a __wild__ animal.
3. An animal's back legs are called its __hind__ legs.
4. Can you help me __find__ my book?
5. A person is a __child__ before he or she becomes an adult.

Choose two words from the box above. Write each word in a sentence on the lines provided below.

6. _____
7. _____

203

Speed Work ·

Birds, Birds, Birds!

Look at the Performance Review, or check the student's fluency chart. Fluency scores (words read per minute) should not fall below 80. If the student scored below 80 words per minute, print a copy of the Speed Work story and have the student read the story silently before reading it aloud. Otherwise, move on to Grammar, Usage, and Mechanics.

Using Verbs

Objectives

• **Identify and use verbs in sentences.**

verb: tells what someone or something does or is.

action verb: shows action you can see (*dance*) or action that is mental and invisible (*think*).

being verb: doesn't show action but tells something about what the subject is.

helping verb: helps the main verb. Some examples: *am, was, has, will, is, were, have, can, are, been, had, might, be.*

Present and **past** forms of verbs do *not* use helping verbs.

Present participle and **past participle** forms of verbs *do* use helping verbs.

Work with students to complete pages 205 and 206 in the *MARK¹² Reading Activity Book*. Read page 205, Get Ready, with students. Have students complete the Try It page. Be sure to discuss students' answers when the page is completed.

Code Work   Name: _____
Long *i* and Sight Words 1

Practice Long *i*

Choose the word from the box that best completes each sentence.
Write each word on the lines provided.

| child | find | hind | kind | wild |

1. Another word for nice is __**kind**__
2. A lion is an example of a __**wild**__ animal.
3. An animal's back legs are called its __**hind**__ legs.
4. Can you help me __**find**__ my book?
5. A person is a __**child**__ before he or she becomes an adult.

Choose two words from the box above. Write each word in a sentence
on the lines provided below.

6. _____
_____

7. _____
_____

203

Code Work   Name: _____
Long *i* and Sight Words 1

Practice Long *i*

Choose the word from the box that best completes each sentence.
Write each word on the lines provided.

| child | find | hind | kind | wild |

1. Another word for nice is __**kind**__
2. A lion is an example of a __**wild**__ animal.
3. An animal's back legs are called its __**hind**__ legs.
4. Can you help me __**find**__ my book?
5. A person is a __**child**__ before he or she becomes an adult.

Choose two words from the box above. Write each word in a sentence
on the lines provided below.

6. _____
_____

7. _____
_____

203

Long *i* and Sight Words 2

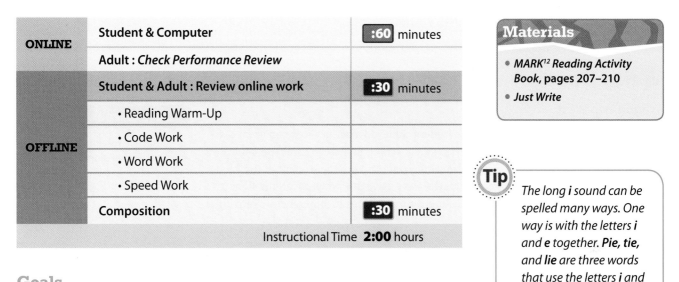

ONLINE	**Student & Computer**	**:60** minutes	
	Adult : *Check Performance Review*		
OFFLINE	**Student & Adult : Review online work**	**:30** minutes	
	• Reading Warm-Up		
	• Code Work		
	• Word Work		
	• Speed Work		
	Composition	**:30** minutes	

Instructional Time **2:00** hours

Tip

*The long i sound can be spelled many ways. One way is with the letters **i** and **e** together. **Pie, tie,** and **lie** are three words that use the letters **i** and **e** together to make the long **i** sound.*

Goals

In this lesson, students will read about life on a wagon trip west. Students will also work with the long *i* sound before working with the sight words *other, people,* and *together*. In today's *MARK¹² Reading Activity Book* pages, you will work with students to reinforce their understanding of the long *i* sound and to reinforce their correct use of sight words. Afterward, students will spend 30 minutes working on composition.

Advance Preparation

For the offline portion of today's lesson, gather the students' composition materials. Based on the Performance Review, if students need to complete Code Work activity 3, you will need the Online Tile Kit or Paper Letter Tiles. If students must complete Word Work activity 2, gather the sight word cards for the following words: *other, people,* and *together*. If students need to complete Word Work activity 3, you will need a timer and the Online Tile Kit or Paper Letter Tiles. If students need to complete Word Work activity 5, gather the second set of sight word cards for the words *other, people,* and *together*.

ONLINE	**Student & Computer**

Students will work online to complete Warm-Up, Code Work, Word Work, and Speed Work activities, and a Wrap-Up assessment on their own. Be sure to read the Performance Review before beginning the offline portion of today's lesson.

Today you will work with students to complete Code Work, Word Work, and Composition activities. Be sure to read the online Performance Review before beginning the Code Work and Word Work activities.

Warm-Up ·

Wagon Trip West

Look at the Performance Review. If the student achieved a perfect score on today's Warm-Up, move on to Code Work. If the student scored 60 percent or 80 percent, print the story and review the comprehension questions with the student. If the student scored less than 60 percent, print the story, have the student read the story aloud, and then work through the comprehension questions together, before moving on to Code Work.

Objectives

• Improve reading and comprehension skills.

Code Work ·

Long *i*

Look at the Performance Review. If the student achieved a perfect score on today's Code Work activities, complete the first two activities from the list below. If the student scored less than 100 percent but more than 85 percent, complete the first three activities from the list below. If the student scored 85 percent or less, complete all four of the activities listed below.

Objectives

• Identify the letters, given the sound /ī/.

• Identify and use /ī/ spelling patterns.

1. Have students complete page 207 in *MARK¹² Reading Activity Book* for more practice on the long *i* sound.

2. Remove the "Give Me a Break" story from *MARK¹² Reading Activity Book*. Fold the pages in half to create a small booklet. Review the following word with students: *scenery*. Have students read the story silently once or twice before reading the story aloud. When students read aloud, make note of any errors, and review those words with the students.

3. Using the Online Tile Kit or Paper Letter Tiles, have students spell the following words: *pie, child, tie, lie, die,* and *kind*.

4. Have students secretly choose three of the words from activity 3. Then have students give you clues for each word while you guess which word is being described. Example: *This is a type of dessert. It can be made with fruit. Some people eat it topped with ice cream.* Answer: *pie*.

Code Work Name: _____

Long *i* and Sight Words 2

Practice Long *i*

Choose the word from the box that best completes each sentence. Write each word on the lines provided.

pie	cried	lie	spied	tie

1. Who ate all of the **pie** _____?
2. The child **cried** _____ when his toy broke.
3. Mom's head hurt so she went to **lie** _____ down.
4. The baseball game ended in a **tie** _____.
5. Jon **spied** _____ on his sister and her friends.

Choose two words from the box above. On the lines provided below, write a sentence using each word. Then read each sentence aloud.

6. _____

7. _____

207

Word Work

Sight Words

Look at the Performance Review. If the student achieved a perfect score on today's Word Work activities, complete the first activity from the list below. If the student scored less than 100 percent but more than 85 percent, complete the first three activities from the list below. If the student scored 85 percent or less, complete all five of the activities listed below.

1. Have students complete page 208 in *MARK¹² Reading Activity Book* for more practice on sight words.

2. Using the sight word cards you created for *other, together,* and *people,* read each word to students and have students write the word on a piece of paper. Give students the sight words, and instruct students to look for any spelling mistakes they may have made. Students should correct the mistakes and then read the list of words aloud.

3. Gather all of the sight word cards students have worked on to date and a timer. Have students read all of the sight word cards as accurately and quickly as possible. Make note of the time, as well as any errors students have made. Use the Online Tile Kit or Paper Letter Tiles to review words read incorrectly.

4. Gather the cards for the sight words *other, together,* and *people,* and up to two additional sight words students have yet to master. Show the first card to students, and ask students to read the word. If students read the word correctly, place in one pile. If students read the word incorrectly, place in a separate pile. On the back of the cards that were read correctly, make a note of the date and put aside. (Once students have read the word correctly five consecutive days, you can remove the word from the pile of cards students are working on.) Review any words students read incorrectly, and keep the cards for next time.

5. Gather the two sets of sight word cards for the words *other, together,* and *people,* and place all of the cards face down on the table or another flat surface. Have students choose a card, read the word aloud, and then choose a second card. After students read the second card aloud, if the two cards match, students should keep the cards. If they do not match, students should return them to the table. Continue until all of the cards have been collected.

Word Work sheet (page 208)

Word Work   Name: _____

Long *i* and Sight Words 2

Sight Words Scramble

Unscramble each sight word. Write each unscrambled word on the lines provided.

1. aailmns — animals
2. eeolpp — people
3. aymn — many
4. reeoghtt — together
5. eohrt — other
6. eihlw — while

Writing Sentences

On the lines provided below, write a sentence for each sight word given above.

7. _____
8. _____
9. _____
10. _____
11. _____
12. _____

208

Speed Work

Seven Tries

Look at the Performance Review, or check the student's fluency chart. Fluency scores (words read per minute) should not fall below 80. If the student scored below 80 words per minute, print a copy of the Speed Work story and have the student read the story silently before reading it aloud. Otherwise, move on to Composition.

Composition ·

Gather students' composition materials and begin where they left off.

Objectives

- Develop composition skills.

Long *i* and Sight Words 3

ONLINE	Student & Computer	**:60** minutes	
	Adult : *Check Performance Review*		
OFFLINE	Student & Adult : Review online work	**:30** minutes	
	• Reading Warm-Up		
	• Code Work		
	• Word Work		
	• Speed Work		
	Classics Session 1	**:30** minutes	

Instructional Time **2:00** hours

Materials

- "The Brothers Grimm" MP3
- *MARK¹² Classics for Young Readers*
- *MARK¹² Reading Activity Book*, pages 211–212

Tip

*The long i sound can be spelled many ways. One way is with the letters **igh**. **High, sigh, fright**, and **slight** are examples of words that use the letters **igh** to make the long **i** sound.*

Goals

In this lesson, students will read about the first passenger railroad. Students will also work with the long *i* sound before learning the sight words *above, here,* and *move.* In today's *MARK¹² Reading Activity Book* pages, you will work with students to reinforce their understanding of the long *i* sound and to reinforce their correct use of sight words. Afterward, you will work with students to complete Classics activities.

Advance Preparation

For the offline portion of today's lesson, download this story: "The Brothers Grimm." Based on the Performance Review, if students need to complete Code Work Activity 3, gather eight index cards and write one of the following words on each card: *bring, flight, high, light, might, splinter, think,* and *winter.* If students must complete Word Work activity 2, create sight word cards for the following words: *above, here,* and *move.* If students need to complete Word Work activity 3, you will need a timer and the Online Tile Kit or Paper Letter Tiles. If students need to complete Word Work activity 5, you will need to create a second set of sight word cards for the words *above, here,* and *move.*

ONLINE   Student & Computer

Students will work online to complete Warm-Up, Code Work, Word Work, and Speed Work activities, and a Wrap-Up assessment on their own. Be sure to read the Performance Review before beginning the offline portion of today's lesson.

Today you will work with students to complete Code Work, Word Work, and *MARK¹² Classics for Young Readers* activities. Be sure to read the online Performance Review before beginning the Code Work and Word Work activities.

Warm-Up ·

Trains for the People

Look at the Performance Review. If the student achieved a perfect score on today's Warm-Up, move on to Code Work. If the student scored 60 percent or 80 percent, print the story and review the comprehension questions with the student. If the student scored less than 60 percent, print the story, have the student read the story aloud, and then work through the comprehension questions together, before moving on to Code Work.

Objectives

• **Improve reading and comprehension skills.**

Code Work ·

Long *i*

Look at the Performance Review. If the student achieved a perfect score on today's Code Work activities, complete the first activity from the list below. If the student scored less than 100 percent but more than 85 percent, complete the first three activities from the list below. If the student scored 85 percent or less, complete all five of the activities listed below.

Objectives

• **Identify the letters, given the sound /ī/.**

• **Identify and use /ī/ spelling patterns.**

1. Have students complete page 211 in *MARK¹² Reading Activity Book* for more practice on the long *i* sound.

2. Have students use the Online Tile Kit or Paper Letter Tiles to spell the following words: *bright, fright, high, sigh,* and *slight.*

3. Give students the index cards you previously prepared. Have them sort the cards into two piles: one pile for words that contain the sound /ī/ and one pile for words that do not contain the sound /ī/.

4. Have students write the opposites of the following words: *dark* (answer: *light* or *bright*), *low* (answer: *high*), *day* (answer: *night*), *left* (answer: *right*), *loose* (answer: *tight*). Have students underline the letters that make the long *i* sound in each word.

5. Have students write a sentence for five of the long *i* words from activities 2, 3, or 4. Then have students read their sentences aloud.

Code Work   Name:

Long *i* and Sight Words 3

The Long *i* Sound

Write each word from the box in the correct column below according to how the long *i* sound is spelled in each word. Then write one word of your own in each column.

bright	child	cries
dried	find	grind
high	tie	tight

i	*igh*	*ie*
child	bright	cries
find	high	dried
grind	tight	tie

Choose one word from each column above. On the lines provided below, write a sentence using each word. Then read each sentence aloud.

1. _____

2. _____

3. _____

211

Word Work

Sight Words

Look at the Performance Review. If the student achieved a perfect score on today's Word Work activities, complete the first activity from the list below. If the student scored less than 100 percent but more than 85 percent, complete the first three activities from the list below. If the student scored 85 percent or less, complete all five of the activities listed below.

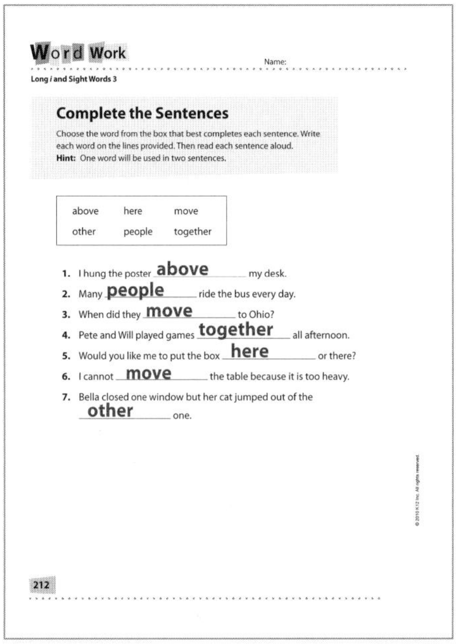

1. Have students complete page 212 in the *MARK¹² Reading Activity Book* for more practice on sight words.

2. Using the sight word cards you created for *above, here,* and *move,* read each word to students and have students write the word on a piece of paper. Give students the sight words, and instruct students to look for any spelling mistakes they may have made. Students should correct the mistakes and then read the list of words aloud.

3. Gather all of the sight word cards students have worked on to date and a timer. Have students read all of the sight word cards as accurately and quickly as possible. Make note of the time, as well as any errors students have made. Use the Online Tile Kit or Paper Letter Tiles to review words read incorrectly.

4. Gather the cards for the sight words *above, here,* and *move,* and up to two additional sight words students have yet to master. Show the first card to students, and ask students to read the word. If students read the word correctly, place in one pile. If students read the word incorrectly, place in a separate pile. On the back of the cards that were read correctly, make a note of the date and put aside. (Once students have read the word correctly five consecutive days, you can remove the word from the pile of cards students are working on.) Review any words students read incorrectly, and keep the cards for next time.

5. Gather the two sets of sight word cards for the words *above, here,* and *move,* and place all of the cards face down on the table or another flat surface. Have students choose a card, read the word aloud, and then choose a second card. After students read the second card aloud, if the two cards match, students should keep the cards. If they do not match, students should return them to the table. Continue until all of the cards have been collected.

Word Work sidebar

Word Work   Name:

Long i and Sight Words 3

Complete the Sentences

Choose the word from the box that best completes each sentence. Write each word on the lines provided. Then read each sentence aloud.
Hint: One word will be used in two sentences.

| above | here | move |
| other | people | together |

1. I hung the poster **above** my desk.
2. Many **people** ride the bus every day.
3. When did they **move** to Ohio?
4. Pete and Will played games **together** all afternoon.
5. Would you like me to put the box **here** or there?
6. I cannot **move** the table because it is too heavy.
7. Bella closed one window but her cat jumped out of the **other** one.

212

Speed Work

A Midnight Surprise

Look at the Performance Review, or check the student's fluency chart. Fluency scores (words read per minute) should not fall below 80. If the student scored below 80 words per minute, print a copy of the Speed Work story and have the student read the story silently before reading it aloud. Otherwise, move on to Classics Session 1.

# Classics Session 1

The Brothers Grimm

Today's story, "The Brothers Grimm," is about Jacob and Wilhelm Grimm and their love of stories. Download the story. Have students listen to the story while following along in *MARK¹² Classics for Young Readers*. Have students listen to the story again before writing a summary of the story.

Long *i* and Sight Words 4

ONLINE	Student & Computer	**:60** minutes	
	Adult : *Check Performance Review*		
OFFLINE	Student & Adult : Review online work	**:30** minutes	
	• Reading Warm-Up		
	• Code Work		
	• Word Work		
	• Speed Work		
	Classics Session 2	**:30** minutes	
	Instructional Time **2:00** hours		

Materials

- *MARK¹² Classics for Young Readers*
- "The Brother Grimm" MP3
- *MARK¹² Reading Activity Book*, pages 213–216

Tip

*The long **i** sound can be spelled many ways. One way is with the letter **i**, followed by a consonant, then by a silent **e**. **Chime**, **strive**, and **wise** are three words that use the letter **i**, followed by a consonant, then by a silent **e** to make the long **i** sound.*

Goals

In this lesson, students will read about a young factory worker in the 1800s. Students will also work with the long *i* sound before working with the sight words *above*, *here*, and *move*. In today's *MARK¹² Reading Activity Book* pages, you will work with students to reinforce their understanding of the long *i* sound and to reinforce their correct use of the sight words *above*, *here*, and *move*. Afterward, you will work with students to complete Classics activities.

Advance Preparation

For the offline portion of today's lesson, download this story: "The Brothers Grimm." Based on the Performance Review, if students need to complete Code Work activity 3, gather a newspaper or magazine. If students must complete Word Work activity 2, gather the sight word cards for the following words: *above*, *here*, and *move*. If students need to complete Word Work activity 3, you will need a timer and the Online Tile Kit or Paper Letter Tiles. If students need to complete Word Work activity 5, gather the second set of sight word cards for the words *above*, *here*, and *move*.

ONLINE Student & Computer

Students will work online to complete Warm-Up, Code Work, Word Work, and Speed Work activities, and a Wrap-Up assessment on their own. Be sure to read the Performance Review before beginning the offline portion of today's lesson.

Today you will work with students to complete Code Work, Word Work, and *MARK¹² Classics for Young Readers* activities. Be sure to read the online Performance Review before beginning the Code Work and Word Work activities.

Warm-Up ·

The Youngest Factory Workers

Look at the Performance Review. If the student achieved a perfect score on today's Warm-Up, move on to Code Work. If the student scored 60 percent or 80 percent, print the story and review the comprehension questions with the student. If the student scored less than 60 percent, print the story, have the student read the story aloud, and then work through the comprehension questions together, before moving on to Code Work.

Code Work ·

Long *i*

Look at the Performance Review. If the student achieved a perfect score on today's Code Work activities, complete the first two activities from the list below. If the student scored less than 100 percent but more than 85 percent, complete the first three activities from the list below. If the student scored 85 percent or less, complete all the activities listed below.

1. Have students complete page 213 in *MARK¹² Reading Activity Book* for more practice on the long *i* sound.

2. Remove the "What Is In a Name?" story from *MARK¹² Reading Activity Book*. Fold the pages in half to create a small booklet. Review the following words with students: *teeth, Birdie,* and *Myrtle.* Have students read the story silently once or twice before reading the story aloud. When students read aloud, make note of any errors, and review those words with the students.

3. Have students look through the newspaper or magazine you gathered, and circle as many words with the long *i* sound as they can find in two minutes. The words can use the *i, ie, igh,* or *i-consonant-e* spellings. Have students read the words aloud. Help students with pronunciations.

4. Dictate the following words to students and have them write the words on a piece of paper: *life, grind, tie, slight.* Have students underline the letter or letters that make the sound /ī/ in each word.

5. Take turns with students thinking of words containing the long *i* sound. Start by giving students a word (example: *shine*). Have students think of a different word containing the long *i* sound. Take turns for one minute or until you run out of words.

Code Work   Name:

Long *i* and Sight Words 4

Practice Long *i*

Choose the word from the box that best completes each sentence. Write each word on the lines provided. Then underline the letters that make the long *i* sound in each word. An example has been done for you.

| dime | child | right | pie | high |
| die | ice | wild | night | nine |

Example: Without water and sunlight, plants will __die__ .

1. Frozen water is __ice__ .
2. A __pie__ is a kind of dessert.
3. A __child__ grows into an adult.
4. The opposite of left is __right__ .
5. The opposite of low is __high__ .
6. The opposite of day is __night__ .
7. If an animal is not tame, it is __wild__ .
8. The number before ten is __nine__ .
9. A __dime__ is worth ten cents.

213

Word Work ·

Sight Words

Look at the Performance Review. If the student achieved a perfect score on today's Word Work activities, complete the first activity from the list below. If the student scored less than 100 percent but more than 85 percent, complete the first three activities from the list below. If the student scored 85 percent or less, complete all five of the activities listed below.

1. Have students complete page 214 in *MARK¹² Reading Activity Book* for more practice on sight words. To complete the page, you will need a timer. As students read the sight words, keep track of how many are read correctly.

2. Using the sight word cards for *above, here,* and *move,* read each word to students and have students write the word on a piece of paper. Give students the sight words, and instruct students to look for any spelling mistakes. Students should correct the mistakes and then read the list of words aloud.

3. Gather all of the sight word cards students have worked on to date and a timer. Have students read all of the sight word cards as accurately and quickly as possible. Make note of the time, as well as any errors students have made. Use the Online Tile Kit or Paper Letter Tiles to review words read incorrectly.

4. Gather the cards for the sight words *above, here,* and *move,* and up to two additional sight words students have yet to master. Show the first card to students, and ask students to read the word. If students read the word correctly, place in one pile. If students read the word incorrectly, place in a separate pile. On the back of the cards that were read correctly, make a note of the date and put aside. (Once students have read the word correctly five consecutive days, you can remove the word from the pile of cards students are working on.) Review any words students read incorrectly, and keep the cards for next time.

5. Gather the two sets of sight word cards for the words *above, here,* and *move,* and place the cards face down. Have students choose a card, read the word aloud, and then choose a second card. After students read the second card aloud, if the two cards match, students should keep the cards. If they do not match, students should return them to the table. Continue until all cards have been collected.

Word Work
Long i and Sight Words 4

Name:

By Sight

See how many words you can read correctly in one minute. Read aloud across the rows. When you get to the bottom of the page, start over. Try to read more words correctly the second time.

above	many	would	love	mother
here	animals	know	very	gone
move	while	together	some	only
other	brother	none	even	down
should	sister	more	look	after
people	baby	held	father	could

Number of words read correctly: _____

214

Speed Work ·

Five Miles

Look at the Performance Review, or check the student's fluency chart. Fluency scores (words read per minute) should not fall below 80. If the student scored below 80 words per minute, print a copy of the Speed Work story and have the student read the story silently before reading it aloud. Otherwise, move on to Classics Session 2.

Have students listen to the story again while following along in *MARK[12] Classics for Young Readers*. Afterward, students should complete the comprehension questions in *MARK[12] Classics for Young Readers* on their own.

W Write

The Brothers Grimm

1. Where did Jacob and Wilhelm Grimm grow up?

   A. Italy
   B. France
   C. Poland
   (D.) Germany

2. What did Jacob and Wilhelm Grimm love doing most of all?

   A. collecting rocks
   (B.) listening to stories
   C. playing hide-and-seek
   D. teasing their brothers and sister

3. Why were Jacob and Wilhelm sent to live with an aunt?

   The boys' father died, and their mother had her hands full with the younger children. For this reason, Jacob and Wilhelm (being the oldest boys) were sent to live with an aunt.

4. As adults, where did Jacob and Wilhelm both work?

   A. school
   (B.) library
   C. factory
   D. restaurant

68   The Brothers Grimm

---

5. Why did Jacob and Wilhelm decide to write a book of fairy tales?

   Jacob and Wilhelm decided to write a book of fairy tales because they couldn't find any already written, and they loved fairy tales very much.

6. What stories did the brothers write down?

   The brothers wrote down the stories they heard while growing up.

7. What did the brothers name their book?

   The brothers named their book *Children's and Household Tales.*

8. List any three Grimm's fairy tales.

   "Cinderella"
   "Sleeping Beauty"
   "Hansel and Gretel"
   "Snow White and the Seven Dwarfs"
   "Rapunzel"
   "Rumpelstiltskin"
   "Little Red Riding Hood"

The Brothers Grimm   69

Long *i* and Sight Words 5

ONLINE	Student & Computer	:60 minutes
	Adult : *Check Performance Review*	
OFFLINE	Student & Adult : Review online work	:30 minutes
	• Reading Warm-Up	
	• Speed Work	
	• Assessment	
	Grammar, Usage, and Mechanics (GUM)	:30 minutes
	Instructional Time **2:00** hours	

Materials

- *MARK¹² Reading Activity Book*, pages 217–222

Tip

The long *i* sound can be spelled with the letter *i* alone, the letters *ie* together, the letters *igh* together, and the letter *i* and a silent *e*, separated by a consonant. **Mild, pie, sigh,** and **stride** are examples of ways to spell the long *i* sound.

Goals

In this lesson, students will read about Elizabeth Cady Stanton. Students will also work with the long *i* sound before learning the sight words *there, against,* and *now.* In today's Unit Assessment, you will administer a test covering all content from Unit 14. Afterward, you will work with students to complete activities on adjectives.

ONLINE	Student & Computer

Students will work online to complete Warm-Up, Code Work, Word Work, and Speed Work activities, and a review game on their own. Be sure to read the Performance Review before beginning the offline portion of today's lesson.

Today you will administer a Unit Assessment and work with students to complete a GUM activity.

Warm-Up ·

Elizabeth Cady Stanton

Look at the Performance Review. If the student achieved a perfect score on today's Warm-Up, move on to Speed Work. If the student scored 60 percent or 80 percent, print the story and review the comprehension questions with the student. If the student scored less than 60 percent, print the story, have the student read the story aloud, and then work through the comprehension questions together, before moving on to Speed Work.

Speed Work ·

Shy

Look at the Performance Review, or check the student's fluency chart. Fluency scores (words read per minute) should not fall below 80. If the student scored below 80 words per minute, print a copy of the Speed Work story and have the student read the story silently before reading it aloud to you. Otherwise, move on to the Assessment.

☼ Assessment ·

Long *i* and Sight Words

Today's Unit Assessment covers all content found in Unit 14. Carefully read the instructions on the student pages before administering the test to the student. If necessary, read the directions to the student. After you have scored the student's assessment, be sure to go online and enter student performance scores in the assessment entry tool.

Part 2. Dictate the following words to students: *hive, child, dries, flight, lights, spied, wild, mind, fries,* and *might.*

Part 4. Dictate the following words to students: *above, against, here, move, now, other, people, there, together, against, now,* and *there.*

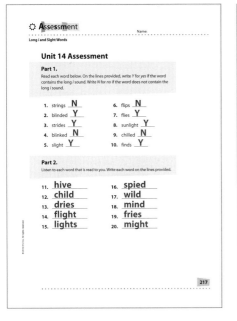

☼ **Assessment** Name:
Long *i* and Sight Words

Unit 14 Assessment

Part 1.
Read each word below. On the lines provided, write *Y* for yes if the word contains the long *i* sound. Write *N* for no if the word does not contain the long *i* sound.

1. strings __N__
2. blinded __Y__
3. strides __Y__
4. blinked __N__
5. slight __Y__

6. flips __N__
7. flies __Y__
8. sunlight __Y__
9. chilled __N__
10. finds __Y__

Part 2.
Listen to each word that is read to you. Write each word on the lines provided.

11. hive
12. child
13. dries
14. flight
15. lights

16. spied
17. wild
18. mind
19. fries
20. might

217

☼ **Assessment** Name:
Long *i* and Sight Words

Part 3.
In each row, underline the word that contains the long *i* sound.

21. <u>kind</u> kids kissed
22. skin <u>skies</u> skips
23. <u>sight</u> sir stink
24. <u>tries</u> trips tricks
25. think things <u>thigh</u>
26. shift <u>shine</u> ships
27. ticked tips <u>tied</u>
28. <u>find</u> finish fins
29. fist <u>fight</u> figs
30. girls ginger <u>grinds</u>

218

☼ **Assessment** Name:
Long *i* and Sight Words

Part 4.
In each row, underline the word that is read to you.

31. after animals <u>above</u>
32. <u>against</u> anything again
33. <u>here</u> held her
34. many <u>move</u> mother
35. <u>now</u> none next
36. out only <u>other</u>
37. put pull <u>people</u>
38. they <u>there</u> that
39. <u>together</u> too their
40. are <u>against</u> and
41. north napkin <u>now</u>
42. the <u>there</u> them

219

☼ **Assessment** Name:
Long *i* and Sight Words

Part 5.
Read each word aloud.

43. together
44. there
45. people
46. other
47. she
48. now
49. move
50. here
51. against
52. above
53. there
54. now
55. against

220

Objectives

- Identify the letters given the sound /ī/.
- Identify and use the silent *e*.
- Identify and use the /ī/ spelling patterns.
- Increase reading vocabulary.
- Read sight words.

Long *i* and Sight Words 5   **245**

Identifying Adjectives and Nouns

- Identify adjectives.

Adjectives are words that describe or modify nouns. They can make sentences more interesting by adding colorful details and lively descriptions. One of the most common ways adjectives describe nouns is that they describe *what kind*.

a *fast* car   What kind of car (noun)?   *fast* (adjective)

Many times, an adjective appears in a sentence before the noun it describes.

The *old* **mug** was filled with *hot* **tea**.

However, when the main verb of a sentence is a *being* verb, any adjective that describes the subject will probably follow the verb.

The **day** was *gray* and *rainy*.

Work with students to complete pages 221 and 222 in *MARK¹² Reading Activity Book*. Read page 221, Get Ready, with students. Have students complete the Try It page. Be sure to discuss students' answers when the page is completed.

G U M Grammar, Usage, and Mechanics   Name: _____

Long *i* and Sight Words 5

Get Ready

▪ **Adjectives** are words that describe nouns.

One of the most common ways adjectives describe nouns is that they describe *what kind*.

a *fast* car	What kind of car (noun)?	*fast* (adjective)
a *great* day	What kind of day (noun)?	*great* (adjective)
a *funny* joke	What kind of joke (noun)?	*funny* (adjective)

Many times, an adjective appears in a sentence before the noun it describes.

The *old* **mug** was filled with *hot* **tea**.

However, when the main verb of a sentence is a *being* verb, any adjective that describes the subject will probably follow the verb.

The **day** was *gray* and *rainy*.

Adjectives can make writing much more interesting by adding descriptive and lively details that help a reader see things more clearly.

That dog is *mine*.

That *spotted, friendly* dog is *mine*.

221

G U M Grammar, Usage, and Mechanics   Name: _____

Long *i* and Sight Words 5

Try It

On the lines provided, label each word as either an adjective (**A**) or a noun (**N**).

1.	**A** exciting	7.	**N** chicken	13.	**N** skateboard
2.	**A** wild	8.	**A** green	14.	**N** snake
3.	**N** teacup	9.	**N** pretzel	15.	**A** confused
4.	**N** shoe	10.	**A** scared	16.	**N** movie
5.	**A** sharp	11.	**N** bluebird	17.	**A** spotted
6.	**N** train	12.	**A** loud	18.	**N** cobweb

On the lines provided, write five adjective + noun pairs using the adjectives and nouns from above. An example has been done for you.

Example: spotted teacup

19. **Answers will vary.**

20. _____

21. _____

22. _____

23. _____

222

Long *o* and Sight Words 1

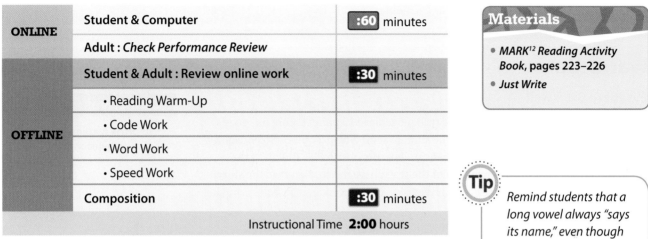

ONLINE	Student & Computer	:60 minutes
	Adult : *Check Performance Review*	
OFFLINE	Student & Adult : Review online work	:30 minutes
	• Reading Warm-Up	
	• Code Work	
	• Word Work	
	• Speed Work	
	Composition	:30 minutes

Instructional Time **2:00** hours

Materials

- *MARK*[12] *Reading Activity Book*, pages 223–226
- *Just Write*

Tip

Remind students that a long vowel always "says its name," even though it may be spelled in a number of ways. The two spellings covered in this lesson are **o** *and* **ow** *for the long* **o** *sound /ō/.*

Goals

In this lesson, students will read about Elizabeth Blackwell, the first female doctor in the U.S. Students will also be introduced to the *o* and *ow* spellings of the long *o* sound before reviewing the sight words *there, against,* and *now.* In today's *MARK*[12] *Reading Activity Book* pages, you will work with students to practice using the *o* and *ow* spellings for the long *o* sound in addition to reading sight words. Afterward, students will spend 30 minutes working on composition.

Advance Preparation

For the offline portion of today's lesson, gather the students' composition materials. Based on the Performance Review, if students need to complete Code Work activity 3, you will need the Online Tile Kit or Paper Letter Tiles. If students must complete Word Work activity 2, create sight word cards for the following words: *there, against,* and *now.* If students need to complete Word Work activity 3, you will need a timer and the Online Tile Kit or Paper Letter Tiles. If students need to complete Word Work activity 5, create a second set of sight word cards for the words *there, against,* and *now.*

ONLINE | Student & Computer

Students will work online to complete Warm-Up, Code Work, Word Work, and Speed Work activities, and a Wrap-Up assessment on their own. Be sure to read the Performance Review before beginning the offline portion of today's lesson.

Today you will work with students to complete Code Work, Word Work, and Composition activities. Be sure to read the online Performance Review before beginning the Code Work and Word Work activities.

Warm-Up 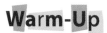 • • • • • • • • • • • • • • • • • •

Elizabeth Blackwell

Look at the Performance Review. If the student achieved a perfect score on today's Warm-Up, move on to Code Work. If the student scored 60 percent or 80 percent, print the story and review the comprehension questions with the student. If the student scored less than 60 percent, print the story, have the student read the story aloud, and then work through the comprehension questions together, before moving on to Code Work.

Code Work  • • • • • • • • • • • • • • • •

Long *o*

Look at the Performance Review. If the student achieved a perfect score on today's Code Work activities, complete the first two activities from the list below. If the student scored less than 100 percent but more than 85 percent, complete the first three activities from the list below. If the student scored 85 percent or less, complete all five of the activities listed below.

1. Have students complete page 223 in *MARK¹² Reading Activity Book* for more practice on the *o* and *ow* spellings of /ō/.

2. Remove the "Old Mo" story from *MARK¹² Reading Activity Book*. Fold the pages in half to create a small booklet. Review the following words with students: *mystery, something,* and *engine.* Have students read the story silently once or twice before reading the story aloud. When students read aloud, make note of any errors, and review those words.

3. Using the Online Tile Kit or Paper Letter Tiles, have students build the following words: *row, snow, stow, slow, mow, shadow, go, no,* and *so.* Have students identify the letters that make the long *o* sound in each word.

4. Challenge students to think of as many words as they can in one minute that use the *ow* spelling for the sound /ō/. Have students choose three of the words and use each one in a sentence.

5. Have students write the following words: *old, open, over,* and *sold.* Ask students to circle the letter that makes the long *o* sound in each word. Have students say as many other words that use *o* to spell the sound /ō/ as they can in two minutes. If students suggest any words in which the sound /ō/ is not spelled with the letter *o* alone, discuss how the sound /ō/ is spelled in those words.

Code Work   Name: _____

Long *o* and Sight Words 1

Practice Long *o*

Underline each word in the box that contains the long *o* sound, as in *go.*

hello	cow	over	row	plow
how	open	flow	plot	stow
sold	porch	storm	tow	told
glow	bold	fork	stop	snow

On the lines provided, write two words that contain the long *o* sound spelled *o* (choose words *not* shown in the box above).

1. **Answers will vary.**
2. _____

On the lines provided, write two words that contain the long *o* sound spelled *ow* (choose words *not* shown in the box above).

3. **Answers will vary.**
4. _____

223

Word **W**ork ·

Sight Words

Look at the Performance Review. If the student achieved a perfect score on today's Word Work activities, complete the first activity from the list below. If the student scored less than 100 percent but more than 85 percent, complete the first three activities from the list below. If the student scored 85 percent or less, complete all five of the activities listed below.

1. Have students complete page 224 in *MARK¹² Reading Activity Book* for more practice on sight words. To complete the page, you will need a timer. Keep track of how many are read correctly.

2. Using the sight word cards you created for *there, against,* and *now,* read each word to students and have students write the word on a piece of paper. Give students the sight words, and instruct students to look for any spelling mistakes. Students should correct the mistakes and then read the list of words aloud.

3. Gather all of the sight word cards students have worked on to date and a timer. Have students read all of the sight word cards as accurately and quickly as possible. Make note of the time, as well as any errors students have made. Use the Online Tile Kit or Paper Letter Tiles to review words read incorrectly.

4. Gather the cards for the sight words *there, against,* and *now,* and up to two additional sight words students have yet to master. Show the first card to students, and ask students to read the word. If students read the word correctly, place in one pile. If students read the word incorrectly, place in a separate pile. On the back of the cards that were read correctly, make a note of the date and put aside. (Once students have read the word correctly five consecutive days, you can remove the word from the pile of cards students are working on.) Review any words students read incorrectly, and keep the cards for next time.

5. Gather the two sets of sight word cards for the words *there, against,* and *now,* and place all of the cards face down. Have students choose a card, read the word aloud, and then choose a second card. After students read the second card aloud, if the two cards match, students should keep the cards. If they do not match, students should return them. Continue until all of the cards have been collected.

Word **W**ork
Name: _____
Long o and Sight Words 1

By Sight
See how many words you can read correctly in one minute. Read aloud across the rows. When you get to the last word, start over. Try to read more words the second time.

now	many	together	above	there
animals	move	people	sister	huge
while	brother	there	above	sister
many	against	together	people	animals
other	huge	baby	brother	against
while	now	other	baby	move

Number of words read correctly: _____

Word Finder
Underline the words *there, against,* and *now* in the rows above.

224

Speed **W**ork ·

Ten Tired, Wet Toes

Look at the Performance Review, or check the student's fluency chart. Fluency scores (words read per minute) should not fall below 80. If the student scored below 80 words per minute, print a copy of the Speed Work story and have the student read the story silently before reading it aloud. Otherwise, move on to Composition.

Composition

Gather students' composition materials and begin where they left off.

Objectives

- Develop composition skills.

Long *o* and Sight Words 2

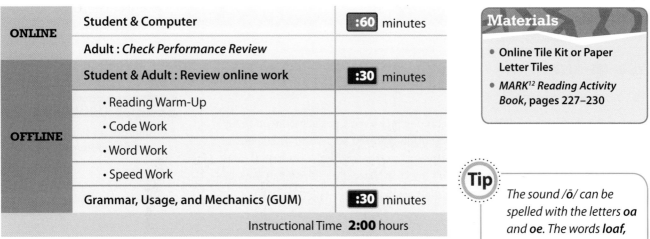

ONLINE	Student & Computer	:60 minutes
	Adult : *Check Performance Review*	
OFFLINE	Student & Adult : Review online work	:30 minutes
	• Reading Warm-Up	
	• Code Work	
	• Word Work	
	• Speed Work	
	Grammar, Usage, and Mechanics (GUM)	:30 minutes
	Instructional Time **2:00** hours	

Materials

- Online Tile Kit or Paper Letter Tiles
- *MARK¹² Reading Activity Book*, pages 227–230

Tip

*The sound /ō/ can be spelled with the letters **oa** and **oe**. The words **loaf**, **croak**, **oak**, **toe**, **hoe**, and **Joe** are examples of these two spelling patterns.*

Goals

In this lesson, students will read about the Pony Express that opened in 1860. Students will also be introduced to the *oa* and *oe* spellings of the long *o* sound before practicing the sight words *every, neighbor,* and *behind*. In today's *MARK¹² Reading Activity Book* pages, you will work with students to help them learn the *oa* and *oe* spellings for the long *o* sound in addition to reading sight words. Afterward, you will work with students to complete activities on the articles *a* and *an*.

Advance Preparation

Based on the Performance Review, if students need to complete Word Work activity 2, create sight word cards for the following words: *every, neighbor,* and *behind*. If students need to complete Word Work activity 3, you will need a timer and the Online Tile Kit or Paper Letter Tiles. If students need to complete Word Work activity 5, create a second set of sight word cards for the words *every, neighbor,* and *behind*.

ONLINE Student & Computer

Students will work online to complete Warm-Up, Code Work, Word Work, and Speed Work activities, and a Wrap-Up assessment on their own. Be sure to read the Performance Review before beginning the offline portion of today's lesson.

Today you will work with students to complete Code Work, Word Work, and GUM activities. Be sure to read the online Performance Review before beginning the Code Work and Word Work activities.

Warm-Up

The Pony Express

Look at the Performance Review. If the student achieved a perfect score on today's Warm-Up, move on to Code Work. If the student scored 60 percent or 80 percent, print the story and review the comprehension questions with the student. If the student scored less than 60 percent, print the story, have the student read the story aloud, and then work through the comprehension questions together, before moving on to Code Work.

Objectives

- Improve reading and comprehension skills.

Code Work

Long *o*

Look at the Performance Review. If the student achieved a perfect score on today's Code Work activities, complete the first two activities from the list below. If the student scored less than 100 percent but more than 85 percent, complete the first three activities from the list below. If the student scored 85 percent or less, complete all four of the activities listed below.

Objectives

- Identify the letters, given the sound /ō/.
- Identify and use /ō/ spelling patterns.

1. Have students complete page 223 in *MARK¹² Reading Activity Book* for more practice on the *oa* and *oe* spellings of the sound /ō/.

2. Using the Online Tile Kit or Paper Letter Tiles, have students build the following words: *Joan, Joe, loaf, goal, toe, road, moan, foe, boat, goat, soak,* and *hoe*. Have students identify the letters that make the long *o* sound in each word (*oa* or *oe*).

3. Beginning with the sample word *boat*, alternate with students for two minutes in thinking of words that contain the *oa* spelling for the sound /ō/. On a piece of paper, write the words in one column. Repeat for the *oe* spelling, beginning with the sample word *toe*. When completed, have students practice reading the two lists aloud to increase their recognition of the spelling patterns.

4. As time permits, have students verbally use *oa* and *oe* words from activity 3 in sentences.

Code Work
Name: _____
Long *o* and Sight Words 2

One Sound, Two Spellings
Write each word from the box in the correct column below according to the spelling of the long *o* sound.

soap	hoe	potatoes	road	throat
toes	boast	moan	Joe	loaf
foe	soak	toast	toad	croak

oa		oe	
soap	loaf	hoe	
road	soak	potatoes	
throat	toast	toes	
boast	toad	Joe	
moan	croak	foe	

227

Word **W**ork ·

Sight Words

Look at the Performance Review. If the student achieved a perfect score on today's Word Work activities, complete the first activity from the list below. If the student scored less than 100 percent but more than 85 percent, complete the first three activities from the list below. If the student scored 85 percent or less, complete all five of the activities listed below.

1. Have students complete page 223 in *MARK¹² Reading Activity Book* for more practice on sight words.

2. Using the sight word cards you created for *every, neighbor,* and *behind,* read each word to students and have students write the word on a piece of paper. Give students the sight words, and instruct students to look for any spelling mistakes they may have made. Students should correct the mistakes and then read the list of words aloud.

3. Gather all of the sight word cards students have worked on to date and a timer. Have students read all of the sight word cards as accurately and quickly as possible. Make note of the time, as well as any errors students have made. Use the Online Tile Kit or Paper Letter Tiles to review words read incorrectly.

4. Gather the cards for the sight words *every, neighbor,* and *behind,* and up to two additional sight words students have yet to master. Show the first card to students, and ask students to read the word. If students read the word correctly, place in one pile. If students read the word incorrectly, place in a separate pile. On the back of the cards that were read correctly, make a note of the date and put aside. (Once students have read the word correctly five consecutive days, you can remove the word from the pile of cards students are working on.) Review any words students read incorrectly, and keep the cards for next time.

5. Gather the two sets of sight word cards for the words *every, neighbor,* and *behind,* and place all of the cards face down on the table or another flat surface. Have students choose a card, read the word aloud, and then choose a second card. After students read the second card aloud, if the two cards match, students should keep the cards. If they do not match, students should return them to the table. Continue until all of the cards have been collected.

Speed **W**ork ·

Ants in Your Pants

Look at the Performance Review, or check the student's fluency chart. Fluency scores (words read per minute) should not fall below 80. If the student scored below 80 words per minute, print a copy of the Speed Work story and have the student read the story silently before reading it aloud. Otherwise, move on to Grammar, Usage, and Mechanics.

A and An

The articles *a* and *an* are used as adjectives to describe nouns. These articles refer to nouns that are part of a general group of persons, places, or things. For example: *I am reading a book.* (It's not a specific book.)

The article *a* is used before words that begin with a consonant: *a* notebook.

The article *an* is used before words that begin with a vowel: *an* egg.

The article *an* is also used when the first *sound* of a word is a vowel sound: *an* hour. (In *hour*, the *h* is silent. The first sound is /ow/.)

Work with students to complete pages 225 and 226 in *MARK¹² Reading Activity Book.* Read page 226, Get Ready, with students. Have students complete the Try It page. Be sure to discuss students' answers when the page is completed.

G U M Grammar, Usage, and Mechanics   Name: _____

Long *o* and Sight Words 2

Get Ready

▪ The words *a* and *an* are called *articles*. These short words are a kind of adjective. Like other adjectives, they describe a noun. *A* and *an* describe by telling us that a noun is one of a group or kind of person, place, or thing.

    Mom told us *a* story.
    Jed found *an* egg.

▪ In English, we use *a* before words that begin with a consonant sound. We use *an* before words that begin with a vowel sound. Notice that it is the first *sound*, not the first *letter*, that tells you which article to use.

    an apple
    a letter
    an hour (The first sound is a vowel sound even though the word *hour* starts with the consonant *h*.)
    a home (The first sound is the consonant *h*.)

229

G U M Grammar, Usage, and Mechanics   Name: _____

Long *o* and Sight Words 2

Try It

On the lines provided, write the correct article to use with each word or words: *a* or *an*.

1. **a** cold
2. **a** shadow
3. **an** ant
4. **an** ice cube
5. **an** hour
6. **a** home
7. **a** bowl
8. **a** rowboat
9. **a** phone
10. **an** ape

230

Long *o* and Sight Words 3

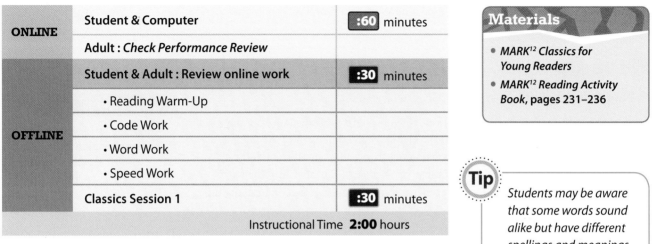

ONLINE	Student & Computer	:60 minutes
	Adult : *Check Performance Review*	
OFFLINE	Student & Adult : Review online work	:30 minutes
	• Reading Warm-Up	
	• Code Work	
	• Word Work	
	• Speed Work	
	Classics Session 1	:30 minutes

Instructional Time **2:00** hours

Materials

- *MARK¹² Classics for Young Readers*
- *MARK¹² Reading Activity Book*, pages 231–236

Tip

Students may be aware that some words sound alike but have different spellings and meanings. These words are called **homophones**. *Some examples of long* **o** *homophones are:* **road, rode; no, know; so, sow; and doe, dough.**

Goals

In this lesson, students will read about a trip to America. Students will also be introduced to the spelling pattern *o-consonant-e* for the sound /ō/ before reviewing the sight words *every, neighbor,* and *behind.* In today's *MARK¹² Reading Activity Book* pages, you will work with students to identify words with the spelling pattern *o-consonant-e* for the sound /ō/ and work with students to identify and write sight words.

Advance Preparation

Based on the Performance Review, if students need to complete Code Work activities 3 and/or 5, you will need the Online Tile Kit or Paper Letter Tiles. If students need to complete Word Work activity 2, gather the sight word cards for the following words: *every, neighbor,* and *behind.* If students need to complete Word Work activity 3, you will need a timer and the Online Tile Kit or Paper Letter Tiles. If students need to complete Word Work activity 5, gather the second set of sight word cards for the words *every, neighbor,* and *behind.*

ONLINE	Student & Computer

Students will work online to complete Warm-Up, Code Work, Word Work, and Speed Work activities, and a Wrap-Up assessment on their own. Be sure to read the Performance Review before beginning the offline portion of today's lesson.

Today you will work with students to complete Code Work, Word Work, and *MARK¹² Classics for Young Readers* activities. Be sure to read the online Performance Review before beginning the Code Work and Word Work activities.

 Warm-Up ·····················

Sailing to a New Life

Look at the Performance Review. If the student achieved a perfect score on today's Warm-Up, move on to Code Work. If the student scored 60 percent or 80 percent, print the story and review the comprehension questions with the student. If the student scored less than 60 percent, print the story, have the student read the story aloud, and then work through the comprehension questions together, before moving on to Code Work.

 Code Work ·····················

Long *o*

Look at the Performance Review. If the student achieved a perfect score on today's Code Work activities, complete the first two activities from the list below. If the student scored less than 100 percent but more than 85 percent, complete the first three activities from the list below. If the student scored 85 percent or less, complete all five of the activities listed below.

1. Have students complete page 231 in *MARK¹² Reading Activity Book* for more practice on the long *o* spelling pattern *o*-consonant-*e*.

2. Remove the "Dragon Tale" story from *MARK¹² Reading Activity Book*. Fold the pages in half to create a small booklet. Review the following words with students: *castle* and *drawbridge*. Have students read the story silently once or twice before reading the story aloud. When students read aloud, make note of any errors, and review those words with the students.

3. Using the Online Tile Kit or Paper Letter Tiles, have students build the following words: *broke, stroke, nose, rose, tone,* and *phone*. Have students identify the spelling pattern that makes the long *o* sound in each word.

4. Challenge students to think of as many words as they can in one minute that rhyme with the word *bone*. Write these words on a piece of paper and have students circle the words that use the spelling pattern *o*-consonant-*e*.

5. Using the Online Tile Kit or Paper Letter Tiles, have students build the following words: *go, hold, below, croak, doe,* and *bone*. Have students identify the letters that make the long *o* sound in each word.

Code Work Name: _____

Long o and Sight Words 3

Find the Right Word

In each sentence, find the word in which the long o sound is spelled with the letter o and a silent e, separated by a consonant. Write the word on the line provided.

1. The old house was made of stone. **stone**
2. My dog has a cold, wet nose. **nose**
3. I hope the boat will float. **hope**
4. Let us go home now. **home**
5. The farmer broke the ground with a hoe. **broke**
6. Do not talk on the phone now. **phone**

Writing Sentences

Choose two words from above in which the long o sound is spelled with the letter o and a silent e, separated by a consonant. On the lines provided below, write each word in a sentence.

7. _____

8. _____

231

Word Work ································

Sight Words

Look at the Performance Review. If the student achieved a perfect score on today's Word Work activities, complete the first activity from the list below. If the student scored less than 100 percent but more than 85 percent, complete the first three activities from the list below. If the student scored 85 percent or less, complete all five of the activities listed below.

1. Have students complete page 232 in *MARK¹² Reading Activity Book*. For items 1–3, dictate the words *every, behind,* and *neighbor* to students.

2. Using the sight word cards you created for *every, neighbor,* and *behind,* read each word to students and have students write the word on a piece of paper. Give students the sight words, and instruct students to look for any spelling mistakes they may have made. Students should correct the mistakes and then read the list of words aloud.

3. Gather all of the sight word cards students have worked on to date and a timer. Have students read all of the sight word cards as accurately and quickly as possible. Make note of the time, as well as any errors students have made. Use the Online Tile Kit or Paper Letter Tiles to review words read incorrectly.

4. Gather the cards for the sight words *every, neighbor,* and *behind,* and up to two additional sight words students have yet to master. Show the first card to students, and ask students to read the word. If students read the word correctly, place in one pile. If students read the word incorrectly, place in a separate pile. On the back of the cards that were read correctly, make a note of the date and put aside. (Once students have read the word correctly five consecutive days, you can remove the word from the pile of cards students are working on.) Review any words students read incorrectly, and keep the cards for next time.

5. Gather the two sets of sight word cards for the words *every, neighbor,* and *behind,* and place all of the cards face down on the table or another flat surface. Have students choose a card, read the word aloud, and then choose a second card. After students read the second card aloud, if the two cards match, students should keep the cards. If they do not match, students should return them to the table. Continue until all of the cards have been collected.

Speed Work ································

One Last Game

Look at the Performance Review, or check the student's fluency chart. Fluency scores (words read per minute) should not fall below 80. If the student scored below 80 words per minute, print a copy of the Speed Work story and have the student read the story silently before reading it aloud. Otherwise, move on to Classics Session 1.

Classics Session 1 ··

Dick Whittington and His Cat

Today's story, "Dick Whittington and His Cat," is an English folktale about a poor boy who earns a fortune through his cat. Review the keywords with students. Read the story with students, and then use the Discussion Questions below as a guide to share ideas about the story. Have students read the story again before writing a summary of the story.

Keywords

in spite of – an expression meaning "even though"
We went outside to play **in spite of** the rain.

garret, n. – a small room under the roof of a house
The **garret** was only six feet across, and you could see the sky through the cracks in the roof.

goods, n. – things made to be sold or traded
There were three kinds of canned **goods** on the grocery shelf: fruits, vegetables, and soups.

advise, v. – to give advice
My father **advised** me to keep my markers in a box so I would not lose any of them.

Discussion Questions

1. Do you think Dick should have believed everything he heard about London? Why or why not? Answers will vary.

2. What kind of person do you think Dick is? What words would you use to describe him? Answers may include that Dick is very kind-hearted. At the end of the story, he gives part of his treasure to the cook who had been cruel to him. He is also brave to travel to London alone. He is a hard worker who is determined to make a good life for himself.

3. Think about some qualities that make a good leader, such as kindness, generosity, and courage. Based on these qualities, do you think Dick would make a good mayor? Why or why not? Answers will vary.

4. What are some words you might use to describe Mr. Fitzwarren? Give evidence from the story to support your choices. Answers may include that Mr. Fitzwarren is kind because he lets Dick live in his home. He is also honest and fair because he does not keep Dick from "a single penny" of his treasure.

5. What are some of your dreams and goals? Dreams take hard work to achieve. Think of one or two things you may do someday to accomplish your goal. (For example, if you wanted to be a musician, you might practice and learn a lot about music.) Answers will vary.

Students should write a summary of the story to complete today's Classics activity.

Long *o* and Sight Words 4

ONLINE	Student & Computer	**:60** minutes	
	Adult : *Check Performance Review*		
OFFLINE	Student & Adult : Review online work	**:30** minutes	
	• Reading Warm-Up		
	• Code Work		
	• Word Work		
	• Speed Work		
	Classics Session 2	**:30** minutes	
	Instructional Time **2:00** hours		

Materials

- *MARK¹² Classics for Young Readers*
- *MARK¹² Reading Activity Book*, pages 237–238
- Online Tile Kit or Paper Letter Tiles

Tip

*The sound /ō/ can be spelled several different ways. Some of the words students will come across in today's lesson are homophones, such as **doe** (a homophone for **dough**) and **toe** (a homophone for **tow**).*

Goals

In this lesson, students will read the story of an immigrant arriving in America. Students will also review spellings of the long *o* sound before working with the sight words *once, come,* and *about*. In today's *MARK¹² Reading Activity Book* pages, you will work with students to reinforce their understanding of the long *o* sound and to reinforce their correct use of the sight words *once, come,* and *about*.

Advance Preparation

Based on the Performance Review, if students must complete Word Work activity 2, create sight word cards for the following words: *once, come,* and *about*. If students need to complete Word Work activity 5, create a second set of sight word cards for the words *once, come,* and *about*.

ONLINE Student & Computer

Students will work online to complete Warm-Up, Code Work, Word Work, and Speed Work activities, and a Wrap-Up assessment on their own. Be sure to read the Performance Review before beginning the offline portion of today's lesson.

Today you will work with students to complete Code Work, Word Work, and *MARK¹² Classics for Young Readers* activities. Be sure to read the online Performance Review before beginning the Code Work and Word Work activities.

Warm-Up  •

New Land, New Life

Look at the Performance Review. If the student achieved a perfect score on today's Warm-Up, move on to Code Work. If the student scored 60 percent or 80 percent, print the story and review the comprehension questions with the student. If the student scored less than 60 percent, print the story, have the student read the story aloud, and then work through the comprehension questions together, before moving on to Code Work.

Code Work •

Long *o*

Look at the Performance Review. If the student achieved a perfect score on today's Code Work activities, complete the first two activities from the list below. If the student scored less than 100 percent but more than 85 percent, complete the first three activities from the list below. If the student scored 85 percent or less, complete all five of the activities listed below.

1. Have students complete page 237 in *MARK¹² Reading Activity Book* for more practice on spellings of the long *o* sound.

2. Using the Online Tile Kit or Paper Letter Tiles, have students spell the following words: *hope, stone, toe, doe, toad,* and *moat*.

3. Have students secretly choose three of the words from activity 2. Then have students give you clues for each word while you guess which word is being described. Example: *It is deep. It is usually full of water. It goes around a castle.* Answer: *moat*

4. Have students write one sentence for each of the words they spelled in activity 2. Review the sentences with students and check the spelling of the long *o* words.

5. As time permits, have students brainstorm a list of as many long *o* words as they can. Ask students to write down the words, and then discuss how the long *o* sound is spelled in each word.

Code Work Name: _____

Long *o* and Sight Words 4

The Long *o* Sound

Write each word from the box in the correct column below according to how the long *o* sound is spelled in each word.

| hope | toad | stone | moat | note |
| foe | road | doe | toe | |

o-e	*oa*	*oe*
hope	road	toe
stone	moat	foe
note	toad	doe

Writing Sentences

Choose one word from each column above. On the lines provided below, write a sentence using each word. Then read each sentence aloud.

1. __Sentences will vary.__
2. _____
3. _____

237

Word Work

Sight Words

Look at the Performance Review. If the student achieved a perfect score on today's Word Work activities, complete the first activity from the list below. If the student scored less than 100 percent but more than 85 percent, complete the first three activities from the list below. If the student scored 85 percent or less, complete all five of the activities listed below.

Objectives
- Read sight words.
- Increase reading vocabulary.

1. Have students complete page 238 in *MARK¹² Reading Activity Book* for more practice on sight words.

2. Using the sight word cards you created for *once, come,* and *about,* read each word to students and have students write the word on a piece of paper. Give students the sight words, and instruct students to look for any spelling mistakes they may have made. Students should correct the mistakes and then read the list of words aloud.

3. Gather all of the sight word cards students have worked on to date and a timer. Have students read all of the sight word cards as accurately and quickly as possible. Make note of the time, as well as any errors students have made. Use the Online Tile Kit or Paper Letter Tiles to review words read incorrectly.

4. Gather the cards for the sight words *once, come,* and *about,* and up to two additional sight words students have yet to master. Show the first card to students, and ask students to read the word. If students read the word correctly, place in one pile. If students read the word incorrectly, place in a separate pile. On the back of the cards that were read correctly, make a note of the date and put aside. (Once students have read the word correctly five consecutive days, you can remove the word from the pile of cards students are working on.) Review any words students read incorrectly, and keep the cards for next time.

5. Gather the two sets of sight word cards for the words *once, come,* and *about,* and place all of the cards face down on the table or another flat surface. Have students choose a card, read the word aloud, and then choose a second card. After students read the second card aloud, if the two cards match, students should keep the cards. If they do not match, students should return them to the table. Continue until all of the cards have been collected.

Word Work sheet (page 238)

Word Work — Name: ___

Long *o* and Sight Words 4

Sight Words Scramble and Sentences

Unscramble each sight word. Write each unscrambled word on the lines provided.

1. roghbein — **neighbor**
2. ecno — **once**
3. moec — **come**
4. eeyrv — **every**
5. inhdeb — **behind**
6. tbaou — **about**

On the lines provided below, write each word from above in a sentence. Then read the sentences aloud.

7. **Sentences will vary.**
8. ___
9. ___
10. ___
11. ___
12. ___

238

Speed Work

Mom's Forever Trip

Objectives
- Increase reading fluency rate.

Look at the Performance Review, or check the student's fluency chart. Fluency scores (words read per minute) should not fall below 80. If the student scored below 80 words per minute, print a copy of the Speed Work story and have the student read the story silently before reading it aloud. Otherwise, move on to Classics Session 2.

Classics Session 2

Dick Whittington and His Cat

Review the keywords with students. Have students reread the story on their own. After rereading the story, students should complete the comprehension questions in *MARK¹² Classics for Young Readers* book on their own. Afterward, if time allows, have students read the story aloud to you.

Objectives

- Improve reading and comprehension questions.

Dick Whittington and His Cat

1. Who is the main character in the story?

The main character is Richard Whittington; everyone called him Dick.

2. What did Dick believe the streets of London were filled with?

(A) gold and silver
B. lost cats and dogs
C. poor boys like himself
D. people from many countries

3. Why did the wagon driver invite Dick to go to London with him?

The wagon driver invited Dick to go to London with him after he learned that Dick was a poor boy with no mother or father. He felt bad for Dick.

4. Who treated Dick poorly?

(A) cook
B. Alice
C. ship captain
D. Mr. Fitzwarren

5. What does Dick want to be when he grows up?

Dick wants to be Lord Mayor of London when he grows up.

6. What were the rats and mice doing that troubled the king and queen?

A. making a lot of noise
B. making nests in the pillows
C. chewing holes in the fine rugs
(D) eating the king and queen's dinner

7. Why was the queen scared to touch the cat at first?

(A) She had never seen a cat before.
B. She knew the cat would try to bite her.
C. She thought the cat's claws would scratch her.
D. She feared the cat might tear a hole in her dress.

8. Why did Dick believe he was being made fun of when he got to Mr. Fitzwarren's office?

Dick thought he was being made fun of because a chair had been placed out for him. He was not used to being treated so well, so he thought he was being fooled with.

Dick Whittington and His Cat   **81**

82   Dick Whittington and His Cat

Long *o* and Sight Words 5

ONLINE	Student & Computer	**:60** minutes	
	Adult : *Check Performance Review*		
OFFLINE	Student & Adult : Review online work	**:30** minutes	
	• Reading Warm-Up		
	• Speed Work		
	• Assessment		
	Composition	**:30** minutes	
	Instructional Time **2:00** hours		

Materials

- *MARK¹² Reading Activity Book*, pages 239–242
- *Just Write*

Goals

In this lesson, students will read about how Hull House acted as a sanctuary to immigrant families. Students will also review the long *o* spellings *o* and *ow* before reviewing the sight words *once, come,* and *about*. In today's Unit Assessment, you will administer a test covering all content from Unit 15. Afterward, you will work with students to complete Composition activities.

Advance Preparation

For the offline portion of today's lesson, gather the students' composition materials.

ONLINE	**Student & Computer**

Students will work online to complete Warm-Up, Code Work, Word Work, and Speed Work activities, and a review game on their own. Be sure to read the Performance Review before beginning the offline portion of today's lesson.

Today you will administer a Unit Assessment and work with students to complete a Composition activity.

Warm-Up ·······································

Hull House

Look at the Performance Review. If the student achieved a perfect score on today's Warm-Up, move on to Speed Work. If the student scored 60 percent or 80 percent, print the story and review the comprehension questions with the student. If the student scored less than 60 percent, print the story, have the student read the story aloud, and then work through the comprehension questions together, before moving on to Speed Work.

Objectives

- Improve reading and comprehension skills.

Speed Work ·······································

Two Trips to the Store

Look at the Performance Review, or check the student's fluency chart. Fluency scores (words read per minute) should not fall below 80. If the student scored below 80 words per minute, print a copy of the Speed Work story and have the student read the story silently before reading it aloud to you. Otherwise, move on to the Assessment.

Objectives

- Increase reading fluency rate.

☼ Assessment ·······································

Long *o* and Sight Words

Today's Unit Assessment covers all content found in Unit 15. Carefully read the instructions on the student pages before administering the test to the student. If necessary, read the directions to the student. After you have scored the student's assessment, be sure to go online and enter student performance scores in the assessment entry tool.

Part 1. Dictate the following words to students: *now, come, about, neighbor, against, once, behind, every,* and *there*.

Part 5. Dictate the following words to students: *there, against, now, every, neighbor, behind, once, come,* and *about*.

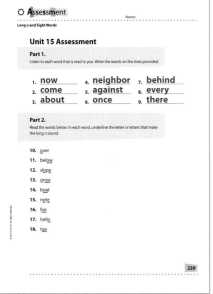

Unit 15 Assessment

Part 1.
Listen to each word that is read to you. Write the words on the lines provided.

1. now
2. come
3. about
4. neighbor
5. against
6. once
7. behind
8. every
9. there

Part 2.
Read the words below. In each word, underline the letter or letters that make the long o sound.

10. over
11. below
12. slope
13. grow
14. boat
15. note
16. foe
17. hello
18. toe

239

Part 3.
Choose the word from the box that best completes each sentence. Write the words on the lines provided.

| against | come | neighbor | there |
| about | every | once | behind |

19. I went to the shop **once** today, not twice.
20. John hid **behind** that tree.
21. Please lean the bat **against** the wall.
22. My **neighbor** is a very nice person.
23. It is time for Mark to **come** home.
24. All the kids are waiting over **there**.
25. I have **about** five dollars in my pocket.
26. I like **every** kind of candy.

240

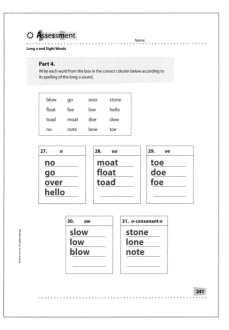

Part 4.
Write each word from the box in the correct column below according to its spelling of the long o sound.

blow	go	over	stone
float	foe	low	hello
toad	moat	doe	slow
no	note	lone	toe

27. o
no
go
over
hello

28. oa
moat
float
toad

29. oe
toe
doe
foe

30. ow
slow
low
blow

31. o-consonant-e
stone
lone
note

241

Part 5.
In each row, underline the word that is read to you.

32. <u>there</u>   then   that
33. again   gain   <u>against</u>
34. <u>now</u>   new   no
35. very   <u>every</u>   ever
36. nested   shoulder   <u>neighbor</u>
37. below   <u>behind</u>   because
38. <u>once</u>   one   just
39. came   <u>come</u>   core
40. <u>about</u>   above   around

242

Composition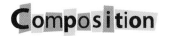

Gather students' composition materials and begin where they left off.

Long e and Sight Words 1

ONLINE	Student & Computer	**:60** minutes	
	Adult : *Check Performance Review*		
OFFLINE	Student & Adult : Review online work	**:30** minutes	
	• Reading Warm-Up		
	• Code Work		
	• Word Work		
	• Speed Work		
	Grammar, Usage, and Mechanics (GUM)	**:30** minutes	
	Instructional Time **2:00** hours		

Materials

- Online Tile Kit or Paper Letter Tiles
- *MARK¹² Reading Activity Book*, pages 243–246

Tip

*The letter **e** alone and the letters **e-e** together are two ways to spell the long e sound. **Be, he, keep,** and **meet** are examples of words that use the letter e alone and the letters e-e together to make the long e sound.*

Goals

In this lesson, students will read about the first cars. Students will also work with the long *e* sound before learning the sight words *please, follow,* and *saw.* In today's *MARK¹² Reading Activity Book* pages, you will work with students to reinforce their understanding of the long *e* sound and to reinforce their correct use of the sight words *please, follow,* and *saw.* Afterward, you will work with students to complete activities on singular and plural personal pronouns.

Advance Preparation

Based on the Performance Review, if students need to complete Word Work activity 2, create sight word cards for the following words: *please, follow,* and *saw.* If students need to complete Word Work activity 3, you will need a timer and the Online Tile Kit or Paper Letter Tiles. If students need to complete Word Work activity 5, create a second set of sight word cards for the words *please, follow,* and *saw.*

ONLINE   Student & Computer

Students will work online to complete Warm-Up, Code Work, Word Work, and Speed Work activities, and a Wrap-Up assessment on their own. Be sure to read the Performance Review before beginning the offline portion of today's lesson.

Today you will work with students to complete Code Work, Word Work, and GUM activities. Be sure to read the online Performance Review before beginning the Code Work and Word Work activities.

Warm-Up

Cars: From Factories to Families

Look at the Performance Review. If the student achieved a perfect score on today's Warm-Up, move on to Code Work. If the student scored 60 percent or 80 percent, print the story and review the comprehension questions with the student. If the student scored less than 60 percent, print the story, have the student read the story aloud, and then work through the comprehension questions together, before moving on to Code Work.

Objectives

• Improve reading and comprehension skills.

Code Work

Long *e*

Look at the Performance Review. If the student achieved a perfect score on today's Code Work activities, complete the first two activities from the list below. If the student scored less than 100 percent but more than 85 percent, complete the first three activities from the list below. If the student scored 85 percent or less, complete all four of the activities listed below.

Objectives

• Identify the letters, given the sound /ē/.
• Identify and use /ē/ spelling patterns.

1. Have students complete page 243 in *MARK¹² Reading Activity Book* for more practice on spellings of the long *e* sound.

2. Using the Online Tile Kit or Paper Letter Tiles, have students spell the following words: *cheek, feet, he, queen, seed, she, teeth, tree, we,* and *wheel*.

3. Ask students to secretly choose three of the words from activity 2. Then have students give you clues for each word while you guess which word is being described. Example: *You have two of these. You walk on them.* Answer: *feet*. If time permits, switch roles.

4. Have students write sentences for five words from activity 2 and then read the sentences aloud.

Code Work   Name:
Long *e* and Sight Words 1

Practice Long *e*
Read each sentence aloud. Underline the word or words in each sentence that contain the long *e* sound. Then read each sentence again.

1. He told me his feet hurt.
2. I like to sleep late on the weekends.
3. Dad asked me to sweep the kitchen.
4. We had a picnic on the soft green grass.
5. Grandpa planted seeds in his garden.
6. Three birds sat chirping on the same tree branch.
7. She does not like when weeds grow next to her flowers.
8. The queen gave a speech.
9. Can we hike up that steep mountain?
10. We will meet under the tree across the street.

243

Word Work ·····································

Sight Words

Look at the Performance Review. If the student achieved a perfect score on today's Word Work activities, complete the first activity from the list below. If the student scored less than 100 percent but more than 85 percent, complete the first three activities from the list below. If the student scored 85 percent or less, complete all five of the activities listed below.

1. Have students complete page 244 in *MARK¹² Reading Activity Book* for more practice on sight words.

2. Using the sight word cards you created for *please, follow,* and *saw,* read each word to students and have students write the word on a piece of paper. Give students the sight words, and instruct students to look for any spelling mistakes they may have made. Students should correct the mistakes and then read the list of words aloud.

3. Gather all of the sight word cards students have worked on to date and a timer. Have students read all of the sight word cards as accurately and quickly as possible. Make note of the time, as well as any errors students have made. Use the Online Tile Kit or Paper Letter Tiles to review words read incorrectly.

4. Gather the cards for the sight words *please, follow,* and *saw,* and up to two additional sight words students have yet to master. Show the first card to students, and ask students to read the word. If students read the word correctly, place in one pile. If students read the word incorrectly, place in a separate pile. On the back of the cards that were read correctly, make a note of the date and put aside. (Once students have read the word correctly five consecutive days, you can remove the word from the pile of cards students are working on.) Review any words students read incorrectly, and keep the cards for next time.

5. Gather the two sets of sight word cards for the words *please, follow,* and *saw,* and place all of the cards face down on the table or another flat surface. Have students choose a card, read the word aloud, and then choose a second card. After students read the second card aloud, if the two cards match, students should keep the cards. If they do not match, students should return them to the table. Continue until all of the cards have been collected.

The following is a reproduction of a worksheet:

Word Work   Name: _____

Long e and Sight Words 1

Complete the Sentences

Choose the word from the box that best completes each sentence. Write each word on the lines provided. Then read each sentence aloud.
Hint: One word will be used in two sentences.

about	behind	follow
neighbor	please	saw

1. James __saw__ Kristin and waved.
2. The book fell __behind__ the bookshelf.
3. Lane told Carl __about__ her track meet.
4. Our __neighbor__ washes his car every weekend.
5. I always say "__please__" when I ask for something.
6. My little brother likes to __follow__ me everywhere I go.
7. The play was __about__ a boy who meets a dog that can talk.

244

Speed Work ·····································

Green City's MVP

Look at the Performance Review, or check the student's fluency chart. Fluency scores (words read per minute) should not fall below 80. If the student scored below 80 words per minute, print a copy of the Speed Work story and have the student read the story silently before reading it aloud. Otherwise, move on to Grammar, Usage, and Mechanics.

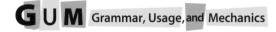

Singular and Plural Personal Pronouns

Objectives

• Identify and use singular personal pronouns and plural personal pronouns.

Pronouns can replace nouns in sentences. A *singular personal pronoun* can replace a singular common or proper noun in a sentence. The singular personal pronouns are *I, me, you, he, him, she, her,* and *it.*

Example: A *bug* bit Ted.

   It bit *him.*

A *plural personal pronoun* can take the place of more than one person, place, thing, or idea in a sentence. The plural personal pronouns are *we, us, you, they,* and *them.*

Example: *Kara and I* are going to summer camp.

   We are going to summer camp.

Work with students to complete pages 245 and 246 in *MARK¹²Reading Activity Book.* Read page 245, Get Ready, with students. Have students complete the Try It page. Be sure to discuss students' answers when the page is completed.

GUM Grammar, Usage, and Mechanics   Name:
Long *e* and Sight Words 1

Get Ready

■ A *noun* is a word that names a person, place, thing, or idea. A *pronoun* is a word that takes the place of a noun. The prefix *pro-* in *pronoun* means "instead of" or "for." A pronoun can be used instead of, or for, a noun in a sentence.

■ A *singular noun* names one person, place, thing, or idea. A *singular personal pronoun* replaces a singular proper or common noun in a sentence. The singular personal pronouns are *I, you, he, she, it, me, him,* and *her.* For example:

   A *bug* bit *Ted.*
   It bit *him.*

   Annie hurled the *football* at Dad.
   She hurled *it* at *him.*

■ A *plural noun* names more than one person, place, thing, or idea. A *plural personal pronoun* replaces a plural proper or common noun in a sentence. The plural personal pronouns are *we, you, they, us,* and *them.* For example:

   The *children* picked the *apples.*
   They picked *them.*

■ Plural personal pronouns refer to more than one person, place, thing, or idea. For example:

   Kara and I are going to summer camp.
   We are going to summer camp.

245

GUM Grammar, Usage, and Mechanics   Name:
Long *e* and Sight Words 1

Try It

Replace the underlined word or words in each sentence below with a singular personal pronoun or a plural personal pronoun. Write the pronouns on the lines provided.

Example: The wagon rolled down the hill.
   _It_ rolled down the hill.

1. Jennifer jumped for joy.
   She _____ jumped for joy.

2. You will find a rake in the shed.
   You will find **it** _____ in the shed.

3. Mr. and Mrs. Jones asked Francis and Phillip to sing.
   They _____ asked **them** _____ to sing.

4. Amber and I watched the horses prance around the ring.
   We _____ watched **them** _____ prance around the ring.

5. Please give the book to Fred.
   Please give **it** _____ to **him** _____.

6. Carlos and Mindy work at the animal shelter every weekend.
   They _____ work at the animal shelter every weekend.

246

Long e and Sight Words 2

ONLINE	Student & Computer	:60 minutes
	Adult : *Check Performance Review*	
OFFLINE	Student & Adult : Review online work	:30 minutes
	• Reading Warm-Up	
	• Code Work	
	• Word Work	
	• Speed Work	
	Composition	:30 minutes

Instructional Time **2:00** hours

Materials

- *MARK[12] Reading Activity Book*, pages 247–252
- *Just Write*

Tip

*The long **e** sound can be spelled many ways. One way is with the letters **e** and **a** together. **Cheap, lean**, and **treat** are three words that use the letters **e** and **a** together to spell the long **e** sound.*

Goals

In this lesson, students will read about life in America during World War I. Students will also work with the long *e* sound before working with the sight words *please, follow,* and *saw*. In today's *MARK[12] Reading Activity Book* pages, you will work with students to reinforce their understanding of the long *e* sound and to reinforce their correct use of the sight words *please, follow,* and *saw*. Afterward, students will spend 30 minutes working on composition.

Advance Preparation

For the offline portion of today's lesson, gather the students' composition materials. Based on the Performance Review, if students need to complete Word Work activity 2, gather the sight word cards for the following words: *please, follow,* and *saw*. If students need to complete Code Work activity 3 and/or Word Work activity 3, you will need the Online Tile Kit or Paper Letter Tiles. If students must complete Word Work activity 3, you will also need a timer. If students must complete Word Work activity 5, gather the second set of sight word cards for the words *please, follow,* and *saw*.

ONLINE   Student & Computer

Students will work online to complete Warm-Up, Code Work, Word Work, and Speed Work activities, and a Wrap-Up assessment on their own. Be sure to read the Performance Review before beginning the offline portion of today's lesson.

Today you will work with students to complete Code Work, Word Work, and Composition activities. Be sure to read the online Performance Review before beginning the Code Work and Word Work activities.

Warm-Up ·

World War I: The Great War

Look at the Performance Review. If the student achieved a perfect score on today's Warm-Up, move on to Code Work. If the student scored 60 percent or 80 percent, print the story and review the comprehension questions with the student. If the student scored less than 60 percent, print the story, have the student read the story aloud, and then work through the comprehension questions together, before moving on to Code Work.

Objectives

• Improve reading and comprehension skills.

Code Work ·

Long *e*

Look at the Performance Review. If the student achieved a perfect score on today's Code Work activities, complete the first two activities from the list below. If the student scored less than 100 percent but more than 85 percent, complete the first three activities from the list below. If the student scored 85 percent or less, complete all five of the activities listed below.

Objectives

• Identify the letters, given the sound /ē/.
• Identify and use /ē/ spelling patterns.

1. Have students complete page 247 in *MARK¹² Reading Activity Book* for more practice on spellings of the long *e* sound.

2. Remove "The Snowman" story from *MARK¹² Reading Activity Book*. Fold the pages in half to create a small booklet. Review the following words with students: *buried, clothes,* and *fruit*. Have students read the story silently once or twice before reading the story aloud. When students read aloud, make note of any errors, and review those words with the students.

3. Using the Online Tile Kit or Paper Letter Tiles, have students spell the following words: *beak, dream, feast, leash,* and *peach*.

4. Ask students to choose three of the words from activity 3 to draw for you. Students should neither tell you which word they are drawing, nor make any sounds or gestures to help you figure out the word. Once you guess the correct word, have students write that word under the picture.

5. Have students choose three words from activity 3 and write a sentence using each word. Students should then read each sentence aloud.

Code Work Name: _____
Long e and Sight Words 2

Practice Long e

Choose the word from the box that best completes each sentence. Write each word on the lines provided. Then read each sentence aloud.

| beak   eat   feel   neat   stream   we   wheat |

1. Bread can be made from **wheat**
2. What did you **eat** for lunch?
3. The bird used its **beak** to peck for food.
4. I **feel** tired in the mornings if I do not get enough sleep.
5. The animals drank water from the **stream**
6. I keep my side of the room **neat**, but my sister does not.
7. Patrick and I will play in the yard after **we** rake the leaves.

Choose three words from the box above. On the lines provided below, write a sentence using each word. Then read each sentence aloud.

8. _____
9. _____
10. _____

247

Word Work •

Sight Words

Look at the Performance Review. If the student achieved a perfect score on today's Word Work activities, complete the first activity from the list below. If the student scored less than 100 percent but more than 85 percent, complete the first three activities from the list below. If the student scored 85 percent or less, complete all five of the activities listed below.

1. Have students complete page 248 in *MARK¹² Reading Activity Book* for more practice on sight words.

2. Using the sight word cards you created for *please, follow,* and *saw,* read each word to students and have students write the word on a piece of paper. Give students the sight words, and instruct students to look for any spelling mistakes they may have made. Students should correct the mistakes and then read the list of words aloud.

3. Gather all of the sight word cards students have worked on to date and a timer. Have students read all of the sight word cards as accurately and quickly as possible. Make note of the time, as well as any errors students have made. Use the Online Tile Kit or Paper Letter Tiles to review words read incorrectly.

4. Gather the cards for the sight words *please, follow,* and *saw,* and up to two additional sight words students have yet to master. Show the first card to students, and ask students to read the word. If students read the word correctly, place in one pile. If students read the word incorrectly, place in a separate pile. On the back of the cards that were read correctly, make a note of the date and put aside. (Once students have read the word correctly five consecutive days, you can remove the word from the pile of cards students are working on.) Review any words students read incorrectly, and keep the cards for next time.

5. Gather the two sets of sight word cards for the words *please, follow,* and *saw,* and place all of the cards face down on the table or another flat surface. Have students choose a card, read the word aloud, and then choose a second card. After students read the second card aloud, if the two cards match, students should keep the cards. If they do not match, students should return them to the table. Continue until all of the cards have been collected.

Objectives

- Read sight words.
- Increase reading vocabulary.

Word Work
Long e and Sight Words 2

Sight Words Scramble
Unscramble each sight word. Write the unscrambled words on the lines provided.

1. oofllw **follow** 2. aeelps **please** 3. asw **saw**

Choose the sight word from above that best completes each sentence below. Write the words on the lines provided. Then read each sentence aloud.

4. **Please** ____ turn off the light when you leave the room.
5. We __**saw**__ the bird dive into the water and catch a fish.
6. If you __**follow**__ the directions, you will not get lost.

On the lines provided, write a sentence using each sight word from above.

7. _____
8. _____
9. _____

248

Speed Work •

Who Is the Baby Now?

Look at the Performance Review, or check the student's fluency chart. Fluency scores (words read per minute) should not fall below 80. If the student scored below 80 words per minute, print a copy of the Speed Work story and have the student read the story silently before reading it aloud. Otherwise, move on to Composition.

Objectives

- Increase reading fluency rate.

Composition

Gather students' composition materials and begin where they left off.

Long e and Sight Words 3

ONLINE	Student & Computer	**:60** minutes	
	Adult : *Check Performance Review*		
OFFLINE	Student & Adult : Review online work	**:30** minutes	
	• Reading Warm-Up		
	• Code Work		
	• Word Work		
	• Speed Work		
	Classics Session 1	**:30** minutes	
	Instructional Time	**2:00** hours	

Materials

- *MARK*[12] *Classics for Young Readers*
- **Online Tile Kit or Paper Letter Tiles**
- *MARK*[12] *Reading Activity Book*, pages 253–254
- **"Snow White and Rose Red" MP3**

Goals

In this lesson, students will read about women winning the right to vote in America. Students will also work with the long *e* sound before working with the sight words *everything, under,* and *whether.* In today's *MARK*[12] *Reading Activity Book,* you will work with students to reinforce their understanding of the long *e* sound and to reinforce their correct use of the sight words *everything, under,* and *whether.* Afterward, you will work with students to complete Classics activities.

Tip *The long **e** sound can be spelled many ways. One way is with the letters **i** and **e** together. **Fierce, shriek,** and **yield** are three words that use the letters **i** and **e** together to spell the long **e** sound.*

Advance Preparation

For the offline portion of today's lesson, download this story: "Snow White and Rose Red." Based on the Performance Review, if students need to complete Word Work activity 2, create sight word cards for the following words: *everything, under,* and *whether.* If students need to complete Word Work activity 3, you will need a timer and the Online Tile Kit or Paper Letter Tiles. If students need to complete Word Work activity 5, create a second set of sight word cards for the words *everything, under,* and *whether.*

ONLINE   Student & Computer

Students will work online to complete Warm-Up, Code Work, Word Work, and Speed Work activities, and a Wrap-Up assessment on their own. Be sure to read the Performance Review before beginning the offline portion of today's lesson.

Today you will work with students to complete Code Work, Word Work, and *MARK¹² Classics for Young Readers* activities. Be sure to read the online Performance Review before beginning the Code Work and Word Work activities.

Warm-Up ·

1920: Women Win the Right to Vote

Look at the Performance Review. If the student achieved a perfect score on today's Warm-Up, move on to Code Work. If the student scored 60 percent or 80 percent, print the story and review the comprehension questions with the student. If the student scored less than 60 percent, print the story, have the student read the story aloud, and then work through the comprehension questions together, before moving on to Code Work.

Objectives

• Improve reading and comprehension skills.

Code Work ·

Long *e*

Look at the Performance Review. If the student achieved a perfect score on today's Code Work activities, complete the first two activities from the list below. If the student scored less than 100 percent but more than 85 percent, complete the first three activities from the list below. If the student scored 85 percent or less, complete all four of the activities listed below.

Objectives

• Identify the letters, given the sound /ē/.

• Identify and use /ē/ spelling patterns.

1. Have students complete page 253 in *MARK¹² Reading Activity Book* for more practice on spellings of the long *e* sound.

2. Using the Online Tile Kit or Paper Letter Tiles, have students spell the following words: *brief, chief, field, pierce, shield,* and *thief.*

3. Ask students to secretly choose three of the words from activity 2. Then have students give you clues for each word while you guess which word is being described. Example: *This is another word for short or quick.* Answer: *brief.* If time permits, switch roles.

4. Have students write sentences using three words from activity 2 and read the sentences aloud.

Code Work   Name: _____

Long e and Sight Words 3

Long e

Read aloud each word in the box. Then write each word from the box in the correct column below according to the spelling of the long e sound. Last, write one new word of your own in each column.

be	steam	yield	screech
least	free	brownie	beans
we	me	greet	shriek

e	ee	ea	ie
be	free	least	yield
me	greet	beans	brownie
we	screech	steam	shriek

Choose one word from each column above. On the lines provided below, write a sentence using each word. Then read each sentence aloud.

1. **Sentences will vary.** _____
2. _____
3. _____
4. _____

253

Word Work ●

Sight Words

Look at the Performance Review. If the student achieved a perfect score on today's Word Work activities, complete the first activity from the list below. If the student scored less than 100 percent but more than 85 percent, complete the first three activities from the list below. If the student scored 85 percent or less, complete all five of the activities listed below.

1. Have students complete page 254 in *MARK¹² Reading Activity Book* for more practice on sight words.

2. Using the sight word cards you created for *everything, under,* and *whether,* read each word to students and have students write the word on a piece of paper. Give students the sight words, and instruct students to look for any spelling mistakes they may have made. Students should correct the mistakes and then read the list of words aloud.

3. Gather all of the sight word cards students have worked on to date and a timer. Have students read all of the sight word cards as accurately and quickly as possible. Make note of the time, as well as any errors students have made. Use the Online Tile Kit or Paper Letter Tiles to review words read incorrectly.

4. Gather the cards for the sight words *everything, under,* and *whether,* and up to two additional sight words students have yet to master. Show the first card to students, and ask students to read the word. If students read the word correctly, place in one pile. If students read the word incorrectly, place in a separate pile. On the back of the cards that were read correctly, make a note of the date and put aside. (Once students have read the word correctly five consecutive days, you can remove the word from the pile of cards students are working on.) Review any words students read incorrectly, and keep the cards for next time.

5. Gather the two sets of sight word cards for the words *everything, under,* and *whether,* and place all of the cards face down on the table or another flat surface. Have students choose a card, read the word aloud, and then choose a second card. After students read the second card aloud, if the two cards match, students should keep the cards. If they do not match, students should return them to the table. Continue until all of the cards have been collected.

Word Work worksheet preview:

Word Work Name: _____
Long e and Sight Words 3

Complete the Sentences
Choose the word from the box that best completes each sentence. Write each word on the lines provided. Then read each sentence aloud.
Hint: One word will be used in two sentences.

everything	about	please
saw	under	whether

1. The dog slept **under** the chair.
2. Joan and I **saw** that movie last week.
3. We sat in the shade **under** the big tree.
4. Will you **please** help me move the table?
5. I packed **everything** I needed for my trip to the beach.
6. Mom told me **about** the things she liked to do when she was my age.
7. Lauren had to decide **whether** to keep the stuffed animal or give it to her sister.

254

Speed Work ●

My Visit to the Big City

Look at the Performance Review, or check the student's fluency chart. Fluency scores (words read per minute) should not fall below 80. If the student scored below 80 words per minute, print a copy of the Speed Work story and have the student read the story silently before reading it aloud. Otherwise, move on to Classics Session 1.

Classics Session 1 ·

Snow White and Rose Red

Today's story, "Snow White and Rose Red," is about two sisters. Download the story. Have students listen to the story while following along in *MARK*[12] *Classics for Young Readers*. Have students listen to the story again before writing a summary of the story.

Students should write a summary of the story to complete today's Classics activity.

Long *e* and Sight Words 4

ONLINE	Student & Computer	**:60** minutes	
	Adult : *Check Performance Review*		
OFFLINE	Student & Adult : Review online work	**:30** minutes	
	• Reading Warm-Up		
	• Code Work		
	• Word Work		
	• Speed Work		
	Classics Session 2	**:30** minutes	
	Instructional Time	**2:00** hours	

Materials

- *MARK¹² Classics for Young Readers*
- "Snow White and Rose Red" MP3
- *MARK¹² Reading Activity Book*, pages 255–260

> **Tip**
>
> *The long **e** sound can be spelled many ways. One way is with the letter **e** and a silent **e**, separated by a consonant. **Adhere** and **extreme** are two words that use the letter **e** and a silent **e**, separated by a consonant to make the long **e** sound.*

Goals

In this lesson, students will read about life in the 1920s. Students will also work with the long *e* sound before working with the sight words *everything, under,* and *whether.* In today's *MARK¹² Reading Activity Book,* you will work with students to reinforce their understanding of the long *e* sound and to reinforce their correct use of the sight words *everything, under,* and *whether.* Afterward, you will work with students to complete Classics activities.

Advance Preparation

For the offline portion of today's lesson, download this story: "Snow White and Rose Red." Based on the Performance Review, if students need to complete Code Work activity 3, gather a newspaper or magazine. If students must complete Word Work activity 2, gather the sight word cards for the following words: *everything, under,* and *whether.* If students need to complete Word Work activity 3, you will need a timer and the Online Tile Kit or Paper Letter Tiles. If students need to complete Word Work activity 5, gather the second set of sight word cards for the words *everything, under,* and *whether.*

ONLINE | Student & Computer

Students will work online to complete Warm-Up, Code Work, Word Work, and Speed Work activities, and a Wrap-Up assessment on their own. Be sure to read the Performance Review before beginning the offline portion of today's lesson.

Today you will work with students to complete Code Work, Word Work, and *MARK¹² Classics for Young Readers* activities. Be sure to read the online Performance Review before beginning the Code Work and Word Work activities.

Warm-Up ·

Life in the 1920s

Look at the Performance Review. If the student achieved a perfect score on today's Warm-Up, move on to Code Work. If the student scored 60 percent or 80 percent, print the story and review the comprehension questions with the student. If the student scored less than 60 percent, print the story, have the student read the story aloud, and then work through the comprehension questions together, before moving on to Code Work.

Code Work ·

Long *e*

Look at the Performance Review. If the student achieved a perfect score on today's Code Work activities, complete the first two activities from the list below. If the student scored less than 100 percent but more than 85 percent, complete the first three activities from the list below. If the student scored 85 percent or less, complete all five of the activities listed below.

1. Have students complete page 255 in *MARK¹² Reading Activity Book* for more practice on spellings of the long *e* sound.

2. Remove the "What a Weekend" story from *MARK¹² Reading Activity Book*. Fold the pages in half to create a small booklet. Review the following words with students: *recycle, pizza, radio*. Have students read the story silently once or twice before reading the story aloud. When students read aloud, make note of any errors, and review them.

3. Have students look through the newspaper or magazine you gathered, and circle as many words with the long *e* sound as they can find in two minutes. The words can use the *e, ee, ea, ie,* or *e*-consonant-*e* spellings. Have students read the words aloud, helping students with pronunciations, if necessary.

4. Dictate the following words to students and have them write the words on a piece of paper: *she, greet, dream, chief,* and *athlete*. Have students underline the letter or letters that make the sound /ē/ in each word.

5. Take turns with students thinking of words containing the long *e* sound. Start by giving students a word (example: *trapeze*). Have students think of a different word containing the long *e* sound. Take turns for one minute or until you run out of words.

Code Work
Long e and Sight Words 4

Practice Long e

Choose the word from the box that best completes each sentence. Write each word on the lines provided. Then underline the letters that make the long e sound in each word. The first one has been done for you.

| athletes | bleed | brief | clean | he |
| here | me | thief | weak | weep |

1. The opposite of she is __he__.
2. Another word for cry is **weep**.
3. The opposite of strong is **weak**.
4. You **clean** something that is dirty.
5. If you cut yourself you might **bleed**.
6. People who play sports are **athletes**.
7. If something is short or quick it is **brief**.
8. Someone who steals from others is a **thief**.
9. Something that is in this place is **here**.
10. A word you use when you are talking about yourself is **me**.

255

Word **W**ork

Sight Words

Word **W**ork

Name: _____

Long e and Sight Words 4

Look at the Performance Review. If the student achieved a perfect score on today's Word Work activities, complete the first activity from the list below. If the student scored less than 100 percent but more than 85 percent, complete the first three activities from the list below. If the student scored 85 percent or less, complete all five of the activities listed below.

1. Have students complete page 256 in *MARK¹² Reading Activity Book* for more practice on sight words. To complete the page, you will need a timer. As students read the sight words, keep track of how many are read correctly.

2. Using the sight word cards you created for *everything, under,* and *whether,* read each word to students and have students write the word on a piece of paper. Give students the sight words, and instruct students to look for any spelling mistakes. Students should correct the mistakes and then read the list of words aloud.

3. Gather all of the sight word cards students have worked on to date and a timer. Have students read all of the sight word cards as accurately and quickly as possible. Make note of the time, as well as any errors students have made. Use the Online Tile Kit or Paper Letter Tiles to review words read incorrectly.

4. Gather the cards for the sight words *everything, under,* and *whether,* and up to two additional sight words students have yet to master. Show the first card to students, and ask students to read the word. If students read the word correctly, place in one pile. If students read the word incorrectly, place in a separate pile. On the back of the cards that were read correctly, make a note of the date and put aside. (Once students have read the word correctly five consecutive days, you can remove the word from the pile of cards students are working on.) Review words read incorrectly, and keep the cards for next time.

5. Gather the two sets of sight word cards for the words *everything, under,* and *whether.* Place the cards face down. Have students choose a card, read the word aloud, and then choose a second card. After students read the second card aloud, if the two cards match, students should keep the cards. If they do not match, students should return them. Continue until all cards have been collected.

Objectives

- **Read sight words.**
- **Increase reading vocabulary.**

By Sight

See how many words you can read correctly in one minute. Read aloud across the rows. When you get to the bottom of the page, start over. Try to read more words the second time.

about	baby	come	everything	follow
held	love	many	neighbor	once
please	saw	there	under	very
whether	above	behind	could	every
here	more	none	other	people
should	together	while	against	brother
move	now	sister	would	animals

Number of words read correctly: _____

256

Speed **W**ork

So Much for My Day in the Sun

Look at the Performance Review, or check the student's fluency chart. Fluency scores (words read per minute) should not fall below 80. If the student scored below 80 words per minute, print a copy of the Speed Work story and have the student read the story silently before reading it aloud. Otherwise, move on to Classics Session 2.

Objectives

- **Increase reading fluency rate.**

Classics Session 2

Snow White and Rose Red

Have students listen to the story again while following along in *MARK¹² Classics for Young Readers*. Afterward, students should complete the comprehension questions in *MARK¹² Classics for Young Readers* on their own.

Objectives

- Improve reading and comprehension skills.

Snow White and Rose Red

1. Based on information in the story, which words best describe Snow White?
   A. clever and sly
   B. **sweet and kind**
   C. loud and chatty
   D. mean and selfish

2. Who did the girls' mother think the child in white clothes was?
   The girls' mother thought the child in white clothes was an angel sent to watch over good children.

3. At night, what did Snow White and Rose Red's mother do while the girls knit their stockings?
   A. **read**
   B. slept
   C. cooked
   D. cleaned

4. Why did the bear come to Snow White and Rose Red's house?
   The bear came to Snow White and Rose Red's house because it was cold. The bear wished to warm himself by the fire.

5. Why is the bear more concerned about hiding his gold from the dwarfs in the spring than in the winter?
   During the winter, with the ground frozen, it is hard for the dwarfs to find the bear's gold. In the spring, the earth is warmer, and it is easy for the dwarfs to dig up the gold.

6. How did Snow White free the dwarf from the tree?
   Snow White freed the dwarf from the tree by cutting off some of his beard that was caught in the trunk.

7. Which of the following did Snow White and Rose Red **not** see the dwarf with?
   A. gold
   B. pearls
   C. **rubies**
   D. diamonds

8. Who does the bear turn out to be?
   A. duke
   B. king
   C. **prince**
   D. emperor

92 Snow White and Rose Red

Snow White and Rose Red 93

282 **Long e and Sight Words**

Long e and Sight Words 5

ONLINE	Student & Computer	**:60** minutes	
	Adult : *Check Performance Review*		
OFFLINE	Student & Adult : Review online work	**:30** minutes	
	• Reading Warm-Up		
	• Speed Work		
	• Assessment		
	Grammar, Usage, and Mechanics (GUM)	**:30** minutes	
	Instructional Time **2:00** hours		

Materials

- *MARK¹² Reading Activity Book*, pages 261–266

Tip

The long e sound can be spelled with the letter e alone, the letters ee, ea, or ie together, and the letter e and a silent e, separated by a consonant. Be, deep, eat, field, and adhere are examples of ways to spell the long e sound.

Goals

In this lesson, students will read about silent films. Students will also work with the long *e* sound before learning the sight words n*othing, almost,* and *over.* In today's Unit Assessment, you will administer a test covering all content from Unit 16. Afterward, you will work with students to complete activities on subject and object pronouns.

ONLINE   Student & Computer

Students will work online to complete Warm-Up, Code Work, Word Work, and Speed Work activities, and a review game on their own. Be sure to read the Performance Review before beginning the offline portion of today's lesson.

Today you will administer a Unit Assessment and work with students to complete a GUM activity.

Warm-Up ·

Before Sound: Silent Films

Look at the Performance Review. If the student achieved a perfect score on today's Warm-Up, move on to Speed Work. If the student scored 60 percent or 80 percent, print the story and review the comprehension questions with the student. If the student scored less than 60 percent, print the story, have the student read the story aloud, and then work through the comprehension questions together, before moving on to Speed Work.

Objectives
- Improve reading and comprehension skills.

Speed Work ·

Waiting on the Kitchen Counter

Look at the Performance Review, or check the student's fluency chart. Fluency scores (words read per minute) should not fall below 80. If the student scored below 80 words per minute, print a copy of the Speed Work story and have the student read the story silently before reading it aloud to you. Otherwise, move on to the Assessment.

Objectives
- Increase reading fluency rate.

☼ Assessment ·

Long _e_ and Sight Words

Today's Unit Assessment covers all content found in Unit 16. Carefully read the instructions on the student pages before administering the test to the student. If necessary, read the directions to the student. After you have scored the student's assessment, be sure to go online and input student performance scores in the assessment entry tool.

Part 2. Dictate the following words to students: _athlete, shield, steam, teeth, she, peach, greed, speech, reach,_ and _grief._

Part 4. Dictate the following words to students: _almost, everything, follow, nothing, over, please, saw, under, whether, nothing, over,_ and _almost._

Assessment

Name: _____

Long e and Sight Words

Unit 16 Assessment

Part 1.
Read each word below. On the lines provided, write *Y* for *yes* if the word contains the long *e* sound. Write *N* for *no* if the word does not contain the long *e* sound.

1. be **Y**
2. needs **Y**
3. held **N**
4. chief **Y**
5. heat **Y**
6. pressed **N**
7. extreme **Y**
8. queen **Y**
9. fresh **N**
10. dreams **Y**

Part 2.
Listen to each word that is read to you. Write each word on the lines provided.

11. **athlete**
12. **shield**
13. **steam**
14. **teeth**
15. **she**
16. **peach**
17. **greed**
18. **speech**
19. **reach**
20. **grief**

Assessment

Name: _____

Long e and Sight Words

Part 3.
In each row, underline the word that contains the long *e* sound.

21.	<u>me</u>	melt	men
22.	felt	<u>feet</u>	fed
23.	<u>beads</u>	belt	best
24.	<u>field</u>	filled	fled
25.	hens	helped	<u>here</u>
26.	tame	<u>team</u>	them
27.	wet	weld	<u>weep</u>
28.	yes	<u>yield</u>	yet
29.	day	dented	<u>deal</u>
30.	<u>we</u>	west	well

Assessment

Name: _____

Long e and Sight Words

Part 4.
In each row, underline the word that is read to you.

31.	about	animals	<u>almost</u>
32.	<u>everything</u>	every	even
33.	father	<u>follow</u>	friend
34.	<u>nothing</u>	none	next
35.	out	only	<u>over</u>
36.	put	pull	<u>please</u>
37.	sister	<u>saw</u>	some
38.	<u>under</u>	unless	until
39.	while	<u>whether</u>	walk
40.	north	napkin	<u>nothing</u>
41.	once	<u>over</u>	other
42.	<u>almost</u>	above	against

Assessment

Name: _____

Long e and Sight Words

Part 5.
Read each word aloud.

43. over
44. nothing
45. almost
46. whether
47. under
48. saw
49. please
50. over
51. nothing
52. follow
53. everything
54. almost

Objectives

- Identify the letters, given the sound /ē/.
- Identify and use silent *e*.
- Identify and use /ē/ spelling patterns.

Subject and Object Pronouns

The subject of a sentence tells who or what the sentence is about. Only certain *personal pronouns* should be used as the subjects of a sentence. These pronouns are:

singular:	I	you	he	she	it
plural:	we	you	they		

In most cases, only certain personal pronouns are used *after the verb* in a sentence. They are sometimes called *object pronouns*. These pronouns are:

singular:	me	you	him	her	it
plural:	us	you	them		

Work with students to complete pages 265 and 266 in *MARK¹² Reading Activity Book*. Read page 265, Get Ready, with students. Have students complete the Try It page. Be sure to discuss students' answers when the page is completed.

G U M Grammar, Usage, and Mechanics   Name: _____

Long *e* and Sight Words 5

Get Ready

■ **Personal Pronouns as Subjects of Sentences**
The **subject** of a sentence tells who or what the sentence is about. What is the subject of the following sentence?

The astronaut blasted off in the rocket.

To find the subject, ask, "Who or what is the sentence about?" Who or what blasted off in the rocket? *The astronaut* is the subject of the sentence. You can replace *the astronaut* with a pronoun, but only certain **personal pronouns** should be used as the subjects of a sentence. These are:

| *singular:* | I | you | he | she | it |
| *plural:* | we | you | they |

So, you could say:

She blasted off in the rocket.   OR   *He* blasted off in the rocket.

■ **Personal Pronouns After Verbs**
Find the verb in this sentence:

The artists draw their sketches on the walls.

The verb is *draw*. What do the artists draw on the walls? Their sketches. You can replace *their sketches* with a pronoun, but in most cases, only certain personal pronouns are used *after the verb* in a sentence. They are sometimes called **object pronouns**. These pronouns are:

| *singular:* | me | you | him | her | it |
| *plural:* | us | you | them |

So, you could say:

The artists draw *them* on the walls.

265

G U M Grammar, Usage, and Mechanics   Name: _____

Long *e* and Sight Words 5

Try It
Underline the subject pronoun in each sentence.

1. <u>We</u> read books to learn about the moon.
2. <u>It</u> has craters.
3. <u>They</u> are really deep holes in the moon's surface.
4. Someday, <u>I</u> would like to visit the moon.

Try It
Underline the correct pronoun in parentheses that completes each sentence.

5. That mean hornet chased (I, <u>me</u>)!
6. We have never met (he, <u>him</u>) before.
7. My father says he has seen (<u>them</u>, they).
8. Andrew is driving into town with (<u>her</u>, she).
9. Kevin and (me, <u>I</u>) would like to write a book together.
10. (Her, <u>She</u>) and Rose will travel together this summer.
11. The governor asked (<u>us</u>, we) to sing at the ceremony.

266

Long *e* Spelled *ie* and Sight Words

ONLINE	Student & Computer	**:60** minutes	
	Adult : *Check Performance Review*		
OFFLINE	Student & Adult : Review online work	**:30** minutes	
	• Reading Warm-Up		
	• Code Work		
	• Word Work		
	• Speed Work		
	Composition	**:30** minutes	

Instructional Time **2:00** hours

Materials

- *MARK¹² Reading Activity Book*, pages 267–272
- *Just Write*

Goals

In this lesson, students will read about family life while a father is away fighting during World War II. Students will also learn the long *e* spelling *ie* before reviewing the sight words *nothing, almost,* and *over.* In today's *MARK¹² Reading Activity Book* pages, you will work with students on practicing words with the *ie* spelling of the long *e* sound as well as spelling sight words.

Advance Preparation

For the offline portion of today's lesson, gather the students' composition materials. Based on the Performance Review, if students need to complete Word Work activity 2, create the sight word cards for the following words: *nothing, almost,* and *over.* If students need to complete Word Work activity 3, you will need a timer and the Online Tile Kit or Paper Letter Tiles. If students need to complete Word Work activity 5, create a second set of sight word cards for the words *nothing, almost,* and *over.*

ONLINE   Student & Computer

Students will work online to complete Warm-Up, Code Work, Word Work, and Speed Work activities, and a Wrap-Up assessment on their own. Be sure to read the Performance Review before beginning the offline portion of today's lesson.

Today you will work with students to complete Code Work, Word Work, and Composition activities. Be sure to read the online Performance Review before beginning the Code Work and Word Work activities.

Warm-Up ·

Life During World War II

Look at the Performance Review. If the student achieved a perfect score on today's Warm-Up, move on to Code Work. If the student scored 60 percent or 80 percent, print the story and review the comprehension questions with the student. If the student scored less than 60 percent, print the story, have the student read the story aloud, and then work through the comprehension questions together, before moving on to Code Work.

Objectives

- Improve reading and comprehension skills.

Code Work ·

E, i, & y

Look at the Performance Review. If the student achieved a perfect score on today's Code Work activities, complete the first two activities from the list below. If the student scored less than 100 percent but more than 85 percent, complete the first three activities from the list below. If the student scored 85 percent or less, complete all four of the activities listed below.

Objectives

- Identify the letters, given the sound /ē/.
- Identify and use /ē/ spelling patterns.

1. Have students complete page 267 in *MARK¹² Reading Activity Book* for more practice on words with the long *e* spelling *ie*.

2. Remove the "Time Out!" story from *MARK¹² Reading Activity Book*. Fold the pages in half to create a small booklet. Review the following words with students: *family, caddy, though.* Have students read the story silently once or twice before reading the story aloud. When students read aloud, make note of any errors, and review those words with the students.

3. Using the Online Tile Kit or Paper Letter Tiles, have students build the following words: *brief, chief, grief, niece, thief,* and *yield.* Have students identify the vowel sound that is contained in each word.

4. Have students verbally use each word from activity 3 in a sentence. Verify students' understanding of each word is correct.

Word Work

Sight Words

Look at the Performance Review. If the student achieved a perfect score on today's Word Work activities, complete the first activity from the list below. If the student scored less than 100 percent but more than 85 percent, complete the first three activities from the list below. If the student scored 85 percent or less, complete all five of the activities listed below.

1. Have students complete page 268 in *MARK¹² Reading Activity Book* for more practice on sight words.

2. Using the sight word cards you created for *nothing, almost,* and *over,* read each word to students and have students write the word on a piece of paper. Give students the sight words, and instruct students to look for any spelling mistakes they may have made. Students should correct the mistakes and then read the list of words aloud.

3. Gather all of the sight word cards students have worked on to date and a timer. Have students read all of the sight word cards as accurately and quickly as possible. Make note of the time, as well as any errors students have made. Use the Online Tile Kit or Paper Letter Tiles to review words read incorrectly.

4. Gather the cards for the sight words *nothing, almost,* and *over,* and up to two additional sight words students have yet to master. Show the first card to students, and ask students to read the word. If students read the word correctly, place the card in one pile. If students read the word incorrectly, place the card in a separate pile. On the back of the cards that were read correctly, make a note of the date and put aside. (Once students have read the word correctly five consecutive days, you can remove the word from the pile of cards students are working on.) Review any words students read incorrectly, and keep the cards for next time.

5. Gather the two sets of sight word cards for the words *nothing, almost,* and *over,* and place all of the cards face down on the table or another flat surface. Have students choose a card, read the word aloud, and then choose a second card. After students read the second card aloud, if the two cards match, students should keep the cards. If they do not match, students should return them to the table. Continue until all of the cards have been collected.

Speed Work

Almost Everything

Look at the Performance Review, or check the student's fluency chart. Fluency scores (words read per minute) should not fall below 80. If the student scored below 80 words per minute, print a copy of the Speed Work story and have the student read the story silently before reading it aloud. Otherwise, move on to Composition.

Long e Spelled ie and Sight Words   **289**

Composition

Gather students' composition materials and begin where they left off.

Long *e* Spelled *ey* and Sight Words

ONLINE	Student & Computer	**:60** minutes	
	Adult : *Check Performance Review*		
OFFLINE	Student & Adult : Review online work	**:30** minutes	
	• Reading Warm-Up		
	• Code Work		
	• Word Work		
	• Speed Work		
	Grammar, Usage, and Mechanics (GUM)	**:30** minutes	

Instructional Time **2:00** hours

Materials

- Online Tile Kit or Paper Letter Tiles
- *MARK¹² Reading Activity Book*, pages 273–276

Tip

*Some students mistakenly use an apostrophe when they write possessive pronouns that end in **s**. Make sure students follow correct usage:* **"That house is theirs"** *is correct, not* **"That house is their's."**

Goals

In this lesson, students will read a brief summary of the U.S. involvement in World War II. Students will also be introduced to words with the long *e* sound spelled *ey* before learning the sight words *children, number,* and *write*. In today's *MARK¹² Reading Activity Book* pages, you will work with students to complete a crossword puzzle and identify sight words.

Advance Preparation

Based on the Performance Review, if students need to complete Word Work activity 2, create sight word cards for the following words: *children, number,* and *write*. If students need to complete Word Work activity 3, you will need a timer and the Online Tile Kit or Paper Letter Tiles. If students need to complete Word Work activity 5, create a second set of sight word cards for the words *children, number,* and *write*.

ONLINE	**Student & Computer**

Students will work online to complete Warm-Up, Code Work, Word Work, and Speed Work activities, and a Wrap-Up assessment on their own. Be sure to read the Performance Review before beginning the offline portion of today's lesson.

Today you will work with students to complete Code Work, Word Work, and GUM activities. Be sure to read the online Performance Review before beginning the Code Work and Word Work activities.

Warm-Up ·

1945: World War II Ends

Look at the Performance Review. If the student achieved a perfect score on today's Warm-Up, move on to Code Work. If the student scored 60 percent or 80 percent, print the story and review the comprehension questions with the student. If the student scored less than 60 percent, print the story, have the student read the story aloud, and then work through the comprehension questions together, before moving on to Code Work.

Objectives

- Improve reading and comprehension skills.

Code Work ·

Long e Spelled ey

Look at the Performance Review. If the student achieved a perfect score on today's Code Work activities, complete the first two activities from the list below. If the student scored less than 100 percent but more than 85 percent, complete the first three activities from the list below. If the student scored 85 percent or less, complete all four of the activities listed below.

Objectives

- Identify the letters, given the sound /ē/.
- Identify and use /ē/ spelling patterns.

1. Have students complete page 273 in *MARK¹² Reading Activity Book* for more practice on words with the long *e* sound spelled *ey*.

2. Using the Online Tile Kit or Paper Letter Tiles, have students build the following words: *valley, jersey, kidney, honey,* and *pulley.*

3. Dictate the following sentences to students and have them write each sentence on a piece of paper:
   Do you have money for lunch?
   Where is the key to the car?
   Do you want to play on the field hockey team?
   Can you drive me down to the valley?
   Review any spelling errors with students.

4. Say the word *turkey* aloud. Have students write the word on paper. Then have students name the sounds in *turkey* - /t/, /er/, /k/, /ē/. Repeat the activity with the words *monkey* and *donkey.*

Code Work   Name: _____

Long e Spelled ey and Sight Words

Long e Spelled ey

Read the clues to fill in the crossword puzzle with words from the box.
Hint: Not every word in the word box is used.

| honey | jersey | key | jockey | monkey |
| donkey | valley | turkey | money | kidney |

Across
1. an animal that lives in a rainforest
2. this is used to buy things
3. this is used to unlock a door

Down
4. an animal that can be used to pull a cart
5. this kind of shirt is worn when playing football or soccer
6. bees make this sweet stuff

273

Word Work ·····················

Sight Words

Look at the Performance Review. If the student achieved a perfect score on today's Word Work activities, complete the first activity from the list below. If the student scored less than 100 percent but more than 85 percent, complete the first three activities from the list below. If the student scored 85 percent or less, complete all five of the activities listed below.

1. Have students complete page 274 in *MARK¹² Reading Activity Book* for more practice on sight words.

2. Using the sight word cards you created for *children, number,* and *write,* read each word to students and have students write the word on a piece of paper. Give students the sight words, and instruct students to look for any spelling mistakes they may have made. Students should correct the mistakes and then read the list of words aloud.

3. Gather all of the sight word cards students have worked on to date and a timer. Have students read all of the sight word cards as accurately and quickly as possible. Make note of the time, as well as any errors students have made. Use the Online Tile Kit or Paper Letter Tiles to review words read incorrectly.

4. Gather the cards for the sight words *children, number,* and *write,* and up to two additional sight words students have yet to master. Show the first card to students, and ask students to read the word. If students read the word correctly, place in one pile. If students read the word incorrectly, place in a separate pile. On the back of the cards that were read correctly, make a note of the date and put aside. (Once students have read the word correctly five consecutive days, you can remove the word from the pile of cards students are working on.) Review any words students read incorrectly, and keep the cards for next time.

5. Gather the two sets of sight word cards for the words *children, number,* and *write,* and place all of the cards face down on the table or another flat surface. Have students choose a card, read the word aloud, and then choose a second card. After students read the second card aloud, if the two cards match, students should keep the cards. If they do not match, students should return them to the table. Continue until all of the cards have been collected.

Speed Work ·····················

Somewhere in the World

Look at the Performance Review, or check the student's fluency chart. Fluency scores (words read per minute) should not fall below 80. If the student scored below 80 words per minute, print a copy of the Speed Work story and have the student read the story silently before reading it aloud. Otherwise, move on to Grammar, Usage, and Mechanics.

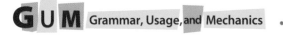

Possessive Pronouns

Like nouns, pronouns can also show ownership, or possession. Possessive pronouns, like all pronouns, take the place of nouns. The possessive pronouns are *mine, ours, yours, his, hers,* and *theirs.*

Work with students to complete pages 275 and 276 in *MARK¹² Reading Activity Book.* Read page 275, Get Ready, with students. Have students complete the Try It page. Be sure to discuss students' answers when the page is complete.

GUM Grammar, Usage, and Mechanics   Name:

Long *e* Spelled *ey* and Sight Words

Get Ready

Possessive Pronouns
If you possess something, you own it. Possessive nouns show ownership or relationship.

Possessive pronouns show possession by telling *who owns something.*

Study this chart of possessive pronouns.

Pronoun	Ownership	Example
mine	belonging to me	The red hat is **mine**.
ours	belonging to us	That house is **ours**.
yours	belonging to you	This cap is **yours**.
his	belonging to him	He lost **his** last night.
hers	belonging to her	Annie found **hers** at school.
theirs	belonging to them	Please bring **theirs** to them.

275

GUM Grammar, Usage, and Mechanics   Name:

Long *e* Spelled *ey* and Sight Words

Try It

Underline the possessive pronoun in each sentence.
Hint: One sentence has two possessive pronouns.

1. That car looks like <u>ours</u>.
2. <u>Mine</u> was over here unless someone moved it.
3. Is that dog <u>theirs</u>?
4. <u>Hers</u> is more colorful than <u>his</u>.
5. Where did you put <u>yours</u>?

276

Long e Spelled *y* and Sight Words

ONLINE	Student & Computer	**:60** minutes
	Adult : *Check Performance Review*	
OFFLINE	Student & Adult : Review online work	**:30** minutes
	• Reading Warm-Up	
	• Code Work	
	• Word Work	
	• Speed Work	
	Classics Session 1	**:30** minutes
	Instructional Time **2:00** hours	

Materials

- *MARK¹² Classics for Young Readers*
- *MARK¹² Reading Activity Book*, pages 277–282

Goals

In this lesson, students will read about life at home after World War II. Students will also be introduced to words that contain the long *e* sound spelled with the letter *y* before continuing to work with the sight words *children, number,* and *write.* In today's *MARK¹² Reading Activity Book* pages, you will work with students to recognize long *e* spelled with the letter *y,* as well as practice using sight words.

Advance Preparation

Based on the Performance Review, if students need to complete Word Work activity 2, gather the sight word cards for the following words: *children, number,* and *write.* If students need to complete Word Work activity 3, you will need a timer and the Online Tile Kit or Paper Letter Tiles. If students need to complete Word Work activity 5, gather the second set of sight word cards for the words *children, number,* and *write.*

ONLINE   Student & Computer

Students will work online to complete Warm-Up, Code Work, Word Work, and Speed Work activities, and a Wrap-Up assessment on their own. Be sure to read the Performance Review before beginning the offline portion of today's lesson.

Today you will work with students to complete Code Work, Word Work, and *MARK¹² Classics for Young Readers* activities. Be sure to read the online Performance Review before beginning the Code Work and Word Work activities.

Warm-Up •

Life after World War II

Look at the Performance Review. If the student achieved a perfect score on today's Warm-Up, move on to Code Work. If the student scored 60 percent or 80 percent, print the story and review the comprehension questions with the student. If the student scored less than 60 percent, print the story, have the student read the story aloud, and then work through the comprehension questions together, before moving on to Code Work.

Objectives

- Improve reading and comprehension skills.

Code Work •

Long *e* Spelled *y*

Look at the Performance Review. If the student achieved a perfect score on today's Code Work activities, complete the first two activities from the list below. If the student scored less than 100 percent but more than 85 percent, complete the first three activities from the list below. If the student scored 85 percent or less, complete all five of the activities listed below.

Objectives

- Identify the sound, given the letter *y*.
- Identify the letters, given the sound /ē/.
- Identify and use /ē/ spelling patterns.

1. Have students complete page 277 in *MARK¹² Reading Activity Book* for more practice on the *y* spelling of the long *e* sound.

2. Remove the "Field Hockey Hal" story from *MARK¹² Reading Activity Book*. Fold the pages in half to create a small booklet. Review the following word with students: *laughed*. Have students read the story silently once or twice before reading the story aloud. When students read aloud, make note of any errors, and review those words with the students.

3. Using the Online Tile Kit or Paper Letter Tiles, have students build the following words: *many, funny, city, jelly,* and *anything*.

4. Dictate the following sentences to students and have them write each sentence on a piece of paper:
    The lady wore a pretty hat.
    Ben read a story to the baby.
    Ned is a happy boy.
    Review any spelling errors with students, and then have them point to the letter that makes the long *e* sound in each word (underlined above).

5. Have students say each word from activity 3 in a sentence.

Code Work   Name: _____

Long *e* Spelled *y* and Sight Words

Long *e*

Read aloud each word in the box. Underline each word that contains the long *e* sound.

cake	many	break
happy	crest	gem
anything	speck	ladybug
heard	story	stretch
feather	babysit	city
pretty	chestnut	jellyfish

Choose three of the words with the long *e* sound from the box above. On the lines provided below, write each word in a sentence.

1. _____
2. _____
3. _____

277

Word Work ·

Sight Words

Look at the Performance Review. If the student achieved a perfect score on today's Word Work activities, complete the first activity from the list below. If the student scored less than 100 percent but more than 85 percent, complete the first three activities from the list below. If the student scored 85 percent or less, complete all five of the activities listed below.

1. Have students complete page 278 in *MARK¹² Reading Activity Book* for more practice on sight words.

2. Using the sight word cards you created for *children, number,* and *write,* read each word to students and have students write the word on a piece of paper. Give students the sight words, and instruct students to look for any spelling mistakes they may have made. Students should correct the mistakes and then read the list of words aloud.

3. Gather all of the sight word cards students have worked on to date and a timer. Have students read all of the sight word cards as accurately and quickly as possible. Make note of the time, as well as any errors students have made. Use the Online Tile Kit or Paper Letter Tiles to review words read incorrectly.

4. Gather the cards for the sight words *children, number,* and *write,* and up to two additional sight words students have yet to master. Show the first card to students, and ask students to read the word. If students read the word correctly, place in one pile. If students read the word incorrectly, place in a separate pile. On the back of the cards that were read correctly, make a note of the date and put aside. (Once students have read the word correctly five consecutive days, you can remove the word from the pile of cards students are working on.) Review any words students read incorrectly, and keep the cards for next time.

5. Gather the two sets of sight word cards for the words *children, number,* and *write,* and place all of the cards face down on the table or another flat surface. Have students choose a card, read the word aloud, and then choose a second card. After students read the second card aloud, if the two cards match, students should keep the cards. If they do not match, students should return them to the table. Continue until all of the cards have been collected.

Word Work
Name:

Long e Spelled y and Sight Words

Choose the Sight Word

Find a word in the word box that has a similar meaning to the underlined word or words in each sentence. Write the word from the box on the line provided. An example has been done for you.

number	over	children	everything
nothing	almost	write	under

Example: The <u>kids</u> walked to the park.
children

1. There was not <u>anything</u> that I could do to help.
   nothing
2. You need to <u>print</u> your name on this form.
   write
3. The cat hid <u>below</u> the bed.
   under
4. A <u>bunch</u> of dogs at the animal shelter have black fur.
   number
5. There are <u>about</u> one hundred people at the fair.
   almost
6. The bird soared <u>above</u> the trees.
   over
7. The fire burned <u>all of</u> it.
   everything

278

Speed Work ·

A New Pet

Look at the Performance Review, or check the student's fluency chart. Fluency scores (words read per minute) should not fall below 80. If the student scored below 80 words per minute, print a copy of the Speed Work story and have the student read the story silently before reading it aloud. Otherwise, move on to Classics Session 1.

Classics Session 1 ·

The Stonecutter

Today's story, "The Stonecutter," is a story about a dissatisfied stonecutter who learns what is important in life. Review the keywords with students. Read the story with students, and then use the Discussion Questions below as a guide to share ideas about the story. Have students read the story again before writing a summary of the story.

Keywords

chariot, n. – a horse-drawn carriage of ancient times
The princess rode through the streets in a beautiful **chariot** lined with silver and gold.

obey, v. – to follow a command or an order
When it comes to riding my bike, I always **obey** traffic laws to help ensure my safety.

wilt, v. – to become limp; to droop
After a week with no rain, the flowers in my garden started to **wilt**.

wither, v., adj. – to lose freshness; to shrivel
The drought left the crops dry and **withered**.

Discussion Questions

1. Why do you think the spirit of the mountain grants all of Taro's wishes? Answers may include that the spirit of the mountain wants Taro to discover for himself what his true calling is.

2. Why do you think the life of a stonecutter suited Taro best? Why do you think being a stonecutter makes him happy again? Answers will vary.

3. Think about Taro's wishes. What do they have in common? Answers may include that each time he wishes to be something more powerful than he was before.

4. What do you think Taro learns by the end of the story? Answers may include that Taro learns that power is not what is most important. He learns to be happy and content with what he has and who he is.

5. If you had a wish, what would it be? Can you think of a reason your wish might not be as good as you originally thought it would be? Answers will vary.

Students should write a summary of the story to complete today's Classics activity.

Long *i* Spelled *y* and Sight Words

ONLINE	Student & Computer	**:60** minutes	
	Adult : *Check Performance Review*		
OFFLINE	Student & Adult : Review online work	**:30** minutes	
	• Reading Warm-Up		
	• Code Work		
	• Word Work		
	• Speed Work		
	Classics Session 2	**:30** minutes	
	Instructional Time **2:00** hours		

Materials

- *MARK¹² Classics for Young Readers*
- **Online Tile Kit or Paper Letter Tiles**
- *MARK¹² Reading Activity Book*, pages 283–284

Tip

If students are uncertain if the **y** *at at the end of a word is pronounced /ē/ or /ī/, suggest they try both pronunciations to see if they recognize the word by hearing it.*

Goals

In this lesson, students will read about civil rights activist Rosa Parks. Students will also be introduced to words that contain long *i* spelled *y* before learning the sight words *because, its,* and *first*. In today's *MARK¹² Reading Activity Book*, you will work with students to use words that contain long *i* spelled *y* and to recognize various sight words.

Advance Preparation

Based on the Performance Review, if students need to complete Code Work activity 3, gather eight index cards. On each card, write one of the following words: *city, funny, happy, story, fly, my, sky,* and *why*. If students need to complete Word Work activity 2, create sight word cards for the following words: *because, its,* and *first*. If students need to complete Word Work activity 3, you will need a timer and the Online Tile Kit or Paper Letter Tiles. If students need to complete Word Work activity 5, create a second set of sight word cards for the words *because, its,* and *first*.

ONLINE   Student & Computer

Students will work online to complete Warm-Up, Code Work, Word Work, and Speed Work activities, and a Wrap-Up assessment on their own. Be sure to read the Performance Review before beginning the offline portion of today's lesson.

Today you will work with students to complete Code Work, Word Work, and *MARK¹² Classics for Young Readers* activities. Be sure to read the online Performance Review before beginning the Code Work and Word Work activities.

Warm-Up

Rosa Parks

Look at the Performance Review. If the student achieved a perfect score on today's Warm-Up, move on to Code Work. If the student scored 60 percent or 80 percent, print the story and review the comprehension questions with the student. If the student scored less than 60 percent, print the story, have the student read the story aloud, and then work through the comprehension questions together, before moving on to Code Work.

Objectives

- Improve reading and comprehension skills.

Code Work

Long *i* Spelled *y*

Look at the Performance Review. If the student achieved a perfect score on today's Code Work activities, complete the first two activities from the list below. If the student scored less than 100 percent but more than 85 percent, complete the first three activities from the list below. If the student scored 85 percent or less, complete all five of the activities listed below.

Objectives

- Identify the sound, given the letter *y*.
- Identify the letters, given the sound /ī/.

1. Have students complete page 283 in *MARK¹² Reading Activity Book* for more practice on words that contain long *i* spelled *y*.

2. Using the Online Tile Kit or Paper Letter Tiles, have students build the following words: *dry, fry, shy, try,* and *myself*.

3. Gather and shuffle the eight index cards that you prepared previously (*city, funny, happy, story, fly, my, sky, why*) and place them face down. Have students choose a card, read it aloud, and then set it aside in either a long *e* or long *i* pile. Students should continue until all cards have been sorted correctly.

4. Dictate the following sentences to students and have them write each sentence on a piece of paper:
   July is a sunny month.
   The baby began to cry.
   Judy has a new washer and dryer.
   Review any spelling errors with students, and then have them point to the letter that makes the long *i* sound in each word that contains the sound /ī/ (underlined above).

5. Have students say each word from activity 2 in a sentence.

Code Work　　Name: _____

Long *i* Spelled y and Sight Words

Long *i*

Read each sentence aloud. In each sentence, underline the word that contains the long *i* sound.

1. Rick wondered <u>why</u> Betty was late for dinner.
2. "Your baby brother is so <u>shy</u>!" Randy said to Kay.
3. We plan to take a trip to Quail City in <u>July</u>.
4. "I would rather go to the fair <u>myself</u>," Gail said.
5. Help me put these wet shirts in the <u>dryer</u>.
6. Jill watched the pretty bird <u>fly</u> to its little nest.

Read the word at the beginning of each line. On the lines provided, write a sentence using the word.

7. cry ___Sentences will vary.___
8. try _____
9. my _____
10. sky _____

283

Word Work ·····················

Sight Words

Look at the Performance Review. If the student achieved a perfect score on today's Word Work activities, complete the first activity from the list below. If the student scored less than 100 percent but more than 85 percent, complete the first three activities from the list below. If the student scored 85 percent or less, complete all five of the activities listed below.

1. Have students complete page 284 in *MARK¹² Reading Activity Book* for more practice on recognizing sight words.

2. Using the sight word cards you created for *because, its,* and *first,* read each word to students and have students write the word on a piece of paper. Give students the sight words, and instruct students to look for any spelling mistakes they may have made. Students should correct the mistakes and then read the list of words aloud.

3. Gather all of the sight word cards students have worked on to date and a timer. Have students read all of the sight word cards as accurately and quickly as possible. Make note of the time, as well as any errors students have made. Use the Online Tile Kit or Paper Letter Tiles to review words read incorrectly.

4. Gather the cards for the sight words *because, its,* and *first,* and up to two additional sight words students have yet to master. Show the first card to students, and ask students to read the word. If students read the word correctly, place in one pile. If students read the word incorrectly, place in a separate pile. On the back of the cards that were read correctly, make a note of the date and put aside. (Once students have read the word correctly five consecutive days, you can remove the word from the pile of cards students are working on.) Review any words students read incorrectly, and keep the cards for next time.

5. Gather the two sets of sight word cards for the words *because, its,* and *first,* and place all of the cards face down on the table or another flat surface. Have students choose a card, read the word aloud, and then choose a second card. After students read the second card aloud, if the two cards match, students should keep the cards. If they do not match, students should return them to the table. Continue until all of the cards have been collected.

Word Work

Long i Spelled y and Sight Words

Sight Word Recognition
Underline the sight word listed as many times as it appears in each row.

1. its	it	sits	its	is	its
2. nothing	nothing	noting	netting	nothing	noting
3. under	under	udder	under	until	udder
4. first	fist	first	firs	fist	first
5. write	white	wife	write	write	white
6. because	became	because	beacons	because	beacons
7. number	number	mumble	rubber	number	mumble
8. almost	almost	almost	almonds	almanac	almond
9. children	chilled	chiller	children	chilled	children

Choose three sight words from the list above. On the lines provided, write each word in a sentence.

10. **Sentences will vary.**

11. _____

12. _____

284

Speed Work ·····················

Lucky

Look at the Performance Review, or check the student's fluency chart. Fluency scores (words read per minute) should not fall below 80. If the student scored below 80 words per minute, print a copy of the Speed Work story and have the student read the story silently before reading it aloud. Otherwise, move on to Classics Session 2.

The Stonecutter

Review the keywords with students. Have students reread the story on their own. After rereading the story, students should complete the comprehension questions in *MARK¹² Classics for Young Readers* book on their own. Afterward, if time allows, have students read the story aloud to you.

W Write

The Stonecutter

1. When Taro was a boy, what did he dream of becoming?

   A. prince
   B. rich man
   C. stonecutter
   D. chariot driver

2. In the beginning of the story, Taro sings while he works. What does this tell you about how Taro feels about his work?

   The fact that Taro sings while he works indicates that he enjoys what he's doing.

3. Which of the following is **not** a reason Taro gives for why he wishes to do something other than stonecutting?

   A. The hammer is heavy.
   B. Sharp chips cut his face.
   C. He does not like rising so early.
   D. Climbing a mountain is hard work.

4. Why does Taro want to be a rich man?

   Taro wants to be a rich man because he wants to wear fine clothes, live in a beautiful house, walk in rose gardens, and not get up so early.

The Stonecutter **101**

5. Why does Taro want to be a prince?

   Taro wants to be a prince because he thinks the prince is greater than he is. Taro wants to ride in a chariot, rule the land, and have servants.

6. Which of the following describes the prince's umbrella and fan?

   A. gold
   B. plain
   C. heavy
   D. colorful

7. Why does Taro wish to be the cloud?

   Taro wishes to be the cloud because he thinks the cloud is greater than the sun.

8. What does Taro finally wish to be?

   A. sun
   B. man
   C. cloud
   D. prince

102 The Stonecutter

ie, ey, & y and Sight Words

ONLINE	Student & Computer	**:60** minutes	
	Adult : *Check Performance Review*		
OFFLINE	Student & Adult : Review online work	**:30** minutes	
	• Reading Warm-Up		
	• Speed Work		
	• Assessment		
	Composition	**:30** minutes	
	Instructional Time **2:00** hours		

Materials

- *MARK¹² Reading Activity Book,* pages 285–288
- *Just Write*

Goals

In this lesson, students will read about the history of the Berlin Wall. Students will also review the long *e* spellings *ie, ey,* and *y*; and the long *i* spelling *y* before continuing to work with the sight words *because, its,* and *first.* In today's Unit Assessment, you will administer a test covering all content from Unit 17. Afterward, you will work with students to complete Composition activities.

Advance Preparation

For the offline portion of today's lesson, gather the students' composition materials.

ONLINE   Student & Computer

Students will work on their own to complete Warm-Up, Code Work, Word Work, and Speed Work activities, and a Wrap-Up assessment. Be sure to read the Performance Review before beginning the offline portion of today's lesson.

Today you will administer a Unit Assessment and work with students to complete a Composition activity.

Warm-Up •

The Berlin Wall

Look at the Performance Review. If the student achieved a perfect score on today's Warm-Up, move on to Speed Work. If the student scored 60 percent or 80 percent, print the story and review the comprehension questions with the student. If the student scored less than 60 percent, print the story, have the student read the story aloud, and then work through the comprehension questions together, before moving on to Speed Work.

Speed Work •

Strawberry, Not Strawberries

Look at the Performance Review, or check the student's fluency chart. Fluency scores (words read per minute) should not fall below 80. If the student scored below 80 words per minute, print a copy of the Speed Work story and have the student read the story silently before reading it aloud to you. Otherwise, move on to the Assessment.

☼ Assessment •

ie, ey, & y and Sight Words

Today's Unit Assessment covers all content found in Unit 17. Carefully read the instructions on the student pages before administering the test to the student. If necessary, read the directions to the student. After you have scored the student's assessment, be sure to go online and input student performance scores in the assessment entry tool.

Part 1. Dictate the following words to students: *many, cry, donkey, thief, honey, story, fly,* and *shield.*

Parts 5. Dictate the following words to students: *children, everything, almost, whether, write, first, its, nothing, number, under, over,* and *because.*

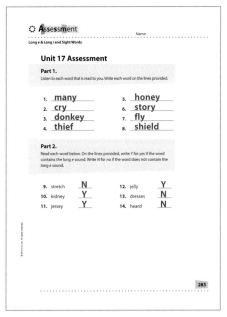

Assessment
Name: _____

Long e & Long i and Sight Words

Unit 17 Assessment

Part 1.
Listen to each word that is read to you. Write each word on the lines provided.

1. many
2. cry
3. donkey
4. thief

5. honey
6. story
7. fly
8. shield

Part 2.
Read each word below. On the lines provided, write Y for *yes* if the word contains the long *e* sound. Write N for *no* if the word does not contain the long *e* sound.

9. stretch   N
10. kidney   Y
11. jersey   Y

12. jelly   Y
13. dresses   N
14. heard   N

285

Assessment
Name: _____

Long e & Long i and Sight Words

Part 3.
Read each word below. On the lines provided, write Y for *yes* if the word contains the long *i* sound. Write N for *no* if the word does not contain the long *i* sound.

15. hitch   N
16. hockey   N
17. skylark   Y

18. frying   Y
19. baby   N
20. shy   Y

Part 4.
Write each word from the box in the correct column below according to the spelling of the long e sound.

| key | chief | valley | happy | field |
| baby | money | niece | hockey | funny |

21. *ie*	22. *ey*	23. *y*
chief	key	happy
field	valley	baby
niece	money	funny
	hockey	

286

Assessment
Name: _____

Long e & Long i and Sight Words

Part 5.
Write each word from the box in the correct column below according to the sound the *y* makes.

| sky | city | many | dryer |
| myself | puppy | ladybug | shy |

24. long *i*	25. long *e*
sky	city
dryer	many
myself	puppy
shy	ladybug

287

Assessment
Name: _____

Long e & Long i and Sight Words

Part 5.
In each row, underline the word that is read to you.

26. chilled   <u>children</u>   child
27. evening   everyone   <u>everything</u>
28. <u>almost</u>   amongst   amiss
29. where   winter   <u>whether</u>
30. ride   <u>write</u>   white
31. <u>first</u>   fern   fist
32. is   <u>its</u>   it
33. <u>nothing</u>   noting   mother
34. amber   nimble   <u>number</u>
35. <u>under</u>   udder   amber
36. of   oven   <u>over</u>
37. begins   <u>because</u>   before

288

Objectives

- Identify the sound, given the letter *y*.
- Identify the letters, given the sound /ē/ or /ī/.
- Identify and use /ē/ and /ī/ spelling patterns.

ie, ey, & y and Sight Words   305

Composition

Gather students' composition materials and begin where they left off.

Long *u* and Closed Syllables 1

ONLINE	Student & Computer	:60 minutes
	Adult : *Check Performance Review*	
OFFLINE	Student & Adult : Review online work	:30 minutes
	• Reading Warm-Up	
	• Code Work	
	• Word Work	
	• Speed Work	
	Grammar, Usage, and Mechanics (GUM)	:30 minutes
	Instructional Time **2:00** hours	

Materials

- Online Tile Kit or Paper Letter Tiles
- *MARK¹² Reading Activity Book*, pages 289–292

Tip

*The letter **u**, followed by a consonant, then by a silent **e**, and the letters **e-w** together, are two ways to spell the long **u** sound. **Fuse, huge, few,** and **nephew** are examples of words that use these two spellings of the long **u** sound.*

Goals

In this lesson, students will read about the first walk on the moon. Students will also work with the long *u* sound before reviewing sight words. In today's *MARK¹² Reading Activity Book*, you will work with students to reinforce their understanding of the long *u* sound and to reinforce their correct use of a selection of sight words. Afterward, you will work with students to complete activities on adverbs.

Advance Preparation

For today's Word Work activity 2, gather the sight word cards for the following words: *because, its,* and *first.* Based on the Performance Review, if students need to complete Word Work activity 3, you will need a timer and the Online Tile Kit or Paper Letter Tiles. If students need to complete Word Work activity 5, gather the second set of sight word cards for the words *because, its,* and *first.*

ONLINE | Student & Computer

Students will work online to complete Warm-Up, Code Work, Word Work, and Speed Work activities, and a Wrap-Up assessment on their own. Be sure to read the Performance Review before beginning the offline portion of today's lesson.

Today you will work with students to complete Code Work, Word Work, and GUM activities. Be sure to read the online Performance Review before beginning the Code Work and Word Work activities.

Warm-Up

1969: The First Walk on the Moon

Look at the Performance Review. If the student achieved a perfect score on today's Warm-Up, move on to Code Work. If the student scored 60 percent or 80 percent, print the story and review the comprehension questions with the student. If the student scored less than 60 percent, print the story, have the student read the story aloud, and then work through the comprehension questions together, before moving on to Code Work.

Code Work

Long *u*

Look at the Performance Review. If the student achieved a perfect score on today's Code Work activities, complete the first two activities from the list below. If the student scored less than 100 percent but more than 85 percent, complete the first three activities from the list below. If the student scored 85 percent or less, complete all four of the activities listed below.

1. Have students complete page 289 in *MARK¹² Reading Activity Book* for more practice on spellings of the long *u* sound.

2. Using the Online Tile Kit or Paper Letter Tiles, ask students to spell the following words: *cube, few, fumes, mule,* and *use.*

3. Dictate the following words to students and have them write each word on a piece of paper: *cub, cut, hug,* and *us.* Ask students to read each word aloud. Then have students add an *e* to the end of each word and read the new words aloud.

4. Have students choose three of the long *u* words from activities 2 and 3 and write each word in a sentence.

Code Work
Name:
Long u and Closed Syllables 1

Practice Long *u*

Read each sentence aloud. Underline the word or words in each sentence that contain the long *u* sound. Then read each sentence again.

1. I added ice <u>cubes</u> to my tea.
2. Julie's new kitten is very <u>cute</u>.
3. We could see <u>fumes</u> coming out of the old car's tailpipe.
4. <u>Mules</u> are <u>used</u> to carry and pull heavy loads.
5. Chris put the television on <u>mute</u>.
6. We only have a <u>few</u> minutes until the concert starts!
7. My mom's <u>nephew</u> is my cousin.
8. We plugged too many things in to the light socket and blew a <u>fuse</u>.
9. The <u>bugle</u> is very loud!
10. I had a <u>huge</u> ice cream cone after lunch.

289

Word Work •

Sight Words

Look at the Performance Review. If the student achieved a perfect score on today's Word Work activities, complete the first activity from the list below. If the student scored less than 100 percent but more than 85 percent, complete the first three activities from the list below. If the student scored 85 percent or less, complete all five of the activities listed below.

Objectives

- **Read sight words.**
- **Increase reading vocabulary.**

1. Have students complete page 290 in *MARK¹² Reading Activity Book*. To complete the page, you will need a timer. As students read the sight words, keep track of how many are read correctly.

2. Using the sight word cards you created for *because, its,* and *first,* read each word to students and have students write the word on a piece of paper. Give students the sight words, and instruct students to look for any spelling mistakes. Students should correct the mistakes and then read the list of words aloud.

3. Gather all of the sight word cards students have worked on to date and a timer. Have students read all of the sight word cards as accurately and quickly as possible. Make note of the time, as well as any errors students have made. Use the Online Tile Kit or Paper Letter Tiles to review words read incorrectly.

4. Gather the cards for the sight words *because, its,* and *first,* and up to two additional sight words students have yet to master. Show the first card to students, and ask students to read the word. If students read the word correctly, place in one pile. If students read the word incorrectly, place in a separate pile. On the back of the cards that were read correctly, make a note of the date and put aside. (Once students have read the word correctly five consecutive days, you can remove the word from the pile of cards students are working on.) Review any words students read incorrectly, and keep the cards for next time.

5. Gather the two sets of sight word cards for the words *because, its,* and *first,* and place all of the cards face down. Have students choose a card, read the word aloud, and then choose a second card. After students read the second card aloud, if the two cards match, students should keep the cards. If they do not match, students should return them. Continue until done.

Speed Work • • • • • • • • • • • • • • • • • • •

The Unicorn Playing the Bugle

Objectives

- **Increase reading fluency rate.**

Look at the Performance Review, or check the student's fluency chart. Fluency scores (words read per minute) should not fall below 80. If the student scored below 80 words per minute, print a copy of the Speed Work story and have the student read the story silently before reading it aloud. Otherwise, move on to Grammar, Usage, and Mechanics.

Identifying Adverbs

Adverbs tell more about verbs. Some adverbs tell *when* an action takes place. For example:

now	then	later	never	sometimes

Some adverbs tell *where* an action takes place. For example:

up	down	inside	outside	nearby

Some adverbs tell *how* an action takes place. For example:

quickly	slowly	happily	sadly	quietly

Work with students to complete pages 291 and 292 in *MARK¹² Reading Activity Book.* Read page 291, Get Ready, with students. Have students complete the Try It page. Be sure to discuss students' answers when the page is completed.

Long *u* and Closed Syllables 2

ONLINE	Student & Computer	**:60** minutes
	Adult : *Check Performance Review*	
OFFLINE	**Student & Adult : Review online work**	**:30** minutes
	• Reading Warm-Up	
	• Code Work	
	• Word Work	
	• Speed Work	
	Composition	**:30** minutes
	Instructional Time **2:00** hours	

Materials

- Online Tile Kit or Paper Letter Tiles
- *MARK¹² Reading Activity Book*, pages 293–298
- *Just Write*

Tip

*The letter **u** alone is one way to spell the long **u** sound. **Bugle, future,** and **pupil** are examples of words that use the letter **u** alone to spell the long **u** sound.*

Goals

In this lesson, students will read about Michael Collins' role in the first walk on the moon. Students will also work with the long *u* sound before working with closed syllables. In today's *MARK¹² Reading Activity Book*, you will work with students to reinforce their understanding of the long *u* sound and closed syllables. Afterward, students will spend 30 minutes working on composition.

Advance Preparation

For the offline portion of today's lesson, gather the students' composition materials. Based on the Performance Review, if students need to complete Word Work activity 4, gather 10 index cards. On each card, write one of the following syllables: *ba, be, cob, do, in, mo, nut, pup, ro,* and *sun.* If students need to complete Word Work activity 5, gather a newspaper, book, or magazine.

ONLINE	Student & Computer

Students will work online to complete Warm-Up, Code Work, Word Work, and Speed Work activities, and a Wrap-Up assessment on their own. Be sure to read the Performance Review before beginning the offline portion of today's lesson.

Today you will work with students to complete Code Work, Word Work, and Composition activities. Be sure to read the online Performance Review before beginning the Code Work and Word Work activities.

Warm-Up  ·

Michael Collins

Look at the Performance Review. If the student achieved a perfect score on today's Warm-Up, move on to Code Work. If the student scored 60 percent or 80 percent, print the story and review the comprehension questions with the student. If the student scored less than 60 percent, print the story, have the student read the story aloud, and then work through the comprehension questions together, before moving on to Code Work.

Code Work  ·

Long *u*

Look at the Performance Review. If the student achieved a perfect score on today's Code Work activities, complete the first two activities from the list below. If the student scored less than 100 percent but more than 85 percent, complete the first three activities from the list below. If the student scored 85 percent or less, complete all four of the activities listed below.

1. Have students complete page 293 in *MARK¹² Reading Activity Book* for more practice on long *u*.

2. Remove the "Triple Trouble" story from *MARK¹² Reading Activity Book*. Fold the pages in half to create a small booklet. Review the following word with students: *serious*. Have students read the story silently once or twice before reading the story aloud. When students read aloud, make note of any errors, and review those words with the students.

3. Have students fold a piece of paper in half and label the left column "short *u*" and the right column "long *u*." Dictate the following words to students and have them write each word in the correct column: *brush, cute, duck, few, fume, lunch, music, mule, plug, used, up, menu, cut, Utah,* and *hutch*.

4. Ask students to write a sentence using as many long *u* words as possible. Encourage students to make the sentence silly. If necessary, students may write a few short sentences. Have students read the sentence or sentences aloud.

Code Work   Name:
Long *u* and Closed Syllables 2

Practice Long *u*

Choose the word from the box that best completes each sentence. Write each word on the lines provided. Then read each sentence aloud.

cute	fumes	huge	mule	nephew

1. Most people think puppies are **cute**
2. The **fumes** from that old car smell awful!
3. The hikers climbed the **huge** mountain.
4. A donkey looks a lot like a **mule** .
5. Blake is my sister's son, so he is my **nephew** .

Choose two words from the box above. On the lines provided below, write a sentence using each word. Then read each sentence aloud.

6. _____

7. _____

8. _____

293

Word Work ·······························

Closed Syllables

Look at the Performance Review. If the student achieved a perfect score on today's Word Work activities, complete the first activity from the list below. If the student scored less than 100 percent but more than 85 percent, complete the first three activities from the list below. If the student scored 85 percent or less, complete all five of the activities listed below.

1. Have students complete page 294 in *MARK¹² Reading Activity Book* for more practice on closed syllables.

2. Dictate the following words to students: *chain (1), gather (2), hunger (2), shorts (1), thunder (2), trash (1), whatever (3),* and *whisper (2).* Have students write each word on a piece of paper, read each word aloud, and write the number of syllables in each word (shown in parentheses). Help students with spellings and pronunciations, if necessary.

3. Dictate the following words to students: <u>basket</u>, *frozen,* <u>itself</u>, *lazy, open,* <u>picnic</u>, *rainfall,* and <u>until</u>. Have students write each word on a piece of paper, read each word aloud, and underline each word that begins with a closed syllable. Help students with spellings and pronunciations, if necessary.

4. Gather the index cards with syllables you previously prepared. Shuffle the cards and place them face down in a pile. Have students turn over one card and say the syllable aloud. If the syllable is closed, have students think of a word that begins with the closed syllable. Have students draw another card from the deck and repeat the procedure until they have provided five closed-syllable words.

5. Have students spend a few minutes searching through the newspaper, book, or magazine you gathered for words beginning with closed syllables. Ask students to make a list of all the words they find.

Word Work

Name:

Long u and Closed Syllables 2

Closed Syllables

Underline the closed syllable in each word.
Hint: Some words have more than one closed syllable.

1. pretend
2. thunder
3. respect
4. moment
5. problem
6. platter
7. ponder
8. apple
9. sudden
10. relish

294

Speed Work ·······························

The Surprise of a Lifetime

Look at the Performance Review, or check the student's fluency chart. Fluency scores (words read per minute) should not fall below 80. If the student scored below 80 words per minute, print a copy of the Speed Work story and have the student read the story silently before reading it aloud. Otherwise, move on to Composition.

 Composition

Gather students' composition materials and begin where they left off.

Long *u* and Closed Syllables 3

ONLINE	Student & Computer	**:60**	minutes
	Adult : *Check Performance Review*		
OFFLINE	Student & Adult : Review online work	**:30**	minutes
	• Reading Warm-Up		
	• Code Work		
	• Word Work		
	• Speed Work		
	Classics Session 1	**:30**	minutes
	Instructional Time **2:00** hours		

Materials

- *MARK¹² Classics for Young Readers*
- "The House in the Forest" MP3
- *MARK¹² Reading Activity Book*, pages 299–300

Tip

*One way to spell the long **u** sound is with the letters **u** and **e** together. **Continue**, **cue**, and **value** are three words that use the letters **u** and **e** together to make the long **u** sound.*

Goals

In this lesson, students will read about the first Earth Day. Students will also work with the long *u* sound before working with closed syllables. In today's *MARK¹² Reading Activity Book*, you will work with students to reinforce their understanding of the long *u* sound and closed syllables. Afterward, you will work with students to complete Classics activities.

Advance Preparation

For the offline portion of today's lesson, download this story: "The House in the Forest." Based on the Performance Review, if students need to complete Code Work activity 2, gather a newspaper or magazine. If students need to complete Word Work activity 3, gather 10 index cards. On each card, write one of the following syllables: *bo, fleep, kin, laif, mit, rupt, sect, sult, ta,* and *ze*. If students need to complete Word Work activity 4, gather 10 index cards. On each card, write one of the following words: *clothing, backpack, flashlight, heater, lantern, plates, raincoat, soap, sunglasses,* and *swimsuit*.

ONLINE	**Student & Computer**

Students will work online to complete Warm-Up, Code Work, Word Work, and Speed Work activities, and a Wrap-Up assessment on their own. Be sure to read the Performance Review before beginning the offline portion of today's lesson.

Today you will work with students to complete Code Work, Word Work, and *MARK¹² Classics for Young Readers* activities. Be sure to read the online Performance Review before beginning the Code Work and Word Work activities.

Warm-Up ・・・・・・・・・・・・・・・・・・・・・・・・・・・・・・

1970: The First Earth Day

Look at the Performance Review. If the student achieved a perfect score on today's Warm-Up, move on to Code Work. If the student scored 60 percent or 80 percent, print the story and review the comprehension questions with the student. If the student scored less than 60 percent, print the story, have the student read the story aloud, and then work through the comprehension questions together, before moving on to Code Work.

Objectives

• Improve reading and comprehension skills.

Code Work ・・・・・・・・・・・・・・・・・・・・・・・・・・・・

Long *u*

Look at the Performance Review. If the student achieved a perfect score on today's Code Work activities, complete the first activity from the list below. If the student scored less than 100 percent but more than 85 percent, complete the first three activities from the list below. If the student scored 85 percent or less, complete all four of the activities listed below.

Objectives

• Identify the letters, given the sound /ū/.

• Identify and use silent *e*.

• Identify and use /ū/ spelling patterns.

1. Have students complete page 299 in *MARK¹² Reading Activity Book* for more practice on spellings of the long *u* sound.

2. Ask students to tell you the ways the long *u* sound can be spelled (*u, u-consonant-e, ue,* and *ew*). Then have students look through the newspaper or magazine you gathered, and circle as many words with the long *u* sound as they can find in two minutes. Have students read the words aloud. Help students with pronunciations, if necessary.

3. Dictate the following words to students and have them write the words on a piece of paper: *cube, few, fuel, music, used,* and *value*. Have students underline the letter or letters that make the sound /ū/ in each word.

4. Have students say two words for each spelling of the long *u* sound (*u, u-consonant-e, ue,* and *ew*). Encourage students to think of words not used in activity 3.

Code Work Name:_____

Long *u* and Closed Syllables 3

Practice Long *u* Spellings
Choose the words from the box that best match each clue. Write each word on the lines provided. Then underline the letters that make the long *u* sound in each word. An example has been done for you.

| argue | curfew | fuel | huge |
| menu | nephew | rescue | humid |

Example: Another word for save is ___rescue___.
1. Something that is very large is **huge**_____.
2. Coal, wood, oil, and gas are kinds of **fuel**_____
3. It is **humid**_____ when the air is damp.
4. When people do not agree, they may **argue**_____
5. The son of your brother or sister would be your **nephew**_____.
6. A **curfew**_____ is a set time a person must be home at night.
7. You look at a **menu**_____ to find out what a restaurant serves.

299

Word Work

Closed Syllables

Look at the Performance Review. If the student achieved a perfect score on today's Word Work activities, complete the first activity from the list below. If the student scored less than 100 percent but more than 85 percent, complete the first three activities from the list below. If the student scored 85 percent or less, complete all five of the activities listed below.

1. Have students complete page 300 in *MARK¹² Reading Activity Book* for more practice on closed syllables.

2. Dictate the following words to students and have them write each word on a piece of paper: *birthday, chapter, fantastic, longer, maybe, shout, shrunk, smooth, switch,* and *whenever.* Have students read the words aloud and write the number of syllables in each word. Help students with spellings and pronunciations, if necessary.

3. Gather the 10 syllable index cards that you previously prepared. Spread the cards face up. Have students separate the cards into two piles, one pile for closed syllables, and one pile for those that are not. After students have separated the syllables, have them explain why the leftover syllables are not closed.

4. Gather the 10 index cards that you previously prepared with the words *clothing, backpack, flashlight, heater, lantern, plates, raincoat, soap, sunglasses,* and *swimsuit.* Now explain that students are going camping. Only items that begin with a closed syllable can be taken. Have students place those index cards in a pile. (Note: Five cards belong in the pile: *backpack, flashlight, lantern, sunglasses,* and *swimsuit.*)

5. Dictate the following words to students, one at a time: *baby, cactus, insect, magnet, moment, napkin, open, pilot, robot,* and *splendid.* If the first syllable in a word is a closed syllable, have students say a silly sentence that uses the word. Students will create sentences for the words *cactus, insect, magnet, napkin,* and *splendid.*

Speed Work

The Burger Palace

Look at the Performance Review, or check the student's fluency chart. Fluency scores (words read per minute) should not fall below 80. If the student scored below 80 words per minute, print a copy of the Speed Work story and have the student read the story silently before reading it aloud. Otherwise, move on to Classics Session 1.

Classics Session 1 ·

The House in the Forest

Today's story, "The House in the Forest," is about acting kindly. Download the story. Have students listen to the story while following along in *MARK¹² Classics for Young Readers*. Have students listen to the story again before writing a summary of the story.

Students should write a summary of the story to complete today's Classics activity.

Long *u* and Closed Syllables 4

ONLINE	Student & Computer	:60 minutes
	Adult : *Check Performance Review*	
OFFLINE	Student & Adult : Review online work	:30 minutes
	• Reading Warm-Up	
	• Speed Work	
	• Assessment	
	Classics Session 2	:30 minutes
	Instructional Time **2:00** hours	

Materials

- *MARK¹² Classics for Young Readers*
- "The House in the Forest" MP3
- *MARK¹² Reading Activity Book*, pages 301–304

Goals

In this lesson, students will read about the inclusion of women's sports in public high schools and universities. Students will also work with the long *u* sound before working with closed syllables. In today's Unit Assessment, you will administer a test covering all content from Unit 18. Afterward, you will work with students to complete Classics activities.

Advance Preparation

For the offline portion of today's lesson, download this story: "The House in the Forest."

ONLINE	**Student & Computer**

Students will work online to complete Warm-Up, Code Work, Word Work, and Speed Work activities, and a review game on their own. Be sure to read the Performance Review before beginning the offline portion of today's lesson.

Today you will administer a Unit Assessment and work with students to complete a *MARK¹² Classics for Young Readers* activity.

Warm-Up ·

Sports for All

Look at the Performance Review. If the student achieved a perfect score on today's Warm-Up, move on to Speed Work. If the student scored 60 percent or 80 percent, print the story and review the comprehension questions with the student. If the student scored less than 60 percent, print the story, have the student read the story aloud, and then work through the comprehension questions together, before moving on to Speed Work.

Objectives

- Improve reading and comprehension skills.

Speed Work ·

Rescued By Music

Look at the Performance Review, or check the student's fluency chart. Fluency scores (words read per minute) should not fall below 80. If the student scored below 80 words per minute, print a copy of the Speed Work story and have the student read the story silently before reading it aloud to you. Otherwise, move on to the Assessment.

Objectives

- Increase reading fluency rate.

☼ Assessment ·

Long *u* and Closed Syllables

Today's Unit Assessment covers all content found in Unit 18. Carefully read the instructions on the student pages before administering the test to the student. If necessary, read the directions to the student. After you have scored the student's assessment, be sure to go online and input student performance scores in the assessment entry tool.

Part 2. Dictate the following words to students: *huge, few, unit, fuel,* and *cute.*

Part 5. Dictate the following words to students: *moment, itself, napkin, open, even, picnic, basket, begin, silent,* and *sunset.*

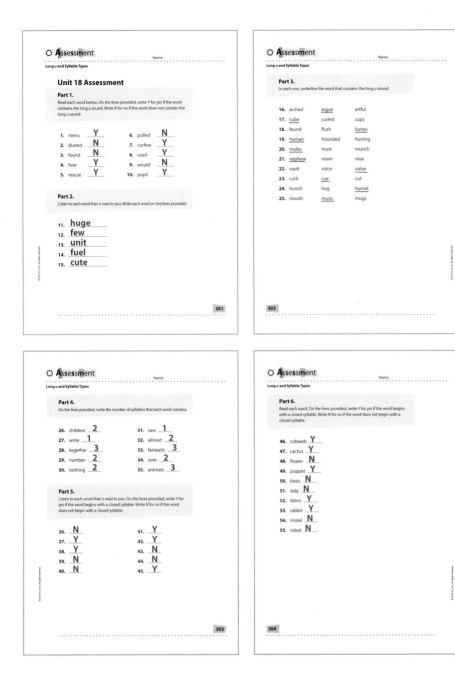

Assessment
Name: _____
Long *u* and Syllable Types

Unit 18 Assessment

Part 1.
Read each word below. On the lines provided, write *Y* for yes if the word contains the long *u* sound. Write *N* for *no* if the word does not contain the long *u* sound.

1. menu __Y__
2. dusted __N__
3. found __N__
4. fuse __Y__
5. rescue __Y__

6. pulled __N__
7. curfew __Y__
8. used __Y__
9. would __N__
10. pupil __Y__

Part 2.
Listen to each word that is read to you. Write each word on the lines provided.

11. __huge__
12. __few__
13. __unit__
14. __fuel__
15. __cute__

Assessment
Name: _____
Long *u* and Syllable Types

Part 3.
In each row, underline the word that contains the long *u* sound.

16. arched — <u>argue</u> — artful
17. <u>cube</u> — curled — cups
18. found — flush — <u>fumes</u>
19. <u>human</u> — hounded — hurting
20. <u>mules</u> — must — munch
21. <u>nephew</u> — never — near
22. vault — voice — <u>value</u>
23. curb — <u>cue</u> — cut
24. hunch — hug — <u>humid</u>
25. mouth — <u>music</u> — mugs

Assessment
Name: _____
Long *u* and Syllable Types

Part 4.
On the lines provided, write the number of syllables that each word contains.

26. children __2__
27. write __1__
28. together __3__
29. number __2__
30. nothing __2__

31. saw __1__
32. almost __2__
33. fantastic __3__
34. over __2__
35. animals __3__

Part 5.
Listen to each word that is read to you. On the lines provided, write *Y* for yes if the word begins with a closed syllable. Write *N* for *no* if the word does not begin with a closed syllable.

36. __N__
37. __Y__
38. __Y__
39. __N__
40. __N__

41. __Y__
42. __Y__
43. __N__
44. __N__
45. __Y__

Assessment
Name: _____
Long *u* and Syllable Types

Part 6.
Read each word. On the lines provided, write *Y* for yes if the word begins with a closed syllable. Write *N* for *no* if the word does not begin with a closed syllable.

46. cobweb __Y__
47. cactus __Y__
48. frozen __N__
49. puppet __Y__
50. basic __N__
51. lady __N__
52. fabric __Y__
53. rabbit __Y__
54. motel __N__
55. robot __N__

- Identify the number of syllables in a word.
- Identify the letters, given the sound /ū/.
- Identify and use silent *e*.
- Identify and use /ū/ spelling patterns.
- Increase reading vocabulary.
- Read sight words.
- Identify and use syllable types.

The House in the Forest

- Improve reading and comprehension skills.

Have students listen to the story again while following along in *MARK¹² Classics for Young Readers*. Afterward, students should complete the comprehension questions in *MARK¹² Classics for Young Readers* on their own.

W Write

The House in the Forest

1. What happened to the grain the woodcutter left as a path for his daughter, Anne, to follow?

   A. It was washed away by rain.
   B. It was blown away by the wind.
   C. It was trampled on by passersby.
   D. It was eaten by sparrows and blackbirds. *(circled)*

2. Which of the following animals did **not** sit beside the fireplace in the white-haired man's home?

   A. hen
   B. cow
   C. dog *(circled)*
   D. cock

3. Why are the animals upset with Anne?

   The animals are upset with Anne because she cooked a nice dinner for the old man and for herself, but she thought nothing of them.

---

4. What does the woodcutter think Anne was doing instead of bringing his dinner?

   A. playing with friends
   B. listening to the birds
   C. swimming in the lake
   D. running after wild bees *(circled)*

5. What creatures ate the beans that the woodcutter dropped for Rose?

   A. deer
   B. foxes
   C. doves *(circled)*
   D. chickens

6. What did Rose do before eating the dinner she cooked?

   Before eating the dinner she cooked, Rose made sure the hen, the cock, and the brindled cow had something to eat and drink.

---

7. What broke the witch's spell?

   A girl (Rose) who came to the prince and servants, who was full of love for animals and for people, broke the witch's spell.

8. Why is Anne **not** allowed to live in the palace immediately?

   Anne is not allowed to live in the palace immediately because she must first learn to be kind to all creatures.

Long *u* & Double *o* and Closed Syllables

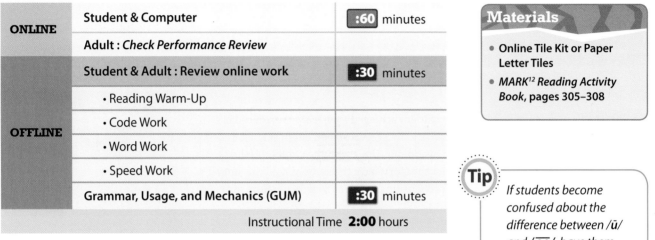

ONLINE	Student & Computer	:60 minutes
	Adult : *Check Performance Review*	
OFFLINE	Student & Adult : *Review online work*	:30 minutes
	• Reading Warm-Up	
	• Code Work	
	• Word Work	
	• Speed Work	
	Grammar, Usage, and Mechanics (GUM)	:30 minutes
	Instructional Time **2:00** hours	

Materials

- Online Tile Kit or Paper Letter Tiles
- *MARK¹² Reading Activity Book*, pages 305–308

Tip

*If students become confused about the difference between /ū/ and /o͞o/, have them listen for the difference between the vowel sounds in **cube** vs. **tube**, and **few** vs. **dew**.*

Goals

In this lesson, students will read about labor leader and civil rights activist, César Chávez. Students will also be introduced to the long double *o* sound spelled *u*-consonant-*e* and *ew* before reviewing closed syllables. In today's *MARK¹² Reading Activity Book* pages, you will work with students to unscramble long double *o* words as well as to break words into syllables.

Advance Preparation

Based on the Performance Review, if students need to complete Code Work activity 2, gather six index cards. On each card, write one of the following words: *stew, tube, rule, chew, blew,* and *tune*. If students need to complete Word Work activity 3, gather six index cards. On each card, write one of the following words: *sunset, handstand, bulldog, itself, nutshell,* and *sandbox*.

| ONLINE | Student & Computer |

Students will work online to complete Warm-Up, Code Work, Word Work, and Speed Work activities, and a Wrap-Up assessment on their own. Be sure to read the Performance Review before beginning the offline portion of today's lesson.

Today you will work with students to complete Code Work, Word Work, and GUM activities. Be sure to read the online Performance Review before beginning the Code Work and Word Work activities.

Warm-Up ···

César Chávez

Look at the Performance Review. If the student achieved a perfect score on today's Warm-Up, move on to Code Work. If the student scored 60 percent or 80 percent, print the story and review the comprehension questions with the student. If the student scored less than 60 percent, print the story, have the student read the story aloud, and then work through the comprehension questions together, before moving on to Code Work.

Code Work ···

Long *u* and Double *o*

Look at the Performance Review. If the student achieved a perfect score on today's Code Work activities, complete the first two activities from the list below. If the student scored less than 100 percent but more than 85 percent, complete the first three activities from the list below. If the student scored 85 percent or less, complete all five of the activities listed below.

1. Have students complete page 305 in *MARK¹² Reading Activity Book* for more practice on words with the long double *o* sound spelled *u*-consonant-*e* and *ew*.

2. Using the Online Tile Kit or Paper Letter Tiles, have students build the following words: *stew, tube, rule, chew, blew,* and *tune.*

3. Gather the six index cards with /ōō/ words you previously prepared. Hold up a card and have students first say the word and then use the word in a sentence.

4. Dictate the following sentences to students and have them write each one on a piece of paper:
   Jack needs a new car.
   That clerk was rude.
   Janet plays the flute.
   There is dew on the grass.
   Review any spelling errors with students, and then have them underline the letters that make the long double *o* sound in the words *new, rude, flute,* and *dew.*

5. Have students compose a two-line poem that contains two of the following words: *blew, chew, crew, dew, flew, new,* or *stew.* Instruct students to place one of the words at the end of each line in their poem.

Code Work   Name: _____

Long *u* & Double *o* and Closed Syllables

/ōō/ Word Scramble

Unscramble each word below. Write the unscrambled words on the lines provided. Then read each word aloud.
Hint: Each word contains the sound /ōō/.

1. tufle   **flute**
2. ewd   **dew**
3. dreu   **rude**
4. nute   **tune**
5. wen   **new**
6. urnpe   **prune**
7. whec   **chew**
8. elru   **rule**
9. wescr   **screw**
10. whert **threw**

Choose two words from above. Write each word in a sentence on the lines provided below.

11. **Sencences will vary.** _____

12. _____

305

ord Work ·

Closed Syllables

Look at the Performance Review. If the student achieved a perfect score on today's
Word Work activities, complete the first activity from the list below. If the student
scored less than 100 percent but more than 85 percent, complete the first three
activities from the list below. If the student scored 85 percent or less, complete all five
of the activities listed below.

1. Have students complete page 306 in *MARK¹² Reading Activity Book* for
   more practice on closed syllables.

2. Dictate the following words to students and have them write each
   word on a piece of paper: *c*o*bw*e*b*, *s*u*ns*e*t*, *b*a*thm*a*t*, *c*a*b*i*n*, *n*a*pk*i*n*, *e*x*i*t,
   and *r*a*bb*i*t. Review any spelling errors with students, and have them
   underline the short vowel in each *syllable* of every word. Then ask
   students to say the words aloud.

3. Gather the six index cards with two-syllable words you previously
   prepared. Hold up one card. Ask students to identify the closed
   syllables contained in the word. Continue for all six cards.

4. After gathering and shuffling the index cards from activity 3,
   demonstrate to students how each word is actually made up of two
   smaller words. Hold up a card and cover up the second syllable with
   your hand and say the exposed syllable. Then, cover up the first syllable
   and say the second, exposed syllable. Have students say the two words
   that make up the word individually, and then as one word. Continue for
   all six cards.

5. As time permits, have students write sentences using words from activity 2.

Word Work

Long u & Double o and Closed Syllables

Name: _____

Break It Up!

Each word below contains two closed syllables. Read each word aloud.
Draw a line between the two syllables in each word.

1. p u m p|k i n
2. c h a p|t e r
3. s u n|s e t
4. i t|s e l f
5. b a c k|p a c k
6. r o b|i n
7. c h i p|m u n k
8. e x|i t
9. r a b|b i t
10. n u t|s h e l l
11. c a b|i n
12. i n|s e c t
13. e n|t e r

306

Speed Work ·

What Do You Know?

Look at the Performance Review, or check the student's fluency chart. Fluency
scores (words read per minute) should not fall below 80. If the student scored
below 80 words per minute, print a copy of the Speed Work story and have the
student read the story silently before reading it aloud. Otherwise, move on to
Grammar, Usage, and Mechanics.

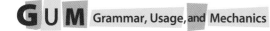

When, Where, and How Adverbs

An adverb can tell *when*, *where*, or *how* an action is happening.

> *When*: I walked to the store *yesterday*.
>
> *Where*: I am standing *outside*.
>
> *How*: I sang the song *loudly*.

Work with students to complete pages 307 and 308 in *MARK¹² Reading Activity Book*. Read page 307, Get Ready, with students. Have students complete the Try It page. Be sure to discuss students' answers when the page is completed.

Objectives

- Identify *when*, *where*, and *how* adverbs.

G U M Grammar, Usage, and Mechanics   Name:

Long *u* & Double *o* and Closed Syllables

Get Ready

☑ An **adverb** can tell *when* an action is happening. For example: Pete went to the zoo *yesterday*. The adverb *yesterday* tells *when* Pete went to the zoo.

Here are some common adverbs that tell *when*.

today	tomorrow	now	then
soon	finally	always	before
later	yesterday	sometimes	never

☑ An adverb can tell *where* an action is happening. For example: Jake is standing *outside*. The adverb *outside* tells *where* Jake is standing.

Here are some common adverbs that tell *where*.

up	down	inside	outside
below	somewhere	nowhere	above
far	near	here	there

☑ An adverb can tell *how* an action is happening. For example: Martin laughed *loudly*. The adverb *loudly* tells *how* Martin laughed.

Here are some common adverbs that tell *how*.

quickly	loudly	sadly	quietly
slowly	softly	safely	weakly
neatly	clearly	calmly	badly

307

G U M Grammar, Usage, and Mechanics   Name:

Long *u* & Double *o* and Closed Syllables

Try It

In each sentence, underline the adverb that tells *when*.

1. <u>Yesterday</u> I ate some plums.
2. We <u>always</u> go to the last game of the season.
3. <u>Sometimes</u> Nick plays at my house.
4. The sun <u>finally</u> came out.

In each sentence, underline the adverb that tells *where*.

5. Ross looked <u>up</u> at the sky.
6. I know my books are <u>somewhere</u>!
7. Put the plate <u>here</u>.
8. We live <u>near</u> the lake.

In each sentence, underline the adverb that tells *how*.

9. Jill ran to the store <u>quickly</u>.
10. Sam spoke <u>softly</u> to me.
11. Tom went into the house <u>quietly</u>.
12. Please speak <u>clearly</u> into the phone.

308

Long *u* & Double *o* and Open Syllables 1

ONLINE	Student & Computer	:60 minutes
	Adult : *Check Performance Review*	
OFFLINE	Student & Adult : Review online work	:30 minutes
	• Reading Warm-Up	
	• Code Work	
	• Word Work	
	• Speed Work	
	Composition	:30 minutes
	Instructional Time **2:00** hours	

Materials

- Online Tile Kit or Paper Letter Tiles
- *MARK¹² Reading Activity Book*, pages 309–314
- *Just Write*

Tip

Remind students that a good way to identify an open syllable is to listen for the long vowel sound in a word.

Goals

In this lesson, students will read about astronaut Sally Ride. Students will also be introduced to the long double *o* sound spelled *ue* and *u* before being introduced to open syllables. In today's *MARK¹² Reading Activity Book* pages, you will work with students to complete a crossword puzzle as well as to identify words with open syllables.

Advance Preparation

Based on the Performance Review, if students need to complete Word Work activity 3, gather 15 index cards. Write one of the following syllables on each card: *ba, be, cab, cac, cob, fro, hab, it, mo, nap, pre, pro, pup, se,* and *sun.* If students need to complete Word Work activity 4, gather a newspaper or magazine.

ONLINE	Student & Computer

Students will work online to complete Warm-Up, Code Work, Word Work, and Speed Work activities, and a Wrap-Up assessment on their own. Be sure to read the Performance Review before beginning the offline portion of today's lesson.

Today you will work with students to complete Code Work, Word Work, and Composition activities. Be sure to read the online Performance Review before beginning the Code Work and Word Work activities.

 Warm-Up •

Sally Ride

Look at the Performance Review. If the student achieved a perfect score on today's Warm-Up, move on to Code Work. If the student scored 60 percent or 80 percent, print the story and review the comprehension questions with the student. If the student scored less than 60 percent, print the story, have the student read the story aloud, and then work through the comprehension questions together, before moving on to Code Work.

Objectives

• Improve reading and comprehension skills.

Code Work •

Long *u* & Double *o*

Look at the Performance Review. If the student achieved a perfect score on today's Code Work activities, complete the first two activities from the list below. If the student scored less than 100 percent but more than 85 percent, complete the first three activities from the list below. If the student scored 85 percent or less, complete all four of the activities listed below.

Objectives

• Identify and use double *o* (ōō) spelling patterns.

1. Have students complete page 309 in *MARK¹² Reading Activity Book* for more practice on words with the long double *o* sound spelled *ue*.

2. Remove the "June Gloom" story from *MARK¹² Reading Activity Book*. Fold the pages in half to create a small booklet. Review the following words with students: *guard, gloomy*. Have students read the story silently once or twice before reading the story aloud. When students read aloud, make note of any errors, and review those words with the students.

3. Using the Online Tile Kit or Paper Letter Tiles, have students build the following words: *blue, due, glue, true, student, tuba,* and *truth*.

4. Dictate the following sentences to students and have them write each one on a piece of paper:
   Sue lost her glue stick.
   It is your duty to help your sister.
   My sister and I argue a lot.
   It was a sunny day in July.
   I am due for a check-up with my dentist.
   Review any spelling errors with students, and then have them underline the letter or letters that make the long double *o* sound in the words *glue, duty, argue, July,* and *due*.

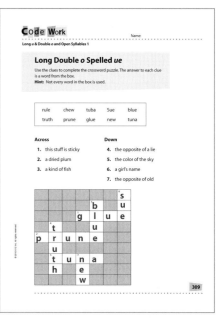

Word Work

Open Syllables

Look at the Performance Review. If the student achieved a perfect score on today's Word Work activities, complete the first activity from the list below. If the student scored less than 100 percent but more than 85 percent, complete the first three activities from the list below. If the student scored 85 percent or less, complete all four of the activities listed below.

1. Have students complete page 310 in *MARK¹² Reading Activity Book* for more practice on open syllables.

2. Dictate the following words to students and have them write each one on a piece of paper: *tulip, robot, begin,* and *relax*. Review any spelling errors with students, and then have them underline the long vowel in the first syllable of each word. Then have students say the words aloud.

3. Gather the 15 syllable index cards you previously prepared. Have students sort the cards into two piles – one pile for open syllables (*ba, be, fro, mo, pre, pro,* and *se*) and one pile for closed syllables (*cab, cac, cob, hab, it, nap, pup,* and *sun*). Then have students explain why the open syllables are open (they end in a long vowel) and why the closed syllables are closed (they end in a consonant and contain a short vowel sound).

4. Have students spend a few minutes searching through the newspaper or magazine that you gathered for words containing open syllables. Students should circle the open syllable(s) in each word they find.

Word Work

Long *u* & Double *o* and Open Syllables 1

Name:

Open Syllables

Say the words in the box aloud. Underline each word that begins with an open syllable.

exit	hotel	relax	insect
tulip	robin	robot	enter
until	begin	itself	secret

Use four of the words you underlined above to complete the following sentences below. Write each word on the lines provided.

1. The **hotel** was closed for the winter.
2. I like to **relax** after working in the yard all day.
3. James forgot his **secret** password.
4. The **tulip** is my favorite spring flower.

310

Speed Work

June Gloom

Look at the Performance Review, or check the student's fluency chart. Fluency scores (words read per minute) should not fall below 80. If the student scored below 80 words per minute, print a copy of the Speed Work story and have the student read the story silently before reading it aloud. Otherwise, move on to Composition.

omposition

Gather students' composition materials and begin where they left off.

Long *u* & Double *o* and Open Syllables 2

ONLINE	Student & Computer	**:60** minutes	
	Adult : *Check Performance Review*		
OFFLINE	Student & Adult : Review online work	**:30** minutes	
	• Reading Warm-Up		
	• Code Work		
	• Word Work		
	• Speed Work		
	Grammar, Usage, and Mechanics (GUM)	**:30** minutes	
	Instructional Time **2:00** hours		

> **Materials**
> - Online Tile Kit or Paper Letter Tiles
> - *MARK¹² Reading Activity Book*, pages 315–318

Goals

In this lesson, students will read about cartoonist Charles Schulz. Students will also be introduced to the long double *o* sound spelled *oo* before continuing to work with open syllables. In today's *MARK¹² Reading Activity Book*, you will work with students to identify words with the long double *o* sound spelled *oo* and to match open syllables.

Advance Preparation

Based on the Performance Review, if students need to complete Word Work activity 3, gather six index cards. On each card, write one of the following words: *belong, even, open, relax, secret,* and *tulip.*

ONLINE Student & Computer

Students will work online to complete Warm-Up, Code Work, Word Work, and Speed Work activities, and a Wrap-Up assessment on their own. Be sure to read the Performance Review before beginning the offline portion of today's lesson.

Today you will work with students to complete Code Work, Word Work, and GUM activities. Be sure to read the online Performance Review before beginning the Code Work and Word Work activities.

Warm-Up

Charles Schulz

Look at the Performance Review. If the student achieved a perfect score on today's Warm-Up, move on to Code Work. If the student scored 60 percent or 80 percent, print the story and review the comprehension questions with the student. If the student scored less than 60 percent, print the story, have the student read the story aloud, and then work through the comprehension questions together, before moving on to Code Work.

Objectives

- Improve reading and comprehension skills.

Code Work

Long *u* and Double *o*

Look at the Performance Review. If the student achieved a perfect score on today's Code Work activities, complete the first two activities from the list below. If the student scored less than 100 percent but more than 85 percent, complete the first three activities from the list below. If the student scored 85 percent or less, complete all five of the activities listed below.

Objectives

- Identify and use double *o* (o͞o) spelling patterns.

1. Have students complete page 315 in *MARK¹² Reading Activity Book* for more practice on the long double *o* sound spelled *oo*.

2. Using the Online Tile Kit or Paper Letter Tiles, have students build the following words: *broom, hoop, pool, spoon, tooth,* and *zoo*.

3. Using the words listed in activity 2, say a word aloud and have students write a word that rhymes with it. Have them underline the letters that make the long double *o* sound in their word. Continue for all six words. After correcting any spelling errors, have students compare their lists. Point out words with alternate spellings of the long double *o* sound (for example, the word *pool* can be rhymed with *rule*, which is the *u-e* spelling, or *cruel*, the *ue* spelling). Discuss how the long double *o* sound can be spelled many ways.

4. Have students compose a silly two-line poem that uses two of the following words: *boo, coo, goo, moo, too,* or *zoo*. Instruct students to place one of the words at the end of each line in their poem. Have students read their poems aloud.

5. Using the words listed in activity 2, say a word aloud and have students draw a picture of it. Have students write the name of the object below their drawing. Continue for all six words or as time allows.

Code Work Name:

Long *u* & Double *o* and Open Syllables 2

Long Double *o*

In each sentence, underline the word that contains the long double *o* sound. Then read each sentence aloud.

1. The strong paint fumes filled the room.
2. "Boo!" shouted Pat as he jumped out from behind the bushes.
3. Joan lost one of her gold hoop earrings.
4. "I lost my first tooth!" said my nephew.
5. Please get home soon.
6. Ken and I like to shoot a few hoops at the park.

On the lines provided, write a sentence using each word given.

7. moon   **Sentences will vary.**
8. zoo
9. pool
10. spoon

315

Word Work

Open Syllables

Look at the Performance Review. If the student achieved a perfect score on today's Word Work activities, complete the first activity from the list below. If the student scored less than 100 percent but more than 85 percent, complete the first three activities from the list below. If the student scored 85 percent or less, complete all five of the activities listed below.

1. Have students complete page 316 in *MARK¹² Reading Activity Book* for more practice on open syllables.

2. Using the Online Tile Kit or Paper Letter Tiles, have students build the following words: *apron, behind, frozen, hotel,* and *unit.* Have students point to and say the letter that makes the long vowel sound in each word.

3. Gather the index cards you previously prepared, shuffle them, and then hold up one card at random. Ask students to identify and say the open syllable contained in the word. Continue for all six cards.

4. Remove the *even* and *open* index cards from the stack. Hold up the two cards and ask students what is special about the open syllable at the beginning of these two words (answer: the open syllable is a single letter). Challenge students to think of other words that contain a single-letter open syllable at the beginning of a word (examples include: *acorn, apron, equipment, event, icon, item, oval, over, unicorn,* and *unit*).

5. Using the words from activity 2, have students write a sentence using each word, or as time allows.

Word Work
Long u & Double o and Open Syllables 2

Make a Word

Draw a line from each open syllable in the first column to the syllable that makes a word in the second column. Then write the words on the lines provided below. The first one has been done for you.

1.	a	cret
2.	se	nit
3.	u	pron
4.	be	zen
5.	re	hind
6.	fro	pen
7.	ho	mind
8.	o	bot
9.	tu	tel
10.	ro	lip

1. apron	6. frozen
2. secret	7. hotel
3. unit	8. open
4. behind	9. tulip
5. remind	10. robot

316

Speed Work

Fresh Air

Look at the Performance Review, or check the student's fluency chart. Fluency scores (words read per minute) should not fall below 80. If the student scored below 80 words per minute, print a copy of the Speed Work story and have the student read the story silently before reading it aloud. Otherwise, move on to Grammar, Usage, and Mechanics.

Good and Well

Sometimes we confuse the words *good* and *well*. The most common mistake is to use *good* when we should use *well*.

The word *good* is an adjective that tells *what kind of* or *what*: Carlos is a *good* writer.

The word *well* is an adverb that tells *how*: Carlos writes *well*.

Work with students to complete pages 317 and 318 in *MARK¹² Reading Activity Book*. Read page 317, Get Ready, with students. Have students complete the Try It page. Be sure to discuss students' answers when the page is completed.

Objectives

- Correctly use good and well.

GUM Grammar, Usage, and Mechanics   Name:

Long *u* & Double *o* and Open Syllables 2

Get Ready

■ Sometimes we confuse *good* and *well*. The most common mistake is to use *good* when we should use *well*.

You will not have this problem if you keep in mind the difference between an adjective and an adverb, because *good* is an *adjective*, and *well* is usually an *adverb*.

Good	Well
adjective	adverb
describes a noun or pronoun	describes a verb
tells *what kind of* or *what*	tells *how*

■ Study these examples.

Mario is a *good* artist. He paints *well*.
What kind of artist is Mario?   *good*, adjective
How does Mario paint?   *well*, adverb

Katie throws *good* passes. She plays basketball *well*.
What kind of passes does Katie throw?   *good*, adjective
How does Katie play basketball?   *well*, adverb

Randy is a *good* dancer. He follows the music *well*.
What kind of dancer is Randy?   *good*, adjective
How does Randy follow the music?   *well*, adverb

317

GUM Grammar, Usage, and Mechanics   Name:

Long *u* & Double *o* and Open Syllables 2

Try It

Complete each sentence by writing the word *good* or *well* on the lines provided.

1. Philip knows how to row a boat **well**.
2. How are you today? I am **well**.
3. Did you get a **good** grade on the math quiz?
4. We can always count on Ben to do the job **well**.
5. Is that milk still **good** to drink?
6. Today is a **good** day to go to the beach.
7. I don't know how to sing very **well**.
8. That was a really **good** movie!
9. Natasha is pretty **good** at hitting the target.
10. How **well** do you know Dr. Martin?

318

Long *u* & Double *o* and Open Syllables 3

<table>
<tr><td rowspan="2">ONLINE</td><td>Student & Computer</td><td>:60 minutes</td></tr>
<tr><td>Adult : Check Performance Review</td><td></td></tr>
<tr><td rowspan="4">OFFLINE</td><td>Student & Adult : Review online work</td><td>:30 minutes</td></tr>
<tr><td>• Reading Warm-Up</td><td></td></tr>
<tr><td>• Speed Work</td><td></td></tr>
<tr><td>• Assessment</td><td></td></tr>
<tr><td></td><td>Classics Session 1</td><td>:30 minutes</td></tr>
<tr><td></td><td colspan="1" align="right">Instructional Time</td><td>2:00 hours</td></tr>
</table>

Materials

- *MARK¹² Classics for Young Readers*
- *MARK¹² Reading Activity Book*, pages 319–322

Goals

In this lesson, students will read about a girl who is surprised with an unusual gift. Students will also review the long double *o* spellings *u-e, ew, ue, u,* and *oo* before continuing to work with open syllables. In today's Unit Assessment, you will administer a test covering all content from Unit 19. Afterward, you will work with students to complete their *MARK¹² Classics for Young Readers* assignment.

ONLINE   **Student & Computer**

Students will work on their own to complete Warm-Up, Code Work, Word Work, and Speed Work activities, and a review game on their own. Be sure to read the Performance Review before beginning the offline portion of today's lesson.

Today you will administer a Unit Assessment and work with students to complete a *MARK¹² Classics for Young Readers* activity.

Warm-Up ·

A Gift for Beth

Look at the Performance Review. If the student achieved a perfect score on today's Warm-Up, move on to Speed Work. If the student scored 60 percent or 80 percent, print the story and review the comprehension questions with the student. If the student scored less than 60 percent, print the story, have the student read the story aloud, and then work through the comprehension questions together, before moving on to Speed Work.

Objectives

- Improve reading and comprehension skills.

Speed Work ·

The Silver Flute

Look at the Performance Review, or check the student's fluency chart. Fluency scores (words read per minute) should not fall below 80. If the student scored below 80 words per minute, print a copy of the Speed Work story and have the student read the story silently before reading it aloud to you. Otherwise, move on to the Assessment.

Objectives

- Increase reading fluency rate.

☼ Assessment ·

Long *u* & Double *o* and Syllable Types

Today's Unit Assessment covers all content found in Unit 19. Carefully read the instructions on the student pages before administering the test to the student. If necessary, read the directions to the student. After you have scored the student's assessment, be sure to go online and input student performance scores in the assessment entry tool.

Part 2. Dictate the following words to students: *cool, clue, drew, truth, moon, rude, clue,* and *tube.*

Part 4. Dictate the following words to students: *tuna, flew, hoop, June,* and *true.*

Page 319

Unit 19 Assessment

Part 1.

Read each word below. On the lines provided, write *Y* for *yes* if the word contains the long double *o* sound. Write *N* for *no* if the word does not contain the long double *o* sound.

1. tune __Y__
2. few __N__
3. due __Y__
4. tooth __Y__
5. cold __N__
6. nephew __N__

Part 2.

Listen to each word that is read to you. Write each word in the correct column according to how the long double *o* sound is spelled in that word.

7. *ew*	8. *oo*	9. *u*	10. *ue*	11. *u-e*
drew	moon cool	truth	glue clue	rude tube

319

Page 320

Part 3.

In each row, underline the word that contains the long double *o* sound.

12. town — <u>tuba</u> — tunnel
13. gutter — goal — <u>glue</u>
14. <u>moo</u> — mold — much
15. could — crown — <u>chew</u>
16. boat — <u>blue</u> — blow
17. <u>flute</u> — float — flour
18. round — <u>room</u> — rotten
19. just — join — <u>July</u>
20. <u>student</u> — stumble — stowed

Part 4.

Listen to each word that is read to you. Write each word on the lines provided.

21. __tuna__
22. __flew__
23. __hoop__
24. __June__
25. __true__

320

Page 321

Part 5.

On the lines provided, write the number of syllables that each word contains.

26. over __2__
27. cheese __1__
28. Atlantic __3__
29. behind __2__
30. until __2__
31. yellow __2__
32. strings __1__
33. volcano __3__
34. faster __2__
35. tulip __2__

321

Page 322

Part 6.

On the lines provided, write the two syllables contained in each word and the type of syllables that they are. Use *O* for "open" syllable and *C* for "closed" syllable. An example has been done for you.

Example: hotel	ho	tel	O, C
36. bonus	bo	nus	O, C
37. pilot	pi	lot	O, C
38. until	un	til	C, C
39. apron	a	pron	O, C
40. robin	rob	in	C, C
41. insect	in	sect	C, C
42. belong	be	long	O, C
43. unit	u	nit	O, C
44. exit	ex	it	C, C
45. student	stu	dent	O, C

322

Objectives

- Identify and use double *o* ($\overline{oo}$) spelling patterns.
- Identify the number of syllables in a word.
- Identify and use syllable types.

Classics Session 1 . . . .

Aladdin and the Wonderful Lamp

Today's story, "Aladdin and the Wonderful Lamp," is the age-old tale of a boy who finds himself the master of two genies. Review the keywords with students. Read the story with students, and then use the Discussion Questions below as a guide to share ideas about the story. Have students read the story again before writing a summary of the story.

Keywords

greet, v. – to meet or say hello to
When my mother came home, I ran to the door and **greeted** her with a smile and a big hug.

mumble, v. – to say words in a low voice
Sometimes, when I am angry with my little brother, I will **mumble** "brat" so that my mother won't hear.

arose, v. – to have risen up from a source
Smoke **arose** from the fire.

sultan, n. – king
The **sultan** lived in the palace and ruled the country.

mad, adj. – crazy or insane
"You want to swim across the Atlantic Ocean without stopping? You must be **mad**!" cried Sally.

wretch, n. – an unhappy person, or a person in trouble
"What a **wretch** am I!" I sobbed. "I have lost my dog."

wrung, v. – twisted together as a sign of being upset
The princess **wrung** her hands as she thought about the prince, off at battle.

Discussion Questions

1. If you were Aladdin, would you have gone down into the cave? Why or why not? Answers will vary.

2. Why does the Princess give the magic lamp away? Does she know it is magic? Answers may include that the Princess gives the lamp away because she does not know it is magic. She believes she is getting a nice, new lamp for an old one.

3. Why is it important to guard the ring and the lamp? Answers may include that it is important to guard the ring and the lamp because bad things can happen if either winds up in the wrong hands. For example, when the magician had the lamp, the Princess was taken from her home and family against her will.

4. What do you think Aladdin learns during this story? Answers may include that Aladdin learns to be thankful for what he has. He also learns to be responsible and to be careful who he trusts.

5. Why do you think Aladdin is not afraid of the genies? Answers may include that Aladdin knows their power. He knows that as long as he makes good decisions and proper wishes, their power can be used for good.

Students should write a summary of the story to complete today's Classics activity.

Double *o* and Open Syllables 1

ONLINE	Student & Computer	:60	minutes
	Adult : *Check Performance Review*		
OFFLINE	Student & Adult : Review online work	:30	minutes
	• Reading Warm-Up		
	• Code Work		
	• Word Work		
	• Speed Work		
	Classics Session 2	:30	minutes
	Instructional Time **2:00** hours		

Materials

- *MARK¹² Classics for Young Readers*
- *MARK¹² Reading Activity Book*, pages 323–324
- Online Tile Kit or Paper Letter Tiles

Tip *Do not confuse an open syllable with a vowel team syllable. An open syllable contains a single letter (be̲hind, fly̲, ba̲con), whereas a vowel team has two or more letters (pe̲anut, wa̲y, si̲gh).*

Goals

In this lesson, students will read important facts about the American flag. Students will also be introduced to the short double *o* sound /o͝o/ before working with open syllables. In today's *MARK¹² Reading Activity Book*, you will work with students to find words with the short double *o* spelling and to distinguish open and closed syllables.

Advance Preparation

If students need to complete Code Work activity 4, you will need to gather five index cards. On each card, write one of the following words: *wood, foot, cook, hook,* and *good.* If students need to complete Word Work activity 3, you will need to gather eight index cards. On each card, write one of the following words: *funny, open, gopher, bacon, even, pretend, remind,* and *she.*

ONLINE	**Student & Computer**

Students will work online to complete Warm-Up, Code Work, Word Work, and Speed Work activities, and a Wrap-Up assessment on their own. Be sure to read the Performance Review before beginning the offline portion of today's lesson.

Today you will work with students to complete Code Work, Word Work, and *MARK¹² Classics for Young Readers* activities. Be sure to read the online Performance Review before beginning the Code Work and Word Work activities.

Warm-Up ·

The American Flag

Look at the Performance Review. If the student achieved a perfect score on today's Warm-Up, move on to Code Work. If the student scored 60 percent or 80 percent, print the story and review the comprehension questions with the student. If the student scored less than 60 percent, print the story, have the student read the story aloud, and then work through the comprehension questions together, before moving on to Code Work.

Objectives

• **Improve reading and comprehension skills.**

Code Work ·

Double *o*

Look at the Performance Review. If the student achieved a perfect score on today's Code Work activities, complete the first two activities from the list below. If the student scored less than 100 percent but more than 85 percent, complete the first three activities from the list below. If the student scored 85 percent or less, complete all five of the activities listed below.

Objectives

• **Identify and use double *o* /o͞o/ spelling patterns.**

1. Have students complete page 323 in *MARK¹² Reading Activity Book*.

2. Using the Online Tile Kit or Paper Letter Tiles, have students build the following words: *cook, foot, good, stood, took,* and *wood*.

3. Say the word *book* aloud. Have students brainstorm words that rhyme with book (for example, *brook, cook, hook, look, shook,* and *took*). Inform students that almost all words with an *o-o* followed by the letter *k* have the sound /o͞o/.

4. Gather the five index cards that you prepared earlier and lay them out flat so students can see them. Read aloud the following sentences, having students point to and say the word on the card that best completes each sentence.
   I need to chop some _____.
   I put a sock on my _____.
   I use the stove to _____.
   I put the bait on the fish _____.
   I think this cake tastes _____.

5. Say one of the following words aloud and have students draw a picture of it: *foot, wood, hook, book,* and *hood*. Have students write the name of the object below their drawing. Continue for all five words or as time allows.

Word Work

Open Syllables

Look at the Performance Review. If the student achieved a perfect score on today's Word Work activities, complete the first activity from the list below. If the student scored less than 100 percent but more than 85 percent, complete the first three activities from the list below. If the student scored 85 percent or less, complete all five of the activities listed below.

1. Have students complete page 324 in *MARK¹² Reading Activity Book* for more practice on open and closed syllables.

2. Using the Online Tile Kit or Paper Letter Tiles, have students build the following words: *pilot, behind, she, study,* and *dry.* Have students point to and say the letter that makes the long vowel sound in each word.

3. Gather the eight index cards you previously prepared and hold up one card at random. Ask students to identify and say the open syllable contained in the word. (Answers: *fun<u>ny</u>, open, gopher, <u>ba</u>con, <u>e</u>ven, pretend, remind, she*) Continue for all eight cards.

4. Have students write down the following words: *at, bleed, dry, he, goat, she, fly, hat, it, not, open, sun, to, we,* and *why.* Ask students to circle those syllables that are open syllables, and then explain why the uncircled ones are not open syllables.

5. Gather and shuffle the index cards from activity 3. Choose a card at random and read it aloud. Have students say a sentence using that word. Continue for all eight cards or as time allows.

Word Work

Double o and Open Syllables 1

Name:

Open or Closed?

Read each word pair. Decide what type of syllable the two words contain, open or closed. On the line provided, write O for open or C for closed.

Example: cup, tub   C

1. go, so   O
2. hit, sip   C
3. mop, hot   C
4. by, my   O
5. up, us   C
6. be, we   O
7. had, sat   C
8. spy, fly   O

324

Speed Work

Your Perfect Day

Look at the Performance Review, or check the student's fluency chart. Fluency scores (words read per minute) should not fall below 80. If the student scored below 80 words per minute, print a copy of the Speed Work story and have the student read the story silently before reading it aloud. Otherwise, move on to Classics Session 2.

Classics Session 2 ·

Aladdin and the Wonderful Lamp

Review the keywords with students. Have students reread the story on their own. After rereading the story, students should complete the comprehension questions in *MARK¹² Classics for Young Readers* on their own. Afterward, if time allows, have students read the story aloud to you.

Objectives

- Improve reading and comprehension questions.

W Write

Aladdin and the Wonderful Lamp

1. Who does the magician claim to be?
   - (A.) Aladdin's uncle
   - B. Aladdin's father
   - C. Aladdin's cousin
   - D. Aladdin's brother

2. What reason does the magician give for **not** visiting Aladdin and his mother sooner?
   The magician claims he was traveling out of the country for many years.

3. Which of the following is the correct order of events?
   - A. Aladdin goes down steps, the earth trembles, Aladdin gathers sticks for a fire
   - B. Aladdin gathers sticks for a fire, Aladdin goes down steps, the earth trembles
   - C. Aladdin goes down steps, Aladdin gathers sticks for a fire, the earth trembles
   - (D.) Aladdin gathers sticks for a fire, the earth trembles, Aladdin goes down steps

128   Aladdin and the Wonderful Lamp

---

4. When did Aladdin finally rub the ring the magician had given him?
   Aladdin rubbed the ring the magician gave him while he was clasping his hands in despair.

5. When did Aladdin and his mother first discover the Genie of the Lamp?
   Aladdin and his mother needed food and decided to sell the lamp to buy some. When Aladdin's mother polished the lamp, in the hopes of getting more for it, the genie first appeared.

6. Why did the Sultan laugh when Aladdin's mother presented him with the gift basket?
   The Sultan laughed because Aladdin's mother thought she was giving him fruit. The basket was actually filled with diamonds, rubies, and sapphires.

7. What did Aladdin want to do before marrying the Princess?
   - A. become rich
   - (B.) build a palace
   - C. buy his mother a house
   - D. own a large piece of land

Aladdin and the Wonderful Lamp   129

---

8. How did the magician get the Genie of the Lamp?
   The magician went into Aladdin's town, pretending to trade new lamps for old lamps. The Princess traded him the old lamp with the Genie of the Lamp for new lamps.

9. Where did the magician keep the lamp during the day?
   - A. in his clothes
   - (B.) under his pillow
   - C. in a basket of jewels
   - D. in the Princess's room

130   Aladdin and the Wonderful Lamp

Double *o* and Open Syllables 2

ONLINE	Student & Computer	:60 minutes
	Adult : *Check Performance Review*	
OFFLINE	Student & Adult : Review online work	:30 minutes
	• Reading Warm-Up	
	• Code Work	
	• Word Work	
	• Speed Work	
	Composition	:30 minutes

Instructional Time **2:00** hours

Materials

- *MARK¹² Reading Activity Book*, pages 325–330
- **Online Tile Kit or Paper Letter Tiles**
- *Just Write*

Tip

*There really aren't any rules that govern the sound of the letters **oo**. When students are in doubt as to how an **oo** word should be pronounced, encourage them to say the word aloud with both sounds, and then decide.*

Goals

In this lesson, students will read about Windsor Castle. Students will work with the short and long double *o* sounds before reviewing open syllables. In today's *MARK¹² Reading Activity Book*, you will work with students to recognize the vowel sound in words with the double *o* spelling and identify words with open syllables.

Advance Preparation

If students need to complete Code Work activity 4, you will need to gather six index cards. On each card, write one of the following words: *cook, foot, wool, fool, hoop,* and *boot*.

ONLINE	Student & Computer

Students will work online to complete Warm-Up, Code Work, Word Work, and Speed Work activities, and a Wrap-Up assessment on their own. Be sure to read the Performance Review before beginning the offline portion of today's lesson.

Today you will work with students to complete Code Work, Word Work, and Composition activities. Be sure to read the online Performance Review before beginning the Code Work and Word Work activities.

Warm-Up ·

Windsor Castle

Look at the Performance Review. If the student achieved a perfect score on today's Warm-Up, move on to Code Work. If the student scored 60 percent or 80 percent, print the story and review the comprehension questions with the student. If the student scored less than 60 percent, print the story, have the student read the story aloud, and then work through the comprehension questions together, before moving on to Code Work.

Code Work ·

Double *o*

Look at the Performance Review. If the student achieved a perfect score on today's Code Work activities, complete the first two activities from the list below. If the student scored less than 100 percent but more than 85 percent, complete the first three activities from the list below. If the student scored 85 percent or less, complete all five of the activities listed below.

1. Have students complete page 325 in *MARK¹² Reading Activity Book* for more practice on words with the double *o* spelling.

2. Remove "The Book of Secrets" story from *MARK¹² Reading Activity Book*. Fold the pages in half to create a small booklet. Review the following word with students: *mystery*. Have students read the story silently once or twice before reading the story aloud. When students read aloud, make note of any errors, and review those words with the students.

3. Using the Online Tile Kit or Paper Letter Tiles, have students build the following words: *broom, book, gloom, good, tool,* and *took*.

4. Gather the six index cards you previously prepared and lay them out so students can see them. Have students sort the cards into two piles: one pile for words with the /o͞o/ sound (*cook, foot, wool*) and another pile for words with the /o͞o/ sound (*fool, hoop, boot*).

5. Gather up the index cards from activity 4, shuffle them, and then hold up one card at random. Ask students to identify the vowel sound contained in the word. Reinforce the short or long vowel sound by repeating the word and exaggerating the /o͞o/ or /o͞o/ sound. Continue for all six cards.

Code Work

Name _____

Double *o* and Open Syllables 2

Double *o* Sounds

Read each word in the word box. Write the words from the box in each column below according to the vowel sound they contain.

Hint: There are six words with the long double *o* sound, and there are six words with the short double *o* sound.

cook	tooth	tool	foot	stood	took
good	root	wood	broom	gloom	hoop

Long Double *o*	**Short Double *o***
root	cook
gloom	foot
tool	good
broom	took
tooth	wood
hoop	stood

325

 Word Work

Open Syllables

Look at the Performance Review. If the student achieved a perfect score on today's Word Work activities, complete the first activity from the list below. If the student scored less than 100 percent but more than 85 percent, complete the first three activities from the list below. If the student scored 85 percent or less, complete all five of the activities listed below.

1. Have students complete page 326 in *MARK¹² Reading Activity Book* for more practice on open syllables.

2. Using the Online Tile Kit or Paper Letter Tiles, have students build the following words: *hello, frozen, paper, she, sunny,* and *unit.* Have students point to and say the letter or letters that make the long vowel sound in each word.

3. Have students write down the following words [shown here with hyphens to indicate syllables]: *o-pen, ro-bot, he, happ-y, a-corn, pi-lot, she, man-y, fry,* and *vol-ca-no.* Have students draw a vertical line to separate syllables in the two- to three-syllable words and then check students' work for accuracy. Next, have students circle those syllables that are open syllables, and then explain why the uncircled ones are not open syllables.

4. Have students make a single list of all their names, and the names of siblings and friends. Have them separate each name into syllables, using vertical lines as in activity 3. Students should then look for and underline open syllables. Discuss how many names end with the letter *y,* which makes the last syllable in those names an open syllable.

5. Using the words listed in activity 3, pick a word at random and read it aloud. Have students say a sentence using that word. Continue for all words or as time allows.

Word Work
Double o and Open Syllables 2

Name: _____

Practice Open Syllables

Read the words in the box aloud. Underline each word that contains an open syllable.

gopher	push	bacon	insect
robin	student	robot	be
exit	sunny	itself	even
she	enter	hotel	basin

Read the words in the box aloud. Underline the letter that makes the long vowel sound in the open syllable in each word.

study	we	remind	pretty
begin	relax	silent	tulip
fly	frozen	unit	paper
over	acorn	secret	hello

326

Speed Work

A Fool for the Pool

Look at the Performance Review, or check the student's fluency chart. Fluency scores (words read per minute) should not fall below 80. If the student scored below 80 words per minute, print a copy of the Speed Work story and have the student read the story silently before reading it aloud. Otherwise, move on to Composition.

Composition ·······································

Gather students' composition materials and begin where they left off.

Double *o* and Syllable Types

Double *o* and V-C-E Syllables

ONLINE	Student & Computer	:60 minutes
	Adult : *Check Performance Review*	
OFFLINE	Student & Adult : Review online work	:30 minutes
	• Reading Warm-Up	
	• Speed Work	
	• Assessment	
	Grammar, Usage, and Mechanics	:30 minutes

Instructional Time **2:00** hours

Materials

• *MARK¹² Reading Activity Book*, pages 331–336

Tip

*Explain to students that, although the silent **e** doesn't have a sound of its own in a vowel-consonant-**e** word, it has an important job to do. Without it, words like **cane**, **bite**, and **cute** would be confused with **can**, **bit**, and **cut**.*

Goals

In this lesson, students will read about tigers. Students will review the short and long double *o* sounds before being introduced to vowel-consonant-*e* syllables. In today's Unit Assessment, you will administer a test covering all content from Unit 20. Afterward, you will work with students on adverbs.

ONLINE	**Student & Computer**

Students will work to complete Warm-Up, Code Work, Word Work, and Speed Work activities, and a review game on their own. Be sure to read the Performance Review before beginning the offline portion of today's lesson.

Today you will administer a Unit Assessment and work with students to complete a GUM activity.

Warm-Up ·

Tigers

Look at the Performance Review. If the student achieved a perfect score on today's Warm-Up, move on to Speed Work. If the student scored 60 percent or 80 percent, print the story and review the comprehension questions with the student. If the student scored less than 60 percent, print the story, have the student read the story aloud, and then work through the comprehension questions together, before moving on to Speed Work.

Objectives

- Improve reading and comprehension skills.

Speed Work ·

Stadium King

Look at the Performance Review, or check the student's fluency chart. Fluency scores (words read per minute) should not fall below 80. If the student scored below 80 words per minute, print a copy of the Speed Work story and have the student read the story silently before reading it aloud to you. Otherwise, move on to the Assessment.

Objectives

- Increase reading fluency rate.

☼ Assessment ·

Double *o* and Syllable Types

Today's Unit Assessment covers all content found in Unit 20. Carefully read the instructions on the student pages before administering the test to the student. If necessary, read the directions to the student. After you have scored the student's assessment, be sure to go online and input student performance scores in the assessment entry tool.

Part 3. Dictate the following words to students: *gloom, brook, moon, coop, wool, spoon, mood, hoop, hook,* and *tooth*.

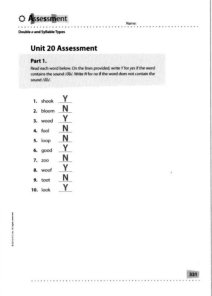

Assessment
Double o and Syllable Types

Name: _____

Unit 20 Assessment

Part 1.
Read each word below. On the lines provided, write Y for yes if the word contains the sound /o͞o/. Write N for no if the word does not contain the sound /o͞o/.

1. shook   **Y**
2. bloom   **N**
3. wood   **Y**
4. fool   **N**
5. loop   **N**
6. good   **Y**
7. zoo   **N**
8. woof   **Y**
9. toot   **N**
10. look   **Y**

331

Assessment
Double o and Syllable Types

Name: _____

Part 2.
In each row, underline the word that contains the sound /o͞o/.

11. foot   <u>food</u>
12. <u>boot</u>   book
13. <u>cool</u>   cook
14. hood   <u>hoop</u>
15. <u>tool</u>   took

Part 3.
Listen to each word that is read to you. Write each word on the lines provided.

16. gloom
17. brook
18. moon
19. coop
20. wool
21. spoon
22. mood
23. hoop
24. hook
25. tooth

332

Assessment
Double o and Syllable Types

Name: _____

Part 4.
On the lines provided, write the number of syllables that each word contains.

26. pretty   **2**
27. scream   **1**
28. animals   **3**
29. glance   **1**
30. sisters   **2**
31. twice   **1**
32. alphabet   **3**
33. boxes   **2**

Part 5.
Underline the vowel-consonant-e syllable that makes the word complete. Then, write the completed word on the line provided. An example has been done for you.

Example:	in	sive	<u>side</u>	inside
34.	mis	<u>take</u>	teke	**mistake**
35.	cos	tome	<u>tume</u>	**costume**
36.	sun	<u>shine</u>	shene	**sunshine**
37.	cup	<u>cake</u>	cace	**cupcake**

333

Assessment
Double o and Syllable Types

Name: _____

Part 6.
On the lines provided, write the two syllables contained in each word and the type of syllables that they are. Write O for "open" syllable, C for "closed" syllable, and V-C-E for "vowel-consonant-e" syllable. An example has been done for you.

Example: inside	in	side	C, V-C-E
38. paper	**pa**	**per**	**O, C**
39. happy	**hap**	**py**	**C, O**
40. basement	**base**	**ment**	**V-C-E, C**
41. gopher	**go**	**pher**	**O, C**
42. rosebud	**rose**	**bud**	**V-C-E, C**
43. fireplace	**fire**	**place**	**V-C-E, V-C-E**
44. tulip	**tu**	**lip**	**O, C**
45. sunrise	**sun**	**rise**	**C, V-C-E**
46. secret	**se**	**cret**	**O, C**
47. snakeskin	**snake**	**skin**	**V-C-E, C**
48. apron	**a**	**pron**	**O, C**
49. baby	**ba**	**by**	**O, O**

334

Objectives
- Identify and use double o ($\overline{oo}$ and $\breve{oo}$) spelling patterns.
- Identify the number of syllables in a word.
- Identify and use syllable types.

Identifying Verbs Modified by Adverbs

An adverb can be used to modify a verb. An adverb used in this way often ends in –*ly*, and it can come before or after the verb in a sentence.

- Identify verbs modified by adverbs.

> The dog <u>ran</u> *quickly* through the woods.
>
> *Silently*, the snow <u>fell</u> on the trees.
>
> My sister *quietly* <u>sang</u> to herself.

Work with students to complete pages 335 and 336 in *MARK¹² Reading Activity Book*. Read page 335, Get Ready, with students. Have students complete the Try It page. Be sure to discuss students' answers when the page is completed.

GUM Grammar, Usage, and Mechanics   Name: _____

Double *o* and *V-C-E* Syllables

Get Ready

■ **Adverbs** are words that can be used to *describe*, or *modify*, verbs. Some adverbs tell *how* the action of a verb takes place. This kind of adverb often ends in –*ly*, and it can come before or after the verb in a sentence. For example:

Janette *spoke loudly* on the phone.
(*How* did Janette speak? Loudly.)

My brother *quietly* cried in his room.
(*How* did my brother cry? Quietly.)

Bravely, the man walked into the lion's cage.
(*How* did the man walk? Bravely.)

Brenda pressed the doorbell *firmly*.
(*How* did Brenda press the doorbell? Firmly.)

■ Study this list of adverbs that end in –*ly* and can be used to modify a verb.

quickly	loudly	softly	slowly
nicely	sadly	carefully	easily
silently	firmly	cheerfully	warmly
rudely	weakly	painfully	bravely
badly	quietly	calmly	safely

335

GUM Grammar, Usage, and Mechanics   Name: _____

Double *o* and *V-C-E* Syllables

Try It

In each sentence, underline the verb and circle the adverb that modifies it.

1. The big tiger <u>ran</u> (quickly) through the jungle.
2. The angry man <u>stared</u> (calmly) at the cop.
3. Jamie <u>yelled</u> (loudly) during the whole game.
4. Bart (carefully) <u>shut</u> the glass door.
5. The butterfly <u>landed</u> (softly) on the flower petal.
6. (Sadly) Mom <u>told</u> us our trip was canceled.
7. Kurt <u>smiled</u> at his dance partner (weakly).
8. My sister <u>whispered</u> (quietly) in my ear.
9. (Carefully) the dentist <u>drilled</u> the tooth.
10. "I won the race!" Jason <u>shouted</u> to his parents (proudly).

336

Schwa and V-C-E Syllables 1

ONLINE	Student & Computer	**:60** minutes	
	Adult : *Check Performance Review*		
OFFLINE	Student & Adult : Review online work	**:30** minutes	
	• Reading Warm-Up		
	• Code Work		
	• Word Work		
	• Speed Work		
	Composition	**:30** minutes	
		Instructional Time **2:00** hours	

Materials

- Online Tile Kit or Paper Letter Tiles
- *MARK¹² Reading Activity Book*, pages 337–342
- *Just Write*

Tip

*The schwa sound is represented by the upside down, backwards **e**, /ə/. The schwa sound, sometimes pronounced like a short **u**, can be represented by any of the vowels. It only occurs in an unaccented syllable.*

Goals

In this lesson, students will read about the first World's Expo. Students will also learn about the schwa sound before learning about vowel-consonant-*e* syllables. In today's *MARK¹² Reading Activity Book*, you will work with students to reinforce their understanding of the schwa sound and to reinforce their understanding of vowel-consonant-*e* syllables. Afterward, students will spend 30 minutes working on composition.

Advance Preparation

For the offline portion of today's lesson, gather the students' composition materials. Based on the Performance Review, if students need to complete Code Work activity 3 or Word Work activity 4, gather the Online Tile Kit or Paper Letter Tiles. If students need to complete Word Work activity 2, gather 15 index cards. On each card, write one of the following syllables (note: some syllables are words): *base, bat, cake, can, fire, grape, hab, lete, mo, place, rose, side, sit, time,* and *ze.*

ONLINE   **Student & Computer**

Students will work online to complete Warm-Up, Code Work, Word Work, and Speed Work activities, and a Wrap-Up assessment on their own. Be sure to read the Performance Review before beginning the offline portion of today's lesson.

Today you will work with students to complete Code Work, Word Work, and Composition activities. Be sure to read the online Performance Review before beginning the Code Work and Word Work activities.

Warm-Up

World's Expo

Look at the Performance Review. If the student achieved a perfect score on today's Warm-Up, move on to Code Work. If the student scored 60 percent or 80 percent, print the story and review the comprehension questions with the student. If the student scored less than 60 percent, print the story, have the student read the story aloud, and then work through the comprehension questions together, before moving on to Code Work.

Objectives

- Improve reading and comprehension skills.

Code Work

/ ə /

Look at the Performance Review. If the student achieved a perfect score on today's Code Work activities, complete the first two activities from the list below. If the student scored less than 100 percent but more than 85 percent, complete the first three activities from the list below. If the student scored 85 percent or less, complete all four of the activities listed below.

Objectives

- Identify the letters, given the sound /ə/.
- Identify and use the schwa sound.

1. Have students complete page 337 in *MARK¹² Reading Activity Book* for more practice on the schwa sound.

2. Remove "The End of Mona" story from *MARK¹² Reading Activity Book*. Fold the pages in half to create a small booklet. Review the following words with students: *radio, aft*. Have students read the story silently once or twice before reading the story aloud. When students read aloud, make note of any errors, and review those words with the students.

3. Using the Online Tile Kit or Paper Letter Tiles, have students build the following words: *about, lemon, ribbon, alone, wagon,* and *awake*.

4. Tell students they will be creating a grocery list from the words you will read. Only items that contain the schwa sound should be added to their list. Read the following food names to students and have students write down those names that contain the schwa sound, /ə/: *candy, pasta, bread, jam, lemons, crackers, lima beans, pizza*. Help students with spelling as needed.

Code Work   Name: _____

Schwa and V-C-E Syllables 1

Schwa Sound

Choose the word from the box that best matches each definition. Write the word on the line next to the definition. In each word, underline the vowel that makes the schwa sound.

alone	lemon	pizza	ribbon	wagon	awake	puma

1. not asleep **awake**
2. a bitter, yellow fruit **lemon**
3. a large, wild, fast cat **puma**
4. fabric used to tie into a bow **ribbon**
5. separate or away from others **alone**
6. a four-wheeled cart used for pulling heavy loads **wagon**
7. an Italian food that is usually round, with toppings of tomatoes, cheese, and spices **pizza**

337

Word Work ∙∙

V-C-E Syllables

Look at the Performance Review. If the student achieved a perfect score on today's Word Work activities, complete the first activity from the list below. If the student scored less than 100 percent but more than 85 percent, complete the first three activities from the list below. If the student scored 85 percent or less, complete all four of the activities listed below.

1. Have students complete page 338 in *MARK¹² Reading Activity Book* for more practice on vowel-consonant-*e* syllables.

2. Gather the 15 index cards with syllables written on them that you previously prepared. Have students sort the cards into two piles: those syllables that are vowel-consonant-*e* syllables and those that are not vowel-consonant-*e* syllables. Then have students come up with as many words as they can in two minutes that use the vowel-consonant-*e* syllables (examples: *baseball, basement, fireball, fireplace, someplace, placement*).

3. Have students make five columns on a piece of paper. Using the letter *c* for *consonant*, label the columns as follows: *a-c-e, e-c-e, i-c-e, o-c-e,* and *u-c-e*. Under each column, have students list as many words as they can think of that fit the spelling pattern. Give students 30 seconds for each v-c-e spelling (examples: *bake, compete, nice, hope, cute*).

4. Using the Online Tile Kit or Paper Letter Tiles, have students build the following v-c-e syllables (which are also words): *home, skate, space, tile,* and *vine*. Then have students create a two-syllable word using the v-c-e syllables. (Possibilities include: *homeland, skateboard, workspace, reptile, grapevine*.)

Speed Work ∙∙

A Simple Idea

Look at the Performance Review, or check the student's fluency chart. Fluency scores (words read per minute) should not fall below 80. If the student scored below 80 words per minute, print a copy of the Speed Work story and have the student read the story silently before reading it aloud. Otherwise, move on to Composition.

omposition ·····································

Gather students' composition materials and begin where they left off.

Schwa and V-C-E Syllables 2

ONLINE	Student & Computer	**:60** minutes	
	Adult : *Check Performance Review*		
OFFLINE	Student & Adult : Review online work	**:30** minutes	
	• Reading Warm-Up		
	• Code Work		
	• Word Work		
	• Speed Work		
	Classics Session 1	**:30** minutes	
	Instructional Time **2:00** hours		

Materials

- *MARK¹² Classics for Young Readers*
- "Mother Frost" MP3
- **Online Tile Kit or Paper Letter Tiles**
- *MARK¹² Reading Activity Book*, pages 343–348

Goals

In this lesson, students will read about the invention of the Ferris wheel. Students will also work with the schwa sound before working with vowel-consonant-*e* syllables. In today's *MARK¹² Reading Activity Book*, you will work with students to reinforce their understanding of the schwa sound and to reinforce their understanding of vowel-consonant-*e* syllables. Afterward, you will work with students to complete Classics activities.

Advance Preparation

For the offline portion of today's lesson, download this story: "Mother Frost." Based on the Performance Review, if students need to complete Word Work activity 2, gather the Online Tile Kit or Paper Letter Tiles.

ONLINE   Student & Computer

Students will work online to complete Warm-Up, Code Work, Word Work, and Speed Work activities, and a Wrap-Up assessment on their own. Be sure to read the Performance Review before beginning the offline portion of today's lesson.

Today you will work with students to complete Code Work, Word Work, and *MARK¹² Classics for Young Readers* activities. Be sure to read the online Performance Review before beginning the Code Work and Word Work activities.

Warm-Up  ·

Ferris Wheels

Look at the Performance Review. If the student achieved a perfect score on today's Warm-Up, move on to Code Work. If the student scored 60 percent or 80 percent, print the story and review the comprehension questions with the student. If the student scored less than 60 percent, print the story, have the student read the story aloud, and then work through the comprehension questions together, before moving on to Code Work.

Objectives

● **Improve reading and comprehension skills.**

Code Work  ·

Schwa

Look at the Performance Review. If the student achieved a perfect score on today's Code Work activities, complete the first two activities from the list below. If the student scored less than 100 percent but more than 85 percent, complete the first three activities from the list below. If the student scored 85 percent or less, complete all four of the activities listed below.

Objectives

● **Identify the letters, given the sound /ə/.**
● **Identify and use the schwa sound.**

1. Have students complete page 343 in *MARK¹² Reading Activity Book* for more practice on the schwa sound.

2. Remove "The Secret Project" story from *MARK¹² Reading Activity Book*. Fold the pages in half to create a small booklet. Review the following words with students: *angel, Hawaii, project.* Have students read the story silently once or twice before reading the story aloud. When students read aloud, make note of any errors, and review those words with the students.

3. Dictate the following words to students and have them write the words on a piece of paper: *afraid, ago, ballad, drama,* and *item.* Have students underline the letter or letters that make the schwa sound in each word.

4. Have students write a very short poem using the words from activity 3.

Code Work
Name: _____
Schwa and V-C-E Syllables 2

Words with the Schwa Sound
Choose a word from the box that means the same or almost the same as the word or words below. Write the words on the lines provided. Then underline the letter that makes the schwa sound in each word you wrote.

| afraid | data | pasta | scuba | wagon | above | drama |

1. cart — **wagon**
2. over — **above**
3. a play — **drama**
4. scared — **afraid**
5. spaghetti — **pasta**
6. information — **data**
7. underwater diving equipment — **scuba**

Sentences
Choose three words from the box above. On the lines provided, write a sentence using each word and then read the sentences aloud.

8. _____
9. _____
10. _____

343

Word Work

V-C-E Syllables

Look at the Performance Review. If the student achieved a perfect score on today's Word Work activities, complete the first activity from the list below. If the student scored less than 100 percent but more than 85 percent, complete the first three activities from the list below. If the student scored 85 percent or less, complete all four of the activities listed below.

1. Have students complete page 344 in *MARK¹² Reading Activity Book* for more practice on vowel-consonant-e syllables

2. Using the Online Tile Kit or Paper Letter Tiles, have students build the following v-c-e syllables (which are also words): *cake, made, note, race,* and *side.* Then have students create a two-syllable word using these v-c-e syllables. (Some possible new words include: *cupcake, handmade, notepad, racetrack,* and *sidewalk.*)

3. Have students secretly choose three of the following words: *backbone, backstroke, baseball, explode,* or *handshake.* Then have students act out each word for you, while you guess which word is being enacted. If time permits, switch roles.

4. Have students write a very short story or poem using as many vowel-consonant-e words as possible.

Objectives

- Identify the number of syllables in a word.
- Identify and use syllable types.

Word Work   Name: _____

Schwa and V-C-E Syllables 2

Vowel-Consonant-e Syllables

Match one vowel-consonant-e syllable from the box to each of the syllables below to form a two-syllable word. Write each syllable on the lines provided. Then read each word aloud.

base	cake	lete	note	tile
race	shake	take	rise	side

1. ath **lete** ____
2. **base** ball
3. cup **cake**
4. hand **shake**
5. in **side**
6. mis **take**
7. **note** book
8. **race** track
9. sun **rise**
10. rep **tile**

344

Speed Work

The Garden's New Friend

Look at the Performance Review, or check the student's fluency chart. Fluency scores (words read per minute) should not fall below 80. If the student scored below 80 words per minute, print a copy of the Speed Work story and have the student read the story silently before reading it aloud. Otherwise, move on to Classics Session 1.

Objectives

- Increase reading fluency rate.

Classics Session 1

Mother Frost

Today's story, "Mother Frost," is about helping others. Download the story. Have students listen to the story while following along in *MARK¹² Classics for Young Readers*. Have students listen to the story again before writing a summary of the story.

Students should write a summary of the story to complete today's Classics activity.

Objectives

- Improve reading and comprehension skills.

Schwa and V-C-E Syllables 3

ONLINE	Student & Computer	:60 minutes
	Adult : *Check Performance Review*	
OFFLINE	Student & Adult : Review online work	:30 minutes
	• Reading Warm-Up	
	• Code Work	
	• Word Work	
	• Speed Work	
	Classics Session 2	:30 minutes
	Instructional Time **2:00** hours	

Materials

- *MARK¹² Classics for Young Readers*
- "Mother Frost" MP3
- Online Tile Kit or Paper Letter Tiles
- *MARK¹² Reading Activity Book*, pages 349–354

Goals

In this lesson, students will read about the Eiffel Tower. Students will also work with the schwa sound before working with vowel-consonant-*e* syllables. In today's *MARK¹² Reading Activity Book*, you will work with students to reinforce their understanding of the schwa sound and to reinforce their understanding of vowel-consonant-*e* syllables. Afterward, you will work with students to complete Classics activities.

Advance Preparation

For the offline portion of today's lesson, download this story: "Mother Frost." Based on the Performance Review, if students need to complete Code Work activity 3 or Word Word activity 2, gather the Online Tile Kit or Paper Letter Tiles. If students need to complete Word Work activity 3, gather a poem students know and enjoy.

ONLINE Student & Computer

Students will work online to complete Warm-Up, Code Work, Word Work, and Speed Work activities, and a Wrap-Up assessment on their own. Be sure to read the Performance Review before beginning the offline portion of today's lesson.

Today you will work with students to complete Code Work, Word Work, and *MARK¹² Classics for Young Readers* activities. Be sure to read the online Performance Review before beginning the Code Work and Word Work activities.

Warm-Up ·

The Eiffel Tower

Look at the Performance Review. If the student achieved a perfect score on today's Warm-Up, move on to Code Work. If the student scored 60 percent or 80 percent, print the story and review the comprehension questions with the student. If the student scored less than 60 percent, print the story, have the student read the story aloud, and then work through the comprehension questions together, before moving on to Code Work.

Objectives

- Improve reading and comprehension skills.

Code Work ·

Schwa

Look at the Performance Review. If the student achieved a perfect score on today's Code Work activities, complete the first two activities from the list below. If the student scored less than 100 percent but more than 85 percent, complete the first three activities from the list below. If the student scored 85 percent or less, complete all four of the activities listed below.

Objectives

- Identify the letters, given the sound /ə/.
- Identify and use the schwa sound.

1. Have students complete page 349 in *MARK¹² Reading Activity Book* for more practice on the schwa sound.

2. Remove "The Big Dipper" story from *MARK¹² Reading Activity Book*. Fold the pages in half to create a small booklet. Review the following words with students: *stumbled*. Have students read the story silently once or twice before reading the story aloud. When students read aloud, make note of any errors, and review those words with the students.

3. Using the Online Tile Kit or Paper Letter Tiles, have students build the following words: *around, mother, occur, salad, across,* and *sofa*.

4. Have students write a very short, silly story or poem using the words from activity 3. Encourage students to incorporate as many additional words with the schwa sound as possible.

Code Work Name: _____

Schwa and V-C-E Syllables 3

Find the Schwa Sound

Choose the word from the box that matches each description. Write the word on the line after the description.
Hint: Some descriptions will match two words. In those cases, write both words.

afraid	banana	ago	collide
alone	item	awake	sofa

1. has a long o sound in the first syllable and ends with a schwa sound **sofa**
2. begins with a schwa sound and has a long a sound in the second syllable **afraid, awake**
3. has a schwa sound in two syllables **banana**
4. has a long i sound in the first syllable and has a schwa sound in the second syllable **item**
5. begins with a schwa sound and has a long o sound in the second syllable **ago, alone**
6. has a schwa sound in the first syllable and has a long i sound in the second syllable **collide**

349

Word Work

V-C-E Syllables

Look at the Performance Review. If the student achieved a perfect score on today's Word Work activities, complete the first activity from the list below. If the student scored less than 100 percent but more than 85 percent, complete the first three activities from the list below. If the student scored 85 percent or less, complete all four of the activities listed below.

1. Have students complete page 350 in *MARK¹² Reading Activity Book* for more practice on vowel-consonant-*e* syllables.

2. Using the Online Tile Kit or Paper Letter Tiles, have students build the following v-c-*e* syllables (which are also words): *use, home, line, space,* and *time.* Then have students create a two-syllable word with each of these v-c-*e* syllables. (Some possible new words include: *useful, homemade, outline, spaceship,* and *timeless.*)

3. Have students read the poem you gathered. As they read through the poem, have them point out any v-c-*e* syllables that they see.

4. Have students write a very short poem of their own using as many words containing v-c-*e* syllables as possible. Students can write additional stanzas for the poem they read in activity 3, write a poem in the same style as the poem from activity 3, or write a completely different kind of poem.

Objectives

- **Identify the number of syllables in a word.**
- **Identify and use syllable types.**

Speed Work

Too Adult

Look at the Performance Review, or check the student's fluency chart. Fluency scores (words read per minute) should not fall below 80. If the student scored below 80 words per minute, print a copy of the Speed Work story and have the student read the story silently before reading it aloud. Otherwise, move on to Classics Session 2.

Objectives

- **Increase reading fluency rate.**

Mother Frost

Have students listen to the story again while following along in *MARK¹² Classics for Young Readers*. Afterward, students should complete the comprehension questions in *MARK¹² Classics for Young Readers* on their own.

Objectives

- Improve reading and comprehension skills.

W Write

Mother Frost

1. Why did the mother care more for the lazy child than the kind child?

The mother cared more for the lazy child than the kind child because the lazy child was her own, whereas the kind child was her stepdaughter.

2. Where did the kind girl find herself after falling into the spring?

(A) field
B. forest
C. cottage
D. bakery

3. At first the kind girl was afraid of the old woman, but then the old woman "won the little girl's heart." What changed the girl's mind?

The old woman "won the little girl's heart" by speaking so kindly.

4. What did the feathers from the old woman's bed fall to earth as?

A. rain
B. hail
C. sleet
(D.) snow

5. Why did the kind girl wish to go back home even though her life with Mother Frost was happy?

The girl wished to go back home even though her life with Mother Frost was happy because she was homesick for her friends.

6. How did the lazy girl prick her finger?

The lazy girl pricked her finger by putting her hand in a thorn bush.

7. Why did the lazy girl refuse to shake the apple tree?

A. She did not like apples.
B. She did not think the apples were ripe.
C. She was scared of the talking apple tree.
(D) She was afraid that some apples would fall on her head.

8. Why was the lazy girl happy that Mother Frost told her to go away?

The lazy girl was happy that Mother Frost told her to go away because she was sure that she would get a golden shower while passing through the gate.

Mother Frost **137**

138 Mother Frost

Schwa and V-C-E Syllables 4

ONLINE	Student & Computer	**:60** minutes	
	Adult : *Check Performance Review*		
OFFLINE	Student & Adult : Review online work	**:30** minutes	
	• Reading Warm-Up		
	• Speed Work		
	• Assessment		
	Grammar, Usage, and Mechanics (GUM)	**:30** minutes	
	Instructional Time **2:00** hours		

Materials

- *MARK¹² Reading Activity Book*, pages 355–360

Goals

In this lesson, students will read about Clara Barton. Students will also work with the schwa sound before working with vowel-consonant-*e* syllables. In today's Unit Assessment, you will administer a test covering all content from Unit 21. Afterward, you will work with students to complete activities on using abbreviations.

ONLINE   Student & Computer

Students will work online to complete Warm-Up, Code Work, Word Work, and Speed Work activities, and a review game on their own. Be sure to read the Performance Review before beginning the offline portion of today's lesson.

Today you will administer a Unit Assessment and work with students to complete a GUM activity.

Warm-Up ·

Clara Barton

Look at the Performance Review. If the student achieved a perfect score on today's Warm-Up, move on to Speed Work. If the student scored 60 percent or 80 percent, print the story and review the comprehension questions with the student. If the student scored less than 60 percent, print the story, have the student read the story aloud, and then work through the comprehension questions together, before moving on to Speed Work.

Objectives

- Improve reading and comprehension skills.

Speed Work ·

2:00 AM

Look at the Performance Review, or check the student's fluency chart. Fluency scores (words read per minute) should not fall below 80. If the student scored below 80 words per minute, print a copy of the Speed Work story and have the student read the story silently before reading it aloud to you. Otherwise, move on to the Assessment.

Objectives

- Increase reading fluency rate.

☼ Assessment ·

Schwa and Syllable Types

Today's Unit Assessment covers all content found in Unit 21. Carefully read the instructions on the student pages before administering the test to the student. If necessary, read the directions to the student. After you have scored the student's assessment, be sure to go online and enter student performance scores in the assessment entry tool.

Part 2. Dictate the following words to students: *about, lemon, item, scuba,* and *alone.*

Unit 21 Assessment

Part 1.
Underline each word in the box that contains the schwa sound.

1.

<u>aware</u>	<u>collide</u>	follow	<u>gallop</u>	hilltop
keyhole	leaky	<u>pencil</u>	<u>ribbon</u>	sister

Part 2.
Listen to each word that is read to you. Write each word on the lines provided.

2. <u>about</u>
3. <u>lemon</u>
4. <u>item</u>
5. <u>scuba</u>
6. <u>alone</u>

Part 3. In each row, underline the word that contains the schwa sound.

7.	almost	<u>adult</u>	after
8.	<u>ballad</u>	backpack	bedroom
9.	camper	counting	<u>connect</u>
10.	<u>dragon</u>	darkness	deeper
11.	<u>afraid</u>	artist	asked
12.	<u>mother</u>	mailbox	manmade
13.	older	onto	<u>occur</u>
14.	safety	<u>sofa</u>	surfing
15.	warmer	weekend	<u>wagon</u>
16.	aimed	<u>ago</u>	arched

Part 4.
On the lines provided, write the number of syllables that each word contains.

17.	alarm	2	22.	gasp	1
18.	butterfly	3	23.	hardest	2
19.	dawn	1	24.	urgently	3
20.	folded	2	25.	awake	2
21.	around	2	26.	wilderness	3

Part 5.
Underline the vowel-consonant-e syllable in each word.

27.	<u>base</u>ment	32.	rose<u>bush</u>
28.	<u>female</u>	33.	<u>side</u>walk
29.	<u>home</u>made	34.	bee<u>hive</u>
30.	mis<u>take</u>	35.	<u>stove</u>top
31.	out<u>line</u>	36.	bird<u>cage</u>

Part 6.
In each row, underline the word that contains *at least one* vowel-consonant-e syllable.

37.	puppet	pumpkin	<u>perfume</u>
38.	<u>campfire</u>	countdown	carload
39.	downhill	dugout	<u>driveway</u>
40.	<u>fireplace</u>	fitness	foolproof
41.	hilltop	<u>hopeful</u>	halfway
42.	<u>nickname</u>	napkin	nearby
43.	paintbrush	<u>pinecone</u>	payment
44.	snapshot	subway	<u>sunshine</u>
45.	<u>tadpole</u>	tiptoe	toothbrush
46.	<u>pancake</u>	penny	piglet

Objectives

- Identify the letters, given the sound /ə/.
- Identify and use the schwa sound.
- Identify the number of syllables in a word.
- Identify and use syllable types.

Schwa and V-C-E Syllables 4   365

Using Abbreviations

Most abbreviations begin with a capital letter and end with a period. However, abbreviations for units of measure usually do *not* begin with capital letters or end with periods. Here are some examples of different types of abbreviations:

Addresses	Units of Measure	Days and Months	Titles
Street (St.)	inch (in.)	Sunday (Sun.)	Ms.
Road (Rd.)	foot (ft)	Monday (Mon.)	Mrs.
Avenue (Ave.)	yard (yd)	Tuesday (Tues.)	Mr.

Work with students to complete pages 359 and 360 in *MARK¹² Reading Activity Book*. Read page 359, Get Ready, with students. Have students complete the Try It page. Be sure to discuss students' answers when the page is completed.

G U M Grammar, Usage, and Mechanics   Name: _____

Schwa and V-C-E Syllables 4

Get Ready

☒ An **abbreviation** is a short way to write a word. Abbreviations save time and space in writing.

Abbreviations for **addresses** begin with a capital letter and end with a period. For example:

Street (St.)	Drive (Dr.)	Boulevard (Blvd.)
Road (Rd.)	Place (Pl.)	Avenue (Ave.)
Parkway (Pkwy.)	Lane (Ln.)	North (N.)
South (S.)	East (E.)	West (W.)

☒ Abbreviations for **state names** consist of two capital letters without a period. For example:

California (CA)	Texas (TX)	Virginia (VA)

☒ Abbreviations for **units of measure** are unusual because, in most cases, they do not use capital letters or end with periods. However, you do use a period to abbreviate *inch* (in.). For example:

foot (ft)	yard (yd)	mile (mi)
pint (pt)	quart (qt)	gallon (gal)
second (sec)	minute (min)	pound (lb)

☒ Abbreviations for **days of the week** begin with a capital letter and end with a period.

Sunday (Sun.)	Wednesday (Wed.)	Saturday (Sat.)
Monday (Mon.)	Thursday (Thurs.)	Sunday (Sun.)
Tuesday (Tues.)	Friday (Fri.)	

359

G U M Grammar, Usage, and Mechanics   Name: _____

Schwa and V-C-E Syllables 4

☒ Abbreviations for **months of the year** begin with a capital letter and end with a period. *May, June,* and *July* do not have abbreviations because they are already short enough.

January (Jan.)	September (Sept.)
February (Feb.)	October (Oct.)
March (Mar.)	November (Nov.)
April (Apr.)	December (Dec.)
August (Aug.)	

☒ An abbreviation for a person's **title** comes before his or her name. When a title is abbreviated, it is capitalized and usually ends with a period.

Title	Use Before the Name of	Example
Ms.	single or married women	Ms. Linda Kaplar
Mrs.	married women	Mrs. Gail Tanner
Mr.	single or married men	Mr. Robert Jansen
Dr.	doctors or dentists	Dr. Maria Gonzalez

Try It

1. Rewrite the following address using abbreviations:
   17 North Fields Lane   **17 N. Fields Ln.**

2. Underline the correct abbreviation for *quart.*
   qu   <u>qt</u>   qrt.

3. Underline the correct abbreviation for *Tuesday.*
   Tue   Tues   <u>Tues.</u>

4. Underline the correct abbreviation for *January.*
   Jan   <u>Jan.</u>   Jany.

360

MARK¹² Reading I Review

ONLINE	Student & Computer	:60 minutes
	Adult : *Check Performance Review*	
OFFLINE	Student & Adult : Review online work	:30 minutes
	• Reading Warm-Up	
	• Speed Work	
	• Assessment	
	Composition	:30 minutes
	Instructional Time **2:00** hours	

Materials

- *MARK¹² Reading Activity Book*, pages 361–364
- *Just Write*

Goals

In this lesson, students will read about the Corn Palace in South Dakota. Students will also review short and long vowels before reviewing syllable types and sight words. In today's Course Assessment, you will administer a test covering content from all previous units. Afterward, students will spend 30 minutes working on composition.

Advance Preparation

For the offline portion of today's lesson, gather the students' composition materials.

ONLINE Student & Computer

Students will work online to complete Warm-Up, Code Work, Word Work, and Speed Work activities, and a review game on their own. Be sure to read the Performance Review before beginning the offline portion of today's lesson.

Today you will administer a Course Assessment and work with students to complete a Composition activity.

Warm-Up ·

The Corn Palace

Look at the Performance Review. If the student achieved a perfect score on today's Warm-Up, move on to Speed Work. If the student scored 60 percent or 80 percent, print the story and review the comprehension questions with the student. If the student scored less than 60 percent, print the story, have the student read the story aloud, and then work through the comprehension questions together, before moving on to Speed Work.

Speed Work ·

Big Sister

Look at the Performance Review, or check the student's fluency chart. Fluency scores (words read per minute) should not fall below 80. If the student scored below 80 words per minute, print a copy of the Speed Work story and have the student read the story silently before reading it aloud to you. Otherwise, move on to the Assessment.

☼ Assessment ·

MARK¹² Reading I Assessment

Today's Course Assessment covers all content found in *MARK¹² Reading* I. Carefully read the instructions on the student pages before administering the test to students. If necessary, read the directions to students. After you have scored each student's assessment, be sure to go online and input student performance scores in the assessment entry tool.

Part 1. Read the following words to students: *act, bump, edge, it, ox, stop, track, us, wish,* and *yet.*

Part 2. Read the following words to students: *at, check, gift, in, on, patch, socks, truck, us,* and *well.*

Part 4. Read the following words to students: *brain, coach, deep, fly, hope, kind, music, stay, weak,* and *fuel.*

Part 5. Read the following words to students: *scram, sprint, strain, scream,* and *stream.*

Part 6. Read the following words to students: *screen, spray, straw, strike,* and *scrub.*

Part 8. Read the following words to students: *is, of, who, said,* and *what.*

MARK¹² Reading I Review

Part 1.
Listen to each word that is read to you. On the lines provided, write a, e, i, o, or u for the short vowel sound heard in each word.

1. <u>a</u>   6. <u>o</u>
2. <u>u</u>   7. <u>a</u>
3. <u>e</u>   8. <u>u</u>
4. <u>i</u>   9. <u>i</u>
5. <u>o</u>   10. <u>e</u>

Part 2.
Listen to each word that is read to you. On the lines provided, write the vowels that are missing from each word.

11. <u>a</u>_t   16. p._<u>a</u>_tch
12. ch_<u>e</u>_ck   17. s_<u>o</u>_cks
13. g_<u>i</u>_ft   18. tr_<u>u</u>_ck
14. <u>i</u>_n   19. _<u>u</u>_s
15. _<u>o</u>_n   20. w._<u>e</u>_ll

Part 3.
Read the words below. In each word, underline the letter or letters that make the long vowel sound.

21. bra<u>ve</u>   26. sh<u>ie</u>ld
22. c<u>o</u>ld   27. t<u>ie</u>
23. f<u>ew</u>   28. m<u>i</u>le
24. h<u>u</u>ge   29. t<u>oe</u>
25. m<u>e</u>   30. tr<u>ay</u>

Part 4.
Listen to each word that is read to you. Write each word on the lines provided.

31. <u>brain</u>   36. <u>kind</u>
32. <u>coach</u>   37. <u>music</u>
33. <u>deep</u>   38. <u>stay</u>
34. <u>fly</u>   39. <u>weak</u>
35. <u>hope</u>   40. <u>fuel</u>

Part 5.
Listen to each word that is read to you. In each row, underline the beginning blend that is contained in each word.

41. sm sn <u>scr</u> spl spr str
42. sm sn scr spl <u>spr</u> str
43. sm sn scr spl spr <u>str</u>
44. sm sn <u>scr</u> spl spr str
45. sm sn scr spl spr <u>str</u>

Part 6.
Listen to each word that is read to you. Write each word on the lines provided.

46. <u>screen</u>
47. <u>spray</u>
48. <u>straw</u>
49. <u>strike</u>
50. <u>scrub</u>

Part 7.
Read each word. Decide what type of syllable the *first* syllable is in each word. On the line provided, write C for *closed*, O for *open*, or V-C-E for *vowel-consonant-e*.

51. hammer   <u>C</u>   56. racetrack <u>V-C-E</u>
52. moment   <u>O</u>   57. homemade   <u>V-C-E</u>
53. frozen   <u>O</u>   58. picnic   <u>C</u>
54. jacket   <u>C</u>   59. baseball   <u>V-C-E</u>
55. open   <u>O</u>   60. winter   <u>C</u>

Part 8.
In each row, underline the word that is read to you.

61. in   it   <u>is</u>
62. <u>of</u>   on   or
63. where   <u>who</u>   with
64. <u>said</u>   so   she
65. we   want   <u>what</u>

Part 9.
Read each word aloud.

66. does   68. gone   70. more
67. were   69. above

Objectives

- Identify and use short vowel spelling patterns.
- Identify and use long vowel spelling patterns.
- Identify and use blends.
- Read sight words.

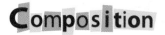

Gather students' composition materials and begin where they left off.

- Develop composition skills.